Togetherness is Our Home

An Orca's Journey through Life

D0874798

Togetherness is Our Home

An Orca's Journey through Life

Dr. Astrid M. van Ginneken

Booksurge Publishing
2007

To my dear Father and Mother

Ad majorem dei gloriam

Contents

Acknowledgements   1

Prologue   3

Map of Tuschka's home waters   6
Family tree of Furka's pod   7

Part I Among the Pod
   1. First Light   11
   2. Exploring the World   23
   3. A Painful Mistake   35
   4. Meeting Friends   44
   5. The Researchers   53
   6. The Big Chase   61
   7. The Meat Hunters   75
   8. Time for Play   89
   9. Korak's Loss   96
  10. Bingor   111
  11. Lifted Spirits   126
  12. Parting of the Ways   131

Part II In the Care of Man
  13. Walls of Loneliness   141
  14. A New Friend   150
  15. A Shy Acquaintance   161
  16. Learning to Perform   171
  17. New Playmates in the Water   187
  18. A Friend is Missing   198
  19. Comfort from a New Friend   209
  20. Adolescence   218

21. The Move   231
22. Voices from her Own Kind   237
23. Durak   249
24. Shachi's Pod   259
25. Wobke   273
26. Kiki's Farewell   282
27. A Hefty Blow   290
28. The Debate   299

Part III The Return
29. The Past Revisited   314
30. Chasing Live Fish Again   325
31. The Puzzle Comes Together   337
32. Beyond the Fjord   347
33. The Reunion   357
34. Bridging the Gap with the Past   373
35. Tragedy and Joy: The Cycle of Life   387

Suggestions for Further Reading   397

Acknowledgements

This book would never have seen the light without the enthusiasm and inspiration of many people. Bertie Roothaan, Toinny Lukken, and Anita van der Mooren, shared their stories and precious experiences with the orca Gudrun, who resided in Harderwijk, The Netherlands, until her transfer to Florida in November 1987.

At Sea World of Florida, I was fortunate to meet Marilyn Mazzoil, Lindsay Rubincam, Jeff Ventre, Mark Simmons, and several others, who shared their perception of the personalities and interrelationships of the orcas, and their fascinating interactions with the whales.

Ken Balcomb, the director of the Center for Whale Research, gave me the unique and wonderful opportunity to participate as staff on his orca project as of 1987. He realized my dream to come to know the orcas of J, K and L pods in the Pacific Northwest. I am grateful for his continued support and appreciation of my work. I also thank his son Kelley Balcomb-Bartok for sharing his enthusiasm and passion for the whales.

Over the years, I have shared many encounters with orcas, and spent many hours 'talking whales' with seasoned staff members David Ellifrit, Candice Emmons, and Adam U. Our insiders talk about the behavior and personalities of the whales were inspiring and have shaped much of my view on these fascinating animals.

My thanks also go to Earthwatch and their volunteers. Their support and enthusiasm were very motivating. The volunteers' questions and eagerness to learn helped me to keep a fresh and inquisitive mind towards everything we observed.

Susan Luff, a relationship therapist studying animal societies, played a key role in understanding the social interactions among the members of an orca pod by asking me the right questions. She, unknowingly, contributed greatly to the book.

Pat Woodfin, a former Earthwatch volunteer, went out of her way to help me get this book published. Her never ending support and efforts were a great stimulus. Ingrid Visser led me to this publisher. Without their help, the publishing of this book would have suffered much more delay.

I am greatly indebted to Charlene Rice, who took on the immense task of carefully reading the entire draft manuscript. She meticulously edited the text to remove errors and make it flow better. Her work was essential for me as a non-native speaker.

Many other people have crossed my path during my time with the orcas. I want to thank them for their enthusiasm, help, and sharing of a good time together.

Most of all, I want to thank my beloved father and mother, who have stimulated me in everything I undertook. They inspired me and made me believe that I could achieve everything I wanted. They always gave me their listening ear, their advice, their support, and their never ending love.

Prologue

This is the story of Tuschka, the killer whale.

Though Tuschka is fictional, her story is based on real events in the life of an Orca, named Gudrun, and from the everyday lives of Orcas in the wild. This story was born from my desire to share 20 years of observing Orcas, both in their natural habitat and in captivity.

For me it first began in 1986 when I visited an exposition on whales at the Smithsonian Institute in Washington D.C. There, on page 5 of the very first Orca book I ever read, a special cord was struck within me. I knew immediately this was a species I wanted to know intimately.

Back in the Netherlands, I started regularly visiting the Orca Gudrun at the Harderwijk aquarium. She immediately stole my heart and changed my life forever.

Then in 1987, I began participating in project Orca Survey at the Center for Whale Research in Washington State. In the years following, I have continued to work with Orcas in Washington, and have had the good fortune of being invited to visit other Orca projects in Norway, Argentina, and New Zealand.

During that time I continued to visit Gudrun following her move to Sea World in Florida. Though she is now gone, I have visited nearly every park in the world that keeps Orcas, except one facility in Canada and one in Argentina.

My time with Orcas has become a fascinating journey of discovery and wonder. I have learned much about this supreme and intelligent predator of the ocean. Piece by piece the puzzle of their lives has begun to fit together and reveal the essence of Orca life to me.

One person in particular — Susan Luff, a relationship therapist studying social animals — without even knowing it helped me put the puzzle together by asking the key question: "how do personality development and dominance relate?" In human societies, dominance of one may suppress the personality of others, thereby causing a seeming harmony. Where there is freedom, there is room for personality development, but there are many different opinions and ways of life.

In orca pods, there is room for personality development and yet, they work together in harmony and live their lives as one cohesive unit. How can such a strong cohesion and consensus exist without suppression?

The answer struck me suddenly as I thought of Gudrun's transfer from the Netherlands to Florida.

During the preparations for her move to Florida, Gudrun squealed in agony and tensed like a string when the net closed in on her in her holding tank. I imagine she must have been reliving the intense trauma of her capture in Icelandic waters. As she squealed, her trainer stepped forward and squeaked to her. In an instant Gudrun relaxed and squeaked back playfully. Swinging in her hammock below the crane, she then playfully returned the calls of her human friend, as if saying: "if you are with me, no harm will come to me…"

If an orca in such unnatural and frightening circumstances can place such trust in a human, how much trust will it place in the matriarch of its own pod? The answer to the question is "trust."

Orcas follow their leader because they trust her completely. Trust also comes from loyalty to each other. In New Zealand, a juvenile female was nearly mortally injured by a boat propeller that made several deep cuts in her back behind her dorsal fin. This female, nicknamed 'Prop', must have been carried and fed by her family for a very long time while she healed. To date — over 15 years later — they still guard her and share food with her. Togetherness is the essence of Orca life.

There are many books and numerous scientific papers on Orcas, but statistics and graphs do not tend to bring the reader really close to an Orca's actual life.

Then what does?

I am human. Whatever I write of Orca life is as I perceive it, created within my own human mind. Yet, it is the only way we can perceive things. As I immersed myself in the lives of Orcas, I felt a growing desire to share my perception of Orca life in the form of this story.

This story is natural history fiction, in which I share what I have heard, read, seen, and experienced. I have added photos of real orcas to give the reader also a visual glimpse of their lives. Because of her special place in my heart, I decided to use Gudrun's life as my main inspiration for Part One and Part Two. Part Three is pure fiction, and was not inspired by the motion picture Free Willy — my story was already in draft form at that time.

Nor is this book a plea for setting all captive Orcas free.

Quite frankly, there are very few candidates left. I realize that reality is probably more unruly than Part Three makes it seem, but I have addressed all aspects of reintroduction that I consider important. Most of all, that recognition has to come from the orca being reintroduced.

Captivity for orcas is controversial. In my opinion Orcas are better off in the wild, but captive Orcas have won widespread sympathy and love, making the species popular and beloved. It cannot be denied that captive Orcas present a unique opportunity for interaction.

It is unforgettable to make contact with an Orca up close. Their intelligence is fascinating and their tenderness and affection are deeply touching. The highest evidence of their intelligence is the fact that humans can befriend Orcas. It is our own intelligence that fascinates them, and it is their refined sense for sincerity and emotion that I believe enables them to perceive our moods and emotions.

It takes little to imagine how rich their lives in the wild must be. When love and respect for the Orca grow, so does the desire for each Orca to have that life. Part Three stems from love for the magnificent Orca. It is what people truly wanted for Keiko. It is what I came to wish for Gudrun.

In my heart Gudrun lives on.

In this book, I simply made my dream come true.

Tuschka's Home Waters

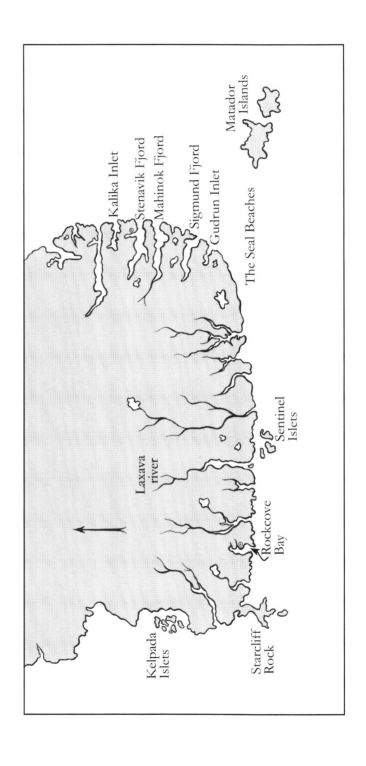

Kalika Inlet

Stenavik Fjord

Mahinok Fjord

Sigmund Fjord

Gudrun Inlet

The Seal Beaches

Matador Islands

Sentinel Islets

Laxava river

Rockcove Bay

Kelpada Islets

Starcliff Rock

Furka's pod at the time of Tuschka's birth

(Numbers indicate age)

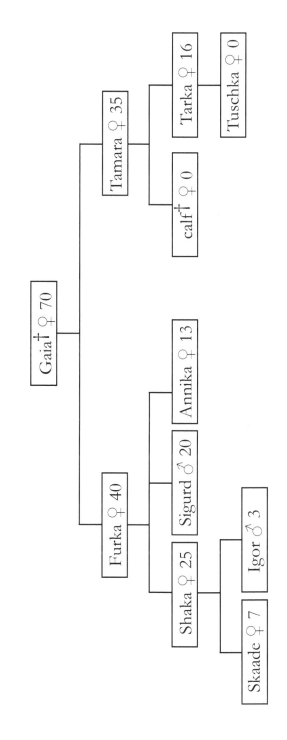

Part I

Among the Pod

1.
First Light

Heavy, gray clouds were racing along the sky and water from the white-crested waves was spraying in the wind. Sigurd's mighty blows were lost in the howling storm: only his tall straight dorsal fin betrayed his presence when he surfaced to breathe. Seven smaller fins cut through the turbulent sea with him. Twenty years ago, Sigurd was born in this family to Furka, who had taken the lead after his grandmother, Gaia, had died. Despite their strength and adaptation to even the most tempestuous seas, Furka was urging them on to reach the calmer waters of a sheltered inlet. For the small pod a long-awaited hour had arrived. Strong contractions seized Tarka's body. She had never experienced these before, but she knew that the new life that had been growing inside her was soon to be born.

Tarka was grateful for the close bodily contact with her family in this fierce storm. She dived and rose with them in unison, trying to conserve energy by staying deep beneath the turbulent waves until she had to grab her next breath. Sigurd swam in front at his mother's flank. Tarka felt her heart stir with gratitude for his skill in guiding the pod through stormy seas. He was a strong, fully grown male and boasted the tall, straight dorsal fin, typical of a mature bull of his kind. Tarka loved the proud beauty of his fin and fully understood, for the first time, its value in these tempestuous waters. With the tip of his six-foot tall fin, Sigurd could touch the surface while most of his body stayed just beneath the zone of heavy turbulence. When he felt a wave pass over, he would signal to his pod to rise for air.

Tarka's pains were becoming stronger, and she felt a desperate need for air. She could not wait for Sigurd's next signal and burst through the surface for a breath. But it was ill-timed, and she inhaled air and spray as a wave broke on her back. She sputtered and tried again, but it was no better. Before she drew a good breath another contraction came. Tarka winced. There was no diving deep now. Still fighting for air, she had lost her rhythm and could not get it back. She felt herself failing to keep up with her pod at this rate – and yet she must! Tarka knew that a baby orca stood little chance in these stormy waters, let alone without help! She kept fighting amidst the bashing waves, but try as she might, she began falling behind…

While the November storm raged on, Tamara would not leave Tarka's side. Tarka heard her voice, urging her to dive with her to calmer water, but she was near exhaustion. She was breathing and sputtering erratically and made no more attempts to dive.

Then, in a sudden upsurge, Sigurd was by her side. Tarka knew in an instant he had come to help her. His powerful presence reassured her at once and within seconds he signaled her to breathe. Tarka inhaled deeply, catching her first clear uninterrupted breath for miles. With each breath, Tarka regained energy. She felt the support of the suction created by his powerful body. Gradually, Tarka found herself moving with him in unison. As she regained her rhythm, he gradually led her on longer dives to relax in the deeper calmer water. Tarka was grateful that Sigurd read her needs unerringly - they still came up more frequently than the rest of the pod - and she began to trust herself fully to his guidance.

Tarka noticed a hesitation in the pace, then a direction change. Instead of heading for the inlet in a straight line, they were now heading straight for shore. Whatever Furka had in mind, Tarka did not take the time to think about it. She needed all her concentration to stay with her escorts.

A fierce contraction made Tarka almost stop dead in her tracks. She was no longer able to continue swimming when they came. To her relief Sigurd and Tamara stayed with her and the five companions in front of her immediately slowed down. Tarka had not felt much urge to push, but the tiny tail flukes of her baby were already born. As the cramp subsided, she only made a few strokes before the next one came. With so little time in between contractions, Tarka felt her energy drain fast. Her dives became ever shorter and shallower.

Fortunately, the tide slackened and the waves became less erratic. Tarka was no longer swimming and rested in between her cramps to conserve energy. She saw Furka's oldest daughter Shaka come over and take Sigurd's place at her side. She knew the experienced female had come to help guide her through her labor. Sigurd hovered at windward side while they lay parallel to the waves, so they would no longer break on their backs, but carry them up and down in the swells.

Both her mother and Shaka supported her with their pectoral fins when another painful contraction started. Each time Tarka pushed, she felt the calf emerge a little further, but most of it slid back when the contraction subsided. She was breathing heavily, trying to regain energy for the next. There it was…, sooner than she had expected and stronger than any of the ones before. Tarka pushed hard and felt her tissue pull tout. She was about to relax a bit when the contraction ended, but this time the baby did not slide back. A sudden tearing pain overcame her. In a wild movement and with a high-pitched scream, Tarka broke loose. She twisted like a corkscrew and pushed with all the strength she had.

Suddenly, a cloud of blood enveloped her and the pain was gone. She took a deep breath and dived immediately to look for her baby. Tamara had already picked it up and Tarka saw her mother help the miniature female to the surface for her first breath. Tarka immediately joined her mother and supported the baby with her pectoral fin. The tiny dorsal fin was still flopped over on her back and the baby's tail flukes were not firm yet. Tarka was drained, but her strong heart beat fast as she proudly watched the little orange chin of her infant break the surface as she came up for her first breath.

When Tarka had rested for a few minutes, Furka set a slow pace towards shore. She was grateful that the tide was slack, but the swells were still carrying them up and down. Tarka longed for calmer water to find rest and nurse her calf. Sigurd was still closely, guiding their surfacing. Tarka heard the strong blows of her mother and Shaka, and she proudly listened to the little puff of her baby.

The steep rocky shore was drawing close. Tarka could hear the water break against it and began to feel the returning waves. As her little calf bobbed against her belly, she felt a new series of contractions, but weaker than the ones before. She pushed and felt something soft pass through. Her mother dived and brought it over. While Tarka nudged the soft red tissue that had nourished her baby, she felt the restlessness in her body cease and knew that her labor was over. Tenderly, she nudged the little female at her side, and followed her family towards the entrance of Gudrun inlet.

* * *

Tuschka shivered when she suddenly found herself enveloped in a cold greenish world. Instinctively, she swam toward the light, but when she broke the surface, it was so different! The light was blinding and there was no water around her head. She sucked in air and sputtered when a small wave washed over her back. Then, something lifted her up and she raised her head high for another breath. Barely conscious of her new environment she hugged against the soft black body next to her. Tuschka heard familiar sounds, but they were louder than she had ever heard them before. Another dark shadow appeared on her left side and she felt herself lifted up again. She recognized the familiar voice of the whale on her left and drew close to her.

Tuschka snuggled against the white soft belly and felt that swimming was easiest when she stayed very close. She felt her own little tail flutter upon every stroke, but it rapidly became stronger. The world around her was full of sounds. Beside the clear eerie calls of her family, there were little splashes, crunches, and clicks. Even in the air world there were scream-like sounds overhead and the strong breaths of her companions.

Tuschka did not know the other members of her pod, but she felt irresistibly drawn to the big, tender mother whale. She tried to follow her mother and each time she rose, she went up with her and arched high next to her mother's dorsal fin. Sometimes, Tuschka could not wait for her mother to go up to breathe and had to go by herself. She did not like these little excursions and immediately snuggled back beneath her mother's belly. There, she felt comfortable and safe and needed little effort to keep up. Almost carried along in her mother's slipstream, Tuschka rhythmically bumped her head against the soft belly and felt the gentle touch of her mother's flukes upon each down stroke.

The sky had turned a scarlet red and the sun had disappeared behind the cliffs when Tarka followed Furka into the small inlet. As the waves changed into little ripples, her companions slowed down to rest. She heard their strong blows and the curious clicks of the younger whales checking out her brand new calf. Although Tarka could hear the others nearby, she was grateful for Tamara's closeness. She was resting at her side when Furka loomed up in the poorly lit waters. Tarka saw the pod leader swim by to take her first good look at the newest addition to her family. Tarka's heart beat fast with pride as the matriarch gave her an approving gentle nudge. Then, she watched the large female gracefully veer off. That night only her mother, Tamara, and Shaka were nearby and Tarka was grateful that they kept the curious younger whales at a convenient distance.

Much of the night had passed by since Tuschka had entered her new cold green world, and she felt hungry. She bumped her mother's belly a bit more vigorously and felt something soft pop out and touch her mouth. A warm liquid squirted out of it and Tuschka curiously explored it. Although it was mixed with a lot of water, the taste was pleasant. She licked the teat for more, but when nothing came, she bumped her mother's belly again. This time she tried to roll her tongue around the soft teat. A thick squirt came and it tasted sweet and creamy. Tuschka was too quick to swallow and felt some of the precious fluid spill outside her mouth.

Tuschka almost forgot to swim and although her mother just glided with her large tail lifted, she had to quickly pump her little flukes to keep her place. Tuschka bumped for more and with each drink she managed to take in more of the rich milk. When she had her fill, she contentedly rubbed against her mother's flank.

The experience was new for Tarka too, but she knew how important it was for her baby's survival. She was grateful for the relaxed time with her calf in the inlet and the opportunity to practice her mother skills without the pressure of foraging. Tarka longed to rest still at the surface, but when she tried, her little calf began to circle around her and zigzag erratically. Her little baby could not stop swimming. Until Tuschka were able to stay in one place, Tarka would keep swimming and guide her.

During the night, the storm had lost most of its strength, but the open waters outside Gudrun inlet were still showing white-caps. Tarka was happy that Furka was in no hurry to leave the protected inlet. Outside, the waves still posed a challenge for her small calf, and none of them was in real need to feed. In the filtered light of the morning sun, she watched Sigurd rubbing himself on a large patch of round stones that extended onto shore. Sigurd was obviously relaxed and joined by Igor, Shaka's juvenile son. Tarka watched as Sigurd let Igor entice him into play, but not for long. Soon the two disappeared in the twilight green.

The little three-year-old male was no match for him, but Sigurd enjoyed it when Igor tried to get his attention. He patiently watched the young male swim back and forth in front of him, squeaking, and nudging him. Sigurd stayed quiet, waiting for a moment to surprise his nephew. When Igor swam by, Sigurd suddenly slapped the water with his big flukes, then rolled over to do the same with his huge dorsal fin. He knew that Igor loved the element of surprise and would continue his game with increasing enthusiasm. He saw Igor dart off, hoping to be chased. But Sigurd did not yet accept the invitation.

Sigurd saw the young male loom up at close range, and kept still. When he felt him bump an instant later, he spun around, swung his tail under Igor, and hurled him into the air. He heard Igor's surprised squeak, but his nephew was not hurt. Sigurd was not surprised when Igor bumped him again. He knew that Igor liked to continue the game, but the big bull never did what the younger whale expected him to. He waited a short moment, just enough for Igor to look back impatiently. Then, Sigurd suddenly opened his jaws, and dashed forward. He saw the young whale turn and swim off fast. With a few powerful strokes of his mighty flukes, Sigurd accelerated fast and Igor found himself in a real chase.

To gain speed, Igor almost cleared the water as he surfaced. The explosive breaths of his big pursuer were close behind. No matter how much he tried, Sigurd gained on him fast. Igor made turns to make the chase more difficult for Sigurd, but his agility surprised him again and suddenly, he felt teeth touch his flukes. He leaped into the air to escape and when he splashed back into the water, Sigurd was nowhere to be seen.

Igor hovered at the surface, puffing from all the energy he had spent. He was tense. Sigurd had to be around, and he had no doubt that Sigurd knew where he was. Igor called him, but there was no answer. Just as he decided to go back to the pod, he felt a sudden upwelling of water beneath him. He looked down to see what was happening, only to see Sigurd charging him at full speed from below. Igor froze a split-second, at a loss how to avoid the imminent collision. Before he made a move, he felt the huge body surging by, missing him by the thickness of a pec. Igor watched Sigurd's huge and powerful body rise into the air, totally clearing the water. For a moment, he seemed to hang still, then turned sideways and fell back with a thunderous crash. Igor was still catching his breath when Sigurd surfaced close to him. His gentle nudge was reassuring, and as he swam off slowly, Igor followed him towards the pod. He was greatly impressed by the keenness, agility, and strength of the large male. He was his example, a master he someday hoped to equal.

The sharp thundering sound of Sigurd's full breach sent a shiver of fright through Tuschka and the little orca hugged against her mother. Her voice was soft and reassuring. Nothing in the big mother whale hinted at concern and Tuschka relaxed under the gentle caress of her pectoral fin. The big orca on her other side was a familiar presence for Tuschka. Her own mother called her mother, even though she did not have the warm tasty milk, but her voice was gentle and her touch was soft. She was almost always there and Tuschka sensed that her mother was more relaxed when she was near.

Tuschka felt a twitch of tension in her mother as she saw a large whale approach. She had no clue who she was, but Tamara glided closer. Although Tuschka was safely tucked in between her companions, she wondered if there was any danger in the newcomer.

Tarka eyed Annika warily. She was undoubtedly interested in her calf, but Tarka did not want to take the slightest risk with her precious infant. For many years, Annika had felt like a younger sister to Tarka and they had played the wildest games. But now, Annika had a different interest. Since she had come into season for the first time this past summer, she had taken a natural interest in babies and motherhood. Tuschka seemed irresistible for her, but Tarka was not sure whether Furka's bold and uninhibited daughter would be careful enough when given a chance to get close to her Tuschka. Besides that, Tarka felt uncomfortable to scold the daughter of the matriarch. She would rather avoid such a confrontation.

Tarka kept Tuschka close under her pectoral fin away from Annika. She was grateful that Tamara understood her concerns and took position in between them. But Annika was not easily discouraged and tried hard to get an unobstructed view. As soon as Tamara moved in between them, Annika veered towards another position. She had not come closer than a body length yet, but her frequent changing of position was a nuisance. Tarka was pleased when she heard Tamara smack her tail on the surface when Annika made another approach. It was an undeniable hint to the younger female to back off. Her mother Tamara had a higher status and was less inhibited towards Furka's daughter. Annika voiced her displeasure, but not convincingly. She backed off a little and settled with keeping parallel at a greater distance. Tarka was relieved. Annika obviously knew that her mother would not stand up for her now.

Tamara was very aware of everything that happened around her daughter Tarka and the baby. She sensed Tarka's needs, and much of the time she kept her and the other youngsters at a comfortable distance. Although Annika did not yet get what she wanted, she learned much from what she saw. It was not much different from when Igor was born: at that time it had also taken a while before she was allowed to touch him and much longer even before she could start to play with him. At that time she had looked at it all through the eyes of a playful girl who wanted to dart off and play with the little baby. She felt the same desire now, but she was also intrigued with the behavior of the brand new mother. For some reason, mothers with newborn babies seemed to want females around who had experience with motherhood. Annika wanted to learn what was expected from a mother whale. Maybe when she behaved like them, she would be allowed closer to the baby.

Tarka had enjoyed three happy peaceful days with her calf after the storm had ended. Tuschka had not mastered all the swimming skills yet, but she pushed easily forward with her small, firm flukes and she had built up much more endurance. Apparently, Furka had judged Tuschka strong enough to keep up with the pod and had decided to leave the bay in search of food. In these dark times when light was short and storms swept the sea, herring and cod were most plentiful. With the calf still so young, Tarka was grateful that Furka decided not to hunt for cod, which required a lot of bottom diving. Instead she was in search of herring, which would come closer to the surface at night. They all followed Furka as she headed for a bank where her mother and their former matriarch, Gaia, had often led them when she was leading the pod.

Furka's mind traveled back… Almost her entire life, Gaia had guided them, making decisions about where to go and what to hunt. Only rarely had they gone without food for more than a week and usually they had found something to eat every day. Furka realized she had mostly taken it for granted that they would find food and she had followed her family for many years without asking herself why they went where they did. She was familiar with the seasonal travels, but Gaia had passed away only one winter ago and not long before then had she begun to actively observe what decisions her mother made, when and where she led them and which priorities she set.

Furka knew her mother was very old when she first showed signs of losing physical strength. She had been beyond child-bearing age ever since she could remember, and even then, Gaia lived to see her great-grand offspring for several years. Yet, she still was the matriarch, who had the complete trust of the whole pod, and her ample experience made up for her decreased stamina. Especially through summer and fall, food was so abundant that Gaia did not need to give all of herself to find and catch it. When they were on the move from one hunt to the other, Gaia would take more pauses to rest. But as long as everybody was well fed, they had enjoyed extra playtime while their old matriarch rested and watched. Gaia had been using her keen senses almost constantly to judge the currents and the depth, and to detect signs of prey. Except for her short naps, Gaia's mind was always working on the next decision.

Just this past winter, Gaia had still been able to lead the family to fishing grounds, but Furka and her sister Tamara had been the first to notice it had become increasingly difficult for their mother to hunt and catch sufficient prey. She gradually lost weight and it was only when she had started to lag behind that they had become fully aware of her needs. Furka remembered herself, as well as Sigurd and Shaka, hunting for her as well as themselves. Though a little reluctant, Gaia had accepted the offerings, which had given Furka hope that her mother would live into another bountiful summer.

For Furka, partly providing for Gaia had not been the only change that winter. Her mother had increasingly been calling upon her for making decisions that she still was more than capable of making herself. Furka had sensed that her mother was preparing her to take over, and at the same time, preparing the pod to accept another leader. She had not been comfortable with the situation and had hunted with even more vigor, hoping that mother would regain her strength and resume her leadership as in the old days. While Gaia was still able to make good decisions, she had given Furka more responsibilities and had been present to advise and correct her. Some kinds of prey were favored over others, but favored prey was not always as easy to catch as less favored prey. Some prey lived far off-shore, requiring a lot of traveling and searching, and when found it was often difficult to herd and catch with their small number. The matriarch always had to make the trade-off between the effort and possible reward of various hunting options.

Sensing that her mother would not be with them for much longer, Furka had learned as much as possible. Winter storms were unforgiving and searches for the scarcer prey were demanding. It had become increasingly difficult for the pod to adapt to Gaia's pace and to provide for her what she was unable to catch. The moment came that the best decision for the family conflicted with their matriarch's physical capabilities. It had been then that Gaia stepped back as their leader. They had all been born in her presence and they had followed her guidance for most or all of their lives. Furka had dreaded parting with her wise and beloved mother and matriarch of them all, who had led them so skillfully through times of bounty and hardship.

They had come close to shore on a windy day when they heard a soft call from Gaia. Furka had been a few hundred yards behind them, heading for a shallow inlet. She relived the moment she had left the pod, urging on to be with her mother… She found her resting with her pectoral fins on a shallow sandbar. Her breathing was frequent and shallow. She rubbed her mother gently and made soft whining squeaks. Gaia had little energy left. With her faithful eyes she looked at Furka, who tenderly lifted her head, and made an affectionate reassuring call. Then, when she blew, her breath carried her familiar voice for the last time. Gaia took no other breath, and when a tidal wave washed her away from her foothold, Furka realized her mother had passed away. Instinctively, she tried to push her body to the surface, but she did not come to life. For a little while, Furka carried her mother's body out to deeper waters, her pod members slowly joining from behind. Then, calling out her sadness, she let go and watched how her teacher, leader, and most of all, mother, went down, disappearing in the darkness of the deep.

Not only Furka remembered the scene as they swam by the place where it had happened. Looking at the playful calf along her side, Tarka realized that one of them had never known Gaia. Furka really had Gaia's place now: she had witnessed all the members of her pod being born and they followed her now as they used to follow their former matriarch.

As for prey, the day had gone by uneventfully. They had spent most of their day traveling along shore in somewhat deeper waters. A few times, Tuschka had heard short trains of small clicks. She did not know what sounds they were, but as she sensed no change of behavior in the family, she did not pay much attention to them. It was obvious the sea was full of sounds: soft crackling sounds, more musical, and high-pitched sounds. She had also noticed little creatures moving gracefully through the air, most of the time making short scream-like calls. Tuschka began to understand that sounds were important to her family.

When evening fell, Tuschka noticed the other orcas move off in different directions. When they were out of sight, she heard their voices farther way. She hugged close to her mother not wanting to lose her. Although she could hardly see anything under water, she could easily tell the directions from which all the voices came. With her mother close by and plenty of tasty milk, Tuschka was content and felt no fear swimming in the dark. It was at the crack of dawn that she heard many trains of clicks, like those she had heard occasionally before. Although many of these clicks came from directions where she had heard family members call, some were soft and came out of what seemed to be nothing. They sounded like little scattered fragments, a sort of echoes of the clicks. Tuschka wondered which creatures made those sounds that were similar, yet different, and coming from ahead. She noticed her mother's excitement grow as she listened intently to the sounds.

Tarka and her companions were echolocating for prey and had just detected a school of herring that had come up from greater depths. As soon as some of the fish came into view, panic spread through the school like a wave. The fish tried to dive and escape, but some of Tarka's fellow hunters had already taken position under the school, making the fish swim towards the surface by surprising them with their white bellies. They herded the school together into a dense ball of fish and took positions to block the fish that attempted to flee. They were moving individually in irregular patterns, making sharp turns and short dives. Tarka mostly stayed at the surface, where she and Tuschka heard the blows of their hunting family all around them.

A few sharp smacking sounds startled Tuschka. When she followed her mother on her dive, she could see where the smacks were coming from: a big orca circled the ball of silver fish and thrust its tail into it with brute force. Numerous fish suddenly floated in suspension, scattered beside the ball that had recovered in a moment. Then, the big orca turned and one by one the floating fish disappeared in its mouth. From the safety of her mother's flank, Tuschka watched the activity for a few more minutes. Soon, the others had joined them at the surface, catching their breaths.

Tarka had not joined in the hunt. She had stayed with her baby, which was not old enough to be left with another female, let alone to be exposed to the fray of a hunt. Hunting with her inexperienced calf at her side would be difficult for her and dangerous for her calf. Tuschka needed her attention most of the time, but her empty stomach reminded her to familiarize her baby with her grandmother. Tarka would not start hunting again until Tuschka would feel comfortable to stay with Tamara for short periods of time. Until then, Tarka would have to be content with a few fish that drifted in her direction.

In the days that followed, Tarka was grateful that Tamara spent more time swimming close to her calf. When they were all resting with Tuschka well fed, Tamara often nudged and rubbed the little baby gently while making reassuring calls. Tarka was pleased to see Tuschka become more comfortable each day with Tamara's presence and tender touches.

One day, Tuschka was playing with Tamara. When she wanted to return to her mother, the little calf was startled not to find her mother where she had expected and hugged under Tamara's belly. A few moments later, when her mother reappeared, Tuschka darted over and bumped her belly for reassurance. The unpleasant surprise had confused Tuschka a little, but she relaxed as her mother rubbed her approvingly. Although mother gradually took a little longer to return, Tuschka soon learned that she would always come back and that the other friendly female was gentle and caring. As soon she was confident that she was never left alone, she moved more freely between her mother and grandmother. At times, Tuschka would swim under Tamara's belly as if she were her mother, but for all the warmth and comfort that Tamara could give her, she did not have the creamy tasty milk that her own mother had for her.

Furka noticed the change in behavior between mother and baby. Tarka had started to acquaint her baby with the other members of the pod. She would soon take turns in hunting and begin to make up for her lost feeding opportunities.

Annika had been eager to explore the little calf, but as their leader, Furka had been hard on her, disciplining her when she had attempted to get too close to the mother and her calf. Now, she decided to take Annika with her and introduce her to the baby orca that fascinated her so much.

When the two females approached, Tarka and Tamara took Tuschka in between them, but they made no attempt to evade the leader and her daughter. They knew very well that Furka was totally in command and that Annika would make no unexpected moves. Tamara contently accepted her sister's gentle rubbing and answered her soft calls. Then she moved over to Tarka and did the same. To ease the young mother, Furka continued on next to Tarka with Annika on the outer side. Tarka noticed Tuschka's curiosity about the two whales that had joined them: she switched from Tamara's belly towards her own and looked inquisitively at the slightly larger female on her right. Her calf's own curiosity was the sign for Tarka to push her up a bit with her pectoral fin. She was pleased that her little Tuschka showed no fear. Furka touched the baby with her pec and fell a bit behind, allowing Annika to approach. Tarka sensed Annika's excitement, yet she was careful not to spoil her opportunity. She moved forward and alongside Tuschka. Tarka felt her baby shy away upon the Annika's approach and tucked her under her flipper. Annika moved a short distance away and called playfully towards her calf. Within seconds, her little baby lost her initial apprehension and Tarka let her glide above and behind her pec. Annika saw Tuschka's curiosity and came gradually closer. Furka was behind, but sounded no warnings. Annika pointed her pec towards the calf to see how she would respond. She did not retreat. Annika gently touched the baby's soft back and was even more thrilled when Tuschka turned her head and nudged the flipper that Annika held towards her. Annika squeaked with delight, encouraging the baby to do it again. A few more times, Tuschka nudged Annika's fin. The young female could no longer restrain herself: she bent her head towards the baby and touched the tiny pectoral fin. Furka called..., but there was no angry tone in her voice. Annika made one more playful squeak and slowed down, falling back to take position at her mother's side. She was filled with delight, even Furka had approved.

As winter progressed, Tuschka learned most of her pod's sounds. She recognized her mother's voice unerringly and was practicing the calls that her mother made most often. The little female also attempted to mimic the clicking sounds she had heard. Although she was just discovering how those sounds were made, she was still far from mastering the technique. She was, however, fascinated by the little echoes of her own attempts. She learned that her family made most clicks during the night or in deep water and she also realized that the scattered "answers" were not made by other orcas far away, but that they echoed back from objects relatively nearby.

After a full moon cycle, Tuschka was round, fat, and full of energy. By now, Annika had become one of Tuschka's favorite playmates. Furka rarely interfered when Annika and Tuschka played together. She only stepped in when Tarka really needed it. Furka knew that Tarka was not used to telling Annika what to do. She had just been weaned when Annika was born and they had played together a lot. They were both used to listening to their mothers and it had never occurred to Tarka to discipline Annika. Furka understood the responsibilities of a young mother, and knew there were times when she wanted Annika to hang back a bit. Tarka had refrained from openly expressing it, because she felt that only her leader and Annika's mother, was in the position to do so. Until now, Furka had used her dominance over Annika to spare the new mother. Yet, as a mother Tarka had gained a higher status in the pod and the time had come for Tarka to learn her new place. Furka interfered less and less, and she saw Annika becoming more obtrusive as her confidence grew. Lately, it was not easy for her to see Annika take advantage of Tarka's shyness. Tuschka sometimes went hours without nursing, because Annika wouldn't let go of the calf.

About a week later, when Annika had failed to return her baby for more than half a day, Tarka lost her patience. She made a sharp call and violently jerked her head sideways showing her teeth. Annika was startled and made an evasive movement, but she did not take the obvious hint. Tarka made the warning again and bumped Annika in her flank. At that moment, the young female did not want to push it any further and took off towards her mother. Tarka watched her go and even though she felt the familiar nudges of her baby under her belly, she felt uncomfortable about her behavior towards the leader's daughter. She was wary when Furka approached her while leaving Annika behind, but Furka called reassuringly. Tarka found it hard to discover her new status and limits. She relaxed as Furka came alongside and nudged her gently. Annika stayed far behind while Furka swam by her side. Their relationship had changed: Tarka felt closer to Furka than ever before. Furka was still dominant, but Tarka sensed that she had gained more respect. She felt Tuschka bump her belly and she lifted her flukes to let her drink. Furka called reassuringly again and Tarka gratefully enjoyed her caress as the matriarch trailed her flipper along her side.

Annika was uncomfortable and avoided her mother's presence. Igor suddenly drew her attention when she felt him nibble on her tail. She wanted to dart off with him and play, but she felt that it was not the right moment to do so. Igor enticed her again. With a shy look into her mother's direction, Annika dove down with him.., at least she was out of sight.

2.
Exploring the World

In early spring, Tuschka was strong and agile enough to keep up with a fast pace. She loved it when they all burst into high-speed swimming, lifting their bodies well out of the water in high arches. Tuschka had no idea why it happened when it happened. For her, the bursts of speed were sheer joy. She did not bother spending the energy: tasty milk was always there when she wanted it. Only recently, Tuschka's gums had started to itch, and when she tried to rub them with her tongue they did not feel as soft as she was used to, but more like bony ridges. Mother wasn't too fond it of if she tried to relieve her itch by biting on her soft teats.

The day was calm and a bright morning sun sent shafts of light in the light blue water. Tuschka saw spots of light dancing on her companions' backs. As she glided alongside her mother, the water carried flavors that she had not tasted before, but everyone was so relaxed that she paid no attention to it. On this early spring day, Tuschka did not know they were approaching Rockcove Bay. She heard a distant background rumble. The mixture of lower and higher frequency grunts was not completely unfamiliar, but she had no clue what they meant. Inquisitive as she was her attention was immediately caught by a high-pitched sound moving closer. She wanted to investigate it and immediately took off in the direction of the sound. She stopped after a few seconds, looking to see if she was followed. No matter how curious she was, she only felt confident enough if a trusted companion came to investigate with her. To her disappointment, she was only called for: no one seemed to share her interest. Reluctantly, she turned around and joined Annika, who had become a good friend and playmate.

While they continued on, the sound became stronger. Whatever made the sound was approaching fast. Tuschka was torn between apprehension and curiosity. Her mother was very aware of the situation and seemed to sense no danger, but she always was right there with her whenever she was experiencing something new. Tuschka scooted over to her mother's side when she veered into her direction. Annika watched her go, but stayed close. By now, she knew her place well.

To their right, the source of the sound slowed down to match their speed. Tuschka caught a few glimpses of a dark stiff object at the surface, much larger than any of them. Something at the rear seemed to produce the sound. It rotated fast, turning the water white. Tuschka did not perceive any apprehension, but her mother positioned herself between her and what she would come to know as a boat. Others in the pod also changed places. Sigurd, who had been a little behind, came forward and started swimming closest to the small boat. Next to him was his mother Furka. They grouped up tight, but made no attempt to get away. Each time they surfaced, Tuschka's view was partly blocked by her mother's dorsal fin and back. She tried to rear herself up a bit to see more. Not knowing why, she heard a sudden burst of sound in the air, coming from the boat. Creatures moving on it produced all kinds of unfamiliar screams and calls…

* * *

On this nice calm spring day Johann, a fisherman from the local community of Rockcove bay, had seen the distant blows of a pod of whales. Although he did not expect a good catch with these predators around, he knew their presence was a good sign. As long as nature could support orcas, he had no reason to worry. Since the weather was so promising, he decided to take his family out and watch the whales for a while. His wife and three children often helped him unload his catch and clean the fish. For them, the orcas' presence was a welcome diversion to every-day life.

The youngest of the family was the first to see the little calf and yelled in excitement: "Dad, did you see that? That female has a baby with her! It's so small still. How old would it be?" On the next surfacing sequence, five pairs of eyes concentrated on the whales. "There it is again," the youngest son said, pointing into the direction of the calf, but his words were lost in the excited screams of his mother and sister. His older brother had a quieter demeanor. He smiled at the sight of the baby orca.

After a few surfacings, the initial excitement was over and the family quieted. Following the whales at a distance of 50 yards, they watched them rise and dive. The orcas traveled at a medium speed of five knots, coming up for air four or five times in a row, followed by a longer dive of approximately four minutes. The fisherman's daughter was endeared by the sight of the male's huge fin almost next to the baby's tiny curved fin. The girl noticed the contrast between the explosive blow of the big male, producing a cloud of vapor, and the small puff of the dolphin-like calf. She realized the big orca had once been as little and wondered how fast the baby would grow. She was determined to get them on film.

"Dad, do orcas just pass through or do they return to certain areas for their food?" the girl asked. "Well, Sarah, I guess they know where to feed, but I have no idea where they go and where they come from. They all look so much alike

I couldn't possibly tell whether I have met certain individuals before. However, several years ago there was a big bull with two smaller whales, which probably were his females. A couple of days later, I was convinced I saw them again: the male had a distinct curl at the tip of his fin and a big nick just below it." Sarah looked carefully at the big male.... "I wish this whale had something distinctive, so we might recognize him if he came back and could see how much the little one had grown." Her father understood what his daughter hoped for, but his doubts grew when he examined the big fin of the male on his surfacing. "That would be nice," the fisherman said, "but even if this bull had a remarkable fin, I don't know if this is a casual group or a male with a harem. These whales show up in all kinds of groups, although there usually are several females to one male."

About an hour later, the wind started to pick up and Sarah put her camera away to protect it from spray off the bow. "I'm thinking of heading back soon, it may get choppy when we round Starcliff Rock. Did you get your picture with the big bull and the baby?" Sarah heaved a sigh, "No I did not get them in one frame, but I do have the mother and her baby and also one of the mother and the father." Suddenly, a gust of wind struck them when they came close to the protruding cliff. The fisherman took the engine out of gear and they watched the whales as they rounded the cliff and headed into the wind. Soon, the fins disappeared and the blows were no longer audible. Johann and his family turned around and headed back to their sheltered bay.

* * *

During the few weeks prior to the great salmon runs it was difficult to find food. Furka had led her family to the edge of the shelf where she had often found a variety of fish. Tarka felt the upwellings and strong currents of the tidal rip they were patrolling in search of food. Her companions were diving in groups of two or three, clicking, listening, and looking to find prey. Tuschka had no need to worry about food yet, but she was interested in what her mother and the other orcas were chasing. She liked the feeling of the strong currents against her body and rolled over in the short waves while her mother paused at the surface. When she dove, Tuschka followed her and darted after nearly every fish that came near. She moved around erratically, not yet knowing when prey was close enough for her to attack. Many little fish were too far away to be prey, and it was also difficult to pursue one fish and stay focused on it. Tuschka interrupted most of her chases because she was distracted by another fish or her mothers' movements. A few times she unexpectedly bumped into her mother's flank. She wasn't aware that she made hunting difficult for Tarka, chasing prey off before her mother even had a chance. Tarka watched her movements carefully and avoided sharp turns, which could hurt her baby severely. The hunt was not very successful for Tarka, but Tuschka had to learn. When she really needed to feed well, she entrusted her baby to her companions.

In the late afternoon, the pod headed towards shore again. The hunt had not been sufficiently rewarding and they still felt hungry. Suddenly, the pod stopped talking. When Tuschka made a few soft calls, no one answered, and her mother signaled that she had better be silent. She listened to the echoes that returned from the clicks others were sending out. They revealed a steep rise of the sea floor. Tuschka saw Furka slow down and then stop. She and Sigurd rose up slowly, poking their heads up in the air to look around. Tuschka peeked around too. They had come upon the Kelpada Islets, a number of little rocky islets, separated by kelp beds. Furka knew that harbor seals often used these islets to haul-out on. She rarely visited the place. They had more often chased the seals for play than for food, but in the first half of spring when food was hard to find, an occasional seal would be welcome.

No seals were present on the closest rocks. The orcas wondered if the seals had left the area, were hiding in the kelp, or had retreated to the higher islets behind. If one of the seals had heard their sonar clicks, the whole colony would undoubtedly be alarmed, but Furka had wisely echolocated softly and almost straight down. As soon as she had detected the rise in the sea floor, she had stopped moving and kept absolute silence. Their number was far from ideal to perform a seal hunt. For prey with a keen sense of hearing, the more whales there were, the more easily the prey would detect them. Furka knew there were orcas, which specialized in hunting seals and porpoises, and those seldom hunted with more than of them. There was an atmosphere of tension and Tuschka hugged close to her mother. With Furka in the lead, Sigurd and Tamara headed off towards the kelp beds. Shaka and Tarka stayed back to keep the youngsters under control.

The three scouts made a wide circle around two rocky outcrops with a kelp bed in between. They listened intently, carefully avoiding making any sound. Nothing revealed the presence of seals yet, but that did not mean they were not there. Tamara stopped swimming and surfaced just enough to breathe. She deliberately released her air gently to avoid a loud blow. It was hardly louder than a seal's exhalation, but it lasted much longer. Tamara hovered at the surface, listening. The seals could stay under for quite a long time, but they too eventually had to breathe. After almost 15 minutes, she heard a little puff, and then another. They were too short to be blows of her orca companions. Knowing there were seals hiding in the kelp, the orcas had to locate them first before they could even try to catch them. Simply moving into the seaweed would eliminate any chance. Furka nudged Sigurd to go around on the other side. She and Tamara closed in on their side of the kelp, each close to one of the two rocky outcrops. After a short silence, they heard Sigurd move into the kelp. The two females listened intently. Suddenly, a small dark shape darted out of the weeds a little underneath and to the left of Tamara. The two made an immediate sharp turn and started their pursuit.

The orcas further out to sea were surprised by the sudden outburst of activity. They echolocated and called when they saw the two females burst into speed. Hearing other whales ahead might make the prey turn around and confuse it. Tuschka spyhopped and saw Furka's whole body fly out of the water. The agile seal had changed direction while Furka leaped out of the water. Tamara had been following a bit behind, and in the poor light of the setting sun, she was again surprised when the seal doubled back and slipped by. She turned instinctively but quickly gave up. Under these conditions, they could catch a seal only by surprise, but for a real chase, they needed good visibility and cooperation.

Sigurd had stayed near the kelp and located the terrified seal. He made no attempt to go after it, however, and waited silently. The seal had fled into the kelp, but did not dare to spend anymore time in the water than necessary. As fast as it could, it crawled onto the rocks, seeking safety on top of them. The outcrop was shallow, barely more than half the height of his dorsal fin above the water surface. Sigurd stole around and turned on his side. The rest of the pod had moved in and watched him from a short distance. No one expected very much of this hunt anymore and although they kept silent, they made no attempt to hide. Sigurd saw the seal watching him, then he slowly moved his strong, curled, flukes backward and in a powerful sideways stroke, he sent a wave of water over the seal's little refuge. The seal almost lost its balance, but found a hold on a little rock between his forelimbs. Sigurd blew forcefully near the frightened animal and slowly turned away to join the others.

The tension had gone and Tuschka followed Igor and Skaade towards the kelp. The young orcas followed each other, rolled over and tugged on the strong kelp leaves. At times, Igor and Skaade pulled on the same piece. Tuschka was watching the tugging game when a black shadow slid by very closely. Startled, she let out a squeak. She had never seen anything big so close to her, except her own kind. It was the seal who had slid off the rock in an attempt to reach the safer ones, closer to shore. For a moment, she was undecided whether to seek safety near Skaade and Igor or her mother, who was much farther away. The playful juveniles were with her immediately, but more out of curiosity than concern. They quickly darted off for some other game. A moment later, her mother was at her side, reassuring her and taking her back to the rest of the family. In the presence of the big loving female, Tuschka immediately regained her confidence and gorged herself with the rich tasty milk. Upon Shaka's imperative call the two playing whales joined the pod. Tightly together, they headed off to another bank, continuing their never-ending search for food.

* * *

In mid-May, the pod turned around from its northerly route along the shelf and headed towards the big mouth of the Laksava River to the south. Furka expected migrating salmon to soon return and start their struggle upstream to spawn. Food had not been particularly abundant over the past several weeks and most of them had lost weight. They were eager to find the nourishing and tasty salmon. Furka had set a good pace and they were traveling with the tide in a tight group. For the last few days they had traveled along the western and southern shore, foraging for food only once.

In late morning, the orcas passed Rockcove Bay again. There were a lot more sounds around them than there had been for quite a while: a variety of rumbles and roars reached their ears. Low rumbles carried for long distances, but these hardly bothered the orcas. The high-pitched shrill sounds of little rotating blades were much more annoying, since they made it more difficult to hear their own calls. Right now, the orcas were silent and did not really care. They were simply on their way to the salmon river.

The pod slowed down when a few members heard faint calls in the distance. Tuschka wondered what was happening and listened intently. The sounds were still way too far to see anything, but they became steadily stronger and puzzled Tuschka. They were very similar to the sounds of her own pod members, yet they were different. Her companions immediately recognized the calls of another well-known orca family on its way to the same river mouth. Excitement was instantaneous. Not only did the other orca family bring a nice diversion, but when hunting together, the two pods would be much more efficient on the hunt. Furka vocalized loudly to voice their presence. A clear reply came almost immediately. Now, the others joined in and while they increased their speed, a concert of orca calls filled the sea.

Furka was aware that the other pod had been swimming ahead of them in the same direction, but more slowly. Upon her call they had turned around and were coming towards her. She called her family to stop before the other orcas came into view. It was enough of a hint for them to line up abreast at the surface. Furka, nor the other adult orcas, needed a single echo to know that the others had done the same. A few younger orcas squeaked in suppressed excitement. Then, after a short pause, Tuschka watched as she saw their own matriarch swim forward towards a similar shadow emerging from the twilight green ahead. The unknown big female radiated a dignity and authority that, until now, she had known only one to have. Tuschka sensed that she was for the others what Furka was for them. Raina, the leader of the other family, had come meet. Tuschka saw the two matriarchs slid by each other, exchanging friendly rubs and nudges. Upon some signal, new to Tuschka, the orcas of both groups approached and intermingled. They caressed, rubbed, and nudged each other, and checked everyone out. Although some of the other orcas were young, there was no one like herself. She was surprised how curious the other orcas were about her. Every single one came over to greet her mother and to take a good look at her, but none of them touched her. Tuschka was not afraid: no orca had ever harmed her. Yet she felt more secure near mom, who would tell her whom she could play with.

It was obvious for Tuschka that the orcas knew each other well. She could not yet fathom that the orcas of both families had shared time in hunting, traveling, and play since they had been as young as she, and their mothers before them. Some of their calls sounded very similar, but others were completely new to Tuschka. The little orca noticed two big males in the other pod, Korak and Stur, and a younger one, whose dorsal fin had begun to grow taller than those of most of the females.

Furka and Raina were happy to share time together after a long time of wandering the ocean separately. Igor and Skaade indulged in play with the three young whales of Raina's pod, while the males sought the company of other males, and females teamed up with other females. For several hours, the orcas just enjoyed being together.

Tuschka watched the big females who gathered around her mother. They were all very friendly and in the relaxed atmosphere, she gave in to her curiosity and ventured a little way from her mother. One of the females, a little younger than Tarka, nudged her gently. She was so much like Annika that Tuschka trusted her naturally and moved over to her. Tarka watched her without worry. She and Nadia had felt a special closeness since they had both carried life within them. Tarka knew that Tuschka awakened the feelings of motherhood in Nadia, who would have her own calf not long from now.

Tarka had not been far away from the two matriarchs, who had spent most of the time together. It was mid-afternoon when she saw them separate. Suddenly their breaches and loud calls startled her: it was time for everyone to group up and move on. They stayed together, but each within its own pod. Raina's family took the lead when they headed for the Laxava River. In anticipation of the first salmon runs, they remained in the vicinity of the river mouth. Meanwhile they took the edge off their appetite with cod and a variety of smaller fish.

When there had been no sign of salmon for several days, Furka left and headed out towards sea again. She decided to forage along the shelf and be ready to follow the first salmon in.

Tuschka bumped her mother's belly in a gentle rhythm when she suddenly heard and felt a low vibrating rumble, unlike anything she had ever heard before. The others had obviously noticed it too, but no one was alarmed. Instead, they seemed to take it as a welcome diversion and headed in the direction of the sound. Some of her companions were echolocating the waters ahead of them. Tuschka joined in, but could not make much of her echoes. Some had bounced off something seemingly big, and the next burst of pulses found no obstacle at all. Full of curiosity the baby orca rose high to peek above the surface, but she saw nothing unusual. After the first several clicks, the rumbling sounds suddenly ceased. Tuschka noticed that everyone changed direction and echolocated once more. Again, she received reflections from something big. While she listened intently to the clicks of the other members of the family, she noticed the reflections came from a different position. Suddenly, it struck her: the big thing moved and her family was trying to follow it. She peeked above the surface again, but saw nothing unfamiliar. Tuschka had never encountered anything of such size that moved.

Her mother increased her pace like the others, and Tuschka started to make small bows while surfacing next to her mother's dorsal fin. Suddenly, she heard a huge blow in the distance. When she jumped up a little higher, she saw giant flukes lift up in the air and submerge. As she descried the huge shape, she was struck by its long, white, and slender pecs, and a mere hump as a dorsal fin. Large grooves lined the underside of its huge lower jaw. It was Tuschka's first encounter with a humpback whale, migrating to its polar feeding grounds. The whale had just come up from a longer dive. The big whale had a companion about a hundred yards further away. Tuschka hugged close to her mother. As big as they were, she could not fathom that the whales viewed them as a potential threat, rather than the other way round. Not knowing why, Tuschka noticed them tense and increase their speed.

Very few times had Tarka seen other orcas attack these whales for food, but her pod had no such intentions. They followed the whales for a little while. Igor and Skaade avoided the giant's tail but they made some playful dives in its slipstream. Tuschka's eyes were drawn to the elongated white flippers, that were much longer herself. The huge blue creatures even dwarfed Sigurd. The two giants had come together now. Tuschka felt the strong suction of their slipstream. Like her, the others followed almost effortlessly. Then, Furka veered off. Tuschka and her mother followed. Skaade and Igor were the last to leave. As the blue shapes dissolved in the blue, Tuschka was not aware that the two pushed on for many more miles until they calmed down from their encounter with her pod.

The orcas been mainly been feeding on mackerel and were heading closer to shore again. Tuschka had accompanied her mother and some of the others several times on their hunts. So far, she had not captured a fish, but Tarka had noticed that her playful hunting had become much more purposeful. For Tarka, that was not the only reason why she felt that time had come for Tuschka to learn more about her future prey.

Since a few days, Tuschka was confused and felt insecure: her mother had surprised her several times by suddenly turning away from her when she tried to nurse. Tuschka was not aware that her teeth sometimes hurt her mother when she took a teat in her mouth. She had first tried to stay at the teat when her mother rolled away and over on her back. But when she tried that, her mother rolled away the next time even before she had had a chance to drink. It was not that her mother didn't want her near. She was very gentle as long as she made no attempt to nurse. Tuschka spent more time with Tamara and Annika, but they had no milk to offer. As dedicated and loving as Tarka was, she was well aware that her calf needed to nurse and was going without milk for longer than was good for her. Her mother heart ached to see her Tuschka seek comfort from others and she stayed close, rubbing Tuschka gently, and talking to her in soft squeaks. She wanted to reassure her calf and make her feel comfortable. Tuschka was grateful for her mother's warm attention, but was still a little reluctant to drink. She did not want to be rebuffed again, but her empty stomach rumbled and she ached for milk. A little hesitant, she took her familiar position under mom's belly and bobbed her gently. There was no sign of refusal. Instead, her mother rolled a little to her side and offered her teat willingly. A little apprehensive, Tuschka carefully touched the teat with her tongue. When her mother did not withdraw it, she rolled her tongue around it and gulped down the squirt of full rich milk. It was also a relief for Tarka, who had felt a bursting tension for most of the day. Tuschka regained some confidence when she was allowed to take a few more gulps. Her mother even nudged and rubbed her approvingly. A little later, when she approached her mother playfully and bumped her belly with a hint of rambunctiousness, she rolled away. Tuschka was taken aback for a moment and then tried again, much more carefully... As she had hoped, mother rewarded her. Tuschka learned quickly that she was welcome to drink as long as she was careful. She soon discovered how to drink without hurting her mother.

Every time Tuschka accompanied members of her pod on the hunt, they immediately swallowed their catch. She could see them grab a fish, but in an instant it disappeared. It came as a surprise to her when she saw her mother approach with part of a fish still hanging from her mouth. Tuschka watched her as she came over and felt a friendly nudge. Mother released the fish in front of her and backed up a little. She looked at the floating fish without making a movement. Then, mother inched forward and in an instant she sucked the fish into her mouth again. Tuschka looked in surprise when mother made the small chunk of fish reappear in front of her for the second time. Tuschka came over and nudged the fish. Mother called encouragingly. She repeated the game and Tuschka came over quickly and nibbled on the fish. While she had it between the front of her jaws, she touched and explored it with the tip of her tongue. The taste was not totally unfamiliar and certainly not unpleasant. It was like the taste of the water when everyone was enjoying a successful hunt. As soon as Tuschka let go, mother sucked it in again and gave it back, encouraging her to imitate her. Tarka and Tuschka went on with their game for quite a while until a loud command from Furka pierced their ears. While they turned to join the others, mother swallowed the little toy, which had become torn and ragged. Tuschka snuggled under her mother's belly. She was contented with her new experience and cherished her mother's closeness.

* * *

A small group of researchers had come the year before to investigate the possibility of a photographic population survey, but they had encountered a lot of logistical problems, especially that of finding a suitable boat. During that first summer, they found out that many orcas were seen near Rockcove bay and that local fishermen might be hired to take them out. Bjorn, the leader of the research team, had recently approached Johann, who was known for his gentle attitude towards the orcas, with the request to take them to the whales as often as they were sighted. Many fishermen, especially those who fished for herring, disliked the powerful black whales that were after the same food. Johann had always had a great respect for nature and he accepted the ways of the whales. When the research leader had arrived at Rockcove bay, Johann had quickly agreed to take them out to the orcas during the next season. He would learn more about these majestic creatures and it even meant some financial support for his family. Since he was one of the professional fishermen, he had only a small boat for recreational purposes, but he wanted to be well prepared for the whale encounters with the research team. A month before the team arrived he had already traded his small boat for a bigger one with a small cabin, where equipment could be stored and people could shelter during bad weather.

* * *

One morning in early June, as the sun appeared on the horizon, the whales were traveling abreast, their glossy backs glistening in the sun. The cool air was filled with the sounds of a gentle breeze and the screams of gulls. At intervals, the explosive blows of the orca family formed an array of plumes, carried away on the wind. The presence of cormorants revealed that they were approaching the Sentinel islands south of the main shore. As usual while on the move, Sigurd and Furka swam at the left side; next to them were Annika, Shaka, Igor, and Skaade; and at the right side were Tuschka, Tarka, and Tamara. They were silent, constantly listening to their surroundings.

The silence was broken when Sigurd called. It took only seconds for everyone to be full of excitement and expectation. As one, they kicked their flukes and sped up. They broke the surface simultaneously with their dorsal fins in line, arching their magnificent bodies high, and creating V's of foam as the water parted at their white chins. They were porpoising, doing close to 20 knots with ease. Sigurd created quite a wake and Igor surfed right behind his big companion. They had been alerted by the sounds and calls of other orcas herding fish. Although the fish were still beyond range for echolocation, the older whales knew a big salmon run awaited them. The hunt would be more successful with more whales and there was no doubt they would be welcome.

A little while later, they heard a variety of calls, mixed with the sounds of slapping fins, tails, and an occasional breach. The water had a slight taste of freshly killed salmon. For Tuschka, the burst of speed was pure joy. Everyone, but her, recognized the typical calls of Raina's pod and Sigrid's pod. They met Sigrid's pod less frequently than they met Raina's. Sigrid led a big pod of almost 30 animals. Seven mature bulls, two adolescent males, 13 adult females, five juveniles, and two calves, less than a year old. Altogether, they formed an armada of 51 whales, of which at least 42 were trained, purposeful hunters.

When Furka arrived with her pod, she called a few times to announce their arrival and she listened to the answers to learn where exactly the other whales were. There was no time to greet and socialize. Now the hunt had first priority, and Tuschka saw her companions immediately move away to take positions among the others. Although the two other pods had already herded the fish into a higher concentration, feeding conditions were still far from ideal. Only a few slower fish close-by were taken on the move. All the voices and slaps told Tuschka that they were covering a very large area, but they were not randomly spread. The majority of them formed a sort of arc, preventing fish from fanning out. The other whales swam somewhat deeper to keep the fish close to the surface. Every few minutes the divers came up and were relieved by others. Seabirds were screaming and following them, eager to dive at scraps of killed fish.

Tuschka followed her mother closely, copying all her movements. She was intrigued by this huge organized mutual effort. As they went, beating the water, sounding, and echolocating, they managed to drive the fish into several tighter groups. As the spaces between them became smaller, the herding became more efficient. Many fish jumped out of the water, only to fall back and follow their congeners in a race for survival. Tuschka sensed the excitement build. The fish became increasingly dense, yet her companions did not give up their formation. At one point, the fish were so concentrated that it became impossible to keep fish from escaping. This was a sign that the time was right to attack and feed. Tuschka could not see much of what happened in the fray of orcas and fish, but each salmon required a dedicated chase. Exceptionally loud clicks from many directions pierced Tuschka's ears and confused the big fish. At the surface, the chase was on with fluke prints, lunges, and dorsal fins that sliced the water in sharp turns. Bodies rolled over, or tails flung through the air when orcas turned and dove near the surface. The hunters took turns eating and herding. Tuschka tried to stay as close to her mother as possible. The whirl of fish and the sounds from all directions were too confusing for her to enjoy her own chasing game. As the orcas gorged themselves, the fish gradually thinned, partly because of the feeding, but mostly because they were no longer herding the prey with the same organized effort.

When the whales finally stopped herding, the fish dispersed. While the water was clearing, Tuschka darted playfully after a few fleeing fish. Then she returned to her mother and bumped her belly. For the last few hours, there had been no opportunity for her to nurse. Tuschka was by no means satisfied when her mother rolled away. She asked for more trying to be as careful as she could, but without success. Mother turned around, instead, with a piece of salmon in her mouth. She spat it out in front of her and backed up a bit. Tuschka sucked it in and spat it out towards her mother, expecting to play the same game as they had done before. Tarka grabbed the piece and swam away with it. Tuschka followed and again tried to nurse, but in vain. Tarka offered her the piece of fish instead and did not wait for Tuschka to give it back. She turned and slowly swam away. Tuschka felt it was not a game. She was hungry and yet, at her attempts to nurse, mother offered her that piece of fish. Tuschka played with it for a little longer and then swallowed a piece of it, a bit surprised with herself. She looked to the side when she heard a reassuring call from her mother. The big whale glided towards her, rubbed her head against her, and rewarded her with a lot of creamy, rich milk. Tuschka understood she had very much pleased her mother, but she did not understand that her first bite of fish was a milestone in her life: liking the taste of fish was the first step in becoming a hunter!

After the rewarding hunt, the whales relaxed and socialized. Tuschka was surprised with all the attention from the whales of Sigrid's pod. Especially the females took a good look at her. A group of young whales rolled, jumped, and chased each other nearby. Their mothers and discipline seemed far away. Orca calls sounded everywhere for miles. Even the adults engaged in games. One of the younger adult females of Sigrid's pod approached her playfully. She swung under her and Tuschka suddenly found herself being pinned on her rostrum and being pushed forward. When she slid off, mother picked her up and did the same. Tuschka felt the sheer power pushing her along and the rhythmical pulses of her mother's strong down strokes. She squeaked in delight and rolled over her mother's back when she pushed her up.

A few more females appeared and Tuschka's attention was suddenly caught by a calf, slightly bigger than herself. It had sighted her too. They swam towards each other and nuzzled. Never before had Tuschka met one of her own kind so close to her own size. They rubbed, made little circles around each other and engaged in little bursts of speed. Soon, Annika came over to gently join their game. She loved to be around the calves and enjoyed herself tremendously at this opportunity to play with them so freely.

3.
A Painful Mistake

Fall had come with much longer nights, heavy rains and strong winds. Tuschka had become used to traveling tight together in big swells with gusts of winds sweeping up spray from the white crests of the breaking waves. Times of bountiful salmon near the river mouth were long past and weeks of scarcity had gone by on their trek along the eastern fjords, but the herring was abundant now and in between storms, hunting was successful. This was Tuschka's second winter and she had learned much from her family of hunters. She was not as proficient as the others, but she helped herding fish and had learned much about using clicks and reading the echoes. Tuschka nursed less frequently, but when she did, she drank lots of Tarka's rich milk. Her weight had doubled and she was about half her mother's length. Tuschka still spent most of the time with mom, but she also traveled with Tamara or Annika, and grabbed every chance to play.

Furka's pod had been following the coast, which had started to curve to the north. It was a relatively calm day when they approached steep rugged rocks. Small and large fjords cut deep into a mountainous barren hinterland. The sky was grey and a drizzle had started. They came upon some seaweed near the shore and played for a while. Annika tried to get strands of the weed in the notch of her flukes and lift them up. Tuschka followed her and tugged at the same strand. Annika, a little annoyed, gave Tuschka a light slap on her nose and turned around. A little startled, she let go and backed up a little. Then Skaade approached and grabbed a strand near Tuschka. In an instant, the three were engaged in a tugging game. Tarka and Tamara were rubbing themselves against the vertical rocks. Some protrusions served excellently to scratch their most itchy spots: the base of their dorsal fin and the underside of their flukes. Furka hovered at the surface, occasionally peeking above the surface to look around. Sigurd was beside her and offered Igor his big pectoral fin to rub on. The juvenile male tried to entice the big one into play, but Sigurd barely responded to the young whale's rolling and bumping. Wanting some rest, the bull gave him a sideways nod. Igor took the hint and joined his mother.

A clear call from Furka got everyone's attention. They stopped their activities and grouped up tight, slowly moving toward the sea again. Swimming close to her mother, Tuschka listened to the echoes of her family's clicks. The reflections revealed many small fish, and her companions picked up speed. The faint but unmistakable echoes revealed a large concentration ahead. Everyone became almost silent, lest they scare the fish, clicking only to assess the distance to their prey. Then, Furka called to start the hunt. They now closed in on the fish and formed a line. Tuschka heard the others on the outside pound their tail on the water several times, and saw the fish flee forward and toward the center of the group. The water was so clear that she could easily see the others form a semicircle around a small part of the big shoal. She already tried to catch some fish that escaped, but the silvery fish were agile and small. In between her distractions she tried to copy the behavior of the adults. When Sigurd went down with Tamara to prevent the fish from diving, they picked up the sound of distant engines. She saw the big male freeze on the spot, listening with full concentration, then continuing on. Tuschka did not know that Furka and the older whales knew the two boats ahead.

Long ago, Furka and her experienced companions had learned to take advantage of their competitors. Late in the afternoon, the boats would position their nets. The matriarch and her pod knew every sound that accompanied the fishing activities. The nets had a similar effect as their herding. Waiting for the fish to be concentrated and then moving in to take a share, proved to be an easy and efficient way to hunt. But, it was not without danger. Some of their kind had been severely injured and a few had even lost their lives when they were close to a fishing boat. The accidents had come suddenly, without warning, and the orcas did not really understand how to detect and avoid the danger. With every bad experience, however, they etched sounds of the boat in their memories and would not approach that boat again. The orcas did not pay much attention to the looks of a boat, but they unerringly registered the subtle differences in the sounds they made. The experienced whales taught the younger pod members which vessels to approach and which to avoid.

The two seiners had located both the orcas and the herring. Quite frequently, the whales were a lead to find the fish. But that was the only aspect of the species that most fisherman appreciated. The wind picked up a bit when the boats separated, and stopped, several hundred yards apart. Furka and her pod continued their hunt, though still alert to any change in the boat sounds. Soon, the orcas had driven some of the fish into a fairly tight ball. Tuschka saw how close the fish stayed together and moved in unison. Each time an orca passed close by a silvery wave went through the ball, as the fish turned away from the whale and back into the ball. Her companions all circled with their white bellies toward the fish and made the fish ball ever tighter. It was clearly the whole purpose of their strategy. With a loud smack, Furka smashed her flukes into the ball and Tuschka watched numerous fish float around, dead or stunned. The matriarch then had an easy time sucking them up one by one. Sigurd struck with even more force and was rewarded with an even larger number of suspended motionless fish. Tuschka followed her mother, and when she did the same thing, she tried to copy her. She moved over to suck up a feebly moving herring. It was easy to swallow. Tuschka was delighted and sucked up a few more. She was thrilled with her success, not knowing that it had been her mother's strike and not hers that had stunned the small fish.

When the herring ball thinned, they all turned, facing into the direction of the boats. Tuschka was curious and started towards one. She wanted to poke her head out of the water near the vessel and hear the excited screams of the creatures on board, but Tarka came after her and brought her back. She was disappointed, but her companions knew what to expect. From one of the big boats, a small one was launched and the orcas recognized the sounds of the nets being unrolled. Hovering at the surface, they rested from their hunt and prepared for the next.

The small boat dragged one end of a huge net away from the main boat. The net was several hundred yards long when fully stretched. With both boats holding the ends, it made a slight curve in the tidal current. The orcas knew that the first fish, hitting the net, would try to swim away from it, but then turn again to join the many newcomers. The orcas waited as more fish encountered the net and swam erratically in confusion. Tuschka was amazed at the large concentration of herring that was forming. She and Igor wanted to dive into the fish, but Shaka and Tarka called them to stay. It was not the right time to start feeding. A few moments later, the small boat dragged its end of the net towards the big boat in a big circle. The circle was not closed yet, but few fish found an escape. Tuschka saw Furka, Tamara, and Sigurd move forward, enter the circle, and gorge themselves. Shaka, Annika, and Tarka stayed outside near the opening with Igor and herself. They grabbed a few escaping fish. The circle was almost closed, when the three whales that had been feeding inside dived and surfaced again outside the net. Now, they all surrounded the net and swam back and forth. Tuschka explored the soft maze that had trapped the fish inside. It gave when she nudged it. One fish was partly stuck through a small hole and struggled in vain to get free. Tuschka delicately grabbed its head and it proved easy to pull loose. While she looked for another, she watched Sigurd dive to gobble up herring that spilled out when the bottom of the net was closed.

A sudden sound close by startled Tuschka. She had a faint memory of it, but she had never heard it so close before. At the same time, the ball of fish kept together by the net, rapidly shrunk. It was the sound of the net being pulled up. Everyone dived, surfaced, and circled around it, grabbing fish that spilled over the edge. Tuschka thought it was over when the net disappeared, but Furka stayed and seemed to anticipate something. Several minutes later, the almost empty net was dropped back and several tangled fish washed out. The orcas were quick to pick them up. After the net had been taken in for the second time, Furka called them together and started to move away. They had been close to the boat for quite a while, but this boat had not harmed them before. Furka preferred to hunt after sunset when the darkness of the night, and the sounds of the wind and the fishing gear, hid much of their presence and activities. In her experience, it was much safer to hunt close to the boats at night than during daytime.

Some nights, they fed near more than one boat, but with two successful hunts on one day, they had been able to eat their complete fill. Satisfied, they moved away. Traveling in close contact with each other, they slowly swam further north, only a mile off the rugged coast. Tuschka had eaten so much fish that she had little need of milk that night. Nevertheless, she swam in her favorite spot beneath her mother, rhythmically bumping her soft, familiar belly.

* * *

The orcas had spent about two months near the fjords and often taken advantage of the activities of the herring fleet. Sometimes, the boats came to them when they had found fish. At other times, they were guided by the sounds of nets being taken in. When the days began to lengthen, the herring became less abundant and Furka led her pod south again. For several weeks, they followed and patrolled the steep rocky coast, crossing the mouths of several smaller and bigger fjords.

One afternoon, they entered narrow inlet. Its mouth was only two hundred yards wide and fairly shallow. The sun was setting when the sound of a starting engine brought an end to the silence. There was nothing alarming about the sound, and the matriarch decided to head on. They moved along the steep rocky shore at a leisurely pace. As Furka echolocated, she was surprised by what seemed a large stationary lump of very concentrated herring. Everyone had read the returning echoes, but their leading female did not speed up in the direction of the unexpected concentration of food. Instead, she echolocated again. Something was strange… There were no other predators near, nor big fishing boats with their familiar sounds.

A small boat was approaching at a higher speed, but the whales ignored the little vessel. Igor was full of excitement and made a high playful surfacing. He dashed forward beyond the matriarch, but she called him back. Just as he heard her call, he descried a net that surrounded the packed fish. In an instant he veered off to the side and barely cleared one of the poles to which the net was attached. A little confused, Igor peeked above the water and saw a long shaft sticking up right by him. A moment later, he heard the small boat heading towards him at a fairly high speed. Just as he dived and turned to join the others, a sharp explosive sound pierced his ears. A shiver went through his body and instinctively, he took off away from the net. The next instant, he was alarmed by the voices of his own family. A faint memory flashed through his mind, but he did not need his memory to understand what the calls meant. The voices did not come from the place where he had left the others behind. Instead, his family was speeding across the fjord on its way out. He heard Shaka and Sigurd call loudly for him. Igor did not hesitate, turned sharply and burst into speed towards them. He did not pay attention to the boat that was between him and his family. As he arched high close to the boat something deafeningly sharp not only hurt his ears, but also sent a sharp, tearing pain through his back. He screamed, diving in a desperate attempt to get away.

Upon Igor's distress call Furka stopped dead in her tracks. The pod was confused, as their leader was suddenly facing the choice between bringing them to safety or coming to Igor's rescue. Shaka and Sigurd did not wait for their mother to make a decision. They were not used to carrying responsibility for the pod as a whole and did not resist their impulse to help. The moment they heard Igor's high-pitched screaming, they burst into speed to come to his rescue. Furka did not call them back. She felt an equally strong impulse to help, but she held her breath and stayed with the others.

The mother and her brother found the young male, whining at the surface, enveloped in a thin cloud of blood. Just in front of his dorsal fin, they noticed a loose flap of skin, revealing some bleeding blubber underneath. The wound did not look big, but it obviously caused the young orca a lot of pain. Sigurd and Shaka took position on each side of Igor and lifted him up between them. The wounded companion quieted when he felt the warmth of the two caring orcas against him and heard his mother's comforting voice. The three were oblivious to the boat, which was slowly moving away. The pod had come to meet the three whales. Furka inspected her daughter's son and greeted him with a soft friendly call. When the last rays of the winter sun disappeared, the pod rounded the rocks that marked the southern end of the fjord's mouth. That night, they moved very slowly with Igor in their midst. The young male hardly moved, giving in to the solace and relief while his mother and Sigurd carried him.

The concentration of fish that the orcas had encountered in the fjord, had been caught by fishermen the day before. The catch was kept in a net in the protected waters of Kalika inlet to stay fresh until it was sold a few days later. This strategy allowed the fishermen to work in a remote area for two or three nights in a row. One crew member always stayed behind in a boat with a small cabin to guard the fish. Torvil was on watch when Furka's pod went by. He was inexperienced and feared the orcas would damage the net and undo the previous day's work. Unlike his more experienced buddies, he did not know that whales rarely tore at nets, and to his knowledge, killer whales were a dangerous species. As soon as he saw the orcas head for the fish, he came over in his small boat and fired a bullet in an attempt to scare them off. Torvil was relieved with the whale's instantaneous response, but he did not realize his boat was between the young orca and his family. Suddenly, the orca surfaced high, at close range, and head on! In fright, he aimed and fired at the fast swimming whale in an attempt to end the seemingly hostile charge. Upon the whale's dive, Torvil froze, staring at the spot where it had disappeared. The next few seconds would tell him if he had succeeded: either his boat would be hit and capsize, or the whale would have changed his mind. Another surge of adrenaline hit him when he heard two strong blows behind him. Guided by his reflexes, he turned and aimed his rifle. When the whales surfaced again he saw them facing away from him and he slowly relaxed his grip. He did not want to draw their attention and kept watching. While he watched, he could not believe his eyes. The two adult whales, one with a huge dorsal fin, surfaced close to each other with the wounded juvenile in between.

Although the scene intrigued the fisherman, he felt his body shiver and he chose to return to the safety of his small dock. His initial satisfaction with his bravery in defending the catch gave way to feelings of wonder and fascination. The scene did not leave his mind. It was plausible that pain had made the wounded orca refrain from attack, but the two big whales could easily have rammed his boat and killed him. Why didn't they? Perhaps they were afraid because of what had happened to their young companion. But if they were afraid, why had they come so close? If their only purpose had been to help their wounded member, it was awfully brave and loyal. Could that be it..? What else could explain this remarkable behavior? That night, his sleep was troubled. The puzzle grew into a strong desire: he wanted to know these mighty predators that every creature feared.

* * *

It was late in the morning when the pod stopped to rest. Carrying Igor had been tiring for Shaka and Tamara came over to relieve her. As strong as he was, Sigurd decided he did not need to change places at this time and stayed with his sister's son. Occasionally, Igor gave soft whining calls. Although she was not carrying her offspring, Shaka stayed right behind, calling frequently to him. The bullet had penetrated the muscles via the thin layer of blubber and had grazed the spine, where it had lodged in a relatively harmless spot. The damage in his muscles caused Igor pain with every move. For Tuschka, the situation was new and difficult to comprehend. She understood that something was very wrong with her playmate, but her mother prevented her from getting close to him. Whenever she had a chance, little Tuschka swam by underneath the three whales, looking up on her side and calling out in hopes Igor would answer her. But most often she only heard her mother or Tamara asking her to stay calm.

The mood in the pod was lusterless. In times when something bothered them, Tuschka felt most secure at her mother's flank. In some way, Tuschka's behavior reflected the mood of the family as a whole. The higher their spirits, the more exploring and brave she was. Now, she was rather timid. The whales heard the familiar sounds of a fishing boat in the distance, but ignored it. For the days to come Igor would need all their attention. They could only hope that his condition would improve fast enough to allow part of them to forage and hunt again.

For the first night and day, Igor had remained virtually passive. Each attempt to move caused him sharp stabs of pain. The second day he was more aware of his surroundings. He felt the pectoral fins of the two adults underneath him, which filled him with a feeling of safety and being cared for. The bodily contact with his escorts made him realize how close Sigurd was. The strong big male had fascinated him since he was very young and playing with Sigurd was always full of surprise and challenge. Never had he been so close to him for so long. While his mother and Tamara voiced affection and encouragement, the calls of the only adult male of his pod were resolute. They conveyed concern, but not worry. The confidence he radiated and his powerful presence made Igor feel stronger inside. Despite the pain, he nudged his big friend, which encouraged Sigurd. Weak but determined, Igor started to move his flukes feebly up and down. As they swam, the bond between him and his family became stronger and the special friendship with Sigurd deepened.

For several days, two companions stayed with Igor all the time and were ready to support him when he needed rest. Most of the time he had his mother and Sigurd on his side. The pod moved slowly, and gradually needed fewer stops. In his companions' slipstream, the injured juvenile managed to keep up by himself for longer periods every day. Having gone without food for almost a week, the need to forage became more urgent. They all were hungry, but food was even more important for Igor. Traveling was strenuous for him and healing took its toll. They were all painfully aware of the problems that would ensue if they did not soon have the opportunity to feed and rest. The initial sharp quality of the pain had changed into a more dull muscle ache. Furka was relieved to see that Igor was strong enough to swim for several hours without resting. Time had come to search more actively for food, but she made sure at least one adult stayed with Igor.

In the afternoon, Annika was the first to hear the sounds of a small engine and nets being unrolled. They all turned into the direction of the sounds. Furka was in the lead and stopped when she was within several hundred yards of the vessel. The orcas were silent and listened. The engine sound was menacingly similar to the one they had heard when Igor had gotten hurt. The matriarch hesitated. The situation was different... Igor had not been hurt during normal fishing activities and the need for food was pressing. She decided to follow the boat and wait for the relative safety of darkness. The sun was low, but had not yet disappeared when the orcas detected an increasing concentration of fish ahead. Swimming against a slow current, they approached within several hundred yards. The small engine had been turned off for a while and their gnawing hunger almost made them forget their initial apprehension. Keeping their distance from the boat, the pod waited. The last rays of the sun cast an orange reflection on their white eye patches.

The young fisherman had joined his mates the day after he had fired his rifle at the young whale. The response to his story had been rather skeptical. The other crew had never witnessed such a thing and they blamed it on faulty judgment due to his fear. Some of them had been teasing him or telling him stories about killer whales that would never forget the ones who harmed them and would someday take revenge. In his heart, the young man hoped to see the whales again from the relative safety of the seiner.

While they waited for the net to fill, he scouted the horizon with his sharp eyes. A scream of surprise almost escaped his throat when he noticed the whales' blows in the distance. He ran to the wheel-house to grab the binoculars and spotted one remarkably tall fin among several smaller ones. When they asked him what he was looking for, he tried to hide his eagerness. The orcas gradually drew closer and he hoped they would get within good observation range before it was too dark to see. He strained to see if there was a sign of the injured juvenile and his two escorts.

The orders to haul in the net caught him by surprise. Reluctantly, he put the binoculars down and prepared to help. Torvil was happy that it was not his turn to get into the small boat. Two whales caught his attention as they surfaced relatively close to the net. After a long dive the two came up heading away towards several other whales. It was then that he saw the male and the female with the juvenile in between. Without hesitation, he yelled and pointed into the direction of the three whales. The skipper right next to him rudely grabbed the binoculars from him and looked. Silence fell. It was obvious to all of them that their skipper saw something unusual. No one wanted to make fun of the situation and risk making a blunder. After watching for more than a full minute, he slowly lowered the binoculars and handed them to one of the others. He didn't say a word. In silence, the binocs were passed from one man to the other. When everyone had had a chance to watch the scene, the skipper nodded confirmation to his newest crew member. Then, with one nod, silence was broken and the pulleys were running again. No one even considered an attempt to repel the whales. In fact, their minds were puzzled and the men seemed to even slow down, distracted as they were by watching the whales.

While the net was being hauled in, the orcas moved closer and waited. Eager for food all the whales except Igor and his companions swam forward and milled near the stern, waiting for the spill and leftovers of the catch. As soon as the six orcas had taken some food, Furka went back and signaled Sigurd and Shaka to take their share. At the same time, she offered a mouthful of fish to the young wounded orca. Igor was thankful and tried to follow Sigurd and his mother when they slowly swam forward to the herring spill. He saw them look back and wait for him, and he was grateful when they took him between them again. Igor managed to grab some dead fish floating close by, but was grateful for the food that the other orcas brought to him. Tuschka witnessed all the attention that was directed to her otherwise playful friend. She felt she was not being watched as closely as she had been the days before, and, playfully, she copied the adults' behavior and brought Igor a fish. She was delighted when he accepted it from her and immediately went for another. Although there were not nearly enough fish to satisfy the pod, most of the fish were dead or injured and easy to catch. At least, they managed to scramble together a meal for their recovering pod member.

The orcas rested most of the night and Igor felt new energy. During the days that followed he gained strength fast. He managed to keep up without needing extra rest, although he still took advantage of the slipstream of an adult companion. Most of the time, he swam at his mother's or Sigurd's side. Shaka frequently caressed him, trailing her pectoral fin along his flank or rubbing chins with him. Now and then, the big male tested his mental and physical health by challenging his interest in a little play. They bumped each other gently, rolled over, and glided underneath each other. At one moment, Sigurd playfully swung under Igor and lifted him up on his belly between his huge pectoral fins. With the attention and loving care of his family, it took less than a month for Igor to regain his health and playful spirit.

4.
Meeting Friends

On their way south, the orcas grabbed every hunting opportunity that presented itself. The herring had become scarce and mackerel was relatively far offshore when they reached the dark volcanic beaches of the south coast. Grey seals had just been calving and were nursing their young on these beaches. In only three weeks, the pups would be weaned and trained to swim. Furka's pod was specialized in hunting and eating fish, but in this period when fish was relatively scarce, the inexperienced seal pups were potentially easy prey. The seal mothers, however, usually defended their offspring viciously. The older whales knew that a furious mother grey seal could inflict nasty gashes.

The orcas patrolled the beaches in search of pups that had escaped the attention of their mothers and had entered the water without them. They had to take the colony by surprise. Being well over a year old, Tuschka had learned enough to take the hint when their matriarch signaled for silence. They could not use their clicks, nor surface too close to the beach, because that would immediately alarm the seals.

A tough breeze made the sound of the orcas' blows less easy to hear. They had stopped about a hundred yards from the beach. It would be too conspicuous if they all moved in, so Sigurd, Tamara and Annika stalked forward toward a group of mother and baby seals, which were splashing and playing around. Visibility was impaired by sand that the seals had whirled up from the bottom, and the orcas had to move very close to see.

A female seal suddenly came into Tamara's sight. She seemed not to have noticed the motionless orca. A pup followed almost immediately. The baby was too far and the mother too close to it to attack. Tamara waited, looking and listening.

Sigurd and Annika were close together. They blew quietly and sank down again. The two whales searched for a pup that was in water deep enough to be attacked without the risk of getting stranded. Annika spotted the dark shadow of an adult seal in front of her. It moved parallel to the beach, in water only barely her own body length deep. She moved forward a little and saw a small shadow beneath and to the rear of the adult. Annika stole after them. She was gaining on them and prepared to attempt an attack before the mother seal would detect her. Annika was aware of the potentially vicious defense of the mother seal, but Sigurd was part of the plan. The big and experienced male had come to follow close behind. Suddenly, the mother seal turned toward the beach. Annika dashed forward and sounded loud. The mother seal instinctively turned around to face the enemy when she saw two orcas charging at her at high speed. One whale would have required enough courage from the mother seal to defend her baby, but two of the voracious beasts were too much for this first-time mother. In a reflex, she snarled and opened her mouth, but Annika and Sigurd did not swerve and when they were within a few yards, the mother seal made a run for her life toward the beach. The pup made an attempt to stay with its mom, but it was not nearly as strong and fast. Within seconds, the baby seal fell behind and Annika was quick to grab it firmly. Yelps of pain escaped the baby seal. It aroused its mother's defensive instinct and she turned back for her pup. Yet Sigurd was prepared and kicked his flukes to gain even more speed. He bumped her hard in the belly to prevent her from inflicting injuries on Annika while she was holding the prey. Annika was relieved. Without Sigurd she might have gotten injured while taking off with the pup, or would have had to let go of it to defend herself.

The mother seal was knocked out for at least a minute, but was not severely injured. When she regained her composure, she looked once more into the direction from which the deadly predators had come and, with a shock, found herself looking into the face of another orca. It was Tamara, who had immediately come over after she had heard Annika's call. When she saw that the female seal posed no threat to anyone, she turned and left her alone. The mother seal headed toward the beach as fast as she could and joined the other seals that had already gathered on their dry refuge.

Although the seal pup did not even make a daily ration for an adult orca, Annika did not swallow it by herself. She and Sigurd swam away from shore to meet the rest of the pod, who were waiting a few hundred yards away. Annika had crushed the pup to death soon after she had grabbed it and she brought the limp body over to her mother. Furka took part of it in her mouth and tore off a large piece. Then, she veered off and offered the chunk to Tarka, who needed the food more than everyone else. She was still nursing Tuschka and especially in these times of scarcity, Tarka's milk was important to Tuschka's survival. Furka went back to Annika and rubbed her head against hers. Her mother's fondness of her made her want to hunt again, even if she did have to share the prey with her family.

Tuschka watched with full attention when she saw how her mother took the meat from Furka. She knew the taste of fish, but she had never tasted meat. She was curious, but also a bit anxious. When Igor had been bleeding from his injury, she had tasted something similar. Yet the young male seemed fine and showed no sign of fear or pain. She watched as her mother swallowed the piece whole. Mother had noticed her apprehension and put her pectoral fin reassuringly over her back. No one in the pod seemed stressed and Tuschka quickly relaxed.

Igor and Skaade became impatient and wanted to satisfy their curiosity near the beach, but the elders held them back. The faster the seals forgot them, the sooner there would be another opportunity to hunt. The pod moved away from shore and approached the dark beaches a few miles more to the west, in hopes of finding seals that had not been recently alarmed. Soon, the gray seals would leave the beaches and head out to sea. If meat was to supplement their meals, it had to be within the next few weeks.

Strong winds howled over the water and heavy breakers had forced the nursing seal mothers and their offspring to move higher up the beaches. A few rocks, carried down by glaciers, offered a lee and the little pups snuggled close to their mothers for protection. The orcas had moved further out to sea in search of mackerel. In the storm, there were no gulls to lead the way to schools of herring, and near the surface turbulence impeded their echolocation. The waves were swept up high with spray blowing up from their crests. The orcas felt the large waves build up and approach from behind. They rose and broke the surface with their white chins showing. They loved the sensation of their bodies being carried upwards in the wave and then gain speed, riding it down. It was an awesome sight when the pod traveled close together and all abreast: nine heads suddenly popping out of a wave, sending explosive plumes of breath into the air. Like torpedoes, their strong streamlined bodies pierced the waves. Sometimes the troughs in between waves were so deep that the orcas seemed to fly through the air, forming a bridge between two waves when they left one to dive into the next. Tuschka was still too small to bridge the gap easily. She tried to build up extra speed for the big jump, but sometimes plunged into the bottom of the trough. It was endearing to see the little orca next to the adults, especially when she traveled between Tarka and Sigurd.

Having traveled for several days without food, the pod spent less time socializing. Most of the time, they traveled in silence, always listening. Tamara and Furka were the first to hear faint familiar calls. They slowed down, and a few seconds later, every member of the pod picked up the sound. It came from several miles behind. Then, they turned around and headed north, almost porpoising towards Raina's pod. When only a mile separated the two groups, the adult females recognized the short high-pitched calls of a new calf. Excitement built as the two pods moved closer together and greeted each other.

The friendly voice, reassuring the calf, came from Nadia. She had recently given birth. Nadia wanted to meet the other baby, but she stopped when she saw Furka and Annika approach. Her calf was only a few weeks old and she was still a little apprehensive. She turned slightly sideways and positioned herself between her baby and the approaching whales. Annika saw her mother nod sideways and hung slightly back. She remembered too well from her experiences with Tarka, that she had better stay calm and make a very careful gentle approach. Furka called affectionately and paralleled the new mother. Nadia quickly felt at ease in Furka's company. An older sister of Nadia had joined on her other side. Annika saw the little calf nurse and surface on Furka's side. The baby peeked briefly at the big female on her left and went underneath her mother's belly to the other side. Annika let herself sink a bit and watched the calf, while she glided on her side underneath it. It was a pudgy little female. Although it was tempting to gently touch the calf, she restrained herself and only made playful friendly calls toward the baby. When her mother left, Annika moved over to take her position, but at that moment Tarka and Tuschka approached. She glided back, sinking a little to have a better view of what would happen.

Tuschka was very curious and found herself blocked by her mother when she tried to swim up to the little baby. When se tried again, her mother gave her a brisk bump, enough to tell her to stay back. Tuschka wondered why her mother gave her such a brusque hint, not knowing that her mother didn't want to upset the little calf with a vocal warning. Tarka and Nadia swam side by side, touching pectoral fins as they swam. Tuschka looked at the infant close to her, and for the first time she saw an orca that was smaller than she.

Annika did not get a chance to swim alongside Nadia, and soon lost interest. Just having come into season, she was restless with an unusual longing for attention. She was on her way to the perimeter of the group when she heard a strong, but friendly voice call to her. She looked back and saw Korak approach her. A wave of excitement went through her. Then, she quickly turned her head forward again and increased her speed. Unconsciously, she knew that the big bull recognized her shy invitation. When she had not wanted any part of him, she would simply have made a brisk nod or slap her tail to warn him away when he came too close. Not so this time... She heard him kick his mighty flukes, and gaining speed fast. He was aiming for her. Her heart beat faster and she suddenly dived and turned to the right. For a moment, it seemed her pursuer had lost her. His call sent a pleasant shiver through her body. She kept silent, but when his pulsing clicks hit her body, she knew he had found her. Annika saw the big male hover for a moment, waiting to see what she would do.

Two older females swam by, but he paid them no attention. Annika had slowed down and was curious about Korak's next action. When she saw him come, she swam away from him again. Korak stopped and called her with a pleading voice. She hesitated, but did not turn around. When he didn't seem to follow her, she slowed down and turned to see where he was. Suddenly, he appeared from below. Her covetous eyes had made him even more excited, and without holding back he sped up and aimed for her. Annika felt the water surge up as the mighty whale approached. A twinge of adrenaline went through her and with a sharp turn, she sped away. She heard the huge bull surface with an explosive blow, and the displacement of water as he lunged in her direction. This time, he was after her in full pursuit.

Tuschka saw Annika speeding by and called to her friend to play. She almost started after her, but just managed to evade the onrushing bull. Annika swam fast, but Korak was gaining on her. Her pursuer was agile enough to follow her every movement. She knew from Sigurd how powerful and agile a large bull could be, but she had never been the target. Korak was only a few yards behind her, and, in a last attempt to surprise him, she pivoted away from him and took off to the left. But the big bull was determined and Annika found herself target of another pursuit. When she broke the surface, Annika heard his explosive blow right next to her. Then, she suddenly slowed and a big wake washed over her as Korak brought his heavy body to a stop.

The two briefly rested, breathing heavily to catch their breath. When his treasure made no more attempts to swim away from him, Korak nudged her flank gently and rubbed against her. Annika felt her heart beat fast and returned an affectionate call. The big bull answered her and glided forward, touching her chin with his. He sank a little and rubbed his head against her chin and chest. While rising for a breath, he glided by her side and she savored the tickling sensation of his pectoral fin as he trailed it along her flank. Then, he rolled over and Annika felt his belly touch hers. She squeaked her delight softly and pressed herself against him. A warm feeling came over her. Korak glided from underneath her and took a deep breath. She followed him upon his dive. In the green water where the light of the sun penetrated faintly, Korak rolled over on his back again. He spread his big broad pectoral fins and embraced the precious young female. He glided up against her from underneath and Annika felt herself being lifted, as he carried her on his soft belly and broad chest. Gently undulating his strong flukes, he took her with him for a while and caressed her with his chin. While he carried her, they became one. They stayed together a little longer and then slowly parted. Annika heard Korak blow loudly and his eyes followed her as she slowly swam away.

Furka welcomed her youngest daughter and nudged her affectionately. The matriarch had been very aware of her lovemaking with Korak near the perimeter of the group. The sun was setting by the time most of the whales had calmed down from their play and other social interactions. The orcas grouped up tight. They lay almost all abreast, hovering in bodily contact with each other. Furka and Raina lay side by side. The little puffs of Tuschka and Nadia's newborn calf contrasted sharply with the heavy extended blows of the big males. The orcas' blows hung over them like clouds of mist in the last bleak rays of the early spring sun.

* * *

48

It was early May when the research team arrived. Johann welcomed them and told them about their sighting of the baby orca. Sarah immediately showed them the pictures she had taken. The leader of the small group looked at the pictures carefully and smiled. "Do you think we will find them again?" Sarah asked eagerly. The big man shook his head: "That's especially what we will be trying, but even when we find a group with a little calf, it may be difficult to tell from these pictures if they are the same whales. I'm happy that you have photographed the mother and that male, although his dorsal fin is very smooth. You may have noticed that each orca has a grey area on its back, right behind the dorsal fin. That area is called the 'saddle patch' and pioneers in orca research have found that each individual orca is unique in the combination of its saddle patch and dorsal fin. You took the picture when the calf was up, but the adult whales were already going down, so their saddles are almost submerged."

Johann and Sarah looked at each other in surprise. Johann thought that only an occasional distinctive fin might help to identify an orca. It was an exciting idea that many more orcas could be distinguished than he ever thought possible. Sarah did not give up easily and asked if there was at least a chance that they would find the baby again. "Certainly, there's a chance. They will probably be around for a while, but I'm hoping that if we meet that calf again, we will be able to confirm that it's the same one. We will take pictures at every opportunity we get and it will probably help when we compare those pictures with yours. The male fin is in focus and its shape and size tell something about that whale's identity. I will also look through the pictures of last summer, although they were taken at least 80 miles more to the east. There, we found approximately 110 different orcas. We photographed about one-third of those more than once."

The group was eager to start their second season. That evening the expedition leader explained how he wanted to asses the size of the population, the structure of the various groupings, and whether or not the whales were occasional visitors or residents to the area. "Although we believe that orcas are most abundant during fall and winter, weather conditions make it often impossible for us to work. In spring and part of the summer, the salmon returning from the sea to spawn up-river attract various pods close to shore. We are happy with your new boat, Johann; it can handle a stiff breeze and will be perfect to work from May through late August."

The research group consisted of Bjorn, the leading biologist, and his wife Ingrid. They were assisted by two university students. Peter was preparing a master's thesis, while Varg was a whale enthusiast who had been invited to participate as a volunteer. The first small salmon runs were expected in about two weeks and the researchers had been using this time to travel along the coast and question local people about orca sightings. They had been handing out forms to fishermen and several harbor masters, to fill out some basic data about number, location, and direction of travel in case they spotted orcas. This information would help the team to search for orcas more specifically.

* * *

Furka slowed down when she approached the bank where her mother had died. It was almost low tide. Memories came back to her and the other adult whales when they joined her for a rest. Tuschka and Igor refrained from playing together. They sensed the different mood. The two hugged close to their mothers, whose mind seemed to have wandered. Having led the pod successfully for a little over two years, Furka felt far more confident, but there were still times when she missed her mother's reassuring presence. They stayed near the bank until the tide was at its lowest. Furka felt her pectoral fins touch the bottom rhythmically, in between small waves that lifted her up. Tuschka had an itch and tried to rub the spot against the bottom, but the sand easily gave way. Her vision blurred as she whirled up the sand. She rose up to look around. Then, Furka took a few deep breaths, dove, and turned away from shore. In silence, the other members of the pod followed her. It was as if their pause near the bank had strengthened their respect for their matriarch.

The long awaited abundance came suddenly. The hunt was on. Furka's pod found themselves in a salmon run, so dense, that they barely needed to concentrate the fish. Tuschka was clicking away, eager for the returning echoes. It was a challenge for her to locate something that moved and then find out if it was what she expected. She dived in together with Tarka. It was a challenge for her to catch one of these relatively big fish herself. She managed to grab one by its tail. The fish struggled and slipped away. Tuschka was surprised by the strength of these fish. She managed to get a better hold on another and held on to it firmly, but she did not know how to avoid its escape when she would release her grip to swallow it down. Her mother had noticed it and came over to help. She crushed the fish quickly by biting its head that was outside Tuschka's mouth. Although it was lifeless, the fish was still too big for her to swallow whole. She shook her head vigorously to tear off a bite-size chunk. Her mother grabbed the other end of the fish and tore it loose. Tuschka worked it around in her mouth and swallowed it down. Mom swallowed the other chunk and Tuschka was full of pride when her mother rewarded her for her accomplishment.

The feeding area was an arena of action. Tuschka had lost sight of her mother in the fray of hunting whales. She was relieved when her mother appeared out of the turmoil. She led her a short distance away to calmer water. Suddenly, Tuschka spotted a slightly wounded fish struggling along. She kicked her flukes and grabbed it in an instant. She shared it with her mother and swallowed her bite-size chunk. Her mother rested and rubbed her approvingly.

Then she rolled over and Tuschka moved close to her. She easily fit between her mother's pectoral fins, and with her small pecs she touched the chest of the big loving female. Tenderly, Tarka bent her head towards her little orca and touched her chin. Tuschka loved it and Tarka touched chins with her again and again. The young female reveled in all the caressing and love she received. In unison, the two rolled over, rose up to breathe and dived again to continue their tender togetherness. Almost unnoticed Tamara had joined them. She rolled over as well and accompanied Tarka to the right. Gracefully, the mother and her calf glided, the bigger orca embracing the smaller one.

As the season progressed, the pod enjoyed several successful salmon hunts. Most of the big runs were heading for the Laxava river, east of Rockcove Bay. Hunting large amounts of fish near shore was much easier than scattered fish offshore. With food being plentiful Tarka gained back her lost weight.

5.
The Researchers

The researchers had found out from the returned questionnaires in early May that whales traveled in a westerly direction in March. Then, during the summer, several groups would hang around in the area of Rockcove Bay to feast on salmon, and in fall, most orcas headed east and north to feed on aggregations of herring near the fjords. Locating and photographing the orcas required relatively calm weather, and such weather was most frequent in summer. The harbor of Rockcove bay was an excellent base to work from.

The morning was calm and crisp when Johann cast off with Bjorn and his team. They headed slightly west and south, staying in sight of land. The crew scanned the horizon with binoculars for blows or dorsal fins. In the early morning, vertical plumes of vapor were usually the first signs of the whales' presence. Johann constantly monitored the most frequently used radio channels for talk that might indicate the presence of orcas. Most salmon fishermen did not appreciate the presence of the big black hunters and made no secret of their location. Without any indication to decide on their course, they chose to head parallel to shore against the tide. If the tales were true that the whales traveled more often with the tide than against it, they might run into them. At noon, Johann shut off the engine and let his craft drift while they had lunch. He listened to the researchers discussing where to go and what to do.

Late in the afternoon, close to Rockcove Bay, Johann's attention was suddenly caught by a large dorsal fin. The crew jumped up at the unexpected sighting and quickly brought out camera gear. Finally, they seemed to be getting the chance to bring home some orca pictures. Johann approached the bull, which was accompanied by two females. There were other whales around, but they were spread out in small groups. The three were relatively easy to approach. Peter took a few notes about their location and looked for any distinctive markings. The bull was large and obviously had been mature for quite some years. His fin had a broad base and the trailing edge had one large wave. Such a curve was common in older males. It happened when the relatively faster growth of the trailing edge, causing the fin to straighten up, continued a bit after the leading edge had ceased to grow. A tiny nick was visible, one third from the base of the big fin. Bjorn estimated the fin to be close to six feet in height. The saddle patch was white-grey with a thin white protrusion extending in the front.

The researchers saw another group 200 yards away. Johann was still approaching them when Ingrid and Bjorn called simultaneously: "look, there's a calf among them!" The little orca surfaced an instant later than her mother, hugging close to her flank. She popped up like a dolphin beside her mother's dorsal fin. Several times, the curious little orca raised her head high to see where the strange sounds had come from. Even the experienced couple was endeared at the sight of her yellowish-orange chin. Varg found it extremely difficult to get a picture of the calf; it surfaced so quickly and at every attempt, he got a tip of the dorsal fin or only the wake of the calf. "Look at how the mother and calf surface," Peter said. "Every time the mother surfaces, the baby comes up a second or so later and always in the same spot. If you see the mother's dorsal, focus on it and keep your finger ready on the shutter. As soon as you see the calf, press it." Varg tried Peter's advice and looked disappointed when suddenly the baby popped up on the far side of its mother. Peter sighed and said: "It won't work any more now. Maybe you will get another chance." But that other chance was not meant for that day.

The wind picked up a bit and the orcas moved closer together. The sun was already setting and Johann felt uncomfortable staying any longer. They needed at least an hour to get home. The team tried to take a few sunset shots, but the orcas did not cooperate. Every time the lighting was perfect, the pod dived. It was late when they packed their camera gear and headed home. Johann had not wanted to interrupt the team while they were taking pictures and notes, but he wondered if they had seen the baby that he and his family had seen last spring. Slowing down to enter the harbor, he asked Bjorn about it. The big man shook his head. "That thought flashed through my mind, but this baby looks even smaller than the one in your picture. By now, that calf should have been noticeably larger. Besides, that big bull we saw today had a slight wave in his fin. It can't have been the same one as in your picture. I will compare today's pictures with yours, but as I said your calf should have been a lot bigger by now." Johann expressed both understanding and disappointment. 'It would have been so nice for Sarah', he thought, 'but the season isn't over yet.'

* * *

Raina and her pod were well beyond Rockcove Bay when they rounded Starcliff Rock and headed north. Furka's family had taken the same direction two days before. In expectation of another salmon run, the orcas worked the tidal rips caused by the many ridges and elevations in the shelf's sea floor.

The two families met close to the Kelpada Islets where seals used to haul out and play in the kelp. The orcas' loud greetings scared the seals away miles before the first whale came into sight. They had all sought refuge on the higher rocky shore. The orcas' excitement was mutual. They accelerated and broke

54

into high speed swimming to cover the last few miles that separated them. They created beautiful V's of white water, parting under their chins. The explosive Poooooh...Pooooh of their blows filled the air. The three male fins in Raina's pod contrasted with the one male fin in Furka's. Sigurd and Korak stood out with their tall dorsal fins and massive bodies.

The orcas made no formal greeting and intermingled quickly. Tuschka was excited but surprised when she and her mother met Nadia with her playful baby: the little female was so much bigger! She was much more curious and explorative. Last time, she was glued to her mother's side and Tuschka was allowed a only few close passes. Now, the baby orca came towards her! Glancing at her mother, who showed no disapproval yet, Tuschka approached the baby. They stopped to look at each other. For a little while they just hung there, almost touching chins. Then, Tuschka rolled over on her side and glided by underneath the baby, looking at her. While she turned, she saw how little Aleta turned to follow. Tuschka waited a moment for the little orca to catch up. Aleta wanted to swim by Tuschka's side as she used to do with her mother. Tuschka slowed a bit and trailed her pectoral fin along the calf's head and back. Aleta enjoyed it and Tuschka felt the baby pushing up against her pec to rub herself. In a fluid movement, Tuschka arched up and accelerated towards the surface. She made a little landing on her belly and was immediately followed by little Aleta, who tried to imitate her.

As Tuschka noticed that Aleta had lost her initial shyness, she started to make more unexpected turns and rolls, encouraging the baby to follow her. Soon, they were making playful circles around each other and Tuschka challenged Aleta's agility with little jumps, dives and rolls. They squealed in delight and were oblivious of their mothers, who watched them play. Tarka felt a temptation to join in, but she wanted to leave the initiative to Nadia, whose baby was the youngest and least experienced.

As soon as Nadia moved forward, Tarka followed. Little Aleta was taken completely by surprise when she suddenly felt herself lifted up and pushed forward on her mother's rostrum. It was special to feel the weight of her body and to experience her mother's strength as she rhythmically kicked her powerful flukes. Aleta was overwhelmed with a feeling of security and care freeness and completely gave herself up to her mother's game. She lay half way on her mother's head, her shiny orange belly and two tiny pecs facing the sun. A skilled swimmer, Nadia subtly kept her baby balanced. When her mother dove, Aleta slid off and found herself enveloped in the blue-green water again. Tuschka followed as she saw her playmate being pushed forward. Still hoping to resume the game that had been interrupted, Tuschka suddenly felt something underneath her. In an instant she was lifted up too. The juvenile female weighed a lot more than Aleta, but Tarka was strong and had no problem giving her daughter a little ride. The ride was very special for Tuschka, to play without holding back. Soon after, she slid onto her mother's back again, trying to steady herself against the leading edge of mother's sturdy dorsal fin. Tarka knew exactly what her baby wanted and gave her several more rides.

Shortly after Nadia and Aleta settled down, Tarka rolled over on her back and without needing a hint, Tuschka glided between her mother's pecs. Then Tarka moved her soft white chin towards her little girl's and the two rubbed each other affectionately. It had been a while since they had played like that and Tuschka loved it. She felt close and yet so free with her mother, who was everything at once in such moments: the one who looked after her and cared for her, but also a playmate with whom she could indulge in unrestrained and exuberant play.

The sharp smacks of two full breaches penetrated everyone's consciousness: games were interrupted, nursing calves were distracted, and those who slept were awake. There was a moment of expectation among the orcas as to what would happen next. Raina's voice filled the void. All attention was focused on her. The two matriarchs took the lead as they headed in a south-easterly direction, toward Rockcove Bay.

* * *

Ingrid was on shore, teaching Varg to identify orcas from photographs when Johann received a call about the orcas' arrival. Without hesitation, he took Bjorn, Peter, and his daughter, Sarah, out to meet them. They were not alone; several commercial fishing boats were operating and there were at least a dozen small boats with sports fishermen. They traveled about four miles before they spotted the first blows. There was a slight breeze and conditions were excellent. As they approached, the whales were in the middle of gorging themselves on salmon. There was no clear travel direction. Instead, most of the orcas were diving, turning and chasing. Bjorn and Peter could hardly do more than attempt to count the orcas, especially the adult males. "There are definitely more whales than there were the other day," Bjorn said. "Do you recognize any of those males?".

They were motoring slowly among the feeding orcas when Bjorn tapped Johann's shoulder to slow down. His attention had been caught by a large male, whose fin just sliced the water almost horizontally as he made a sharp turn in pursuit of his prey. A few seconds later, the fin rose up and Bjorn spotted a large wave in the trailing edge. "Try to stay with him. I want to see if it is the one we saw last time with that small nick in his fin." The next several surfacings gave the crew a better look. "Peter, that must be the same one! Let's try to find that mother and calf again." Bjorn asked Johann to stay with them until after the hunt was over. It was mid-afternoon when the whales started to form several groups. The researchers noticed that there were at least three full-grown bulls and a younger one, whose fin was still growing. There were several juveniles, but it was a while before Peter spotted a small group at starboard, containing two adult females, a calf and a small juvenile. A large male, not the one with the nick, came up from behind and positioned himself between their vessel and the group. Johann closed in on them, but made no attempt to get closer than about 50 yards. Sarah was excited to see the baby orca. She had understood that it could not be the calf she had seen the year before, but she wondered about the somewhat bigger juvenile traveling among them. Bjorn and Peter managed to get pictures of the five whales. "Johann, this male reminds me of the picture you showed me. Too bad he is so smooth. That will make it more difficult to confirm a possible match. I'm wondering about the mother with that larger baby too. The small calf might be the one we saw the other day, since that bull with the notch is swimming ahead of us. I would not be surprised if this big salmon run attracted several local groups. We should try to photograph as many different individuals as possible."

Sarah was a little shy with the two other men on board. She was so happy to have been invited and she did not want to distract the researchers with her questions. The girl enjoyed watching the whales surfacing. The larger juvenile had almost white markings, but the smaller calf still showed a yellowish color on her eye patch and chin. In contrast to the strong blows of the adult females, the two young whales made little "puffs" as they popped up right after their mothers arched to dive. The four radiated a harmonious closeness, with the big male a caring escort. Upon Bjorn's directions, Johann systematically went from group to group until they felt they had sufficiently documented the orcas. It was late in the afternoon when Johann turned to head home. Sarah continued looking at the majestic creatures until the fins, and then the blows, disappeared from sight. In her heart she wished she could go beyond the boundaries of her life and follow them, to be with them and share their alluring, mysterious life.

When he heard Peter and Bjorn enter the house, Varg dashed out of the office to meet them: "How was it? Did you see the whales that we had the other day?" Bjorn smiled at the enthusiasm and winked at Ingrid, who had just entered the room: "Well, it depends on how many pictures you have ready to compare them to." Varg turned to get the results of his day's work, but he stopped as Bjorn continued. "There were more whales than we saw last time. I guess there were some 20 or more. I'm hoping that you have already printed some photos of that big male and the female with her baby. We feel quite confident that we saw the same male today. We may also have seen the same mother and calf pair, but they were traveling alongside another female with a somewhat older juvenile, and between them and our boat was a different large bull. Perhaps this big salmon run attracted several groups from around the area." Varg entered the office again and showed them two pictures. "Yes, that must be the one we saw today," Bjorn said. "See that nick here, and the stubby finger on the saddle?" Peter nodded. He volunteered to download the pictures of the day and they all looked forward to actually matching the whales.

The following morning, Johann and Sarah stopped by to ask about the findings of the previous day. Bjorn gave them a hearty welcome and confirmed what he had expected. "The bull is definitely the same. The female is also. Her fin has a relatively curved and pointed tip and she has an easy, distinctive saddle. These orcas will be the first ones, to which we will give identity numbers," Bjorn announced proudly, "although we cannot make these official before the end of the season. The male will probably be A1 and the female A2. The letter denotes the pod and the number designates the individual in that pod. Although we do not have a clear picture of the calf's saddle, we give it the same letter because of its age."

Bjorn saw that Sarah had brought the pictures that she had taken a year before, and took them from her. "Good that you brought those along. I've been wondering if the other female and her juvenile may be the ones you saw a year ago." Bjorn bent over some photos in a binder and studied them thoroughly. "It might be them, but I cannot say for sure," he mumbled. "The saddles of the adults aren't visible on your photo, because they have already started their dive, but the female has two small parallel scratches behind her saddle near the spine and the fin shape looks identical. The male's dorsal fin looks the same as the one that escorted the group yesterday, but we've no other clue to match him." He smiled at Sarah, regretfully, while he handed the photos back to the girl. "Will you give them numbers too?" Sarah asked. "I would indeed like to, but I don't feel comfortable calling them A too, because I'm certain they were not with the group we saw the previous time. It is possible that two families met each other. For the time being, they will receive B numbers. We will assign a number to the calves when we have identified all members of the respective pods. I want the youngest whales to have the highest numbers. We may meet the families proper some day soon and that will help us to know who belongs to which pod." Sarah and Johann thanked the biologists for sharing their findings with them and left. The recognition of several of the orcas had made the whole study much more meaningful for them. What an exciting idea that orcas could be identified and perhaps even followed over the years. It would be so rewarding to see the baby grow up.

* * *

As the summer wore on with so many opportunities to practice, Tuschka became much more proficient in catching salmon. She was not as experienced as the adult members of her pod, but she also needed less food. She was more than capable of catching what she needed. It had been almost a month since she had taken a sip of her mothers' milk, and only now did she realize it had been the last one. Although Tuschka often interacted with other whales when they were resting or socializing, she still preferred to swim with her mother when they were on the move.

With the salmon disappearing, the orcas had to rely on opportunities that presented themselves. Tuschka would no longer be able to fall back on her mother's milk, but she had built up a lot of reserves during this summer. As strong and healthy as she was, she had the best chances a young orca could possibly have.

6.
The Big Chase

The orcas' foraging efforts gradually shifted to the east. They eventually left the shore and went out into the open sea. Furka led her pod past a deeper ocean bed towards the autumn feeding grounds. A few difficult weeks lay ahead, but then the herring shoals would congregate and feed them through the winter.

On a day in late September, the sun rose in a hazy sky. The moist air hung low in a thin fog, enveloping the orcas' blows. Furka was in the lead with Shaka and Tamara following close behind. Sigurd brought up the rear. They traveled in silence, completely attuned to the sounds around them. Then Furka slowed down. Something had alerted her. Tuschka pressed against her mother and listened. There it was again... All members of the pod heard it, but not everyone was quick to interpret it. Only Annika and the adults recognized the sounds as the vocalizations of pilot whales. These black whales were bigger than dolphins, but smaller than themselves. They were traveling in a big group, and they were fish-eaters like themselves. Their dorsal fins, both male and female, were curved backwards and bore some resemblance to the fins of juvenile orcas.

Having recognized the sounds, Furka increased the pace. A big group of pilot whales might indicate food nearby, although they might be also searching for it, just like they were. Nevertheless, Furka wanted to take her chances at it. After about an hour, they caught up. An initial nervousness spread through the big group of pilot whales, but they quickly relaxed when the orcas seemed not to be after them. They, too, knew that not all orcas hunted their kind for food. Some of the lead pilots had detected a concentration of mackerel ahead. The pilot whales were clicking frequently to assess the situation. When they started herding the fish, the fog gradually lifted.

Furka had been traveling behind with her pod, waiting for an opportunity to separate some of the fish for her pod to round up. As they were few, it would pay to wait until the pilot whales had succeeded in concentrating part of the fish. At that point, Furka wanted to move forward and encircle a share. Faint and broken among all the sounds of the whales, the birds, and the moving fish, were the sounds of boats, but they paid no attention to them. When the pilot hunt became more organized, the orcas concentrated on their prey so hard they did not notice the engine sounds behind them.

Tuschka traveled alongside her mother. She was curious about the new sounds she heard and became impatient to see the animals that made them. It was a while before the first pilot whales came into sight. The appearance of the dark creatures was new for her, but she felt no fear. During her short life she had often been called back from her curious ventures, but other than her vague memory of Igor's injury, her companions had never shown fear of anything.

Tuschka had grown into a chubby, fearless, and playful orca. She looked at the whales moving gracefully in front of her and wanted to find out how they would respond to her. Tuschka suddenly took off ahead and saw one of the pilot whales turn to look backwards. She hesitated a moment, but as she went after the pilot again, her mother called her back. Reluctantly, she turned around.

The orcas concentrated on the movements of the pilot whales and the mackerel ahead. They were eagerly awaiting their leader's signal to move forward and separate their portion of the fish. Tuschka became impatient. Her excitement built, just like everyone else's, but the expected action did not follow. Her attention was suddenly drawn by the sounds of boats behind. Sensing that her mother would not let her move off again, she moved over to Annika and joined her. She saw her mother watch her, but she soon focused again on the hunt that drew near. After a little while Tuschka tried to draw Annika's attention to the boats behind her. but her big companion was more interested in the hunt. When Annika did not respond, Tuschka slipped away while her mother was not looking. Annika noticed it but didn't look where she went.

Tuschka curiously approached one of the boats and poked her head out of the water close to it. A few hoarse yells came in response. One creature on the boat pointed at her with a long shaft, but a companion grabbed it and moved it down. She dove again and swam under the boat, popping up on the other side. This time they ignored her. It was then that Furka's signal pierced the water. Tuschka heard it and hesitated to join the pod again. She felt she might get away with it if she stretched her adventure a little longer.

Hardly more than a minute after Tuschka had left Annika's side, the orcas suddenly moved in on the fish, pounding their tails on the water. Sigurd, Tamara, and Annika pressed up on the pilots at their flank and started the separation maneuver. It was then that Tarka noticed Tuschka was not with Annika. She immediately called her calf, but her call was lost in the noise of the hunt, which was suddenly accompanied by the beating of paddles on the water and the hoarse shouts of men. Tuschka turned toward her family, but shuddered as a paddle landed close when she surfaced. She quickly dove and dashed away beyond the stern of the boat. From a safer distance she looked for her family but did not see them. The noise both below and above the water was intense and she suddenly felt panic not knowing where her mother and the others were. She called and swam to where all the activity was, but she ran into the beating paddles again and backed off. Somehow, the experience was unlike any other before. Strangely enough these boats were hostile. Tuschka, being close to only two years old, nervously tried to find a way past the boats, constantly calling out to her mother.

The promising hunt was interrupted almost immediately after the boaters had started to speed up and beat the water. The whales suddenly found a large number of boats approaching fast behind them. The noise of engines was deafening and above the water the air was filled with screams. The boats moved in, forming a line behind the whales with very small gaps in between. Around each boat the water was pounded to foam. They heard pilot whales emit distress calls and the whole group surged forward at high speed to move away from the boats.

The orcas had been taken completely by surprise and felt distressed by the scene. They, too, increased their speed, but more than anything else they were concerned about their missing calf. The boats increased speed too, and although the orcas managed to still stay ahead of the boats, they were continuously calling and looking for Tuschka. As the pilots had done with the mackerel, the boats did with them. While they were in full flight, their pursuers gradually drove them closer together and moved up on their flanks. An explosion blasted through their ears, followed by the screams of a pilot whale in agony. Some pilots immediately moved to the sides of the wounded animal and tried to urge it on, but within seconds one of them felt a stabbing pain in its peduncle and turned away with pain flashing through its body at every thrust of its flukes. Men were hurling metal shafts at the nearest whales, discouraging them to turn around and break through the ranks.

Tuschka kept a great distance between herself and the terrible scene in front of her. She called desperately for her family, only to hear the roars of engines and the screams of terrified whales. She started to tire and was filled with fear, but pushed on in hopes not to lose her family.

The wild chase was directed towards West Matador Island and its shore was a little more than a mile ahead. Furka and her companions were at the far left of the hunting group. They still had energy left to stay ahead of the boats, but they noticed a steep rise in the ocean floor and sensed the danger of being beached. Most of them felt fear for the first time in their lives. Tarka could no longer resist to turn around and search for her baby. She told the pod with a short call that was barely audible in the noise, nudged Tamara, and took off towards the boats.

The desperate mother thrust herself forward at full speed, her heart beating in her chest. A strong bond and feelings of concern and caring had overcome her fear. She did not know what to expect, but she pushed on in a desperate attempt to find her calf. Close to one of the boats, Tarka came up for air. Two objects hit the water almost on top of her. One missed, while the other raked her spinal ridge. Tarka flinched and dove deep, speeding forward below the surface until her lungs almost burst. All the time Tarka called for her little orca. She finally surfaced and found herself alone, the rage of the chase behind her. Although she felt relieved at being out of immediate danger, she was confused and looked around. She kept on calling while swimming in an undirected pattern. Then she heard a faint call... She called out loud, moving to where she had heard the sound. There it was again... It was the desperate call of a young orca... her own baby! At that moment, fear and fatigue left the young mother. She sped toward where she had heard Tuschka call. Tuschka, too, had heard her mother's loud call and raced towards her with all the energy she had left.

In less than half a minute they saw each other emerge out of the blue-green. Tarka swerved a little to avoid bumping into her calf too hard. She voiced her happiness and Tuschka squealed her relief and joy. The two rubbed and nuzzled each other affectionately. Tarka took Tuschka under her pectoral fin and a warm feeling overcame her when she felt the familiar bumps under her belly. The joyful reunion of the mother and her baby made the two whales forget for an instant the tragic scene that had moved close to shore. They were together, but soon they realized that the others were in great danger. Drawn by their lifelong bonds, the two turned and followed the boats. Tuschka swam as if she were glued to her mother's side. Tarka called, but her calls were lost to the rest of their family.

Tamara rushed forward toward Furka and then to Sigurd, calling for Tarka, who did not respond. The water was less then 50 feet deep and becoming steadily shallower. Furka and Tamara knew how serious the situation was and Sigurd faintly remembered a similar scene. The matriarch veered off to the left, attempting to evade the beach ahead. In the act, they increased the gap between them and the pilot whales.

The orcas noticed some boats swerve and come after them, leaving gaps of various sizes between them. Not knowing what had happened to Tarka, Tamara had turned around. Echoes of clicks were lost in the commotion and some orcas scanned the surface in despair to assess the situation. When they saw a large gap, Furka and Sigurd made a sharp turn and dashed towards the opening. In a moment, all the others followed. As they urged on the big gap narrowed, but several smaller ones opened up. The water was filled with screaming whales and the taste of blood. There were only two choices: death on the beach or a chance ahead. Furka crossed the ranks unhurt, followed by Shaka and Igor.

Sigurd hung back a moment, watching who managed to get away. The gap had become too small for the rest to follow. He called loudly and they veered away before they were within range of the sharp shafts that were hurled at them. Another gap had formed and the remaining four of them headed for it at full speed. Again, the boats were closing the gap, but they continued, diving when they were near the boats. Several spear like shafts came right down above them. Skaade screamed when she felt a tearing pain behind her pectoral flipper. She flinched and turned. Sigurd bumped her hard and pushed her forward, momentarily losing precious speed. Within a second he felt a sharp stab in his back. He thrust his tail in the direction of the pain, slapped the water and dove. Speeding on, they stayed down for as long as they could hold their breaths.

They surfaced... There were no lances, no chase, only screams and roars that were moving away from them. The orcas hugged close and while slowing down, they gradually came round. Skaade whined and nudged Shaka. She had a deep gash in her flank behind her left pectoral fin, but her ribs were unhurt. A little blood trickled off, leaving a thin red cloud. Shaka called reassuringly and calmed her. Sigurd had been stabbed in his back, about four feet behind his dorsal fin, while he had helped Skaade to escape. It had been a spear without a barb and it had dislodged when he thrust his tail toward the boat. In their flight, Sigurd had not been conscious of the pain, but now he felt a deep burning pain that intensified at every movement. He stopped swimming and rested. Seven of them had managed to break free, but Tarka and Tuschka were still missing. Furka called, followed by Tamara.

Tarka and her calf had stayed within a few miles of the chase and swam back and forth. In the distant roar, Tarka heard faint calls. She needed no encouragement. She called loudly and sped forward with Tuschka at her flank. Within moments the two saw seven shadows approach. The current carried the taste of blood, but they were all there. Tarka and Tuschka greeted their family with exuberance. Skaade let out a squeak of pain when Tuschka bumped her. The other members of the pod returned the happy and warm nudges and rubs more quietly, but not less meaningfully. They felt worn out and as they swam away from the tragedy, the noise faded. Hugging close, rubbing and gliding alongside each other, they moved on with Skaade and Tuschka in their midst.

For several days the orcas traveled relatively slowly and close together. Skaade and Sigurd were still in their midst. The first day, their wounds had attracted a few sharks which had followed them for hours, but they had made no attempt to attack. When evening fell, she had stopped bleeding, and soon afterwards the sharks had left. The orcas had allowed some time for Sigurd and Skaade to make an initial recovery. Having gone without food for almost a week, Furka increased the speed to search a larger area more quickly. It was the first time that Tuschka experienced what it was to have an empty stomach. She could no longer fall back on her mother's milk, and she was more aware than ever before how important foraging was. Skaade had no problem keeping up. She had a relatively shallow wound that hurt only when she made big movements with her pectoral fins. It was Sigurd, who labored to stay with the group. The spear had penetrated deeply. The powerful bull had managed to keep the slow speed of the past days with relatively small strokes that kept the pain at a tolerable level. But the new pace was a torture for the big orca. Every stroke sent tearing pain through his entire back. Furka noticed his trouble and stopped almost every hour to give him a few minutes of rest, but the need for food became ever more urgent as time wore on.

Tuschka sensed the tension among her companions. She rubbed against her mother and made soft moaning calls, asking for extra attention and reassurance to make up for the overall mood of concern. Her mother nudged her gently and caressed her with her pectoral fin. The familiar, affectionate voice of her loving mother calmed her. Furka and Shaka had been swimming with Sigurd in between them to offer him some advantage of their slipstream. When they tired, Tamara and Annika took over. Sigurd was very well aware that his pod could not cover as much area as they wished. He did not want to be a burden on them, and after giving his escorts an affectionate nudge, he slowed down and fell back. Furka called for him and turned around to urge him on, but he refused to follow her forward toward the others. Everybody slowed down and Furka tried again to spur him on. She called and pleaded, but he bumped her gently, telling her to go and take her lead spot. With her responsibilities weighing heavily, Furka looked at him once more and reluctantly swam away from him to join the pod. She was both mother and leader, but she had to give priority to the latter.

Furka took her lead position and set a brisk pace. Tamara turned around and joined Sigurd, who had already fallen behind a quarter mile. They could stay in acoustic contact for several miles, but Tamara had come to offer some protection in case hungry sharks noticed the injured lone orca. The pod had by no means given up on Sigurd, but they made an attempt to find food while taking some care of him as well. When needed, Tamara could cover many miles in little time to get to the pod and return with them. In case they fell back beyond hearing range, Tamara could double it by taking a position in between.

Sigurd swam about five knots and refused to rest. He vocalized barely and occasionally rubbed his chin on Tamara's peduncle. With fatigue, the pain intensified, and in late afternoon his tail felt like lead. His breathing became heavier and more frequent and Tamara stopped to let him rest. Sigurd, exhausted as he was, gave in to her: he stopped moving his aching tail and gratefully rested his head on Tamara's back.

The rest of the pod had detected a small school of mackerel and Furka decided to make an attempt to concentrate them. With Skaade not yet capable of hunting effectively and without Sigurd's participation, they would need everyone else to give the hunt at least some chance. When they managed to eat something, they would have a little time to stay with Sigurd. Furka called loudly...

Tamara and Sigurd heard Furka's call. It was obvious the leader needed them, but Tamara knew that only she could go. She glided forward, letting Sigurd support himself, and turned to face him. He returned her gentle nudges. Then, Tamara turned and kicked her flukes. In a moment she was out of sight. Sigurd heard her call toward the pod to announce that she was coming. A movement of his flukes to resume swimming painfully ended his soothing rest. He faintly heard the sounds of foraging orcas and set a slow pace in their direction.

The orcas had surrounded a relatively small amount of fish. Skaade tried hard to help and it was fortunate that Tuschka had become much more proficient in a cooperative hunt. This time, they fed one by one, the others trying to keep the fish together. With few whales and only a small concentration of fish, this was the best they could do. How different from those summer days, when they had been feasting with several pods at once on large runs of salmon! The feeding was over quickly and had taken the edge off their hunger.

No fish were near to start another chase. Tuschka was skimming the surface for small pieces of fish and sucked them in. While doing so, she noticed the birds diving down on the leftovers. Most of them immediately took wing again, but some lingered in their attempt to swallow a piece of fish. Yet, every bird with something in its beak was beleaguered by greedy congeners trying to steel it. Many birds trying to fly up with their prey often dropped it in the attempt.

Just as Tuschka sucked in a small piece, her attention was attracted by the legs of a bird close by. She hesitated a moment, then made a grab for it. The moment she closed her teeth on the thin legs, she was startled by the strange feeling of the moving bird feet in her mouth and let go. The terrified bird took its chance and was off in a moment. For a few seconds, Tuschka thought her experience over. It had triggered her curiosity and she searched for another bird. She found a second one, but it took off before she was close enough. Her game did not last long, as Furka decided to move on. It was not the right time to play.

Evening fell and, the otherwise so strong, Sigurd labored to keep on going. He had not heard his family's voices for a while and wondered how far he had fallen behind. A dull pain had spread to the areas around the stab and in the center he felt a throbbing sensation. The rusty spear point had caused a local infection, which caused Sigurd even more pain and a slight fever. Coming up for air almost every minute, the lone bull plodded on, his huge dorsal fin barely going under on his dives. In the dark, his pod found him. They surrounded him and he was grateful for their support while he rested. Tuschka and Igor nudged the big bull, otherwise so strong and indefatigable. In the company of his caring pod, Sigurd was fighting his infection.

For two days, the pod covered little distance and spent much time with their ailing bull. Igor and Tuschka tried to entice Skaade and Annika into play, but they failed to entice them in more than a few rolls and gentle nudges. The mood was gloomy. Igor swam over to Sigurd, who drifted most of the time with his eyes closed. He stopped a few feet short of him and called plaintively to the big orca. Sigurd moved his head a little in the direction of his juvenile companion and opened his eyes. For a moment, they looked at each other. When Igor moved closer to his friend, Shaka moved in and gently pushed him away. Sigurd saw what happened and closed his eyes again. In his feverish condition he was less alert, and much of the day he dozed off. While slumbering, Sigurd was temporarily freed from his suffering.

Far too soon for the big male, the pod found itself torn again between the care for their companion and the need for food. As they had done before, they resumed traveling with Sigurd in their midst. He had regained some energy and managed to keep up in the slipstream of two females for a few hours. Close to the afternoon, the pain worsened and the throbbing sensation returned. This time, Annika stayed with him when he fell behind. For two weeks, they traveled, rested, and fed on whatever they could find. Sigurd, however, had not eaten anything during that period and spent time by himself while the pod was foraging. Although he was very well fed when he got stabbed, he gradually lost weight. His neck was sunken behind his blowhole. Since food was scarce and difficult to get, his companions were often many miles away.

Sigurd had been by himself for most of the day when the wind picked up in the evening. White-caps appeared on the waves and strong swells developed. He had traveled in storms countless times, and it had never caused him any trouble. Not so long ago, he had been guiding Tarka when she was in labor. Now, no one was near. He was too exhausted and too frequently in need of air to dive to calmer water between his surfacings. Staying near the surface, he rose high to breathe and tried to avoid waves running over his blowhole when he inhaled. Sigurd called a few times, but his calls were lost in the turbulent waves. That night, he needed his family more than ever, but there was no solace. Darkness enveloped the bull, buffeting with the waves.

The strong wind and the swells abated at dawn. The pod had spent most of the night in one area. They had called for Sigurd several times without a reply. In the morning, Furka decided to turn around. It was still a bit early for herring, but if they traveled slowly, they might as well start on their way. It had been the first night in Furka's life that her pod had not been complete. They had lost contact with Sigurd and had no idea how far apart they were. Furka wondered whether he was still alive. With no other lead than the spot where they had left him, the pod headed west.

The storm had been hard on Sigurd, but despite the pain and the fatigue, he still had the strength and the willpower to fight for his life. The morning finally brought relief and the big bull floated at the surface, drifting with the current while he rested. He gave in to the comfort of slumber, which temporarily took away the pain and the loneliness. He suddenly woke up when something rough touched his flukes. He felt a shot of pain when he jerked his tail away and saw a shark dash off. Fully alert, he watched the shark make a few wide circles before it took off. It was not his time yet. Sigurd had just dozed off again when a faint call woke him. He listened intently and waited. A few gulls flew screaming over his head.

Furka and her pod continued on against the tide. Her call had not been answered. She wondered if she was traveling in the right direction. Finding one orca would be like finding a needle in a haystack, but Furka knew that Sigurd was familiar with their seasonal movements. That common knowledge was the only hope for the orcas to find each other. A few minutes later, Furka and Shaka called again. This time, Sigurd recognized their voices without any doubt. He answered with as strong a voice as he could manage, to tell them he was there. All members of the pod veered a little to the right and burst into speed. Sigurd heard the greetings of his family and started moving toward them, drawing some energy from his excitement.

When only half a mile separated them, the pod spotted his mighty dorsal fin. Sigurd felt their sonar pulses. He voiced again. Furka rushed forward even more, with Igor in her wake. Then, Sigurd saw their dark shapes appear in the twilight green. In an instant, Furka was with him. She rubbed up against him and called affectionately. She lavished all her maternal love on him without holding back. For a moment, Sigurd felt no pain. He responded warmly, and returned her affectionate rubs and calls. Shaka and Annika came over next, and Igor bumped his flank playfully when he saw the big bull. The whole pod surrounded Sigurd and every member greeted him with enthusiasm.

Sigurd was not in good shape, but he was alive and showed a strong will to live. Igor breached playfully, and Skaade and Annika followed. The tension was broken and the young orcas indulged briefly in playful leaps and chases. Tuschka nudged Sigurd's pectoral fin and then bumped Tarka's belly for affection. Furka saw her son's fatigue and the sunken area behind his blowhole. They were all hungry, but no one needed food more than he. Sigurd was grateful when he felt his mother glide under him and lift his chin. He nudged her back in response. Then, he entrusted himself to her and rested his head on the caring female.

The pod spent the rest of the day and the night in one area. Furka stayed with Sigurd all the time, supporting him and caressing him gently. In the morning, they grouped up tight with Sigurd in their midst. Tamara took the lead and set a slow pace, while Furka and Shaka traveled on both sides of Sigurd. He only needed to gently undulate his tail to keep up. He still felt pain when he moved his tail, but there was no longer the throbbing sensation, and the pain had lost its sharp character. The ample periods of rest and his family's presence and attention were beneficial for him. His fever went down and the whole pod knew that their companion was recovering. Although they all felt the pangs of an empty stomach, the mood in the pod had lightened. The brave bull was aware of the difference and felt mentally stronger. The worst of the battle had been fought. Sigurd was regaining his health.

Three days later, the pain had gone down so much that Sigurd could manage a normal travel speed without too much effort. His pod still kept him in a central position and Furka spent much time at his side. The sunken area behind Sigurd's blowhole had become even more pronounced and his flanks were not filled out anymore. Although his wound was healing well, the infection and fasting had taken their toll. Sigurd had not eaten for nearly a month. If food were not available for him soon, his condition would relapse. The need to find prey became pressing.

It came as a surprise, more welcome than ever, when they heard the calls of Raina's pod. Together, they would be much more successful in herding fish. The greeting was warm, but brief. The other whales immediately noticed Sigurd's condition and refrained from socializing with each other. The two pods did not mix, but formed two tight groups, close behind each other. Raina took the lead when they all set out in search of food. Late in the afternoon, the screams of gulls announced fish in the area. Soon, the orcas located a medium-sized school of mackerel. As usual, the orcas formed a wide line and started to drive the fish into a higher concentration. Igor accompanied Tamara and Sigurd on their dives. He loved to spend time with the big male, who gradually began to take more interest in him again.

When they started to feed, Sigurd tried to grab what he could, but he had not yet regained his normal speed and agility. Missing fish that otherwise would have been certain prey confused and annoyed him. He had to content himself with the capabilities of a young hunter with little experience, yet he had the appetite of a starved bull. Fortunately, his companions managed to keep the fish together long enough to get their fill and Sigurd managed at least half a meal. When the feeding was almost over, Furka and Tamara came over and offered Sigurd a few fish that they had kept in their mouth. Annika snatched a fish out of the rapidly dispersing school and offered it to Sigurd as well. He accepted the fish as he had done many years ago when he was a calf learning the taste.

The two pods stayed together for several days and after a few more successful hunts they spent more moments resting and socializing. Although Sigurd had not yet replenished his reserves, his condition improved quickly. When most of the orcas had dozed off, Igor and Tuschka nudged Sigurd and bumped his flank gently. He welcomed the two playful youngsters. In response, he dove down and turned upward, with the two juveniles in his wake. With his regained strength Sigurd built up speed with powerful strokes of his large curled flukes. Then he broke the surface and rose in a mighty breach. In the air, he curved his body and fell back on his side with a thunderous crash. Igor's splash, a split second later, was lost in the turbulence that Sigurd had created. Tuschka surfaced in a playful belly flop close to the same spot. The other orcas had been taken by surprise. Furka and Tarka kicked their flukes and vented their joy, breaching almost simultaneously. Sigurd came to the surface belly up and Igor rubbed up against his side. Then, more breaches followed in the distance, … by Raina's pod! In a burst of exuberance most of the orcas engaged in breaching, some of them doing several in a row. Sigurd rolled over and exhaled with a strong blow. He saw his mother and sisters come over and felt a warm feeling of satisfaction when they voiced their excitement over his demonstration of regained health and strength. Their worry had come to an end. They all knew that he was again as they knew him: their mighty bull and their caring Sigurd, ready to travel and hunt with them and to aid whoever needed him.

7.
The Meat Hunters

A year had passed since Sigurd and Skaade had recovered from their injuries, and the pod had returned on their northerly trek along the rugged shore on their left. Food had been sufficient, but not overly abundant. Tuschka was now a little over three years old. She was not as fat and rounded as she had been at the beginning of fall, but she was in good shape. Although she had learned how important hunting was, she still loved to play. Whenever possible, she tried to coax her mother, Igor, Skaade, or Annika into play. Igor was in for it most often, but with nearly the size of her mother and the temperament of a young bull, he was sometimes a little rough. Tuschka liked games that really challenged her, but Igor was her superior in many respects; it was a delicate matter for him to push the games to her limit, but not beyond. Tuschka had played a lot with Aleta during the many days they had hunted with Raina's pod. The past several weeks, however, they had spent much more time by themselves and Tuschka often longed for her younger playmate.

Heavy clouds were retreating when sunrise shed a soft orange light over the eastern sky. Furka and her family traveled in silence. They had been feeding that night and the orcas were relatively relaxed. Tuschka had saved a piece of fish and went from one to the other to see who wanted to play suck and spit with her. When no one showed interest, she played with it by herself. They had come close to shore and approached a kelp bed. Tuschka saw several birds sitting on the rocks, but some flew when they came close. Her companions slowed down and started to roll and rub in the long strands of seaweed. It was an excellent area for hide and seek, but no one was interested.

Tuschka took off, glided underneath Sigurd's chin and started to explore a kelp bed that lay a little ahead. She poked her head out of the water and watched the birds circling in the air. The remainder of her fish was dangling from her mouth, contrasting sharply with her white chin. One of the birds spotted it, came down close and veered away, just when the young orca sank down. It caught her attention and she rose up a bit, waiting to see if it would happen again. Within seconds another gull swooped down and almost touched the piece of fish. Tuschka snatched at the bird, but it was too swift. She dived and explored the kelp bed. A little later, she spotted the legs of a bird nearby.

She stole closer and touched the surface carefully with the little thready fish exposed. The bird was disturbed for a moment and Tuschka immediately sank down, leaving the fish adrift. She opened her mouth a bit and stayed motionless, just below the surface. The bird settled down again. Then, it spotted the piece of fish. The gull flapped its wings to make a fast dash for the small prey. This was the moment Tuschka had been waiting for. Before the bird took wing, Tuschka seized her target by its legs and dragged it under. The startled bird let go of its prey and struggled to get away, but this time Tuschka was determined and held on to the unfamiliar animal, despite the strange feeling in her mouth. She did not immediately think about eating the bird, but, excited as she was with her new game, she squeaked in delight. She gave a few tugs at the frightened victim and let go. She watched as it made its way to the surface. Just when it was about to take wing, she grabbed it again and made another little tug. The gull screamed in distress and in an instant others nearby took wing. This time, she gave the bird a lucky escape.

Her mother nuzzled her warmly when she returned. The others were still taking a late morning nap, lying close together, all facing the tidal current. Tuschka listened to her companions' regular and slow breaths, and snoozed off. She woke as her pod gradually awakened. A few of her companions rubbed and scratched themselves against the rocks. Without a sound, Furka moved forward and set a slow pace. Soon, they took their familiar travel positions and followed their matriarch further north.

* * *

The days were lengthening again by the time they had reached the most northern point of their annual journey. Although herring was still their main food, the large congregations were already dispersing in smaller schools and moving further away from shore. The unpredictable weather often kept the boats away and left them with few opportunities to take advantage of the fishing nets. Most of the time they traveled in silence. Tuschka was getting restless, not only because she was hungry, but also because of the monotony of the last several days. She was not the only one, but the others seemed to resign themselves to it. Annika was already looking rounder and more full. Her appetite kept increasing and she became a little agitated now that food was not available every day.

In late afternoon, with scattered clouds hanging over a slightly choppy sea, faint high-pitched sounds reached the orcas' ears. Alerted, Furka veered a little east into the direction of the sounds. Tuschka had heard such sounds on several occasions before, but she was not as familiar with them as the other members of the pod. She knew the sounds as coming from dolphins, but only a few times had she really been close to them. Either they had ignored them or the dolphins had moved away from them. Tuschka felt an urge to dash ahead and explore. She exhilarated and squealed her curiosity, but her mother told her to stay before Furka needed to. It was striking how suddenly the sounds ceased. Intuitively, Tuschka felt that she had something to do with the sudden change. Her companions' clicks returned no echoes. After a few minutes, a few hesitant calls were audible, but this time Tuschka didn't even think of making a sound. They all listened intently as the sounds gradually increased. The experienced hunters recognized the calls as coming from feeding dolphins and they were hoping to find some food for themselves too.

Guided by their ears, the orcas approached the dolphins in silence. When they sounded no more than a 100 yards away Furka echolocated again. As expected, the dolphin's calls ceased again. The orcas detected several small concentrations of herring and headed straight for them. The dolphins grouped together and the orcas heard them take off. The pod split up in two groups, and each immediately started to circle one of the small, but relatively high concentrations of herring that the dolphins had left behind. They swam very tight circles around the fish. The rapid turns of the silvery fish caused a continuous play of reflections.

Tuschka saw Tamara initiate the attack. She slowed down, her belly facing the fish, when she suddenly hit the ball full force with her flukes. Her powerful stroke made a sharp sound. Tuschka saw how most of the fish where Tamara had hit, were floating around limply. She watched the strong female turn and start to suck them in one by one. In half a minute, she had swallowed more than a mouthful. Tuschka heard a sharp call directed at her, and quickly took up her task of keeping the fish concentrated. The next to strike was Annika, and then Sigurd. The powerful bull created an even sharper sound as his tail crashed into the fish. Tuschka saw him suck in the dead and paralyzed fish and snapped a few for herself as she continued to circle around. As soon as the remainder of the ball was nicely under control, Tarka struck. Tuschka copied her mother, but she did not create any sound. She did hit a few, but they were lost in her mother's kill. Tuschka was not nearly as efficient as the adults, but she was becoming more proficient in the strategy. For her, Igor, and Skaade, it was tempting to just dive into the tight ball of fish with an open mouth, but it was disappointing how few of the agile fish they caught that way. It was obvious that the powerful fluke strokes of their adult companions were far more successful.

The white sided dolphins had been reluctant to leave their prey. They were facing the same problem as the orcas of herring becoming gradually harder to find. The dolphins knew that some pods of orcas attacked their kind. Orcas always made them wary, even though most of them fed primarily on fish. This time, being hungry like the orcas, the dolphins had been waiting at a safe distance to assess the predators' intentions. It soon was evident that the orcas were after the fish. Well-fed, these orcas posed them no threat and could even be fun to play with. When the pod was finishing up with feeding, the dolphins returned cautiously.

Tuschka was playing with Igor and darted away, inviting him to chase her. A few dolphins were startled by the fast swimming juvenile and quickly made way for her, but in an instant they picked up the orcas' playful mood. The much bigger male, who was in pursuit, created a strong wake and some of the dolphins took his sides and started to ride his wake. Tuschka heard the mixed voices of Igor and the dolphins. She turned her head to look back and saw Igor heading for her at high speed. She kicked her flukes hard, but did not manage to keep the distance. Her agile adolescent playmate was gaining on her fast, still accompanied by the playful dolphins. Just before he touched her, Tuschka veered upwards and leaped in the air. When she dived back into the water, Igor was awaiting her and playfully skimmed along her flank with his jaws. Tuschka turned around, rubbed him under his chin, and took off again. He turned and followed.

The wake of the young female was not nearly as attractive as Igor's, but some dolphins thought her a suitable playmate. Tuschka's excitement built as one of the dolphins joined her. The animal was streamlined and swift, and surfaced in graceful bows. Completely distracted by her new companion, she forgot about Igor, who was close behind. Tuschka nodded sideways and wanted to nudge the dolphin, but it instantly dived and disappeared. Disappointed, she slowed down, upon which Igor quickly veered aside to avoid a collision. He turned and found his playmate looking around bewildered. She almost ignored the gentle bump of her companion, who felt the sudden change in her mood, but didn't understand why. Nudging her playfully and gliding alongside her, he obviously tried to perk her up and shift her attention back to play. It didn't take long for Tuschka to lose her disappointment. When Igor started to move away from her, she followed. As soon as he noticed her coming after him, he quickly sped up. Tuschka tried hard to gain on him. Igor could swim faster if he wanted to, but he loved the game of letting the juvenile female come very close and then accelerating again to stay out of her reach. Tuschka knew the game, but nevertheless she didn't give up trying to catch him.

The fast-swimming orcas were attractive to the dolphins, and three of them started to ride on Igor's wake. Tuschka saw the graceful creatures in front of her and it stimulated her even more to stay close behind. Two other dolphins joined and were swimming almost parallel to her as Igor let her gain on him. Tuschka watched the dolphins and was excited with their company. Yet she didn't even consider an approach. She just wanted the game to last, and kept on going. Distracted again by her smaller streamlined companions, Tuschka continued her fast swim, but she no longer focused on Igor. She was just looking at the dolphins next to her. Igor saw Tuschka's excitement with the dolphins. Coming up from behind, he accelerated and paralleled her. Tuschka was surprised with the propulsion of his wake and looked at him. Two more dolphins were riding his wake. He kept her pace, positioning himself just a little ahead of her. Tuschka was tiring of her prolonged fast swim, but the slipstream of her bigger companion gave her new energy.

Skaade heard the two orcas' excited calls mixed in with the high-pitched sounds of the dolphins. She darted away towards them. It was a special sight: the bigger and smaller orca with four white sided dolphins riding their wake. Tuschka was disappointed. Her fast approach had scared the dolphins away. They slowed down for a brief rest. Having regained some energy, the trio increased its speed again to see whether the dolphins would return. Within moments, the sleek creatures were back: five in total. Igor was in the lead with Skaade and Tuschka on each side and just a little behind. Two dolphins started to make little leaps out of the water just ahead of the orcas, while the other three stayed parallel to them. The swimming formation was most strenuous for Igor as the leading whale, but he had the most stamina of the three. The excited orcas surfaced higher and higher and eventually broke into full porpoising. It was a beautiful scene of strength, energy and grace. The water ran up the orcas' chins and pecs, and as a group, they created larger and smaller white-crested V's of water. Some dolphins left and changed places with others. Annika felt tempted too, but before she appeared, the trio slowed down, and she found them breathing heavily at the surface. After a short rest, the four slowly swam back to join the rest of the pod.

It was late January and Furka had been leading her pod south for almost a week. The orcas were traveling quite close to shore when they approached Kalika inlet. Although it was familiar, it made them uneasy as it revived the traumatic memory of Igor's injury. Sigurd was traveling closest to shore. He echolocated into the direction of the inlet and found it empty. Although nothing threatening seemed to be present, there was no sign of fish either. Even if there had been, they would not have considered using the natural trap.

Tuschka was traveling at Tamara's side. Her mother was near, swimming with Annika and Skaade. Recently, Annika had felt changes inside her, but she did not yet understand the stirring from within. She had a hard time to satisfy her growing appetite, and she sometimes felt a tension near her teats. Annika was less into active games, but she was all the more affectionate. She loved to rub and glide along the others and her desire for caresses never seemed satisfied. Annika was not aware that she had started to identify more with the adult females in the pod. Her fondness for babies and juveniles was taking on a slightly different quality. She began to love them not so much as playmates, but as young ones of her own kind who needed love and care. The three females were a special trio. Instinctively, Annika felt drawn to Tarka, who was what she would soon become... Skaade, in turn, felt attracted to Annika, because she was experiencing the awakening of puberty.

The low afternoon sun lent a misleadingly warm glow to the cold late winter sky when the pod approached the mouth of a relatively large fjord. They knew the big inlet as a home to fishing boats, that would leave to set their nets or seek refuge from bad weather. Conditions were extremely calm and the orcas had planned to wait and see if one or more boats would leave that night and set their nets.

Inconspicuous against the dark rocky shore, the sleek black predators passed a rocky outcrop, marking the northern side of the mouth, and entered the fjord. There were some engine sounds coming from deeper inside, but no boat was coming out yet. They continued further into the craggy inlet. Shaka and Igor were the first to detect a medium-sized concentration of the nutritious herring. It was a difficult task for only nine orcas to bring all the fish tight together. The orcas' appetite made it tempting to take on too many fish, but Furka was aware of the threat of faulty judgment. She sharply called to Igor when she noticed that the young male was trying to annex more fish, instead of taking his place between Shaka and Skaade. The young optimistic orca responded without hesitation. Whereas tolerance and creativity dominated during play, discipline ruled the hunt. Furka's judgment proved right. As the orcas drew smaller circles around the silvery gregarious fish, their concentration increased rapidly. Many gulls appeared on the scene.

The sound of an engine suddenly alerted the orcas, but they did not interrupt their hunt. Although the ball of herring was dwindling rapidly under the attack, it was still worth a few more well-aimed strikes. While they were finishing up, they heard the sound of an approaching boat. They had enough appetite left for another meal and listened to the boat. When it passed by about two hundred yards from them, they grouped together and started following from behind. Only a mile from where they had been hunting, the boat slowed down and stopped. Furka continued her approach and echolocated to find out whether herring were near. A different engine sound sent a shiver through the whales and Furka stopped. They were all silent. They had heard that sound when Igor had gotten hurt, but they had also heard it shortly after, near a vessel where they had been feeding without problems. The orcas were apprehensive, not certain whether the sound meant danger. Feeling somewhat uneasy, Furka started moving again in the direction of the fishing boat, that was setting the net.

The fishing boat had just left Stenavik harbor. On board was Torvil, the young fisherman who had been deeply impressed by the care of two adult orcas for a younger one that had been wounded by his hand. Since that time, he was even more motivated to stay at sea. The orcas fascinated him and every time they came near the boat to feed on the spill, it was an opportunity for him to observe them and learn more. Most fishermen were not very happy with orcas near their nets, but as long as they didn't interfere with the fishing, they left them unharmed. Being a hard worker and much more skilled than he was the season before, Torvil had gained more respect from his fellow crew members. Although herring were often located with the depth sounder, Torvil always scanned the sea with his binoculars for signs of whales or feeding gulls. Such activities could indicate the presence of herring from a far greater distance. The captain preferred to set the nets in places where no whales were present, but even then, the sound of reeling nets often attracted them.

The small powerboat had stopped and the net was fully stretched. Now it was time to wait for the fish to swim into the trap.

Torvil was excited to spot a pod of orcas drifting with the current into the direction of the net. He knew they were waiting for the fish to become more concentrated. His pal in the small boat started the engine to prepare for pulling the net into the circle. Torvil was watching the orcas and it struck him that the whole pod suddenly dived when the engine was started. Why? It came to his mind that some people had told him about orcas remembering those who had done them harm. He wondered if there was some truth in that. Could this pod be the one at which he had been shooting? The only thing he quickly realized was that this family also had one adult male. If they were the same, would they remember the small boat? Many seiners used such boats. Would the slight differences between these boats be distinct enough for the whales to recognize? And if they recognized it, what were they up to? Were they leaving or preparing to attack. The young man watched in silence. No one was aware of the tension that built in him while the orcas stayed down. The dive seemed to take forever. He was partly relieved when the first two adult females came to the surface to breathe. The orcas had barely changed their position. Quickly the others followed. He counted nine.

The sun had disappeared and the orcas were no more than black silhouettes against a background of reflecting water. The fishermen saw the whales dive. They didn't know where the whales were, but they pictured in their heads what was going on below. Torvil and his fellow crew member, Ruben, watched the periphery of the net closely. They were not aware that the big male and a female had slipped inside to feed, nor that one of the youngsters was exploring the net on the outside.

Ruben, saw the strong tugs at the net and grabbed a rifle to stop the whale from damaging the net. Torvil had not seen him reaching for the gun and as Ruben aimed for the spot, he suddenly saw it from the corner of his eye. At that moment, one of the orcas burst through the surface. In a flash Torvil noticed a whitish scar in front of its dorsal fin. With a single reflex he hit the barrel of the rifle from underneath just as his crewmate pulled the trigger. The sharp explosion took everybody by surprise and everyone looked at Ruben.

Furka and Shaka had just surfaced when the sharp sound blasted through their ears. With a yelp of fright they dived. To Igor, who had just pulled his ensnared teeth free, the sound almost felt like another stab. He kicked his flukes and took off without paying attention to his direction; he just wanted to get away from the boat. The others heard the same sound, but it was muffled by the water. Sigurd and Tamara immediately recognized it and gave a penetrating call. In an instant, they slipped out of the net from underneath and followed the others at high speed, staying down as long as they could hold their breaths.

The other men on board had seen the whales' instantaneous response to Ruben's shot. Yet they did not know why the shot had been fired in the first place. "Why was that?" one of them asked. Ruben didn't even hear the question. Heavily annoyed, he turned to Torvil: "Are you crazy, how dare you interfere?!" Torvil calmly said: "There was no need to shoot at that whale." Rubin was enraged. "That animal was tugging at the net. God knows how much damage it has done already. Haven't we been told to shoot if orcas touch the net? Well, that one did more than just touch it! Didn't you shoot last season for the same reason?" "Yes I did," Torvil replied, "and I had no reason: that orca was already swimming away from the net before I fired." Ruben was not at all satisfied: "I've always known you had something with those beasts. If it were up to you, you would rather have a hundred whales around and torn nets!" Ruben kicked Torvil hard. The young man squared off and saw the captain coming. With a heavy voice he asked for an explanation. Torvil kept silent while Ruben told his story. In the meantime one of the men had pulled in enough of the net to show the small hole the orca had made. When the captain looked at Torvil, the young man said: "I know the orders when the orcas seem to damage the nets, but there was no need to hit. It is enough to shoot, especially when the orcas are familiar with the sound." "How are you so certain that these orcas were?" the captain asked. "I recognized the orca I shot last winter by the scar on his back. But even if I hadn't known, don't they deserve at least enough respect from us to try a warning first?" Torvil knew he might have pushed it too far with the captain, but he had to know where his commander stood. All men were staring at him. The captain looked Torvil firmly in the eye. After a few seconds, he gave a confirming nod. "So be it," he said and waved his arm to call everyone back to work.

A few miles away from the boat, Igor came to himself. He had hurt himself a bit when he had been jerking with his teeth ensnared in the net. There were a few gashes in his gums and he licked the blood that trickled inside his mouth. Just as he realized no one was near, he heard his family call for him. They were not very far away. Without hesitation, he turned and swam fast in their direction. He was warmly welcomed. Seeking some comfort, Igor rubbed against his mother and nudged her flank. Sigurd tasted some blood and swam by to look his friend over. He noticed the shallow gashes in Igor's lower jaw and understood that the wounds were minor. They checked each other out and were relieved to find that none of them had been severely injured. Furka was quiet. she felt unsatisfied about her judgment. She and the others had been feeling uneasy about the sound all along, but she had underestimated the danger, because the conditions were so different from when Igor had been hurt. The experience was etched in the matriarch's memory, and not only hers. They would never again come close to that sound.

* * *

The pod had been patrolling the beaches for several days in an attempt to catch a few careless seal pups. They never stayed long in one place, leaving as soon as the seals had detected them. Mainly at night, between moving from one colony to the next, Furka led her pod away from shore in search of mackerel. In this period of late winter and early spring, opportunities to feed were unpredictable and they fed on whatever they could find. Annika, especially, had a hard time. The new life growing inside gave her an insatiable appetite. She was losing blubber and her contours now clearly betrayed her pregnancy. Tuschka had noticed Annika's increased affection for her and she frequently glided alongside, brushing against the larger female and rubbing heads with her.

One day, shortly after daybreak, Furka was heading to shore again. They had been out at sea for most of the night, but hunting had been unsuccessful. She decided to try one of the seal beaches that they had left several days before. The first time they were there, the pups were still very young and had not yet ventured into the water. With only three weeks of nursing, however, the pups would soon have to work on their swimming skills. The orcas were about three miles away from shore when they picked up faint unusual sounds. Furka did not stop swimming, but called softly for silence. Not knowing yet what she was hearing, she did not want her pod to reveal its presence.

The sound grew stronger, but was still several miles away. No one thought of seals any more. Listening intently, the orcas moved on until they were a little less than a mile from the beach. Furka stopped and rose up high to peek around. Shaka and Tamara followed. They understood the source of the sound as sudden as the long high pitched call that penetrated the sea. The seals' response was equally instant. The few that were in the water made for the beach as fast as they could. Tuschka felt the tension build, but she had no idea what was happening. It was a sound that triggered a strange sense of familiarity, but she did not remember hearing it from anyone of her own kind. Instinctively, she pressed close to her mother, seeking reassurance. Her mother nudged her, but made no sounds. The penetrating call was followed by a few others and after a few seconds of relative silence, they heard a sort of muffled moan. Tuschka shivered. She had never heard anything like that before and somehow, the sound conveyed fear, pain, and despair.

Sigurd nudged Igor and they both swam forward, positioning themselves between the others and the source of the sound. All of them, except Tuschka, had recognized the approach of orcas in full pursuit of about the largest prey they could possibly take: a humpback whale. Although the predators were orcas, none of them had the intention of joining the hunt. Unlike themselves, these orcas led different lives and preferred warm-blooded prey. But scarcity of food turned them all into opportunistic feeders. Where Furka's pod would not pass up an opportunity to grab a seal if other food was scarce, these hunters would fall back on fish if they had to. Furka's pod had no need to fear, but it was obvious the seal hunt would be unsuccessful for the rest of the day. Tuschka quickly sensed that her companions knew what was happening. Although she understood there was no immediate danger, and although her initial apprehension gave way to curiosity, she felt unerringly that it was not a situation to investigate by herself. She listened with full attention to the sounds growing rapidly louder.

The ill-fated whale had been traveling with two others when the orcas appeared. They had increased their swimming speed and initially stayed together. One of them, a young male, had soon veered away, however, and left. A few orcas had followed the young male, but he was in good shape and the predators had quickly returned to the two remaining females. The baleen whales were no match for the orcas in speed, but the predators numbered only six and showed respect for the powerful strokes of the humpbacks' flukes. They tried to exhaust their victims and focus on the one that would tire soonest. The humpbacks had not been swimming full speed. Instead, they tried to stay together and save energy to strike out at any orca that made an attempt to get a hold on them. They knew this small number of orcas would attack only if they got separated. One of the humpbacks slowed down a bit and felt teeth rake her tail. She kicked it forcefully free. As strong as the humpbacks were, the orcas were cautious not to get injured.

Although the predators traveled far below their top speed, the chase tired them too. To keep pressure on their prey, the orcas relieved each other frequently, leaving four at all times in active pursuit. The orcas, few in number, were not investing all this energy in pursuing large, healthy whales: they had soon detected the slight wheeze and prolonged inhalation of one of the two females.

The chase had been going on for nearly two hours when another small group of orcas came to join forces. Seven fresh strong orcas appeared on the scene, doubling the pressure on the humpback whales. The orcas were no longer swimming behind the two baleen whales. Half of them had positioned themselves alongside and ahead of the wheezing humpback. Noticing that the predators were concentrating on her companion, the other whale grabbed her chance: she veered off and gathered all her energy to break free. The orcas made no attempt to follow. Instead, they quickly joined the other flank of the laboring whale. The humpback saw her companion go and knew the battle was lost. With so many orcas around her and so little energy left, she knew they would soon attack, and she would fail the strength to fight them off. But her will to live was strong and she pushed on.

Two orcas started blocking her way. She could do little more than keeping her mouth shut tight and veer up to avoid a collision. Suddenly, she felt a sharp tug at her flukes. She kicked violently and freed herself again. The next instant, she felt teeth stab her left pectoral fin, but managed to jerk that free too. The thin skin was torn, but in her fear she didn't even notice she was bleeding. When she veered up for air she felt the heavy weight of a big orca on top of her. She tried to shake it off, but the orca was quick to follow her movements. When she forced herself to the surface, the sleek predator slid off, and the tired humpback breathed heavily.

The humpback female dived again, in a desperate attempt to get rid of the orcas. Yet the attackers were many, and fast, and relieved each other. Few of the orcas followed her down and she felt the pressure subside somewhat, but her dive didn't last long. Most of the orcas simply followed her near the surface, waiting to impede her rise when she would come up for air. The exhausted female arched up, only to look up at three heavy black bodies blocking her way...

The scene had come within visual range of Furka's pod. They saw the large whale breathing heavily and jerking her tail, shaking off one of her attackers. She was losing energy rapidly and would no longer be capable to fight off her besiegers.

The big whale veered a little to the side in a futile attempt to avoid the bodies blocking her ascent. Still below the surface she felt a heavy weight on her head and she jerked sideways in an attempt to shove it off. A second agile whale assisted and positioned itself on her blowhole when the first whale shifted. The humpback female was in desperate need of air and her lungs almost burst. There was no choice other than sheer force to break her way through to the surface. While she pushed upwards, most of her breath already escaped and bubbled towards the surface beneath and around her attackers. More orcas had gathered around her head and she panicked, still unable to inhale. With the whale making barely any forward motion, it was easy for the orcas to get a hold on her.

A big experienced female orca bumped the humpback's soft throat hard. The forceful blow came unexpected and in a reflex the humpback briefly opened her mouth a little. That was exactly what the orca female had wanted to achieve and she was quick to sink her teeth in the soft lip of the lower jaw. The kick from below had helped the big baleen whale to reach the surface, because the thud had also thrown the orca on her blowhole off balance. But before she managed to finish her desperate breath, a sharp tearing pain tugged her under again. As she felt water enter her blowhole, she snapped it shut, but only for seconds. She jerked against the pain and managed a breath as two other orcas got a hold on the other side of her jaw. She tried to push forward and upward, but lacked the strength to shake off her attackers. Panic overwhelmed her, feeling tearing pain and craving for air.

She knew there was no hope. In a final desperate attempt, the female humpback made a violent roll upon which two orcas tore off a part of her lips. At the surface, she took a breath and part of a second one before the predators blocked her blowhole again and grabbed another hold on her. Blood was streaming from the big wounds in her mouth and she could no longer effectively protect her vulnerable tongue from the attackers. One of the orcas grabbed her left pectoral fin, but she made no attempt to tear it loose. The orcas on and around her head caused far greater pain. She clenched her jaws together, but as a big bull orca managed a hold on her throat and pulled hard, she gave way. The need for air was unbearable and again she let go huge bubbles of air, that burst to the surface explosively. As two smaller orcas managed to grab her tender tongue, the desperate and suffering humpback female surrendered. Pain overwhelmed her and giving in to her need to inhale, she opened her blowhole, only to feel a mass of water streaming in. Then, as a final mercy, blood loss and drowning blurred her consciousness. A long, almost protracted moan escaped as she opened her blowhole to release a mix of air and water.

The battle was over. The once so majestic and strong whale rolled over belly up with eight or nine orcas violently tugging and tearing loose the pieces they liked most. They preferred the tongue above all, but also valued the lips and part of the throat and belly. After the second group of orcas had appeared on the scene, the struggle was over in less than half an hour.

Furka's pod had witnessed the ordeal of the humpback, whose death agony had turned the water red. There was a taste of blood everywhere. Tuschka had never witnessed a scene like this before. Although she was captivated by it, she felt no desire to investigate it more closely. Skaade and Igor had experienced it twice before, but not from such a short distance. None of them had ambition to be involved. They would rather hunt for fish.

After the humpback female had surrendered, one of the orcas made a loud long call, which was immediately repeated by the others in the hunting party. They all made that same characteristic call. It sounded jerky, starting high and ending low: "eee-eeeee-ee-eee-ooo" "eee-eeeee-ee-eee-ooo". It rang their victory through the sea.

The humpback was far more than the 13 orcas could eat. When they had fully gorged themselves, they abandoned their prey. One of the bulls broke the surface in a majestic breach and was followed by a few others. A juvenile who had taken only a few bites of the whale meat did a series of belly flops. The mood among the strange orcas was totally different and Tuschka felt a desire to swim over and join in the game. She had not really played for a while and the juvenile orca seemed such a nice companion. But without giving it a try, she felt she was not expected to take off. Instead, she made a little jump right by her mother's side. Tarka understood and rubbed her head against her. As the mood in the pod relaxed, she pinned Tuschka on her rostrum and pushed her up playfully. In the distance, they heard the 13 orcas move away in an easterly direction.

8.
Time for Play

Spring had not been very generous to the orcas and Tuschka had come to understand fully how dependent they were on finding food. All their wanderings served just that. Tuschka loved to participate in the hunt. She had her own place now and was no longer the shadow of her mother. As her pod moved on, Tuschka recognized more and more: she had come to associate the fjords with herring and the beaches with seals, but she did not yet know how to find these places herself. She still took it for granted that others led the way.

Still heading in a westerly direction, Furka's pod noticed the change in taste of the water, so typical for Rockcove Bay. They were traveling in a loose formation while they searched for food. Furka was in the lead with Sigurd close behind. Shaka and her offspring brought up the rear. Igor was only slightly shorter in length than his mother, but he still had the slender build of a young orca. He was agile and fast and loved to be next to Sigurd as the cunning male challenged his skills. Whether it was hunting or play, Igor still learned from every experience. He became more aware of Sigurd's part in the pod. He noticed how the strong powerful bull positioned himself between the pod and any potential danger, such as an unfamiliar boat. He always seemed to make sure that anything that wanted to get close to Tarka and Tuschka would find him first. He radiated protection and security. Igor remembered how comforting and encouraging it had been to have Sigurd near him when he was wounded. The confidence of the young male grew with his size, and deep inside him a calling awakened to protect his family. Instinctively, he spent more time near Skaade and Shaka when the pod was on the move.

* * *

One day in mid-May, the screaming of a huge congregation of birds guided the orcas to a large school of mackerel. Upon Furka's signal, the orcas took turns feeding. It was tempting for Sigurd to extend his turn to feed in the center of the ball and satisfy his ravenous appetite, but it was second nature for him to share. The mighty bull needed almost twice as much as the adult females of his pod and six times as much as Tuschka. He had to rely on his great hunting skill to catch what he needed. After Sigurd, Igor smacked his flukes into the fish, but managed to knock out only two. Tuschka darted forward and snatched one of them. Igor noticed her in the corner of his eye and turned sharply to chase her. Tuschka sped away, but the young male gained quickly on her, and she felt a hint of aggression. She squeaked for her mother, who answered her from a small distance away. Tuschka turned toward her mother and suddenly felt Igor's teeth rake her tail. He did not really hurt her, but she yelped in surprise and let go of the fish. As suddenly as he had started the chase, he gave it up and sucked in his kill. Tuschka, seeking comfort under her mother's belly, had been taken aback by Igor's reaction. Although some tension was tangible in the pod after having gone without food for nearly a week, she had not expected the young male to be so defensive of his catch.

When Tuschka regained some confidence, she became aware of engine sounds that gradually had grown louder. She approached and echolocated. Several small echoes revealed fish, suspended in the water right next to the boat, but without a net. They seemed easy prey. A little apprehensive about the situation, she nudged her mother and pushed her gently toward the boat. Tuschka echolocated again; the echoes piqued Tarka's curiosity and she sent a few more clicks to investigate. She called to the others and joined her offspring in the direction of the boat. Within two body lengths of the boat, they saw that the suspended fish were attached to thin threads. There also were threads without fish, but with a small glistening object dangling at the end.

Tuschka approached at close range, but when she was about to nudge one, Tamara rushed forward and called sharply. Tuschka immediately backed off, not understanding the reason for the sharp warning. When her experienced companion was beside her, she softly and gently repeated her warning. Then Tamara let her body sink a bit and approached one of the fish from below. Tuschka saw her carefully close her mouth around the tail and pull. The fish stayed on the thread at first, but when Tamara gave two little jerks, it suddenly came loose with a little gush of blood coming from its head. The mackerel floundered briefly and lay limp across the big female's jaws. Tuschka squeaked in delight when Tamara offered it to her. She wanted to follow the example of the grandmother orca, but Tamara still held her back. To Tuschka's surprise, several fish, still hanging on their threads, rose up towards the surface and disappeared. The two whales followed and popped their heads out of the water simultaneously. A burst of screams startled Tuschka. She had been so engrossed in her new experience that it came totally unexpected. Her curiosity aroused, Tuschka spyhopped again, this time a little further away. She saw the creatures moving on the boat and screaming again. The yells and shrieks conveyed excitement and she felt it had something to do with her.

Beneath the surface, she noticed several threads coming down with small silvery things hanging down from them. She echolocated on them, but they did not seem edible. Tuschka moved over towards another fish, immediately followed by Tamara and Tarka. Tamara made her stop and repeated what she had previously done: approach the fish from below and grab it carefully by the tail. She watched Tamara jerk gently, but it did not immediately come off the thread. Then, to Tuschka's surprise, she let go and encouraged her to follow her example. Under Tamara's watchful eye she carefully took the tail of the fish between her teeth. She pulled a little and felt the tension in the thread. It gave, but the fish did not come off. Tuschka pulled a little harder, and suddenly felt tugs that she didn't cause herself. Instinctively she held on and kept her position. Suddenly, the fish came off. She squeaked triumphantly and showed it to her companions. Then her eye caught other fish that were leaving the water again. With her prey still in her mouth, the young orca followed and spyhopped to see where the other fish had gone. Again she was greeted with shouts, but at the same time, she saw how several fish dangled in the air briefly before they disappeared over the edge of the boat. The creatures on the boat pointed at her and she gazed at them briefly. Then, she sank back down and swallowed her fish.

When the threads reappeared with the silvery objects, Tamara immediately swam over to one. She nudged it before Tuschka's eyes and made a warning call while she bobbed her head up and down. The young female did not know what was so dangerous about those things, but she clearly understood what her teacher meant and made no attempt to explore it further.

Since Igor had chased her after the mackerel hunt, Tuschka had felt slightly uncomfortable and had been avoiding him by keeping her mother in between them. Igor had noticed it too and felt he had responded too aggressively towards his younger companion. He found Tuschka fairly wary as he approached her, but he neared slowly and made friendly calls to the young female. Like all of them, he didn't like tension with other members of the pod. Although she still felt a little uncertain, Tuschka sensed Igor's good intentions and she wanted very much to restore her playful and unreserved relationship with him. Igor did not push it and started to join Tarka's other side. Every now and then, his voice was friendly and her mother made no attempt to make him leave.

Tuschka began to relax and moved over to her mother's other flank. Tarka tapped her reassuringly with her pectoral fin. Now, she was close to Igor, who looked like an adult in her eyes. The young male closed in a little more and briefly trailed his pectoral fin along her side. With his gentle touch, Tuschka lost the last of her apprehension. She moved over and swam underneath him, brushing his chest with her back and dorsal fin. Then she turned around and nudged his chin with hers. Igor responded affectionately, suppressing a desire to start a game with her. The pod was not in the right mood for that. The two young whales, only slightly more than three years apart, but very different in size, caressed each other while they made graceful rolls and turns. It felt like a reunion for them after the brief period of alienation, and to reassure their bond, Tuschka swam close to him for much of the day.

The orcas had been feeding off and on, but did not feel satisfied at all. They longed for the bounty of late spring and summer and to indulge in play with other orca families. The mood was not depressed, but rather dull as they changed their direction back towards Rockcove Bay. Noticing Annika growing more heavy with her advancing pregnancy, Sigurd had started to feel more protective towards his youngest sibling and spent more time in her proximity. She was a beautiful young female, but he did not look at her as males from other pods used to do. She was his sister, carrying precious young life within her. Sigurd's attention did not escape the expectant female. The presence of her strong confident brother gave her an extra feeling of security.

Tuschka and the others had noticed the sounds of distant small boats, that often predicted the return of the salmon. Yet they did not hear or taste a sign of the highly eligible prey. Sigurd dropped back a bit and joined Igor, who immediately perked up in the big bull's presence. The two bumped each other in greeting as a few faint calls caught their attention. None of the whales had been vocalizing and they had all picked up the sound. Almost instantaneously, Furka slowed down and turned her head slightly towards the direction from which it had come. Another eerie call penetrated their ears. It sounded familiar to all of them and Tuschka squeaked with delight, too excited to leave the initiative to one of the higher-ranked whales. Furka glanced in Tuschka's direction but did not call for silence. Just as Tarka bumped Tuschka in warning, the matriarch voiced a loud greeting to their congeners, who were approaching from the east.

The response was sudden and unmistakable: Raina's strong voice sounded a greeting in return. It was immediately followed by another call, a little softer, commanding to her family to group up. Furka did not need to give the same message to her own pod. As if Raina had spoken for them both, the two orca families tightened together and kicked their flukes to a speed of 12 knots to quickly bridge the three miles that still separated them. Tuschka porpoised ahead. The three and a half-year-old juvenile had burst into speed and seemed motivated to "win" the race. After about half a mile, she slowed down a bit, but was still in the lead, with Furka close behind.

The two pods had not met in almost two months and they were eager to spend some time together. Together, they would need more food, but there were also advantages of hunting together. Micro-algae had started to grow and were decreasing the underwater visibility. When the two pods were less than a few hundred yards apart, they did not see each other, but sound told them everything. Although full of excitement, Tuschka dropped back a little and joined her mother's flank. It was one thing she had not waited for Furka to announce their presence, but she was definitely not supposed to be the one to take the initiative in greeting.

Both pods slowed down and formed a line with all the whales abreast. Raina's voice pierced the waters, immediately followed by Furka's. Just a few seconds later, all the other whales moved forward and voiced their greetings. The sea vibrated with the excited calls of the two orca families. They intermingled and rubbed and bumped each other affectionately. Tuschka and Aleta did not need much time to find each other. Aleta had grown since they last met, but she was noticeably smaller than Tuschka. The two were the closest in age and they loved to play together. Tuschka moved her head down just as she was about to bump into Aleta, and glided underneath her younger playmate. Tuschka liked chasing games, especially when the challenge was almost equal. She made a sudden and sharp turn and darted off. Aleta needed no encouragement and darted after her. Tuschka had the advantage of the initiative and had no problem staying ahead. Just as she looked around to determine what to do next, she saw Korak and Sigurd to her left and veered in their direction.

The two bulls were so engrossed in each other's company that Tuschka's sudden appearance took them by surprise. She dashed by underneath the two big males, turned and broke the surface in a small belly breach. Coming down, Tuschka hid behind Sigurd's flank. Barely more than a second later, Aleta ran into the two bulls, and had a little fright not seeing Tuschka. She stopped short of Korak and called. Tuschka did not answer, but Aleta quickly spotted the flukes of her playmate behind the other big bull. She knew Korak well, but she did not feel as close and familiar with Sigurd. She dove down to swing wide underneath the two giants and just as she spotted Tuschka, the latter kicked her flukes and pushed herself up on Sigurd's broad back. Korak did not interfere, but waited to see what his companion would do. Sigurd seemed not to mind it at all. Tuschka thought she was going to slide over Sigurd's back, just in front of his dorsal fin, but then she felt him rise up again and move forward. She felt herself pinned against the sturdy dorsal fin as she was dragged along. She squeaked with delight at the exciting ride. She slid back a little, but with the leading edge of the tall dorsal fin behind her flipper, she managed to hang on a little longer.

Aleta followed in Sigurd's wake, hoping to continue her game with Tuschka. Sigurd slowed down and Tuschka washed off. Korak watched it while he hovered at the surface. As Sigurd came to a stop, Tuschka immediately made another attempt to get on his back. She slid up, bumped into the broad base of his great dorsal fin and slid off again. Aleta was watching and felt tempted to do the same. She glanced at Korak, who was hovering a few yards behind. Tuschka noticed her and squeaked to Aleta to join in. She hesitated. She bumped Tuschka gently and then nudged Sigurd. The big male responded friendly and he sank down a bit to encourage the juveniles. Tuschka kicked her small flukes, and this time, she had so much speed that she slid off on the other side. She turned around underneath Sigurd and started to push Aleta up, poking her rostrum into the soft little belly. Sigurd did not move, waiting to see if Tuschka would try again. When she did, Aleta overcame her initial apprehension and the two juveniles pushed up in unison. This was exactly what Sigurd had waited for: he rose quickly, felt one of the two little orcas slide back against his dorsal fin and gained speed. Tuschka, who was in front, started to slide off, but Sigurd noticed it, rolled on his side, and supported her with his huge pectoral fin. Both juveniles squeaked with excitement. They felt a little kick with each stroke of Sigurd's powerful flukes.

Korak had been following behind as his younger companion carried the two little females along. He felt a bit left out and was ready to leave. Sigurd dived suddenly and turned around towards Korak, nudging him sideways. Tuschka and Aleta had become so exuberant that they did not hold back in Korak's presence. The two started chasing each other, using the two big males to play hide and seek. They glided underneath, slid over their broad backs, dashed by in front of them and almost collided as they both slid up on Korak's back from opposite directions. No longer feeling left out, Korak playfully scared Aleta by suddenly opening his mouth as she brushed his rostrum. She swerved away from him and he went after her.

Tuschka and Sigurd followed. Aleta was no match for her big pursuer and Korak gained on her fast. She tried to escape and breached, but as she fell back, Korak pinned her on his rostrum and elegantly balanced her as he pushed her forward. Sigurd suddenly halted and Tuschka felt herself dragged forward in the wave he created. As she paralleled him he signaled her to follow. He dived down several times her body length and arched upwards. Then he quickly accelerated with Tuschka in his wake. For every single stroke Sigurd made, Tuschka made three. Helped by his slipstream, she managed to stay with him as they sped upwards. The huge orca broke the surface, and the smaller one a moment later. Sigurd was so large that Tuschka was already fully out of the water while Sigurd still climbed higher. When his majestic body was fully in the air, he seemed to hang there for a moment with his striking black and white markings standing out against the blue sky. Then he turned sideways, arching his flank towards the surface with his head still pointing upwards. Tuschka's small splash alerted several whales nearby as if it was a warning about the bigger one to come. Just a moment later, Sigurd came down with a thunderous crash, throwing up walls of water at least 10 feet high. Tuschka was a little dazzled with Sigurd's breach so close and let out a squeak of surprise.

Sigurd liked to surprise juveniles when he played with them, but he knew exactly what their limits were and he never took risks with them. To reassure his young playmate, he nudged her warmly and rubbed his head against her. Then Tarka came into view and waited patiently for Tuschka to join her. Tarka had spent some time with Nadia when all the activity and exuberant calls of their offspring had made them wonder what kind of exciting game they were playing. Both mothers trusted the two males completely with their babies. In their presence no harm would come to them. As they had done many times before, Sigurd and Korak had not only looked after them well, but they had also given the juveniles an exhilarating diversion. Both Nadia and Tarka knew how much they needed distraction after such a sparse spring.

The encounter between the two families had a enlivening effect on all of them. Korak had joined Sigurd again after he had turned Aleta back over to Nadia. The two juveniles did not spend much time with their mothers. It was too special to be together.

Annika gave most of her attention to Kujira, who also was pregnant. Kujira was a little older than Annika and the relative scarcity of food had also accentuated the contours of her belly. With their clicks, they investigated each other's belly. They picked up some contours of the bones, especially the spine, and got a rough estimate of the size of the other's unborn baby. The two expecting mothers did not engage in wild chasing games, but stayed at the perimeter of the gathering. One of the younger whales had almost run into them and they felt more comfortable in a relatively quiet spot.

After more than two hours of playing and socializing, the orcas calmed down. In the late afternoon, they formed a tight group and rested. Almost in bodily contact they hovered at the surface. Korak and Sigurd were still side by side, close to Kujira and Annika. The orcas synchronized their breathing and a cluster of plumes rose into the air at regular intervals. The sound of their blows, slow and heavy, was accompanied only by the occasional call of a bird swooping by.

9.
Korak's Loss

The two pods had been together for two days, but they had found no food source that enabled them to take advantage of their larger number. Reluctantly, the families broke up again to spread their forays over a larger area. Furka's pod was feeding on some cod to the north of the Kelpada Islets when some adults suddenly stopped their activities. Some reddish flash in the corner of their eyes had caught their attention. They looked around to see where it was, but it had disappeared. They waited briefly to see if it would happen again. Just as they were about to give up, another dark reddish object came by, followed by a few more. Sigurd echolocated and a few fragmented echoes confirmed his thoughts. Shaka looked at him with a knowing look: they had found the long awaited salmon!

Everyone was alerted and facing south, full of tension and ready to burst into speed. The only encouragement they were waiting for was Furka's go. The matriarch kicked her flukes and, like newly shot arrows, the pod burst in full porpoising in the direction of the salmon. They did not yet know whether they would find a big run, but the arrival of the first of the nutritious fish announced the abundance of early summer.

The burst of action was spectacular: even before they broke the surface in unison, their blows heralded their surfacing. Streams of white bubbles exploded into plumes of white vapor, left behind in the air. Water ran up their chins and off their dorsal fins in an almost solid vertical spray. Sigurd's tall dorsal fin waved a little as it broke free of its watery weight. Most of the whales came out of the water so high that their pectoral fins cut through it. Tuschka was almost enveloped in a white foamy V as she porpoised along. Even Annika, heavy as she was, kept up with her family. During their brief dives, they noticed that the number of fish flashing by increased steadily.

Furka, Sigurd, and Tamara were in the lead, with Furka just slightly ahead. Not more than half a body length behind Sigurd was Shaka, flanked by Igor and Skaade. Annika was in the center and Tamara was immediately followed by Tuschka and Tarka. They were so tight that they seemed to touch. This way, more than half of the pod benefited from the suction of the whales in the lead and on the outside. When they needed to keep it up for a while, they took turns in the lead positions to share the hardest work. They did about 25 knots and it was now that their sheer supremacy as top predator was patently obvious. Their size and power, combined with their speed and disciplined teamwork, made them invincible.

After several miles Furka slowed down and the orcas felt themselves carried along by their own wake. The run was not very dense and big. It would not be easy to scramble a meal together with only nine of them, but Furka decided to give it a try. She could not afford to risk waiting, only to find that suddenly the opportunity had passed. How much they wanted to be with Raina's pod now!

Furka quickly signaled what hunting strategy to follow. There were not enough of them to form a head-on trap for the fish. It would be too easy for the agile salmon to veer quickly away from the predators and break through their ranks. Instead, the orcas started to chase them from behind in two lines. Annika, Tarka, and the three younger whales made up the second line, close behind the first. With the hunters on their 'heels', an escape sideways slowed the fish down and made them easier to catch for other predators in the line. Those that completely turned around and escaped the first line, ran into the second. It was quite an energy consuming strategy, but the most successful with so few whales.

The lead whales blasted strong sonar pulses. Even to Tuschka, the sharp sounds came as a surprise. Being smaller than the others, Tuschka was not as quick to swallow her prey. She had to shake it quite vigorously to get some bite-size chunks. Tarka quickly rushed over to bite off the parts sticking out from Tuschka's mouth. There was no time to lose. As soon as Tuschka had swallowed something, she had to race ahead again to take her position between her mother and Annika.

With the orcas swimming just a bit faster than the fish they were hunting, the density did not change much. The size of their meal depended on their endurance. As hungry as they were, there was no question when to stop: they would go on until they either were satisfied or exhausted. The hunters often smacked their tail or a pectoral fin on the water to maintain pressure on the fish. Annika tired faster than the others, but she was not yet satisfied. She went up for air more often than the others and pushed hard to keep the pace. Shaka switched position with Igor and came alongside the heavy, pregnant female to share a fish with her.

Sigurd was getting his fill. He was so big that swallowing the fish hardly required any effort. The strong bull still had energy left and he caught several fish to help satisfy Annika too. She was grateful and concentrated more on staying with the others than on actively pursuing fish. After nearly an hour of chasing, turning, and snapping around, the majority of the pod had managed to satisfy their appetite and fatigue rapidly dominated. As the fish continued south, the orcas grouped together to rest. They felt spent. Silent but satisfied, they rested closely together. Shortly after sunset, Furka started a slow pace toward the destination of most of the salmon: the Laxava river.

Since that first salmon run, Furka and her pod had not ventured far from Rockcove Bay in expectation of more. The small village was teeming with activity and small boats buzzed around during most of the day. Although the engine sounds made it harder to pick up faint sounds, they did sometimes lead them to the fish. The whales had learned over the years that the boats often gathered around the fish. A larger concentration of boats, or a group of boats all heading in the same direction, was enough reason for them to go ahead and explore. Most often, however, the orcas found the fish first.

In late June, Furka's pod was gorging themselves on a run, so dense that they did not even have to work together. Suddenly, a relatively loud call revealed the presence of Raina's pod feeding on the same run. Furka did not call the hunt off. Knowing they would have ample time to be together, the nine orcas indulged in feeding.

When they had satisfied their ravenous appetites, Furka led her group out of the main route of the salmon run and listened to determine whether Raina and her pod were still actively feeding. She decided to rest a little before calling to them. From a distance, she noticed Korak's tall dorsal fin. He seemed to rest, which was remarkable for such a big bull. Would he have eaten his fill in even less time than most of his companions? His sister Kujira surfaced near him.

The two pods met at the edge of the big run. The greeting was warm, but not as exuberant as usual. Although it was obvious that the other pod welcomed Furka and her family, their mood seemed a little subdued. Furka did not need much time to find out what had happened. After she had greeted Raina and a few others, she noticed that Ruka was missing. At the same moment, she understood the behavior of the big bull, who had been resting at the surface while the others were still feeding. He hung back a little behind the pod and had not yet joined in the greeting. Furka approached him and called softly. He turned his head to look at Furka, but he remained silent. Kujira came over, touched him gently in passing and greeted Furka. The matriarch sensed Korak's depressed mood. He had lost his mother, the one with whom he had the strongest bond.

* * *

Since they had last met, Raina had tried her luck in the opposite direction, but the pod had soon been slowed down by Korak's mother, Ruka. The older female had begun to come up more frequently for air and had problems keeping up with her pod. Korak had noticed it from the earliest signs on and had helped his mother by giving her the benefit of his wake. Yet her condition deteriorated relatively fast and within two days, the pod had to wait several times a day for Korak and Ruka to catch up with them. Raina's pod, too, had suffered from the relative scarcity of food, and the pressure to find prey had weighed equally heavy on them.

Ruka felt she was a burden to her family and she pushed hard to stay with them. The long days of traveling had taken their toll on the older female, who had already begun the previous winter with fewer reserves than the others. Being underweight, she spent even more energy to stay warm. When she developed a fever, she was no longer capable of keeping the pace. One night, Raina's pod stayed in a protected bay, close to the river mouth. Raina had hoped the rest would give Ruka new strength. If food were not found within a day or two, there would be no recovery for their ailing companion.

The next morning, it was obvious that Ruka would not be able to stay with them for long. It was difficult to decide what to do. Raina wanted the pod to stay together, but if they all went without food for too long, they were risking the same fate. Waiting consumed little energy, whereas active searching did, but no one knew how much longer it would be before the salmon arrived.

Reluctantly, Raina left the bay mid-morning, leaving Korak and Ruka behind. The presence of her strong son was comforting for Ruka, yet she felt he had refrained from foraging on her behalf. They rubbed each other tenderly and Korak supported Ruka much of the time: she rested her chin behind his dorsal fin with her pectoral fins on either side of his body. Every now and then, they called softly to each other, but most of the time they were silent. Korak was very aware of his mother's frequent and shallow breathing that betrayed her weakness.

They had been together for over 30 years and for almost three quarters of that time they had swum side by side, breathing in unison. Even though he had surpassed her in size when he was only 10 years old, his mother had always been a reassuring and comforting presence for him. Whatever mood he was in, whatever the pod did, she had always meant a warm welcome. Now, she was so close to him, so much in contact with him, and yet it was so different. For the first time in his life, she depended on him and there was little he could do. Korak felt heavy in his heart. He felt how her former strength was leaving her. For a moment, his aching stomach made him wonder where the pod was and when they would return.

The weak blow of his mother immediately brought his attention back to her. She moaned a little and he felt her slide off a bit. Korak sunk down a little and turned to face his mother. She went under for a moment, but came up by herself for another breath. Korak nudged her tenderly and called softly to her to comfort her. He gently lifted her chin a bit and touched her with his tongue. Ruka responded and touched her son's tongue with hers. For a while they tenderly caressed each other with the tips of their tongue. They had done that many times in the past, in playful games like suck and spit, or to reinforce their bond. It was strenuous for Ruka to support herself, but the precious moment made her fatigue fade to the back of her consciousness. The two cherished each other's closeness. For a moment, his mother's loving and caring tenderness felt as it had always felt: as if nothing could part their ways. Ruka lifted her head for another breath and caressed Korak once more, but tired rapidly. Korak sensed her need and lifted her to the surface. This time he did not support her on his back. He wanted to be near her face and let her chin rest on his broad pectoral fin.

Night fell as the two drifted at the surface. Soon after dark, Korak was awakened from a light slumber by the familiar calls of his pod. He waited in silence, so as not to disturb his mother. He felt her lift her chin a bit and take another breath. Raina and Kujira immediately approached the two and the matriarch noticed how weak Ruka had become. Their hunt had not been very successful, but she decided to stay with their sick family member. Ruka's neck was sunken and her ribs visible as ripples beneath her skin. Raina caressed her and called her. Ruka responded weakly. Her breathing had become even more shallow and the fever was blurring her consciousness. Raina and Kujira supported her body in between them. Kujira moaned a little at her mother's side. Raina had insisted the pregnant female join the hunt, not expecting to find Ruka so sick upon her return. Korak was grateful for the support of the two females. It gave him the opportunity to be face to face with his mother in what he felt were their last moments together.

Almost losing consciousness, Ruka called softly to Korak. He answered and nudged her to reassure her that he was there. He tenderly lifted her chin to help her take another breath. It did not yet come. He pushed a little to encourage her. Ruka opened her eye just barely. Korak rubbed his cheek against her and caressed her once more with his tongue. When her mouth opened a little, he found hers one more time. Then her breath came, like a deep sigh. Korak pushed her up a bit higher, making sure his mother's blow hole was well in the air, but she remained silent. It had been his mother's last breath. She gently bobbed with the ripples. Still resting on her three companions, she seemed just slumbering. She was almost weightless in the water and still with them. Raina caressed her companion for the last time and slowly let her slide off her pectoral fin. As Kujira did the same, a little later, Korak felt her slowly sink. He swam underneath her and lifted her up on his broad back. He swam by his pod members, who silently watched him carry her by. The big male still had his pod, but it would never be the same. Korak could not yet part with his mother, who had been closer to him than any other orca ever was. Now he wanted only to be with her. With her pectoral fins still embracing him, and her weight and warmth on his back, she was still there for him. Feeling comfort in his closeness with her, he carried her into the night.

* * *

When Furka looked at Korak, she knew better than most others what he was going through. Losing one's mother left a void that was never filled, but unlike a female a male did not have his own offspring to provide comforting diversion and closeness. After his mother's passing, Korak would never again have someone who would give him that special unconditional acceptance and warm intimacy. He had his place in the pod and his presence was appreciated, but he would never again experience the same closeness. For now, Kujira was closest to him, but soon she would have a calf to tend to. Although he would spend much time with them and give them protection, Kujira's calf would be closer to her, just as all the other members of his pod had ones who were closer to them than he.

For Furka, the loss of her mother had been more difficult for her than for most females. She still had intimacy to share with her offspring, but she had to face the responsibility of being leader. Although less so than in the very beginning, she still had moments when she longed for the security and experienced guidance that Gaia had given her. Making decisions sometimes meant difficult choices between the interest of her pod and her maternal impulses. In a different way, both Furka and Raina shared some loneliness with Korak. Raina was very understanding of Korak's grief, but, unfortunately, being mother and leader at the same time, Raina had less opportunity than others to give extra attention to the sad male. Still, she often made an effort to reassure and encourage him.

Furka knew she could not offer any lasting solace. Yet she felt an urge to divert him and give him some attention. Although not a member of Korak's pod, Furka did not hesitate to approach the big male. She was respected as a whale of high rank and it was unlikely that Korak would show any adverse response to her. He acted aloof, seemingly not wanting company, but Furka knew that he would be grateful for the proper kind of attention. He was not into superficial or playful interaction, but deep inside he was craving for tenderness and affection. Furka called softly to him and saw him turn his head in her direction. She met him slowly head-on, and rubbed her head and body against him before she swung around to take his side. She trailed her pectoral fin along his flank and encouraged him to follow her. They surfaced together to breathe. Mostly in silence, Furka kept him company, caressing him tenderly from time to time. Several times, Korak expressed his appreciation with a little nudge or a gentle call. Furka's presence was not only a comfort for him, but also deterred the unrestrained approach of boisterous young males, who would have wanted him to join in their game. After a little while, Raina appeared in the blue-green twilight and joined them. She rubbed Korak while she glided underneath him and took Furka's other flank.

The three whales were together for only a few minutes when faint distant calls suddenly took them out of their semi slumberous state. Just as Furka had found Raina, feeding relatively close by on the same run, the big concentration of fish apparently had attracted Sitka's pod as well. The two leaders looked at each other knowingly: whether or not their companion was in the mood for it, they had to take control in the greeting activities with the other big pod. Furka nudged Korak one more time, leaving him with Raina. Kujira joined her brother and mother as the two pods formed a tighter group. Keeping position against the tide, the 23 orcas listened to the sounds of the other hunters drawing near.

* * *

The research team had returned for another summer. They had learned much about the area and they had agreed with Johann that they could use his boat without him whenever he preferred to go out fishing. Johann enjoyed the trips with his scientific guests, but a few times these trips had conflicted with the demands of his true profession. The researchers' payments were a certain source of income, but not enough to make a living. The problem was that the presence of salmon often coincided with that of the whales. Several times Johann had tried to do some fishing either before or after a trip, but that had not been very successful. After a full season of working together, he knew his boat would be in good hands. Without being skipper, he would be paid less, but that would be more than compensated for by a good catch.

It was still early in the morning, but well after dawn, when Johann received a call about a large run of salmon, heading for the river. His first impulse was to take out his fishing boat and leave the research team the smaller vessel. While he was dressing, Werner called and said he had heard some talk on the radio about many whales feasting on the fish. The blue sky, the calm weather, and the almost certain presence of orcas held a promise for a very special day. After a little hesitation, he decided to dedicate the day to the whales and take his family along as well. Johann quickly walked over to Bjorn's place and found them at breakfast. Varg nearly burst with enthusiasm as he heard the report. Since it would be a little cramped in the smaller boat with eight people and gear, he suggested to work from the bigger boat. "She's slightly less maneuverable, but I think it will still work," Johann said. "It is fine with me," Bjorn responded. "If there are many whales, they're either feeding or socializing. In either case, they will be difficult to photograph anyway. But, their behavior may be all the more exciting!"

Soon after leaving the small harbor, they were among several small boats heading in the same direction. Johann checked a few times by radio on the whales' position. Their number was estimated to be around 50! After about an hour, Peter was the first to spot two male dorsal fins. As soon as they were less than half a mile away from the first group, Johann slowed down to just a few knots. They found the whales just as Bjorn had predicted: there were several small groups and some single orcas, swimming in an unpredictable pattern. "There must be several pods here," Bjorn said, "and it seems that they aren't feeding. According to the depth sounder they aren't with a high concentration of fish at the moment. With a big run so close and no one pursuing it, I assume they've eaten their fill already. They may hang around together for a while, but I've no idea for how long. I suggest we try to document the males first; they're the easiest to spot and will give us some indication of the pods that are present".

They approached one of the two males Peter had seen first. At closer range, he looked strong and majestic, though without very distinctive markings. He allowed the boat to parallel him at a distance of only 30 yards and the crew was impressed by the power he radiated: the appearance of his fin tip heralded his slow and dignified rise, his blow was strong and explosive, and his massive muscular body created suction in the water near his flanks. Then, a little forward kick of the huge fin announced his dive. His blow hole snapped shut, seemingly almost too late. His fin cut a V through the water, leaving no marks when it disappeared. The only sign he left behind was a slick, almost oily patch made by the movement of his flukes. Although the team had taken the pictures they needed, they stayed with him for a while. They were sure the big bull was very aware of their presence. Yet he was so tolerant. They all felt close to him. He was not just an animal they were observing; another mind was accompanying them.

Johann's family was as excited as the researchers, but in their own way. They were not scientifically involved, though they had picked up many things along the way and had started to develop a personal interest in some distinctive individuals. Sarah had a special interest in the young calf she had seen on her first day out with the scientists. They had sighted it since and she hoped she would be able to see it grow up. Deep inside, she wondered about the calf she had seen that special day in early spring. Would it still be alive? And if so, had they seen it again without recognizing it? She and her brother were happy to share this encounter on their father's big boat. Their mother was in the galley, preparing some hearty soup for the crew.

By afternoon, Bjorn saw the whales form two groups, moving in a southern direction. He picked up his binoculars and looked ahead. "I think they are done feeding. They may be grouping up to meet other whales in the distance. Let's follow them. We've got photos of the males and most other individuals of these groups." About 10 minutes later, the groups they were following and the oncoming group almost came to a stop. "Look," Varg yelled, "the lead whales are swimming forward to meet….." "Wow," Varg continued excitedly, "it was as if someone gave a starting signal. One moment they just hung there and the next it's all action!" As restrained expectation finding its release, the orcas burst into an exuberant display of activities. Like fireworks, many orcas leaped into the air, falling back with great splashes. A few times, two or even three whales breached at the same time. Some calves were doing several jumps on their own.

Sarah saw several juveniles playing together and was endeared by the young orcas rolling, bumping, and chasing each other, making several bubbly squeaks at the surface. Several females, which she presumed to be their mothers, were resting at the surface nearby. Johann had shut down the engine and they watched the orcas while they enjoyed a late afternoon snack. Since most of the fishing boats were a mile or more away, Bjorn decided to drop a hydrophone. As soon as the rubber-coated receiver was lowered into the water, the air was filled with the squeaks, clicks, and groans of dozens of orcas. Johann's family was dazzled; the sounds were so clear and so varied. They ranged from high-pitched eerie calls, long whines, and abrupt squeaks and clicks, to low groans. Seeing the whales was one thing, but hearing them live made their presence much more tangible. Even when the nearest whales were down, the observers were part of their underwater world filled with orca conversation. They envisioned the dark bodies under water, gliding along talking to others they could not see, yet knowing who and where they were. Often a call was repeated several times in rapid succession. "Would it be members of the same pod, communicating that way?" Peter asked Bjorn. "I'm not sure, but it's very plausible. It's remarkable that those repetitions involve one type of call. And if the repeats are indeed answers, it's a limited number of whales that respond. They may be checking on each other's position that way."

They had lost a little ground while the hydrophone was in the water. When everyone had amply enjoyed the richness of the orcas' vocal repertoire, Bjorn hauled it in and kept it ready in case another opportunity would present itself. Within several minutes they were amidst some 70 whales. Fins popped up everywhere around them and there was no consistent direction to any of the small groups. Bjorn advised Johann to cut the engine again to listen. While the voices of the whales filled their ears again, they all tried to capture on film the breaches, spyhops, tail slaps, chases, and many other activities.

For Johann's family and the research team, the big gathering of orcas, which they called a 'super pod', symbolized a celebration of the exceptionally big salmon run that marked the beginning of summer. Despite long summer nights, the team realized that they could not stay with the whales much more than another hour. The warm orange sunlight and the calm water were excellent to capture the special, even romantic, atmosphere of the encounter.

Peter was talking to Ingrid when his attention was suddenly caught by a small group of orcas chasing and bumping and rolling over each other. Several spyhopped as they came closer to the boat. "Look at that!" Peter suddenly yelled, as he saw a whale with a distinctive scar on his back dive under the boat.

At the same time, a very loud train of clicks hit their ears. Although the loudness of these clicks took everyone by surprise, the others in the boat had also noticed Peter's sudden reaction and wondered what he had seen. It was obvious that one of the whales had echolocated on the hydrophone at a very short range, but what else had attracted Peter's attention? Everyone turned around to face the direction where they expected the orcas to surface again. They came up about 30 yards from the other side of the boat. The whales differed slightly in size. The first two to take a breath were clearly immature. As the third whale came up in a high arch, Peter pointed at the orca: "look at that strange scar on the back, in front of the dorsal. I thought there was a nick in its fin. It is important to document that whale if we can. It might be the one we know got wounded."

Light conditions were far from optimal, but Bjorn asked Johann to try to get alongside the group for a picture. He joined Johann in the wheelhouse, helping him by keeping an eye on the target group. The hydrophone was quickly taken aboard and within two minutes they were heading after the five orcas. It was not difficult to gain on them, but the surfacings of the playing whales were totally unpredictable. "This is like chasing a rabbit," Johann commented. "I can't promise that you'll get what you want." Bjorn nodded, but did not respond otherwise, which made it clear to Johann that the researcher was not prepared to give up.

For Johann's family it spoke for itself that the train of clicks had been made by a curious orca who had wanted to check out the hydrophone. It dawned slowly on them, however, that the speaker had been much more puzzling for the orcas: how strange it had been for them to hear their own voices in the air. Perhaps that was the reason, they had spyhopped so close to the boat.

Their attention was caught by two adult whales heading for the rambunctious group. The two men didn't welcome the approach at first, because it would become more complicated to pick one orca out of a bigger group. The newcomers' arrival, however, had a dramatic effect on the behavior of the playing orcas. The game ended abruptly and after a few seconds, two whales took off, each with a juvenile at their flank. The other crew had noticed it too. "It seems like their mothers came to get them back," Peter commented. The three remaining orcas stayed together and set off at a slow pace. Just when Johann managed to get parallel to them, the arrival of the boat caught the orcas' attention. They turned around and surprised everyone when they came up in the stern wake. Several seconds later, they popped up in front of the boat. "They seem to be playing with us," Bjorn said, as he stepped out of the wheel house. He asked Johann to maintain his course and instructed the others to take different positions on the boat. "If Varg takes the stern, Peter and Ingrid a side each, then I'll take the bow. Be prepared for a close pass and try to get what you can".

Bjorn was frustrated when he missed a shot of the scarred orca surfacing in front of the bow. When the whale surprised him a second time, the researcher discovered the pattern and was fully concentrating on the spot where he hoped it to pop up again. With his finger on the shutter release, he was tense with anticipation. The orca came up just as he had expected and he yelled excitedly: "I got a shot of his back. It'll show the saddle on both sides and the scar, but not the fin. It may be hard to get a shot on the si.." Before he had finished his sentence, they caught a glimpse of a breach on starboard side. "That's a male!" they heard Ingrid speak up loudly. The orca splashed down and as it came up for a breath, they all spotted the scar in front of the dorsal fin and a little to the left of the spine. Although no one had managed to get the breach, both Varg and Bjorn clicked their cameras on the surfacing. The young male's fin did indeed have a small triangular nick in the upper part. Johann slowed down as they watched the orcas swim away. The light was fading rapidly. In silence, they drifted, looking at the misty plumes and fins silhouetted against the setting sun, and listening to the sound of their blows carrying far over the flat, calm waters. As the orcas' presence faded, they headed home.

The team was excited when they managed to match the young male with the scar on his back. Bjorn explained to the young girl that within several years, the young orca would grow a large dorsal fin like the majestic fin of the big male in his pod. The adult male had a smooth fin with a broad base and despite his lack of distinctive markings, the team had some excellent shots of his saddle patch, showing several shallow rake marks. Those would be sufficient to distinguish him from similar males on good quality photos.

On behalf of his daughter, Johann asked the team if they had recognized any of the juveniles. "There were two juveniles in that group that dived under the boat near the end," Bjorn responded. "They may very well have been the two calves that we documented in A and B pod. They were far too big to be new calves and far too small to be anyone else. Since there were more than those two pods, it's still possible that they belonged to the other groups." Bjorn read from Peter's eyes that his remark had made him think of something. "What are you thinking about, Peter?" Bjorn asked. "Well, I was thinking of those two mothers that came to get the calves. I didn't take pictures, because it was too far away, but they headed toward that male A1 which spent most of his time away from the main activity. I wonder if that tells us something." "Now you mention it, I remember that too," Bjorn said. "But even then, only one female in his pod has a juvenile that size and that isn't the one Sarah has in mind. We still have much of the summer ahead of us. If that young orca is alive, I'm sure we'll find out."

* * *

Two months had gone by with many good salmon runs and being well fed, the orcas spent a lot of time playing, resting, and socializing with other pods. As in most summers, Furka's pod spent much time with Raina and her family. Annika had become really heavy and everyone expected her to give birth some time soon. Although she had lost some of her agility, she had not experienced any difficulty with feeding in such abundance of food. She had built enough reserves to nurse a calf through the winter.

Skaade spent a lot of time with Annika. For a couple of days, Skaade had been feeling different; she was more affectionate than she normally was and she felt strangely attracted to Sigurd. The big male returned her nudges tenderly, but didn't allow himself any more. Skaade's behavior was not lost on him and he sensed immediately that his sister's daughter was going through her first cycle. He found her attractive, but being related to her, he didn't give in to his feelings.

Korak had noticed the young female too, but he had not taken any initiative to approach her. Since the loss of his mother, he felt depressed and a little less confident too. Most of the time he chose to be near Kujira, although he welcomed the company of Raina and some other adult females. Tarka noticed the quiet male, but his inhibited behavior did not discourage her. Since many summers, they shared a special fondness for each other, and Tarka was aware of the effect Ruka's passing still had on him. Korak was not into any chasing games with younger whales, but Tarka knew he was especially receptive to tenderness. She read him unerringly and quietly glided by his side. Her presence and gentle caress began to warm his grieving heart.

As Sigurd approached to greet his friend, he veered away so as not to disturb the two. While he returned towards the main group, his attention was drawn by a young female in Raina's pod, who had come into season. Sigurd felt attracted to Undina, a young female in Raina's pod, who had not yet had a calf. Undina was shy and wanted no part in the often impatient and obtrusive advances of younger males.

Sigurd had noticed Undina's shyness and carefully explored her interest in him. While she swam with her mother, he quietly followed her from behind, keeping a small distance. Undina was very aware of him, but she did not show any interest. She was insecure and afraid to elicit disapproval from others in the pod. Sigurd patiently kept his position, occasionally looking at her. Undina watched him out of the corner of her eye: he was masculine and strong. His pectoral fins were large and broad and his curled flukes moved effortlessly up and down. He radiated power, yet he was so self-controlled. When she looked him over and caught his eye, she felt a little shiver of titillation. Hours followed, but while they continued on, Undina's excitement and confidence built. She looked at him for a few seconds, then averted her eyes. Sigurd understood her subtle gesture. He rose up to breathe and dived to take his position again.

The large bull continued patiently. Then, when Undina's mother veered away approvingly, he moved closer. Undina did not back away. Sigurd stretched his large pectoral fin out to touch her and noticed by the way she glided how much she enjoyed his caress. Under his gentle touch, she began to move more freely. She rolled a little sideways and began to rub parts of her body against the edge of his pectoral fin. A few moments later, Sigurd bent his head a little towards her and when their eyes met he nudged her tenderly. Then, she suddenly tensed. Within seconds a younger bull loomed up. At the sight of Sigurd, he stopped short, creating a wave. Undina's eyes went from one male to the other, but her apprehension was short-lived. Sigurd gave the younger male a sideways nod, which was enough to make him leave.

Undina and Sigurd were by themselves again. As if nothing had happened, Sigurd continued his courtship. He was six feet longer than Undina and more than twice as heavy. With his size and power, he gave the young female a strong feeling of security. As if in a graceful dance, the two orcas rolled and glided, rose and dived, rubbed, and nudged each other. Sigurd read Undina unerringly, knowing by the way she glided, when she was ready for him. Then he rolled over on his back and took her between his big pectoral fins. Undina felt herself being lifted on his chest, gliding in unison with the effortless and calm undulations of his tail. Undina was delighted to feel Sigurd carry her. She felt his closeness and wanted his embrace to last. She pressed her chin against his and Sigurd nudged her warmly in response. While he carried her, they shared their pleasure in the twilight green.

Raina's voice broke the enchanted moment. A little reluctant, but contented, Sigurd glided from underneath Undina, rolled upright, and nudged her to follow. The two swam side by side, enjoying their special closeness a little longer. While Sigurd escorted Undina to her mother, he noticed Korak and Tarka bringing up the rear. It was not his companion, nor Korak's relative position in the pod, that struck Sigurd; it was the unmistakable change in his buddy's demeanor. He was no longer the dejected male, the quiet presence of the past several months, but a whale that had regained his purpose in life. Tarka's affection had touched him from within. She had always been patient and sensitive. Her cycle was incipient and she brought out his feelings so well that he overcame his inhibitions. Tarka's closeness obviously not only satisfied him as a male, but also filled some of the emptiness that he had experienced since his mother had died.

For several days Furka's and Raina's pods stayed together, and all that time Korak and Tarka delighted in each other's company. Raina was relieved to see the biggest male in her pod in a better mood and resuming activities that bespoke his mental recovery.

10.
Bingor

Summer and its abundance of salmon were coming to an end. The days were shortening and the opportunities to feed became less frequent. Boat traffic had quieted down as well. Raina and Furka had not been together for over a week. It had been harder on Korak than on Tarka when they first parted in late August. Since then, the two pods had shared a few more hunts. Gradually, the big male was coping better with the new situation, although he had not yet found a comfortable place in the pod Especially when they were feeding, some did not allow him his former place in the order. At first, he held back and waited for others to give him a signal. Raina sometimes did, but he soon discovered that he needed to stand up for himself more. It was not a simple matter of age. His mother had largely determined his rank in the pod. Now she was gone, he had to find out for himself which females really did take a dominant stand over him and which attempted to only briefly. Korak paid close attention to Stur, the oldest of the other males, and managed to put himself in a position similar to his.

Tuschka was almost four years old and had been hunting successfully during the past summer. The juvenile female was round and fat, and like the others, well prepared for winter. Although she had grown much, she missed a companion to play with. Skaade had grown into a young adult female and although Igor was still playful, he was already the size of an adult female. Tuschka was not a real match for him and when they played, it often became rougher than she liked.

Furka did not venture far from shore. Annika was so heavy that labor had to be imminent. There was a brisk wind from the east with partly clouded skies as Annika felt her first contractions. Furka and Shaka were at her side as Sigurd took the lead to a protected place.

In the shallow bay, protected from wind and waves, Annika turned to find her calf in a cloud of blood. The pudgy young male had his little dorsal fin still draped over his back. He seemed a strong baby and was already making his way upwards as Annika gave him a little push towards the surface to let him take his first breath. Furka immediately took position at the baby's other flank and voiced a mixture of relief and praise. Skaade had watched everything from as

111

closely as possible, but in a moment, all members of the pod knew they had a brand new family member. Annika proudly looked at the miniature orca next to her, bobbing his head up to take shallow puffs.

Tarka had sensed Tuschka's intense curiosity and took her close by her side as she made a pass underneath the new mother and her baby. Annika held her pectoral fin beneath the calf, but Tuschka did notice the outline of the little male against the light. With her first curiosity satisfied, Tuschka veered off with her mother to give Annika and her baby quiet time together.

After the strenuous labor, the afterbirth came easily. Another cloud of blood appeared, and the big placenta, that had provided nourishment to the baby orca for so long, very slowly sank down. Tuschka saw Skaade follow it and touch it. She pushed it with her rostrum for a little while. Tuschka came over to investigate. The blood tasted a little strange, but it felt very soft. She nudged it a few times, but stayed back when Skaade brought it over to her big sister.

Furka stayed with Annika through most of the night. While they stayed in the protected bay, she had more time to spend with the first-time mother. Little Bingor had been breathing well and after a few hours, he had started to explore his mother's belly. Although Annika had never nursed a calf before, she had witnessed it many times. She squirted some milk upon the little bumps under her belly. A little spilled when the miniature orca tried to drink and Tuschka noticed a faint familiar taste.

Shaka relieved Furka just before dawn. Skaade joined Annika's other flank, while Sigurd hovered at the surface behind them. When sunrise shed light on the newborn male, his tiny dorsal fin stood firm, showing a few ripples near the base of its strongly curved rear edge. Bingor had nursed several times and was gaining skill. Annika was constantly swimming around with him, and his swimming skills were improving quickly. His strokes became stronger and he discovered which spot near his mother gave him the best advantage of her slipstream. Convinced that all was going well, Furka encouraged Annika to follow her around inside the bay. She wanted Bingor to practice nursing at slightly different speeds, which would be important while the pod was traveling.

After two days in the protected bay, the weather was still holding well and Furka decided to head slowly east to where the herring would congregate a little later in the season. In a relatively calm sea, Bingor had ample opportunity to build up stamina and adapt to the long hours of traveling. Furka was leading her pod relatively close to shore. The dark grey beaches were monotonous and deserted, and the orcas paid no attention as they continued their journey to the herring grounds. The land changed as they came to an area where the end of a massive plateau glacier reached the sea. There were no icebergs, nor the impressive rumble and splash of large chunks of ice breaking off. Most of the ice melted on its final miles to the sea and the glacier just produced melt water near shore. The fresh run-off lent a strange taste to the water. Very few birds roamed the sky and the orcas' warm moist breath seemed to be the only sign of life in this barren area. The silence was almost like a prelude to a storm: the burst of life that would soon follow the arrival of the herring. Thousands of gulls of different kinds would gather to feed on the rich fish and many dolphins, porpoises, and pilot whales would gather to hunt as well. The herring would feed all these creatures until early spring.

Soon after the 10 orcas had passed the glacier, the shoreline angled to the north, but the orcas didn't follow it. The older whales knew that the herring was further offshore and more to the northeast. Only later on would they move westward again to follow the herring into the rugged fjords. Bingor managed to keep up well with the pod and was nursing on the move. It occurred to Furka and Tamara that he nursed fairly frequently, but that in itself was not uncommon during the first weeks of life when a young orca had to build up a good layer of blubber against the cold. Several times, they heard the voices of dolphins and porpoises foraging in the area. Tuschka was eager to go off and investigate, but her older experienced companions were quick to interpret the sounds of their smaller relatives. They weren't feeding, so they continued on their course.

Two weeks had gone by since Furka had left sight of shore. During the late afternoon, the sound of an engine broke the relative silence of waves and wind. Not sensing any threat they continued on. Suddenly, Furka and Sigurd slowed down and came to a stop. Within seconds, the two tensed. Some wondered what had caused the sudden apprehension in their matriarch. Furka moved a little down and forward, and echolocated. The echoes revealed an incline in the sea floor, indicating shallower water to the left from where they were. The engine sounded much closer, but it also had a higher pitch. It was heading their way at an increased speed. The situation brought on an undefined feeling of distress. Suddenly, the recognition was there! It sent a shiver through them: it had been here where they had been chased, where they had barely escaped disaster, and where Skaade and Sigurd had become hurt. Without a call, Furka turned 90 degrees, kicked her flukes and took off, not in full porpoising, but with a brisk pace. The orcas outdistanced the boat quickly and they continued on for at least 15 minutes after the engine sound had disappeared. Finally, assured that no danger was near, they slowed down to relax.

The herring had not yet arrived in any density and the orcas had been feeding a few times on cod. Although there were 10 of them, only eight could participate actively in the hunt, since one of them had to stay at the surface with Bingor. Furka and Shaka took turns relieving Annika to give her opportunities to feed. They both had Bingor bumping their bellies, but neither of them was able to feed him. Each time the baby returned to his mother, he impatiently asked for milk. Skaade was swimming next to her mother, watching little Bingor. The miniature orca curiously peeked at her. To her surprise, he suddenly scooted over to her, and she felt excited when the little orca bumped her belly as well. She stretched and glided along, imitating Annika when she nursed him, but she couldn't keep his attention for very long. Tuschka watched him return to Annika when she rose up from a long dive. Tuschka longed to play with him. Since Bingor was among them she felt different. Although she had met several orcas younger than herself when they shared time with other pods, it was a special experience for her to no longer be the youngest in her family.

In the few days that passed since the orcas had left the area of their tragic experience, Bingor began to nurse more frequently. Annika gave in to his begging, but she felt that she didn't have to give much during each feed. The little male was still very active, but the more experienced females felt that he was acting a little strange. Bingor was bumping his mother's belly ever more vigorous and, at times, he seemed to poke his rostrum almost into Annika's mammary slits as if craving food. His appetite seemed insatiable.

Bingor shivered. Annika tried to reassure him, but he remained restless. Her baby still kept up, but he was breathing more frequently. Annika and Furka watched him closely and realized that their little calf had picked up a fever. It became obvious that all the frequent nursing didn't satisfy Bingor. Annika looked full and round after the bountiful summer and nothing even hinted at her not having enough reserves to feed a baby orca, but Bingor's restlessness and vigorous bumping kept Annika constantly awake. Furka slowed the pace and decided to give Annika more opportunities to rest. Perhaps that would increase the young mother's milk production. At the same time, she didn't want to demand much from a calf that was fighting a fever. Annika, Furka, and Shaka kept a constant watch over Bingor, trying to comfort the calf, who went from belly to belly in search for food.

Annika tried hard to take care of him. She never refused when he asked her for milk, but she was painfully aware that she could not make him satisfied and content. Tuschka felt some tension in the pod. Something obviously was not right with Bingor, but she could not yet comprehend what was wrong. The baby orca had started to make short high-pitched calls that bore some resemblance to the sounds Annika often made for him. The young worried mother tried to comfort him with gentle nudges and rubs, and she often took him protectively under her pec. Bingor obviously enjoyed the loving caresses, but he often was too restless to stay in one position for long. When the pod was resting, the tiny male surfaced all around his mother, in small dolphin-like bows. His white markings were a warm orange and his little puffs contrasted with the much heavier blows of his companions. Even Tuschka's blows were strong compared to his.

Bingor had been so round and fat at birth. Now, the once so pudgy male was becoming leaner every day. Furka nudged her daughter's belly as if she were a calf. Annika was surprised when her mother continued. Why would she want the milk that her calf needed so much? Giving in to her prodding, she reluctantly let go of a few drops. Furka tasted… The milk lacked the creamy fattiness it ought to have. Furka's mood sank as she came to the realization that Annika wasn't able to produce the fatty, rich milk that Bingor needed to grow, not to mention recover.

Bingor tried to nurse as much as possible, but he no longer experienced a content and satisfied feeling. He had a playful nature, but his hunger pangs often distracted him. Lately, he had started to feel cold and tried to swim himself warm. Annika had felt him shiver several times when she held him close to her. The fever and his efforts to fight off the cold drained him even faster of the little reserves he had left. Bingor started to tire quickly, but as much as he tried to drink, he never got his fill.

Tamara was very aware of the problem: it revived memories of her own first baby. She had painfully watched her little baby waste away. There had been no one who could help out, just like now. None of the females in the pod was lactating, so none of them could help to relieve Bingor's needs. Even Tarka's milk had dried long ago.

Bingor weakened rapidly, and the pod had to stop frequently for him. Furka and Annika took him in between them to make swimming as easy as possible for him. Resting had not improved Annika's milk supply, and the matriarch felt that her youngest grand-offspring was in serious difficulty. Little Bingor shivered, but had no energy left to play around his mother for warmth. He huddled against her for comfort, making little soft squeaks. Annika called warmly to him and tried to perk him up. The miniature orca revived after resting, but tired fast. The mood in the pod was depressed. They made little progress, tightly gathered around their little weakening pod member.

Bingor, feeling weaker, made fewer attempts to nurse, and by daybreak, he had become more lethargic. Furka and Annika almost carried him in between them. Several hours later, Sigurd took over to relieve the matriarch. The fever didn't cause Bingor any pain and its reverse effect on his appetite gave him a pleasant illusion of satisfaction. As his small body started to lose the fight, the fever abated a little. Bingor felt the cold leave him and to the amazement of all, he perked up. Feeling no hunger and chills, he affectionately bumped his mother's belly. Annika felt a surge of hope. When he nudged her, she gratefully squirted her milk in his mouth. A fair amount had built up in a few hours. Bingor took most of it in and enjoyed the sweet taste. This time, his soft gentle bumps conveyed his contentment. Annika squeaked her delight and nudged him tenderly as he surfaced in a little bow. The little orca took another breath and rubbed cheeks with his mother. Annika rolled over and picked him up on her chest between her pecs.

His revival was short-lived and Annika felt his little body relax. She lifted him up well above the surface and felt him take a shallow breath. The young mother still carried him, holding him between her flippers. She called to him in encouragement, her voice bubbling to the surface. Annika felt her baby's feeble nudge as he weakly pressed his chin against hers. Then, with a soft call, the little orca breathed his last. Annika pushed up to encourage him, but Bingor didn't take another breath. She felt him lying limp, and slowly sank down to pick him up on her rostrum. She pushed him up gently, but there was no response. Annika let out a long plaintive call and wailed her grief. Furka came alongside her daughter, nudging her gently and touching the baby orca, his little body still warm. For a moment, they both carried their smallest pod member in between them. Then, Furka made way for Sigurd and softly called the other orcas to follow her. Annika felt desolate. She didn't want to part with her baby, yet she was exhausted from caring and worrying so intensely. Sigurd swam alongside his sister and after a little while she accepted his comfort and let him share in carrying her baby. The strong patient male rubbed Annika tenderly and a little later, he gently balanced Bingor on his rostrum with his sad, drained sister at his flank.

* * *

Torvil, the young man who had been working on a seiner during the herring season, had been the subject of many discussions after his incident with the whales in the fjord, and also later on, for his subsequent interference with Ruben's shooting. His fascination for the orcas, which he had never showed openly, had become the subject of satire and laughter. Although the captain had treated him with usual respect, life among the other crew members had been fairly miserable and Torvil was happy to leave when the season was over. Back on shore, he discovered that the gossip had spread quickly and he heard many twisted versions of the events. Torvil usually didn't comment on what he heard, but the situation filled him with dread for the upcoming season. Several times he had put off joining a crew when he felt that one or the other would make a fool of him in front of the other men.

Finally, he traveled to a small village near Kalika inlet where he had hit the young orca. There, a small family operating a seiner, took him on. His wages were not as good, but he was happy to have a fresh start. The captain, Arjen, worked with his two sons and another older man, Sem, who probably wouldn't last another season. The man had lost much of his physical strength, but he had an amazing knowledge of the area and his experience was highly valued.

Torvil felt drawn to the man and wondered what he knew about orcas and how he felt about them, but he refrained from touching the subject. The unpleasant experiences of the past winter had made him reluctant to show his thoughts and feelings. Torvil was sure that the first encounter with the controversial predators would reveal much of the attitude of his new crew, but as much as he wanted to see them, he also feared an adverse reaction.

Toward the end of October, the lone seiner left the small harbor. The weather had been grey but steady for the past several days. The crew had suffered some delay, waiting for an engine part, and they were happy to finally cast off. On their second day at sea, Sem, the old man, called loudly and pointed south. He had the eyes of an eagle and it took Torvil more than a minute to notice the plumes of whale blows more than a mile away. The sight made him catch his breath and his heart beat faster, but no one noticed. With anxious expectation, the young man waited for the events to follow.

The captain immediately changed course towards the whales and slowed down considerably. Torvil knew that orcas often led fishermen to the fish. It was obvious that his new captain didn't want to disturb the whales too much in their activities. If they were concentrating herring, they might benefit from each other. Some whales had learned to use nets as a trap to herd fish into. The orcas would take their share, but that sacrifice was more than compensated for if their activities led to extra fish in the net. It was an entirely different matter, however, if the orcas appeared when the nets were taken in. Some captains, however, were so greedy that they tried to drive the whales away as soon as they started to close the net, no matter if they had been a help earlier.

When they were no more than half a mile away from the orcas, Sem raised his hand and Arjen put the engine in idle. "They aren't feeding," Sem said, "but they aren't traveling either." Torvil was fascinated. The orcas seemed to stay in one area, making short shallow dives. He wondered how the old man knew so quickly that they were not feeding 'Of, course', Torvil realized. 'If they were feeding, there would've been swarms of gulls to pick up the scraps.' "Well Sem," Arjen said calmly, "what do you suggest we do? Shall we wait and see, or do you advise to leave and continue our search for fish?" Sem paused for a moment. "It doesn't make much difference, I think. Whales spend most of their time searching for food. If they don't travel or feed now, they will soon. If any food is near, they'll find it probably before we do. Let's wait for a little while. Perhaps their behavior will give us some clue." Torvil was excited. This man was really close to nature. He was one of the few who observed nature keenly and had learned to interpret her signs in a time when there were no high-tech instruments to aid the fishermen. The fact that he had worked with Arjen for many years was encouraging. It meant that Arjen respected this attitude and valued it.

Torvil hesitated to grab his binoculars. What would they think? Just as he decided to run inside and grab them, he briefly noticed something in front of the big male. The next moment it was gone. About half a minute later, he saw something orange pop up and disappear. The young man looked at Sem, who was watching intensely. Again, Torvil saw a tiny orange shape. When he saw the outline of a tiny pec, it suddenly struck him: "a calf," he called out loud, pointing in front of him. Sem nodded in confirmation. Torvil felt a little embarrassed as he understood that Sem had already seen it. "Maybe this is what's keeping the orcas busy," the experienced man commented. "The baby is obviously very young. Perhaps it has just been born. I have seen very young calves several times before, but then the orcas were usually traveling with the newborn in their midst. Right now, that male and his female companion are a bit separate from the group. Perhaps they are resting. I expect them to gather and move off soon." Torvil was fascinated and he could hardly believe that the man talking was his fellow crew member. As they drew slowly near, they saw the baby orca pop up several times in what appeared to be a playful manner, letting itself be balanced on its side on the big bull's rostrum. Yet, both Sem and Torvil sensed that something was strange. With the engine idling, they could hear the blows of the two whales, the female followed by the male: pooo-hup .... pooo-hoo-hup...

Suddenly, the two observers understood; the big bull was carrying a dead baby with him! It was a sad sight. They were close enough to see the little calf, such a perfect, beautiful miniature orca. It was obvious that the two whales had acquiesced to the calf's death: they were not actively attempting to revive it. No one knew for how long the two orcas had been carrying the baby. Somehow, it seemed they could not yet part with their infant. Why had they not abandoned it?

The mood in the pod was dejected. They all knew that Bingor had fought to survive, but had lost the battle. Tuschka hugged close to Tarka for comfort. She saw Igor rub his mother's flank, and Skaade seeking comfort in Shaka's company. Tamara joined Tuschka's other side. The juvenile female wallowed in the comfort and security of the two caring females.

Annika was almost oblivious to the boat until the change in engine sound caught her attention. She spyhopped to check it out. Sigurd followed her and felt Bingor slide off his rostrum. The baby orca slipped along his chest and was caught on one of his big pecs. Neither Annika nor Sigurd noticed any sign of danger and the boat with the low rumbling engine quickly faded from their consciousness. Annika was the only one who occasionally voiced her grief with a soft sorrowful cry. Since several years, the young mother had loved to be around young calves and play with them. She had been so delighted to have a calf of her own, and now, her little baby lay limp, carried along on her brother's rostrum. She was painfully aware of the emptiness under her belly. Even though the frequent nursing of the past week had been strenuous on her, she missed the familiar bumps of the little male, who had frolicked around her so playfully during his first weeks of life. Annika nudged her baby, caressing him gently. She rolled over on her side and ran her cheek under Bingor's soft little belly. The miniature orca, so perfectly formed, bobbed up and down a little with the movement of the waves. It was difficult to comprehend that he would never swim, hunt, or play with them.

Sigurd patiently stayed with Annika, caressing her occasionally. He was aware that Annika paid no attention to her surroundings and he made sure they stayed within a hundred yards of the pod. Furka had kept the other orcas together and away from Annika to give her time to accept her loss and to share some undisturbed and intimate moments with her little offspring. Yet they had to face reality. Nature would not be considerate. Over the past several days, they had barely eaten anything and they would soon have to resume foraging. Furka was the first to turn and approach Annika and Sigurd slowly. The matriarch came alongside her grieving daughter and gave her a tender nudge. Annika pressed her head against her mother and whined a little. Furka returned the call with understanding, but at the same time she had to make Annika ready to part with Bingor. She came forward a little to take the calf from Sigurd's rostrum. Annika moved in and lifted her baby up, not wanting to let her mother take it away from her. The matriarch and leader empathized with her daughter and made no attempt to force it. For some time, they carried the little male together. Then, Annika acquiesced in parting with her precious calf and rubbed herself against Bingor. She nuzzled the little head and touched it with her tongue. With a call full of helplessness and sorrow, the young mother turned away and hugged against her brother for comfort. Slowly, Sigurd led Annika a little away from the others, knowing it was their turn to part with their little pod member.

As soon as Sigurd and Annika had separated from them, the other orcas lined up abreast of Furka. Upon a seemingly imperceptible sign, they surfaced and blew with her in unison. After their next surfacing, Furka, still carrying the calf with her, left the line and turned around. When they all saw their matriarch face them, they made a circle around the little calf. In turn, they came forward, touching their little companion gently. Shaka was first, followed by Skaade. Then Tamara and Tarka came, finally followed by Tuschka and Igor. Furka made a shallow dive and picked Bingor up on her rostrum again. She swam a little forward and, again, the others formed a straight line on either side of Furka, surfacing in unison with the matriarch. When their leader swam forward and turned to face them, they broke their formation to make another circle, around the limp little orca. Furka lifted the baby up in their midst. Then, with a soft sad cry, she sank down and backed away, leaving Bingor to her family. This time, the others nudged, rubbed and caressed their tiny pod member in no apparent order. The baby orca almost seemed to come to life with the gentle pushes.

Until now, Tuschka and Igor had barely had a chance to interact with the newborn. Especially Tuschka had been awaiting her opportunities eagerly. Now, they could touch Bingor freely, but it was not the same. They felt that the little male gave no responses and just drifted, bobbed, and turned in reaction to their caresses. Tuschka had never experienced one of her own kind dying and it was difficult for her to comprehend. She did, however, feel the absence of life in the baby orca that had been so playful until recently. Instinctively, she lifted Bingor to the surface. But deep inside she knew this wouldn't bring him to life. Furka came up beside her and took the baby from her. Tuschka watched their matriarch turn around and swim away in silence. They all watched their leader fade into the dark green waters.

Furka needed a final moment with the calf for herself. All others had parted with the smallest member of their pod. Now, it was her turn. Bingor had not been with them for long, but he belonged to the pod as much as any of them. Furka balanced the weightless little body on her rostrum and caressed it tenderly. She rolled over and took it on her chest between her pecs. Finally, she touched the baby orca with her chin. Then, she moved forward and felt him slide along her belly and touch the edge of her flukes. As she turned upright, she got a final glimpse of the orange tinted belly as Bingor faded in the darkness of the sea.

Both Torvil and Sem had been watching the male and the female carry the dead baby with them. Such a perfect, beautiful miniature orca that would never grow up. As the female and her male companion moved a little away, they focused their attention on the highly unusual behavior of the bigger group: seven orcas surfacing abreast forming a small circle, twice. Torvil watched the scene intently. Something in their midst had their undivided attention. He almost gasped as he saw the tiny pec and the orange eye patch of the little calf pop up in the center. Sem and Torvil looked at each other briefly, amazement showing in their eyes. They had thought the baby orca was still with the male and the female, who were now further away. The whales were gently pushing and rubbing the little dead calf. Once more, the men caught a glimpse of the calf. Then, moments later, heavy clouds packed together, enveloping the orcas in darkness.

The crew stood in silence. The scene had left a special impression on all of them. A little later, Arjen went inside to prepare for leaving. He put the engine in gear and picked up some speed. He steered the boat in the direction of where the male and the female had disappeared from sight, and they soon spotted the tall male's dorsal fin. The orcas were moving slowly, and both Torvil and Sem watched the two as they passed by. Both men were lost in their own thoughts. Torvil was impressed with what he had seen, but in a way it didn't surprise him. In fact, it fitted very well in the events that had awakened his fascination with the orcas. He vividly remembered the young orca, that had been wounded by his hand, and how its pod had come to help it and carry it with them while it was recovering. It was then that the young fisherman had begun to grasp something of the strong bonds that kept a pod together. But at that time, the orcas had been carrying a live companion, that evidently had not been mortally wounded. Today, the whales were carrying and caressing a dead baby that would never come back to life. Apparently, the attachment to each other, even to one who had been with them briefly, was very strong. So strong, in fact, that their behavior was not only driven by reason; it would be worth caring for a companion who had a chance to recover and hunt with them again. But how could they benefit from this lifeless calf? Apparently, orcas were receptive to more than just the harsh rules of nature. There was room for some sort of emotion in their lives.

Torvil's thoughts traveled back to the moment when he had suddenly recognized 'his' orca by the scar on its back. That same whale had been tugging at their net. Torvil felt both happiness and relief that he had been able to repay some of his debt by preventing Ruben from inflicting another gunshot wound.

The scene had been new even to Sem, who had met the strong, sleek predators many times. Torvil was itching to talk to Sem, to ask the seasoned man what he was thinking, but he was still too shy to start a conversation about the whales. All crew members were very quiet for the rest of the day. The event with the orcas had left each of them with certain thoughts and questions, but none of them wanted to be the first to reveal them. Man at sea didn't show emotion easily. It was considered a weakness if they did. The thought that creatures of the sea would be capable of any such feeling had never occurred to any of them. To most of them, it probably still was farfetched. But to Torvil, the sequence of events had been so compelling that he was convinced there had to be more to the mind of these creatures than just being predators.

* * *

Furka returned to the others, who were still close together, but no longer in a circle. Silently, she swam by each of them, stroking them gently in passing. Then, she called them to follow her and led them in the direction where she had left Sigurd and Annika. The matriarch was heavy-hearted, but she refrained from showing it too much. She wanted to encourage and motivate her pod to resume foraging. A mutual hunt would not only provide necessary food, but also a beneficial diversion for the sad pod. Furka took the lead and silently joined her daughter's right flank. The caring mother gave a comforting nudge. Annika saw that her mother had not returned with her calf. She felt an urge to turn around and look for him, but as her mother gently blocked her way, she acquiesced and continued on in silence. For a while, the trio formed the lead, but gradually, the other orcas moved forward until they surrounded them. Sigurd had been a comforting presence for Annika for several hours, but as he noticed Shaka moving in close from behind, he backed away to let his two sisters be together. During the last several months of Annika's pregnancy and Bingor's short life, the strong Sigurd had felt protective and had stayed close to them. Now, his sister's depressed mood and reduced vigilance continued to call upon his special attention.

Tuschka felt uncomfortable with the sad atmosphere. She bumped her mother's belly, rubbed herself along her pecs, and nibbled a bit on her mother's dorsal fin. Tarka sensed her offspring becoming impatient and she tried subtly to divert her young daughter without bothering the others. The two moved a bit more to the rear, so they would be out of sight for at least Annika and her close companions. In her heart, Tarka welcomed the diversion. She not only lifted the spirits of her juvenile daughter, but her own as well. For the rest of the night, they just traveled at a relatively slow pace and close together. Furka had not yet asked her companions to spread out in an active foraging formation, but all the time she was listening for signs of prey and watching for gulls when she surfaced.

* * *

A few days had gone by before Arjen and his crew found a good concentration of herring. The first catch had been satisfactory and they were on their way to one of the fjords to dump the fish in a stationary net. That way, they could stay out of port longer and save up several catches before selling the fish. No one had yet spoken about the encounter with the orcas. When Sem and Torvil were changing clothes, Torvil brought it up. Somehow, he felt a little more confident after he had actually worked together with his new crew mates to successfully bring in a catch. In addition, it seemed that he could address the subject more casually now than immediately after the unusual event. "Sem," Torvil asked, "when we spotted that pod, we immediately went over there. Were you planning to follow them in case they would start foraging?"

The old man looked up for a moment. "Yes," he said. "You're a good observer. They weren't feeding, otherwise there would've been birds around." Sem felt that Torvil wanted to know more and continued: "The electronic equipment on board can do things that we wouldn't even dream of in my younger years, but it still can't compare with those uncanny hunters. We know the main migration patterns of the fish and we can detect how deep and how dense they are when we have found them, but the whales are far better at finding them. It is essential to their survival. Hunting is their life. They are so well adapted to their environment that they will be hard to beat. As long as we've no clue to the presence of the fish, we might as well follow them. In my opinion," the older man continued, "small pods are usually found to hunt denser schools than bigger groups, but I may be biased. With fewer hunters it just seems more difficult to start out with some loose fish." Torvil understood that Sem didn't just watch. He noticed many details and managed to put the pieces of the puzzle together using both his own observation and empathy with the creatures he observed. "Would you call that a big pod?" Torvil asked. "No, that was a small group. On average, we see 15 or 20 whales at a time."

The young man felt that Sem was in the mood to speak more openly and he decided to ask him straight away about the question that had been troubling him. "What does Arjen expect us to do when orcas feed around, or even inside the net?" Sem looked cautious. "What would you consider reasonable?" he countered. Torvil flushed a little, which didn't go unnoticed by Sem. Torvil felt that the older man looked straight through him, aware that it was a problem for him and wanting him to speak up. How wise. A simple answer would still leave questions. Although a little shy, Torvil was grateful that Sem helped him to bring up the subject he craved to discuss. Yet he decided to stay on the safe side. "As long as they don't damage anything, I think it's reasonable that they have a little share: especially when they lead us to the fish." "And what if we find the fish first, or if they start tugging at the net?" Sem asked. Torvil felt uncomfortable, but he understood that the conversation would take a satisfactory turn only if he spoke his thoughts openly.

Sem saw the young man struggling. There was something that made him hesitant and he sensed his younger companion was afraid to give himself away without being understood. "Don't think you will be fired if you think differently," he encouraged, "and no one else needs to know if you don't want them to." Torvil looked Sem in the eyes and felt he could trust him. "I don't think it makes any difference who finds the fish first," the young man said. "One day, we attract the orcas, the next day they give us a lead. Often, it's fish that we spill anyway. The benefit is both ways. It's only fair." Sem nodded, but waited for Torvil to continue. "It may sound strange, but even if they come to feed inside the net before the purse is closed, I don't really mind. They sometimes use the net to herd fish into. In that case, we catch more anyway. I must admit, though, that I find it very difficult to decide what to do when they start tugging at the net. Fortunately, it rarely happens; and when it does, I do not know if they are purposely trying to tear it or that they get stuck somewhere and try to get loose again. Has it ever happened to Arjen's nets?" Torvil asked. Sem nodded. "We had it a few times. Th.." "What did you do?" Torvil interrupted in his eagerness. "Arjen was reluctant to shoot and decided to wait and see. He had a rifle ready, though, in case it started getting bad. We saw only a few tugs and when we hauled the net in, there was hardly any damage. The orcas had led us to the fish and I could see that Arjen was happy he hadn't used the rifle. We had a little more damage on another occasion, but it was still easy to repair. We do indeed think their teeth may get stuck sometimes, probably when they pull on fish sticking halfway through the maze. We have never had reason to think they try to damage the net on purpose".

"It seems you have dealt with the problem before," Sem said. "Tell me what happened". Torvil cleared his throat and started telling Sem about his first encounter with the orcas when he was on guard near the stationary net. "..and when that whale came at me at high speed, I was so terrified that I shot. But what I saw then was amazing. The whale dived and was still down when I saw two of his companions heading for me. I was sure they would attack, but they didn't. Instead, they had come for the wounded whale and picked it up between them. Later on, I am sure we met that pod again: two whales were swimming with a sick one tucked in between them." "That is remarkable," Sem responded, "but it doesn't surprise me after what I saw the other day with the dead calf. I wonder if your whale survived." "You wouldn't believe it!" Torvil continued. "The next season, orcas were circling the net closely as we were closing the purse. We saw a few tugs on the net and Ruben immediately aimed the rifle. Then, when the orca surfaced, I saw a distinctive scar on his back, just in front of the dorsal fin. Without thinking, I kicked Ruben so he actually shot into the air. I am almost certain it was that same whale. His pod counted about eight or nine whales with one big male in it. That was also the one who traveled near him when he was still wounded."

"What happened after that shot?" Sem asked. "They all took off instantly, at great speed. Ruben was very angry at me. We had orders to shoot if orcas actually grabbed the net. The captain asked why I reacted that way and I told him I recognized the whale I had shot. I said they deserved at least a warning. The captain never spoke it out loud, but I felt he was on my side. Perhaps that was the reason why the crew ridiculed me. They said I would rather have torn nets and healthy orcas than the other way round." Torvil paused a moment, then continued. "Well, I wouldn't like to see the nets torn, but I do appreciate healthy whales. To be honest, Sem, with what I have seen, I am fascinated by them." "I can imagine that, Torvil," the older man said. "I bet the behavior around that dead calf fascinated you too, perhaps even more than me." "Oh yes," the young fisherman said, grabbing Sem by one of his shoulders. "That calf would never come to life and yet they carried it so gently. It gave me the impression of some sort of funeral, lining up and forming a circle around it. I had the feeling that the female and her mate, or whoever that male was, had taken time to part with the baby first, before giving the rest of the pod an opportunity to part with it." Sem nodded in silence. Then, he looked Torvil firmly in the eye. "There is much more to those predators than we seem to know. Don't worry, Arjen respects the orcas, probably even more now. He won't harm your whales," Sem said, giving Torvil a meaningful tap on his shoulder.

Torvil watched Sem as he went up to the wheelhouse and felt a tremendous relief wash over him. He had finally been able to talk about it and he had been understood. Even more, he was still respected and didn't have to worry about the orcas the next time they met. The young man took a few minutes to fully realize how fortunate he was. Taking a deep breath and in a good mood he followed his older friend.

11.
Lifted Spirits

Tuschka and her family had found herring fairly soon after Bingor had died. Initially, Annika had needed some encouragement to participate, but the diversion of hunting lifted her spirits. Her sad, withdrawn behavior gradually improved. The mood in the entire pod lifted as Annika was getting over the worst of her grief. The young adult female had a very playful nature and none of them had ever known her to be so depressed. They felt relieved that her interest in her surroundings was returning. Sigurd and Furka had spent most of their time with her during the first several days. They felt that Annika wanted the companionship and affection mostly from the ones who were closest to her. The presence of the matriarch and the powerful bull had discouraged the younger whales from approaching Annika, but now Furka started to encourage a change of companionship for her.

Many weeks had passed by since Tuschka had last played with Annika. Igor, as large as he had become, had been her biggest playmate. Even Skaade had been more interested in the young calf than in playing with her. Now, Tuschka was almost shy to approach Annika, but her curiosity about the young adult female had been growing. Would she want to play with her if she could get close? Tuschka saw Sigurd drop back a little, leaving Annika's left flank unattended. She slipped away from her mother, looking back for a moment as if expecting Tarka to call her back, but she didn't. Tuschka approached Annika from the side. The bigger female did not respond, but she didn't move away either. Tuschka started to swim alongside and as she saw Annika turn her head slightly towards her, she tentatively nudged her pectoral fin. Tuschka felt how Annika returned her touch and tenderly trailed her pec along her flank. She felt a surge of excitement and took the caress as an encouragement. She swam forward and rubbed her head underneath Annika's chin. Annika responded warmly. Although Tuschka was enormous compared to Bingor when he died, she was noticeably smaller than any of the others, and the affection of the youngest member in her pod aroused Annika's motherly feelings. Somehow, Tuschka touched Annika in a special way. Her juvenile companion was both playful and affectionate, and filled part of the emptiness she felt. Tuschka came up for a breath, dived, and gave a playful nudge against Annika's belly. Then, she moved forward and rubbed herself between her big friend's chest and pecs.

126

Annika loved it. The feelings that had been locked up inside her since the loss of her calf suddenly found their way out. They both felt a special closeness. They rolled and turned around each other and indulged in a lot of rubbing and caressing. Tuschka squeaked in delight and Annika returned the playful calls.

Annika's response took the whole pod by surprise. Furka voiced her happiness and expressed her excitement even more strongly with a triumphant leap into the air. As the matriarch fell back with a tremendous splash, Shaka and Skaade followed. Then Sigurd kicked his flukes. Tuschka and Annika felt the suction of the big male building up speed, and they, too, joined in. Sigurd broke the surface just before them, and they felt themselves almost carried along in his wake. As the majestic male soared into the air, Annika and Tuschka broke the surface in a playful back dive, almost in unison.

All members of Furka's pod felt as if a heavy burden fell away. For a brief moment, the orcas indulged in affectionate play. After a while, Furka gently summoned her pod to resume foraging. They all were still very aware of the loss of their youngest family member, but they were relieved that Annika was mentally recovering. The subdued mood was fading and they all found solace in reinforcing their bonds.

Everyone was aware that Tuschka had brought about a remarkable change in Annika's attitude. From being withdrawn and taciturn, she now welcomed affection and opportunities to play. Tuschka took delight in her renewed friendship with Annika and for much of the time the two were inseparable. Tarka understood and left them be. She knew that Annika found comfort for herself in lavishing her motherly instincts on Tuschka, while her juvenile daughter enjoyed the extra attention and playful interactions. When they were on the move, Tarka spent much time with Tamara, while Tuschka enjoyed an occasional sip from Annika's milk.

Late one morning, Furka and her pod were heading north and a little west towards the many fjords of the eastern shore. The hunting had been good and Tuschka was playing chase with Annika. She was not yet as fast as her bigger companion, but she was very agile, which made the chase still challenging for Annika. As her pursuer was closing in, Tuschka suddenly arched upwards and flung half her body into the air in an evasive turn. She brushed by Annika's pec in the opposite direction. Tuschka was startled when Shaka suddenly appeared in the dim light, and she barely managed to avoid a collision. For a moment, she had failed to concentrate on Annika, who had taken advantage of the event and playfully raked her flukes. Tuschka let out a loud squeak of surprise, but Tarka found her to be fine. Tuschka briefly snuggled against her mother's flank, but soon relaxed when Annika gently came alongside. It was only then that she became aware of the sudden alertness in the pod. Distant, but unmistakable, she heard the familiar voices of her own kind.

It took Tuschka just a few moments to recognize the calls from Raina's pod. She bumped Annika in her excitement and made a playful half breach between the two adult females. The other orcas were closer to shore and not feeding. Both pods had been traveling by themselves for many weeks and they were happy with the diversion and the opportunity to hunt together. Tuschka was excited at the prospect of playing with Aleta. She had to restrain herself from bouncing ahead of Furka to find her.

The orcas were impatient and as soon as Furka and Raina called their mutual greetings they dashed forward to meet. Kujira quickly found Annika and the two greeted each other warmly. Annika immediately noticed how heavy the expectant mother was and Kujira noticed that Annika was not in the company of a young calf. The streamlined slender body of her friend, who had been more advanced in pregnancy than herself, and her slightly swollen mammaries, bespoke her calf's ill-fated end. Having lost her own calf made Annika feel different towards Kujira. She did like the other young female, but they were no longer sharing their pregnancy, nor was there the joy of showing her newborn calf. The pain of her loss came to the surface as she nudged Kujira's bulging belly. It was obvious that she would give birth soon. For a moment, Annika wanted to withdraw, but Kujira understood Annika's mood unerringly and tenderly comforted the female, whose motherhood had been so short.

Although it had never become like the old times, Korak had found a position in the pod again. He held a less prominent place, but he had regained much of his personality. He still spent most of his time with his sister, Kujira, who was close to giving birth. As Sigurd came over, he greeted him with enthusiasm. The company of the other large male was a welcome diversion for him. The two swam off a little away from the main group. They surfaced and dived in unison, sending their breath into the air in explosive blows. In the presence of Sigurd, Korak felt as he had in the past. It was relaxing for him to be with a befriended male, who looked at him as he always had. Although Sigurd had been aware of what had happened to Korak, it had not changed his feelings towards the big male of Raina's pod. For the two males, being from different pods, hierarchy or position did not play a part in their relationship. They interacted simply because they liked each other.

As Korak swam alongside his companion, he felt his former confidence return. For months he had not been as spontaneous as he used to be. Right now, with Sigurd, he felt a desire to loosen the reins. Korak bumped his companion's flank, kicked his powerful curled flukes and took off ahead. Sigurd immediately took the invitation and dashed after Korak. The two bulls were similar in size and skills, and it was exciting for Sigurd to be challenged by an equal. Playing with Igor was fun, but the younger male had never been able to push Sigurd to his limits. Sigurd pumped his flukes up and down, but barely gained on his target. He broke in porpoising to gain speed, but Korak immediately noticed Sigurd's change in strategy and also started porpoising to keep his head start. Both males felt that it would soon become a matter of stamina if they continued like that. Korak suddenly slowed down and turned head on to his onrushing pursuer, but Sigurd immediately understood what Korak was up to: the big bull would veer off at the last moment knowing that his opponent could not make a quick direction change at high speed. Sigurd slowed down too. It was tempting to quickly bridge the distance between them, but it would be more effective to wait for Korak's next move. As Sigurd approached, both felt the tension building. Korak knew that if he veered away too soon, Sigurd would be quick enough to turn. But if he waited too long, his opponent would be too close to evade. When less than a body length separated the two bulls, Korak dived straight down. It was more difficult for Sigurd to track him with sound alone than on sight.

As Korak went up for air, he had gained some distance again, but he realized that in his act to make his pursuer lose track of him, he had also lost track of his pursuer. Sigurd could see the outline of the other large bull against the surface, while he himself was hiding deep. Korak burst to the surface, blew, and kept up his speed for a moment longer. Then, he slowed down to scan around for Sigurd. The latter took advantage of Korak's hesitation and made a run for him while he was looking a little away. Korak suddenly noticed the upwelling beneath him. He turned quickly and saw Sigurd in full charge. With no time to accelerate away from him, Korak lunged aside, brushed Sigurd's chin with his dorsal fin and lunged for his contender's flukes. Sigurd broke the surface and dived in one big spin. The two bulls no longer engaged in a full chase, but spun around in an attempt to grab a part of each other. They had no intention to hurt. Just a light rake would conclude the playful chase. In a lunge, Korak opened his mouth towards Sigurd, but there was no venom in his action. Sigurd bent his head down and nudged Korak's chin with a meaningful and reassuring intent.

The two majestic males rested at the surface, side by side. Korak's fin was just a hint taller than Sigurd's, and the wave in his trailing edge contrasted with Sigurd's straight and somewhat less mature fin. They had both enjoyed the game. It had brought the two adult males closer again after the relatively quiet period since Ruka had passed away. The challenge they had been for each other had boosted Korak's confidence and they felt a special satisfaction as they leisurely approached the other whales. Stur and Brutus greeted them and they noticed the change in the largest male of their pod. Korak faced them with his former confidence and in some way it restored the familiar secure balance in the pod.

For most of the afternoon, the two pods stayed in the area where they had met, playing and resting together. Especially Furka's pod, had welcomed the diversion. When twilight fell, the two pods grouped up and headed northwest towards a large fjord. Each pod had its own favorite places to forage and hunt. The fjord they were heading for was one that Raina often visited in winter. Furka knew Mahinok fjord well, but she preferred rather smaller fjords when they were hunting by themselves. With fewer orcas to join the hunt, she was always on the lookout for big crevasses, miniature bays, or rocky outcrops that could serve as a natural trap for fish. Now, with 23 whales, Furka was more than willing to follow Raina to one of her favorite hunting grounds.

It was already dark when they reached the mouth of the large fjord. Over a mile into the fjord, they located some herring, but the fish were not very dense. The night was uneventful and the orcas passed a small harbor as they went several more miles into the fjord. They didn't find the large quantities of fish they had hoped for, but they didn't know whether the fish were still to come or less abundant this season than they had been before.

On the third day, the two pods located herring in a fairly concentrated layer at a depth of several hundred feet. It required more cooperation and effort to hunt successfully at that depth. The orcas wouldn't have the surface as a natural trap, but with their larger number, they decided to give it a try. The feeding was intense, but relatively brief. Hunting at that depth with many deep dives was quite strenuous.

The two pods had stayed together during the following night, but in the morning they exchanged a few rubs and parted. Tuschka was reluctant to leave Aleta and tried to ignore her mother's prodding, but Tarka was determined. When she began to push her away from her buddy, Tuschka voiced a few pleading calls, then gave up, and followed her mother.

12.
Parting of the Ways

Another year had passed when Furka continued north again towards the rugged coast. Herring on their way to the fjords were likely to cross their path. The pod traveled tight, listening and echolocating for any sign of prey. In the strong wind, it seemed like the orcas were riding the white-capped waves. They lifted their heads high when breaking the surface. Beneath the turbulent waves, they recognized the sound of a familiar fishing boat.

It was certainly possible to hunt in this rough water. They had done it many times before. Less than a body length below the surface, there was little left of the turbulence. Nevertheless, feeding near a net and waiting for the spill was easier. Furka decided to try her luck. She slowed down to listen where the vessel was heading. It was approaching at fairly high speed and the pod simply let itself drift with the tide.

The orcas soon detected the school of fish the vessel was heading for. The boat had already reached the perimeter of the school, but continued on a little ahead of the fish. The pod moved along in the same direction. A little later, they heard the sounds of the small skiff, pulling out the net. Furka waited. She wanted to hunt after dark and approach the net when fish were closer to the surface .

It was well after sunset when Furka started moving closer. She guided her pod to a position facing the semicircular net. They came upon a few fish heading for the trap. The tide was slackening and it was obvious that most of the school had passed by. Furka, Sigurd, and Tamara went ahead to determine the amount of fish near the net. There was a moderate density, but it was not at all spectacular. The three stayed down as they investigated the net from one end to the other. Still under water, they returned to the others. Furka contemplated whether she would wait for the spill at the end or dive in and start feeding now. Although the pod was impatient, she decided to go ahead with her most experienced companions and call the rest if she considered it safe. They intended to feed near the net and leave again without coming up for air.

Three of them took a deep breath and dived with her. An instant later, bright lights almost blinded the five orcas waiting further away. Furka, Tamara, Shaka, and Sigurd saw the sudden bright beams pierce the water ahead of them. They caught a glimpse of a few silvery fish crossing the beams. Furka immediately turned away from the net and called the others back as well. At a safe distance, they surfaced and shied away from the blinding lights. The lights disappeared quickly, but left them in doubt whether they should continue to feed or leave the vessel. None of them had ever experienced this before. Every ship had one or two lights, but never had there been such bright light.

After a while, the four adults cautiously returned to the net. The fish had become more concentrated, but there was no sign of the net being closed yet. Furka called for the other five orcas to approach. While they started feeding, three of them swam back and forth to prevent the fish from turning and leaving the net. The orcas expected the net to be closed anytime, but to their surprise it stayed open. They had never before fed near an open net for that long, yet they continued as long as they sensed no danger. Gradually gaining confidence, they began to surface right along the edge of the net. Finally, they heard some splashing, quickly followed by the familiar sound of a small engine. When the two ends of the net were being pulled together, most of the orcas slipped underneath the edge to the outside. Tamara and Sigurd quickly checked the size of their escape route through the bottom and stayed inside to take advantage of the rapidly increasing density of the fish. The two were highly alert to the net being closed, but that event, too, took longer than usual.

Although the pod was getting close to being satisfied, Igor and Tuschka had slipped inside the circle too. Tuschka had never done that before, but the relaxed atmosphere and the presence of the other orcas inside the net had been too tempting. She immediately noticed the larger amounts of fish, but it was still not so easy to catch them. She smacked her tail, but hardly stunned any. As Tuschka approached the maze, she found a fair number of fish entangled in it and it proved much easier to pull on those. Tamara heard her squeak nearby and she felt her grand-offspring's little tugs at the net while she pulled a fish free herself.

The circle was still quite large when the orcas suddenly heard an unusual squeaky sound. Sigurd dived and echolocated on the edge of the net. The sound was not very familiar, but he had been expecting their escape opening to be closed off soon. He nudged the net and, feeling rhythmic tugs, he gave a signal and slipped away. Tamara and Igor followed him quickly. Tuschka heard his call too, but paid no heed. Until now, she had never had to.

In the pitch black, Tarka didn't see her offspring, but she was reassured when Tuschka answered her call relatively nearby. The squeaky sounds in the background had quickly faded from Tuschka's attention and she was engrossed in pulling at a big fish that was caught in the maze behind its gills. The young female was jerking at the fish, which was starting to tear. She was not really hungry anymore and the pulling had become a game in itself. Tarka heard the playful squeaks close by and felt the jerks at the net. She came over to play tug with her baby and almost felt a shock when she found Tuschka's rostrum on the other side of the maze. Tarka urged Tuschka to instantly follow her down. The juvenile noticed the concern in her mother's voice and, suddenly, she too realized that the net separated them. Without the slightest hesitation, Tuschka followed her mother down, but the maze stayed in between them. Tarka started to panic and circled around the bottom of the net, desperately searching for an opening. There was none. The absence of the squeaky sound suddenly struck her and Tarka knew the net had been closed. Tuschka came to surface for a breath when the bright lights came back on. She didn't pay any attention and dived down to find her mother again.

The whole pod was alarmed. They all circled the net and everyone was calling towards their youngest pod member. Among all the calls of her companions, Tuschka unerringly recognized her mother's. In the beam of one of the spotlights, she saw mother's familiar white eye patch. The two stayed together, swimming back and forth, but not finding any way to reunite. Tuschka pushed her rostrum into the maze nudging her mother and calling out her fear. Tarka tried to comfort her precious offspring, but her calls were fraught with concern and a hint of panic. Tuschka pressed against her mother for reassurance, which the dedicated and loving mother was unable to give.

Both Tarka and Tuschka had temporarily lost each other before. Panic had dominated everything. Now, they saw, heard, and touched each other, but deep inside they felt that something was terribly wrong. Tuschka was trapped and they all were suddenly faced with the fact that they could not swim away from the trouble. At the time when they were herded toward shore, they had been able to escape, albeit with injuries. But now, Furka and all the others were at a loss. The orcas swam all around the net, intensely searching for a way out, but to no avail.

Suddenly, Tuschka heard several splashes above her. She looked up and saw the outline of the small boat in one of the light beams. Tuschka followed her mother away from the light , but when she finally had to surface, several splashing creatures were approaching her. She felt a surge of adrenaline. She dived again, frantically calling for her mother. They soon found each other on either side of the maze. Sigurd came over too. He and his companions had been searching in vain for an escape route for Tuschka. The big bull went down again and started tugging at the net near the bottom, but it gave easily and didn't tear. The material was heavier than usual and he was not even aware that he had already acquired several bleeding cuts in his gums. Tuschka didn't leave Tarka's flank, but the circle had become much closer, and her attention was suddenly caught by the creatures that had entered the water. She cried in fear and pressed her head against her mother, who whined in shared desperation. Despite that one terrible experience in the past, Tuschka took Tarka's presence for granted. She was always there to give her comfort and protection.

None of the orcas knew what was going to happen, but they were very aware of the fact that they were not in control of the situation. The deepest possible fear overcame them: the fear of death and separation.

Tarka tried to lead her Tuschka away from the skiff, but she found little room to maneuver. The net had become very shallow too. Not knowing what to do, Tarka and Tuschka nudged and rubbed each other through the maze, calling out affection and despair. Both came up for air when Tuschka suddenly stiffened, upon something touching her. She heard many screams, like the ones she had heard in summer. Tuschka voiced her distress, then stiffened, paralyzed with fear. Two more creatures approached her other side and started to push her away from the edge, away from mother!

Tuschka heard her mother call, mixed with all the other concerned voices of her pod. She responded in a weak, stifled voice. Her soft calls conveyed that she was losing hope. Tuschka kept still, barely moving her flukes. She noticed the strange creatures manipulating her, but they were not really hurting her. Although she didn't feel any pain, the situation was unlike anything she had experienced before, and being unable to get to her family was most distressing of all. Suddenly, she felt another netlike structure being pulled around her head. For a moment, she feared she would drown, but managed to take a breath. Tuschka was overwhelmed by all the rubbing and pushing she felt. Something touched her belly and she felt her pec being grabbed and lifted up. Most important of all was that she could still breathe. Then, something pulled on her other pec. She struggled a little, only to find that she could barely move. Tuschka still heard the voices of her mother and the rest of her family, and cried plaintively in return. Then, she suddenly felt her full body being lifted and the voices of her family vanished. All around her were shouts, creaky sounds and rumbles. In a final attempt to reach her mother, she made a long imploring call. She stopped as she faintly heard a voice that sounded like her mother's. Then, it faded away. The contact was broken. She was alone. No one heard her cries, no one came to her rescue. Tuschka had never felt so helpless and so desolate.

Tarka had been watching from the edge of the net and saw how something large rose up along the side of the vessel. They noticed that Tuschka was no longer in the water. They had stopped hearing her and they could no longer locate her with their sonar. Furka and Sigurd spyhopped next to Tarka. Among all the confusing noise, the desperate mother heard the soft, plaintive call of her offspring, but there was nothing she could do. Her companions, too, recognized the feeble cry of their youngest pod member. Tarka returned a long whine and saw the large dangling bundle, from where she had heard her baby's voice, disappear over the edge.

The net was soon being pulled up, but the orcas were oblivious to the spilling fish. They swam back and forth, calling for Tuschka, circling around the vessel that had taken her. None of them had ever left the pod other than by death, but Tuschka had not died. She was with that vessel and they could do nothing to bring her back.

The orcas felt uneasy around the fishing boat that had taken away their Tuschka, but their strong bond made them stay. They could not comprehend that Tuschka was not with them. Tarka was totally upset and restless, swimming from one to the other. She kept calling for her precious baby, but there was no answer and the familiar affectionate bumps under her belly failed to come.

Dawn announced the break of day with a red sky in the east. The whitecaps of the previous afternoon had given way to a calm sea. The pod traveled in a tight formation, still following the boat from behind. Annika felt close to Tarka. The event had brought the loss of Bingor to the surface again. In a very different way, they had both lost their first and only offspring. But not only Tarka and Annika shared their grief. The whole pod felt depressed and deeply troubled with the tragic event. Tarka was in the lead with Annika and Tamara at her side. Furka and Sigurd followed, with Shaka and her offspring bringing up the rear. The matriarch was heavy-hearted. In her sad, troubled mind there was no room for any other decision than to follow the dismayed mother behind the vessel that carried their Tuschka with it.

* * *

When Arjen saw another seiner head towards shore, he called them on the radio to ask how the fishing had been. "Just a moderate catch," was all they replied. It was Torvil, who suddenly spotted the orcas behind the seiner. At first, he had simply assumed that the vessel was passing the pod, but when he watched it a little longer, he could not escape the impression that the orcas were following the boat. He went downstairs to inform Sem about it. The experienced man came up, and after several minutes of careful observation, he agreed with Torvil's suggestion. "It's strange," the older man said. "I've seen whales following when vessels were disposing of discards, but in this case there is no sign of such a thing. If it isn't food that's attracting them, I wonder what it could be."

Arjen was watching it too, but he had not commented on it yet. Sem requested him to ask the crew over the radio, which helped Arjen to give in to his own curiosity. "It seems like you're being followed by a pod of orcas," the taciturn captain brought up. "Yes, we noticed that too," they replied, without further comment. Arjen felt the reluctance of the other side to reveal more, but he did not give up yet. Although it was not customary to meddle in other matters than fishing, he justified his persistence from the standpoint that the presence of orcas was always related to fishing. "What's keeping them so interested?" the captain inquired. There was a short pause on the other side before the answer

135

came: "It may have to do with our remarkable catch last night." "I thought your catch was only moderate," Arjen countered, but he didn't press any further. Instead, he said: "Well, we'll take a closer look at those whales. Perhaps they'll take us to another remarkable fishing ground". Arjen didn't give them a chance to voice whether or not they appreciated that. After all, it was quite common for two or three fishing boats to follow each other while under way.

The seiner with its retinue was traveling at a good pace and it took Arjen and his crew almost an hour to close in on the orcas. They had the feeling that the other seiner had increased its speed. Arjen pulled alongside the whales at a distance of about 80 yards. Because of the calm sea it was relatively easy to observe the orcas with binoculars. Torvil was excited at the opportunity to watch the predators more closely. It occurred to him immediately that this group had just one adult male. There were about seven or eight whales and the pod inevitably made him think of the group with the wounded orca and the incident with Ruben, when he was sure he had recognized that same whale by its scar. The young fisherman tried to study the orcas in detail. He wished he had some way of remembering the ones he had seen. He had noticed subtle differences in the shape of their dorsal fins, but what help would that be? There were probably hundreds of whales out there with fins just like those.

Torvil was happy when Arjen pulled a little closer. The clear sky offered fairly good light on the orcas. While they were traveling in tight formation, frequent spyhops and high surfacings revealed an obvious restlessness. The men were convinced that the pod was indeed following the seiner, because it seemed unlikely they just happened to be traveling at the same speed for such an extended period of time. "Perhaps those whales had some good feeding near that boat last night. That might be a reason to follow it around for another opportunity," Sem said. "But, I must say that I've never seen them stay around any boat for long after feeding was over."

Arjen's oldest son had shifted his attention to the seiner ahead of them. It's name was Hydetor. The angle was not ideal for observing the deck, but he saw quite a lot of activity around something on deck. He took the wheel to give his father a better opportunity to look. "It doesn't look like they're working with fish," Arjen said. "It's unclear, but there seems to be a big elongated canvas structure on deck. It may simply be some sort of fish container, but it looks different from any I've seen before."

Arjen and the others were suddenly startled by Torvil's shouts. Sem was the first to stand next to him. "You wouldn't believe it, but I saw the orca with the scar! I'm sure it's the same whale. He's among the three orcas in the rear. They're similar in shape and size, but he's the one closest to us. There's also a small nick in his fin that I hadn't been aware of." Torvil handed his binoculars to Sem, but he was too impatient to give the man much time to see for himself. "At first, I thought it was sun glare, but nothing shines like that on any of the whales. It's too white and just in front of the dorsal fin. I'm sure it's that scar I told you about." Sem was still straining to get the proper whale into view. "I just got the rear group in the viewfinder," Sem said. "I hope to see it on the next surfacing." The young fisherman waited impatiently for the older man's judgment. Sem suddenly lowered the binoculars and nodded with a serious expression on his face. "I'd never have seen it if you hadn't focused my attention on it, but it's definitely something abnormal in the orca's skin. I don't know 'your whale', but if you recognize it as such, who am I not to believe you? There won't be many orcas with a scar in that spot and living in a pod of eight whales with only one male."

Torvil's excitement was so evident that Arjen even came out to ask him if he, perhaps, had found the answer to the orcas' behavior. "No," Torvil said, taken by surprise. "I uh, I think I've seen the same pod before." The young man expected little understanding from the captain, knowing how similar all the whales were, but he had nothing else to say. Arjen gave him a questioning look, then turned to Sem. "One orca has a remarkable scar," he said calmly. "Torvil has seen a whale with just such a scar in the past." The young man stiffened, fearing that his friend would bring up his past shooting. Arjen nodded understandingly. "And did you see the same behavior in this group at that time?" the captain asked Torvil. "No, I can't recall such behavior. They left .. after feeding. Most orcas are difficult to tell apart, he added. To see one so strikingly similar, is special in itself." The captain raised his eyebrows and nodded: "It surely is".

Since the seiner was heading in the direction of Stenavik harbor, the crew would probably not set the net this night. Both Sem and Arjen expected that the orcas would sooner or later give up and resume foraging. They saw no obvious reason for staying around any longer. In fact, their action had already been fairly obtrusive, given that plain inquiries over the radio had not provided any clarity. Arjen realized that the crew of the other boat might even have seen that they were being observed with binoculars. He felt a little uncomfortable about the circumstances, but it was not a familiar boat and they seemed to be hiding something.

After having observed the orcas for about half an hour, Arjen veered away. He made a note in the log and resumed his original plans. Torvil watched the pod until the fins, and finally the blows, faded in the distance. He wondered when he would see them again.

* * *

For several hours, the pod had been following the seiner. The orcas traveled mainly in silence, totally engrossed in the tragic loss of the previous night. Furka was among the first to have an awakening awareness of her surroundings. Like the others, the matriarch had not heard a sign of life from their youngest pod

137

member for quite a while. They all missed Tuschka, each in a different way, but no one missed her more than Tarka. Furka went a little ahead and slipped in between Annika and Tarka. The matriarch touched the despondent mother tenderly with her pectoral fin. She was grateful for it, but did not respond. Furka felt that she was not ready to stop following the boat. She nudged Tarka and rubbed her head under her chin. Tarka subtly nudged her appreciation. Furka was relieved that Tarka had not completely withdrawn. As long as she was receptive to her, it was likely that Tarka would sooner or later acquiesce to her lead. Furka decided to leave Tarka in peace for a while. After having eaten their fill the night before, there was no urgent need to hunt. The matriarch kept her position next to Tarka, making an effort to give the depressed mother some comfort.

By mid-morning, it became clear that the seiner was heading for the big fjord where they had been feeding with Raina's pod. The fjord was not one that Furka frequented, but it certainly held a potential for finding food. As long as they were not heading too far away from potential feeding grounds, the leading female was accepting of Tarka's compulsion to follow the fishing boat.

The pod was aware that they entered the fjord. The steep, rocky walls produced typical echoes upon echolocation. Sigurd and Shaka were suddenly surprised by faint echoes, that didn't come from their own sonar pulses. In a few moments, the pod was alert and listened intently. It was obvious that some other pod was nearby, but they wondered who they were. Furka felt that the company of a well-known family would be a welcome diversion, but she was not into meeting less familiar groups. Since it was a fjord that her pod didn't visit often, she decided to stay silent and wait for any further cues.

Furka slowed down, but Tarka kept on going. Preferring silence over calling her back, the matriarch picked up speed again. A distant, but clear call pierced their ears. It was a relief for most of them to recognize Raina's voice. The other pod was obviously heading out of the fjord on the other side of the fjord's entrance.

The vessel was only half a mile away from the harbor and was slowing down. Furka nudged Tarka and tried to make her stop. The troubled mother was confused. She sensed what the matriarch wanted from her, but it gave her a feeling of capitulation to leave the boat that had taken her Tuschka. Tarka heard another call of Raina's pod and recognized Nadia's voice. She felt torn between her urge to stay with the boat and to give in to her pod leader. She hesitated. Tuschka was not with her. The taking of her offspring had left her empty and dejected. To separate from her pod would make it far worse. They were her companions for life and she realized she needed them more than ever. With a feeling of finality, the grieving mother gave a soft plaintive cry. Then, reluctantly, Tarka veered aside and turned around to follow Furka, who had been waiting for her.

Part II

In the Care of Man

13.
Walls of Loneliness

A little later, Tuschka felt her belly touch ground. She felt strangely heavy out of the water, and it was an effort to breathe. The net was taken away from her head and people started rubbing her all over. Tuschka lay there, panic-stricken, unable to comprehend what was happening to her. She felt her heart beat in her chest and although she did not move, she became aware of a strange rocking movement. It gave her an uneasy, almost nauseous feeling.

After a while, Tuschka tried to understand what she saw. Directly below and beside her, everything was white. She could barely look up, but she saw some sky above the edge of the white screen that blocked most of her view. Ahead, she saw mainly grey and brown shapes. The objects were motionless and did not look like anything she had seen before. A dark figure bent over her and Tuschka squinted to protect her eyes. As the man disappeared, she was again aware of the rumbling sounds, the weird rocking, the splashing of water in the distance, and strange voices close by.

"Perfect individual, isn't she?," one of the men said. "She's nice and young. Old enough to have been weaned and young enough to be transported with minimal risk. I'm sure she will adapt quickly. What's her breathing rate?" Another young man was sitting nearby, keeping the whale wet and timing every breath. "Let me see... She's been taking a breath about every 20 seconds for the last several minutes," he replied. The older man tapped the young female gently. "That's quite frequent for an orca, but it's not surprising under these circumstances. She'll be stressed and probably quite hot as well. As soon as we have her in the container, the water and the ice will cool and calm her. I'll be relieved once we have her in the tank."

The older man's name was Bob. He had taken the initiative in the whole venture. He walked towards the stern and looked at the orcas following the boat at a distance of about 50 yards. Another local crew member stood staring at the same. The expedition leader saw that he was a little uneasy. "That must be her pod," Bob said, nodding in the direction of the orcas. "It's amazing they're still following us." "They've been doing that since we took that juvenile on board," the local man said. "They may cause trouble if we don't drop their companion." "What kind of trouble, Chris? Are you afraid?" The younger man shifted position, feeling he was about to be ridiculed. Yet he was eager to know the opinion of the expedition leader. If his fear was unfounded, it would make him feel a lot more comfortable. "I saw a movie, several years ago, about a male orca that lost.." "Ah," Bob said. "You mean 'Orca, the killer whale', about a male who kills several people and finally sinks the boat to avenge the loss of his pregnant mate!" Chris nodded. "Well, I wouldn't take it that seriously. Orcas do have good memories, like their cousins, the dolphins, but I've never heard of them taking revenge. Many fishermen shoot at them, don't they? And how many boats have been sunk by them?" The young man shrugged his shoulders, not knowing what to say. "But killer whales can attack anything, can't they?" "They're the top predators of the sea, but there's no account of wild orcas having killed humans. Come on Chris, relax," Bob said, resting his hand on his shoulder. "Those whales won't do you any harm." The expedition leader gave him a smile and walked back to the young orca. Bob seemed so convinced and so relaxed that there had to be truth in his words. Chris looked back at the whales, still following. He wondered if they were closer, but if so it was not obvious. 'I hope Bob is right about you guys,' he thought to himself, and walked away to divert his mind.

Shortly after the vessel had entered Stenavik fjord, Chris noticed that the orcas, who had been following them since the capture, were slowing down. They seemed to hesitate before he saw them turn around and head towards the southern side of the fjord's entrance. The young man was relieved to see them go, but he wondered for how long they would be gone. He was not very eager to board the same vessel again in the near future.

There was a lot of activity on shore. People were walking back and forth. A crane was parked near a truck with a steel container for the whale. Having been contacted by radio, a team on shore had prepared for the seiner's arrival. Everyone was eager to make the whole procedure as smooth as possible. The sooner the valuable orca was in her future tank, the better her chances. The captors were very well aware of the risk of transportation. Out of the water, the otherwise weightless creature suffered under the pressure of its own weight and had difficulties dissipating its heat. Young orcas could endure it much better than large adults, but after a few hours their condition would inevitably deteriorate.

Two people had constantly watched over the juvenile female. They sprayed her with water regularly, and they had also rubbed her skin with zinc oxide to prevent it from dehydration. As soon as the boat had docked, the crane was brought into position to hoist the orca into the container. The new holder was partly filled with water and ice to alleviate gravity and provide cooling. Furthermore, it was heavily padded to minimize the chance of injury in case of rough handling or violent movements of a panicking whale.

Tuschka felt tired and hot. She became a little restless under her uncomfortable circumstances, but stiffened as she suddenly felt herself being lifted again. The situation was similar to the moment she had been taken from the water, away from her family. Other than that, she could not relate to anything she had experienced before. Feeling alone and physically helpless, Tuschka did not even attempt to resist. She surrendered to the situation in a resigned mood. The rocking she had experienced during the past several hours changed into a strange swaying feeling. Some sharp edge irritated her near the front of her flipper.

Tuschka was taken by surprise when her belly touched water. Instantly, she moved her tail and called for her family, only to find that the wet environment meant no return to freedom. Her movements were just as restrained, and the immediate muffled reflections of her sonar revealed that she was closed in by walls of some unfamiliar texture. Tuschka could barely see beyond the canvas that was still holding her, but she felt much less heavy, and the cool water was soothing. Although she was still unable to comprehend what was happening, the new comfort took the edge off her paralyzing fear.

Although Tuschka felt utterly alone without her family, she noticed that one or more of the land-based humans constantly stayed near her. Their presence as such caused Tuschka no fear. The biggest shock had been the abrupt separation from her pod and the sudden inability to move. As a top predator, Tuschka had never experienced an attack by other animals that lived in the sea. In fact, it surprised her that these land creatures had no fear of her. They seemed to approach her without any reservation. Yet it made Tuschka uneasy that she was not in control of the situation. She had no way to evade them or fend for herself in case she needed to.

A sudden reverberating sound caught her attention, together with several jerks. She gave a little shriek in response. One of the men made some incomprehensible sounds as he reached over and rubbed her back. Tuschka did not associate the gesture with the loving caresses of her mother, but in some way it had a comforting and reassuring effect on her.

As the truck slowly drove to the airport, Bob stayed right next to the young orca. He was wearing a dry suit and sat on the edge of the container, holding on to one of the poles that where placed across the top. He had to make sure he could not be hit by the orca's tail, nor be wedged in between her body and the wall when the truck took a curve. The orca was submerged for about two thirds of her body, so she would have no trouble keeping her blowhole at the surface. Every time the whale blew, Bob felt a moist spray touch his face.

After about one and a half hours the truck finally reached the airport. The orca's condition seemed stable. He heard very soft little whimpers, which made him think of the dolphins at his aquarium. How would they get along? In the wild, orcas occasionally attacked dolphins and porpoises, but they had also been observed in more playful interactions with their smaller relatives. "Good girl," he said, tapping her gently. "Keep it up. It won't be long before you can swim again."

Tuschka felt exhausted and stiff. After nearly 20 hours, the rumbles, vibrations, and jerks hardly made an impression on her any more. After a final hoist, Tuschka experienced the relief of water again. Partly numbed and not very alert to her surroundings, she did not even realize that she was not lowered back into her small container. It was not until she felt several strong nudges and pushes that she became aware of her increased freedom of movement. As the canvas sling gave way underneath her, Tuschka lost her balance for a moment and rolled over to her side. She felt someone help her as she tried to right herself again. She wriggled a little sideways. Her muscles ached from stiffness and her balance was uncertain, but she finally swam out of the hands of those who had been holding her.

Tuschka was in the water and she had room to swim, but it did not resemble her home waters. There were bright lights and everything around her was a light blue. Tuschka echolocated and sharp echoes returned, revealing a stone wall several yards ahead. She veered aside and scanned her surroundings, but the echoes only bounced back and forth around her. Tuschka followed the wall, taking in more detail with every round. She discovered that the wall had round and straight stretches with sharp angles in between. There were also rectangular structures in the wall that were not solid, but similar to very thick rigid wire mesh. In the background she heard a very faint drone.

After several rounds, Tuschka realized she was circling. The new container was far bigger than the one she had just left, but it did not come anywhere close to what she was used to. It was very shallow and after a few strokes straight ahead, she had to turn to avoid hitting the wall. She could keep swimming, but only if she kept changing course. Tuschka could see very well and kept an eye on the people near the edge. Each of them had four extremities and they hung vertically in the water with their heads above the surface. Their movements looked rather clumsy. She watched as they climbed out of her enclosure.

After all the manipulation she had been through and the loud reverberating sounds she had endured, it was suddenly very quiet. Stretching her muscles made her feel a lot better. Tuschka was still too restless to stop swimming. The only familiar thing she could cling to was to swim.

Suddenly, Tuschka saw the light dim and she did not feel familiar enough with her enclosure to rely completely on what she could see. Just a few sonar pulses were enough to help her keep track of where she was. During the past day, her immobilization and the periods of difficult breathing had dominated her consciousness. Being able to swim again, she was painfully aware of the absence of her mother and the rest of the pod. Tuschka called softly for her mother with a plaintive voice, filled with grief, and devoid of hope.

Night had fallen. Tuschka was still swimming her circles. She spyhopped a few times and noticed it was not completely dark. There was one light casting a faint shine on her surroundings. She saw a sloping wall with a strange uniform relief that reflected the light in a regular pattern. When she dived again, she was struck by some soft sounds. She listened intently. The voices did not come from orcas, but from dolphins. Where were they? With the reflecting walls it took Tuschka some time to locate the source of the sound. She ended up near the wire mesh construction. The young female had never hunted dolphins and did not associate them with food. Yet they were usually shy and elusive. Only a few times had dolphins felt confident enough to play with her. Tuschka called to them, but the only response was silence. Like most dolphins, these seemed unhappy with her company. After a while, Tuschka heard their voices again and squeaked back, but to no avail. She gave up and resumed her circles. By morning she began to feel hungry, but where could she go to find food?

The light of dawn slowly penetrated the high dome that covered the pools. A man of about 35 years old walked over to relieve a colleague, who had been watching the young orca during the second half of the night. "How's she been doing, Tom," he asked. "She's pretty restless. Hasn't stopped swimming, except for one moment near the gate. She looks good though." Richard was the head trainer. He had helped during the orca's transportation and had gone to bed after an exhausting day. After six hours of sleep, he had returned to the park to see how their newest acquisition was doing. "I've taken some fish out of the freezer for her. I wonder if she'll accept it. You can go home now and get some sleep." Tom was tired, but his excitement kept him going. "I'd like to watch when you try to feed her," the younger trainer said. "Ok Tom, have some coffee then. I'll get you when I'm ready for it."

Richard sat down and picked up the notepaper to continue timing some blows. He was excited with the new arrival. He looked at the energetic, more than 12 foot-long orca. Her glossy black and white markings were beautiful. She was much bigger than their oldest dolphin male, but he knew she was still young, probably somewhere between four and five years of age. He loved the sound of her strong blows and the robust curved dorsal fin. Richard had seen a captive orca once before. It had left a deep impression on him. The prospect of training one himself was a great thrill. He stood up and walked over to the edge of the holding pool. Within seconds, he saw the black shadow pass in front of him, beneath the surface. She blew on the opposite side. Richard bent over and tapped the water with his hand. The whale did not stop or come over to him.

145

What a difference with his trained dolphins, who vied for his attention. She was a truly wild animal. It would be a long haul to make her a skilled performer, but he was eager to take on the challenge.

Tuschka heard a series of weak sounds, like soft thumps. Then, still submerged, she saw two people appear near the edge of her enclosure. Wary of anything strange, she stayed down and surfaced as far away from them as she could. When she came up, she saw they looked like those that had been with her since she had found herself entrapped in the net. Yet the juvenile orca did not fathom that the tragic event had been their initiative. From her perspective, they had not harmed her, but she was still far from trusting them. On her next surfacing, she noticed for the first time that the men near the edge of her pool were standing on two legs. In her young mind the image of a human being began to take shape. As she continued her circles underwater, she kept an eye on them. She was aware of every movement they made.

Richard and Tom were back near the edge of the pool with the thawed mackerel. "Bob would be excited if we could tell him she accepted fish. Let's see if she's interested," Richard said. He tapped the water, but there was no response. He waited for the orca to surface and tapped the water again. "Come on," he encouraged, holding the fish out to her. Both men noticed some hesitation prior to her dive. "I think she looked at you, Richard," Tom said. "Try it again."

Richard waited for the whale to surface. As soon as he saw the tip of the dorsal fin break the surface, he tapped the water and held the fish out to her. The orca did not dive immediately, but stayed at the surface for a few seconds. "She's definitely interested," Richard said. They both watched as the young whale passed by underneath them. "She's probably not comfortable surfacing right next to us, nor do I expect her to take her first fish from my hand. I'll throw one near her in just a moment, but I want to attract her attention first. It's important that she associates us with food." "I'll go look downstairs," Tom said as he headed for the viewing window.

Tuschka noticed the fish dangling from the man's hand. The sight of the fish reminded her of her empty stomach, but it did not occur to her to approach and take it. In a situation so unfamiliar and with no one to fall back upon, she did not have nearly the courage that she used to have in the company of her pod. Otherwise inquisitive, she was timid now and craving reassurance.

She flinched slightly as an object hit the water close by. In a flash Tuschka saw a fish floating near her head. Moments later, another fish landed in front of her. Being hungry, it was tempting to investigate the fish, but tense with all the activity near her tank, she only looked as she passed over them. The men's presence confused her. There had been many humans around during her stressful hours of immobilization. They had been in control then: manipulating and hoisting her. Could that happen again? She realized she could not get away from them. Yet it had gotten better, step by step. After having been dry, heavy and hot, she could at least swim now. They had eventually given her the relative freedom of this enclosure. Had they been helping her in their way?

When the whale passed the window, Tom caught his breath. "What a big animal," he thought, "and so graceful." He was in awe as he saw the beautiful orca swim by. Her size impressed him too. He watched her elegant movements and wondered how long it would take to make contact with her. He was determined to make friends with this new treasure. He was distracted for a few minutes watching her when he suddenly recalled he had come down to check on the fish. He scanned the tank carefully. Just as he thought the fish had disappeared, he saw them near one of the grids on the bottom. They whirled around a little as the orca passed by. She seemed oblivious to the fish. He wondered what they could do to stimulate her. Probably, she simply needed time to settle down a little more.

He leaned on the window sill, following the streamlined, black and white creature. Instead of surfacing, he saw her swim by and tilt her head slightly towards the tank floor. Was she looking at the fish? She repeated the behavior twice and resumed her surfacing pattern. Tom walked upstairs. "It seemed she was looking at the fish. When she stayed down, I saw how she tilted her head. I've the feeling it's just a matter of time. She's still very restless." Richard looked at him and nodded. "Come on," he said, "we'll try later." He threw in another fish and walked away, looking back to see her surface once more.

As soon as everything was quiet again, Tuschka's attention was immediately drawn to the two fish on the bottom. She was hesitant to stop and investigate the potential food, afraid to be caught off guard. Eventually, she relaxed enough to give in to the temptation. Although she was used to hunting live fish, she had often swallowed fish that had been killed or paralyzed by powerful tail slaps of her family members. She carefully nudged one of the fish, then sucked it in. It tasted strange, as did the water she was in. The fish was also pappy, not as firm as she was used to. She spat it out again and played a little with it. Then, she let go and tried the remaining one. It was the same.

Tuschka was not anywhere near starvation. In the past, she had fasted much longer than she had now, but then there had not been a choice. Although she felt uncertain with the strange tasting fish, she had learned how vital food was to survive and how important it was to grab as many opportunities to feed as possible. She nibbled a bit on the fish and swallowed it. Having made her decision, she quickly grabbed the other one. It made little difference in her appetite. Unable to find any more, Tuschka resumed her circles.

She was immediately alert when she heard the voices of the dolphins again. They were louder than before and accompanied by a lot of splashing. Tuschka swam to the wire mesh structure and listened again. When she called to them, there was immediate silence, but not for long. Tuschka pressed against the steel gate, but it did not yield the way the nets did. She wished she could investigate the waters on the other side. If there were dolphins out there, could her family be there too? Tuschka called for her mother, but there was no response. Then she made the sound that all the members of her pod used to tell each other where they were when they were foraging far apart. There was no answer. Tuschka listened intently. The dolphins started to whisper again. Where was everyone? Tuschka cried for help with all her heart. Her loud distress calls had startled the dolphins and silence returned. The spark of hope that the voices of the dolphins had given her vanished. Desolation overwhelmed Tuschka and she moaned softly, hovering near the gate.

As Tom came in, he found Richard near the edge of the pool and saw the young orca slowly move away from the gate. Richard had a big smile. Tom looked at him questioningly. "She did take the fish! Paul has checked the fil.." "Terrific!," Tom interrupted enthusiastically. "She's eating!" His eyes gleamed as he looked at the beautiful animal. He was not very experienced yet, and he thought it would probably be a while before Richard would let him work with the young orca by himself. Yet, he was hoping that the head trainer would soon involve him in his training sessions with the orca to teach him how to work with her.

Having overcome her initial fear to eat the first few fish, Tuschka did not hesitate to suck up more fish that came down into the water. Yet this fish was not floating free. When she was about a foot away from the fish, Tuschka sucked, but it did not slip into her mouth. She rolled aside, noticed that it was being held, and passed by. The situation reminded her of the moment that Tamara and her mother had taught her to take fish off a line. This was not exactly the same and she contemplated if she would try the same strategy. When she had picked the fish off the lines, she had been taught to approach from below and grab the end of the tail to pull it loose. This fish was hanging head down.

Tuschka made a small circle and stopped below the mackerel. She tried once more to suck, but without success. With utmost caution, Tuschka nudged the fish and hesitated briefly. Then, she cautiously grabbed the head just behind the gills. She barely needed to pull for the fish to give way. She dived down with it, away from the man, and swallowed it. She heard another tap and saw a new fish dangling down in the same spot. This time, Tuschka did not hesitate. She gracefully swung underneath the fish and picked it up by the head. To her great surprise, several fish fell into the water simultaneously. Gratefully, she quickly sucked them in.

148

Richard was beside himself with joy: the orca was taking fish from his hand! She had been so close that he could have touched her... 'That will be the next step,' he thought. He dumped several fish in the water at once to reward her, and he was thrilled to see her suck them in effortlessly. He got up and looked at the beautiful orca with great satisfaction and full of expectation of what was to come.

The other trainers had all come to see the new addition to the collection. They had all been excited, but in a different way. Some worked only with the pinnipeds and they did not look at the whale with the prospect of working with her. Two of Tom's direct colleagues were more experienced and were likely to be involved sooner in the training process. They appeared less eager than him. Was it because they would get their chance soon, or was it because their years of experience with the dolphins had dulled their initial enthusiasm? Tom was off for the weekend, but the orca was constantly on his mind. He wondered if the whale would turn out to be clinging or not. If three trainers, and perhaps Bob as well, had already acquainted themselves with the whale, how receptive would it be towards him? One by one, the personalities of the dolphins crossed his mind. Each of them was different. Although they responded to all trainers who worked with them, they definitely had their favorites. It occurred to Tom that the youngest dolphins were the most accepting of changes and the most interested in the visitors. Two of the younger dolphins really liked him, even though he was new to them at the time he was hired. His fellow trainers would have a head start. That was true, but orcas were big dolphins and this orca was young...

14.
A New Friend

Tom had returned from his weekend off and was eager to see the orca. He was excited that she was eating well, although it was hard for him to accept that he was not yet part of it. For the coming week, he had been assigned night shifts to watch the orca and take some notes on her behavior and breathing intervals.

Tom made himself comfortable in a chair close to the edge of the pool. After most of the lights had been turned off and his colleagues had gone home, he somehow felt closer to the mysterious and beautiful orca. There had not yet been opportunities to attract her attention. During day time, he was busy with a lot of chores and when he had training sessions with the dolphins, he was always supervised. Even during playtime sessions, he felt watched and his actions judged.

He listened to the strong blows, which sounded deep and pronounced in the high dome of the indoor stadium. He was already happy just to be near this new whale. With nobody around, he could relax and give in to his wishful thinking.

After a few days Tuschka began to realize her family was nowhere near, not even out there with the dolphins, whose voices had become familiar to her. The hope that her mother would come for her began to dwindle, but it did not make her miss Tarka and the pod any less. In the silence of the night a deep feeling of desolation stole over her. There was a total absence of purpose. In the pod, she had a place and a task and it was always clear what she was expected to do. Not that the long forays for food had always been that exciting: it had often annoyed her when no one wanted to play or when they called her back from something that she wanted to investigate. In between the precious playtimes, discipline ruled the pod. But how preferable that was to this! No matter how boring traveling could be, her presence had been important to her family. There always was the unconditional and loving commitment of her mother. The pod had wanted her among them and had shown concern. They had been her home, her comfort, her purpose, her future.

Lost in her sad thoughts, Tuschka slowed down and found a ledge near the gate to rest her head. Softly, she wailed her utter loneliness.

Tom had almost fallen asleep when the orca's soft long cries woke him. He quickly spotted her dark shadow in a corner of the tank. She was no longer swimming and her voice conveyed a desolation, so intense that it pierced his heart. It filled him with compassion and an urge to comfort her. There was no room for Richard's rules and instructions in his mind. Just a few yards away from him was a creature in need. He was not her kind. Could he somehow reach her? Quietly, he got up, stepped over the public fence, and knelt down near the gate. He looked down at the orca, who seemed oblivious to his presence. She blew and he felt her breath touch his face. Just hovering at the surface, her glossy back reflected the faint light.

"Eeeeeuee," only a few seconds had passed when the young orca made her soft high-pitched whine. Tom saw a few miniature bubbles escape from her blowhole. She was so close and yet he felt how lonely she was. He sensed the presence of a mind in the orca, craving for contact. "Eeeuup," Tom imitated tentatively. After several seconds of silence, he tried again.

The man's strange cry interrupted Tuschka's sad deliberations. She noticed him sitting close to her beside the pool. He was the first of his kind who had ever made a sound like that. It was unfamiliar, but somehow she felt addressed. The atmosphere was different now then during the daytime when she had constantly been on guard. She turned towards him, wondering what he was up to. She sought his eyes, but they were difficult to find, silhouetted as he was against the light. Tuschka heard him call again, awkward and strange, but with obvious intent. She sensed an alien mind wanting to make contact. It was the first hint of concern she had experienced since she had been separated from her family. It was what she was craving for. No matter how unusual, no matter who it was: if there was any creature caring for her, she wanted contact with it. In response, Tuschka returned his unusual call.

Tom saw the orca stir and direct her head slightly towards him, the tip of her white chin reflecting in the light. Her movement encouraged him. She was paying attention! He bent over to be closer to her. "Eeeeuee," her answer touched him deeply: it seemed an imitation of his own attempt. She had acknowledged him, so personally! "I wish I could understand what you say to me," he whispered, "but I know you must feel lonely and out of place."

The orca's message was not lost on the man. Tom changed position, moving slowly so as not to scare her. He stretched out on the walking ridge, lying down on his belly, facing the orca at much closer range. She did not draw back. He made another call to her and felt goose bumps upon her prompt answer. She kept talking back to him! The fascination he had felt for the young orca from the moment she had arrived grew into empathy and warm affection for her. He whispered several more words and saw her rise higher, until he found her eye. She tilted her head slightly sideways as if trying to see him better. Barely more than two feet separated them. Tom felt an urge to stretch out and touch her, but he did not want to break the special moment. It was something not to be forced. It was up to the orca to tell him when she was ready for it. He looked at her with compassion. "I feel we can become friends, my beautiful orca. I will be there for you. I cannot replace your family, but I will do all I can to make you feel less alone." The orca made a soft call and Tom tried to copy it. He knew they were both aware that their language was neither human nor orca, but it was the beginning of what would become their unique way to share minds.

Quietly and a little stiff from lying on the cold, damp concrete, Tom sat upright. The young orca blew, a sound which the trainer playfully copied. It was much deeper than the small puffs of the dolphins.

The sound of a door in the distance caught the attention of both of them. Tom got on his feet, ready to go back to his seat. He did not want the night guard to find him there. As if the orca understood, she dived and started swimming again. Tom felt a surge of excitement. He could hardly believe what had happened and assured himself that he was not dreaming. It was tempting to share this precious moment with someone, but he knew that the incipient friendship between him and the orca could prosper only if it remained their secret.

A dark shadow blocking the light reminded Tom of the guard he had heard. "How's she doing, Tom?," the tall man asked with a deep voice. "I think she's doing O.K.," Tom answered, a little startled by the slight hoarseness of his own voice. He wondered if the guard sensed his mood. "Still doing her circles, hey?" The young trainer nodded, happy that the dark hid the expression on his face. The guard stayed several minutes to watch, while Tom timed a series of surfacings. "I guess I'll continue my round. See you tomorrow night." He tapped Tom lightly on the shoulder and left.

Tom realized he would be relieved soon. He walked to the railing and watched the orca swim by. She surfaced on the opposite side and lifted her head briefly before she dived. Had she seen him? Close to where he stood, she stopped and came up. She did not spyhop, but hovered at the surface in front of him. Tom made one of his orca cries again to acknowledge her and tell her that he appreciated that she was there. She answered him softly. "I have to leave soon," he said quietly. The orca did not move. Tom took a few steps along the railing. The attentive orca noticed it. She did not want him to leave and called to him once more. The young man stopped, looking at her. He felt almost guilty about leaving. He had made contact with her, promised her that he would be there and try to make her feel less alone. But he had no other choice. He could only hope she would soon learn that he would be gone only temporarily and that he would always return.

Tom could barely sleep when he got home. He knew he needed the rest, but he could hardly wait to get back to the park. He loved to work with the dolphins, but never before had he been so fascinated. The orca had stolen his heart, but what was it that made her so special? Was it the thrill of working with a species with such a controversial reputation, or was it the personality of this particular orca? Were they all like her, or was she special? He had no comparison, but it did not matter. To him she was special.

Then something struck him. The interaction between them had been spontaneous. No one had tried to manipulate her, to make her act the way humans wanted. In the absence of a supervisor, he had been able to let his feelings flow freely. He concluded that both her personality and his spontaneity had contributed to their sharing of minds. She was a special orca who had been receptive to a voice that came from the heart. He felt privileged to have reached her, but he realized at the same time that it was the special circumstance of a night watch that had made it possible. He dreaded the end of his watch. How could he face her with the attitude of a trainer? How would she feel if he suddenly acted differently, like the others who only had their own purpose in mind? He suddenly no longer regretted that it would be a while before he became involved in her training. Instead, he hoped it would not be too soon. For the time being he would use every opportunity to work on his relationship with her. Then, he would somehow try to find a way to make clear to her that he was a friend who had to 'work' with her from time to time.

The next evening when Tom arrived for his night watch, he tried not to show his excitement. Night watches were regarded as boring chores and it would raise suspicions to show he liked them. But he did not want to pretend too much reluctance either. It was a delicate balance.

Tom brought out his chair and sat down. The orca was swimming in circles. The young man waited until the tranquility of the night had descended upon the park. He wondered if the whale would remember last night. Would she have another sad moment and hover near the gate, as she did the night before? It was tempting to call to her, but he wanted her to be in the right mood. If the whale was not resting she might not be as receptive. Tom wanted so much to make contact again that he feared being disappointed. He waited for a long time, but there was not much change in her behavior. She switched direction several times and her breathing pattern was repetitive: she would surface four or five times with small intervals in between, followed by a longer dive of approximately three minutes.

After half an hour of recordings, Tom got up quietly and walked to the railing near the edge, making sure he did not create a silhouette against the light. It was the only unobtrusive way he could think of to see if she was interested. The orca continued her circles without hesitation and passed him by below the surface. His eyes followed the black shadow. He hoped she would surface near him, but instead she blew near the opposite side again. A little disappointed, Tom kept watching. He was indecisive; why was the orca not showing more interest? 'She is probably not into contact', he thought to himself. Well, if that was so, he would not intrude into her world. He did not want to try to wring responses from her only because he wanted them, and he realized that if she was not interested, she would not even let him do so. No, he would be patient and wait for a special hint from her.

Tom did not feel at peace with his reasoning. The tank could not be that interesting. She was not tired, otherwise she could have chosen to rest. What was on her mind? Tom had read about the orcas living in pods and he wondered if these intelligent creatures had some kind of imagination: could this young orca think of her family in a more tangible way than just some indefinable feeling of loss? Dolphins had moods, this whale seemed to be no different. Would depression have dulled her curiosity? Then Tom suddenly realized that the young orca probably did not associate him with the events of the previous night. How could she? He realized orcas were a highly acoustic species, but visually, he had not been more than a black shadow. He had not yet identified himself for her by making any of the sounds of the night before. 'I will make one call to her,' he decided. 'When she comes up...'

"Eeeuup," Tom called softly as he heard the orca blow. Her response left him in no doubt. She was clearly startled by the sound and threw her head up a little to see where it came from. Tom watched and felt goose bumps rise as the orca popped up in front of him. There she lay, waiting for him as if wanting a confirmation. He made another soft cry, and with her answer the special connection had returned. Tuschka had turned sideways to parallel him and he saw how she tilted sideways to look at him. Tom walked along the railing towards the gate that separated the holding tank from the performance pool. There, the lighting would be much better for the orca to see him. When he climbed over the railing, he saw the whale slowly heading towards him. Carefully, Tom sat down. He watched the orca, now drifting still nearer, inch by inch. Then, when she was only three feet away from him, she rose in a small spyhop. He felt a wave of excitement as he could see her small dark eyes looking at him. A soft plaintive cry escaped from her blowhole. Tom bent over and returned his best imitation of her cry. By copying her sounds, he tried to make her understand that he wanted to share what she felt.

Tuschka inched closer, taking him in. The man was a strange creature with a slender dark body in an odd folded pose. She quickly found his eyes in a light colored, mainly smooth head with a patch of fur on the top and sides. He looked like the men working with her during the day, but his voice and behavior were very different. Now, she took in the details of his appearance. It was natural for her to pick up subtle differences. Although she knew her family members best by their voice, she did not have the slightest problem in identifying them by eye if they were within visual range.

154

Over the last few days, Tuschka's diversion had come only from men. The dolphins she often heard had never come in sight. This man intrigued her, even though he had no fish. He was the only one of his kind who had made sounds with some remote resemblance to her own. She felt that he wanted to communicate with her. Somehow he radiated some comfort.

Tom lay on his belly and looked at her. She was so calm and so patient. What would she want him to do? How could he keep her interested? Dolphins liked to be touched and rubbed once they became accustomed to people. This orca was just beginning to learn about man. The young trainer lowered his hand into the water and saw the young whale sink a little to take a look. He waited for her to regain her confidence and spoke softly to encourage her. He also made soft shallow imitations of the juvenile orca's blows. The whale rose again and surprised him when she suddenly made a gurgling sound with her blowhole. He saw a few tiny bubbles appear with the sounds. Tom tried to copy the sound, but it was not easy. The orca came a bit closer and repeated the sound as if to teach him. The young man squeezed air between his lips, compressed his cheeks and made all kinds of grimaces in his attempt to imitate her, but none of his tries was very good. He smiled at the orca, which was still watching him. She made another, more melodious, call, which was easier for Tom to copy. Then, she did the bubbling version again. Tom felt that the young orca was playing with him, challenging his vocal skills. The imitations contained no words. Yet there was no question that they were communicating. The sounds conveyed mutual acknowledgement and were full of the desire to interact, to learn, and to explore the other's alien mind.

Tom pulled his hand up and rested it on the water, making very small subtle movements to catch her attention. His desire to touch the orca burned inside him. She was only a foot away from him, but he was determined to let her take the initiative; he did not want to abuse her trust and take her by surprise. Tom tried the bubble sound again, but he laughed at his own attempt. Yet it struck him when she repeated his version of it. She had understood what he meant! "You' re already playing games with me, smart girl. You'll soon find out how clumsy I am, not only with my voice," Tom said softly. "But I'll try to think of games and other things to fuel your curiosity."

Without any correction by her family, Tuschka's interest and longing for contact began to overcome her natural apprehension. She saw the tiny fingers of his hand move in front of her and heard his gentle voice. She too felt a growing desire to make physical contact, but what would it be like with a creature so different? She inched forward.

Tom saw her approach and made a soft cry to encourage her. "Yes, you can trust me. I won't do you any harm." Only a few inches separated them. His eyes were glued to her rostrum and he held his breath without knowing it. Tuschka blew as if to draw final courage. He saw the tip of her rostrum glide under his hand, but did not yet feel contact. He concentrated and waited. Then he felt a touch, light and brief. Had it really been the whale? He felt his heart beat in his chest. His fingers were almost too cold for subtle feeling. He suddenly was aware of his need for air and drew another breath, trying not to move too much. Then, unmistakably, the young orca touched his hand. This time it was a little longer. When he moved a finger to feel her skin, she sank down a bit.

Suppressing his excitement, Tom stayed calm and did not make any unexpected movements. A sense of trust was awakening in the young orca. He saw her tilt her head a little upwards, then felt her gentle nudge. He felt the orca's round rostrum fill the palm of his hand and lift it up. He saw her rise and tears welled up when their eyes met. Trembling with emotion, the young man moved his fingers over her soft velvety skin. She pressed a little more and vocalized softly. Tom tried to return the call, which conveyed so much affection, but his voice stuck in his throat. Her gentle movement betrayed the supreme mastery of her great strength, and engendered in him a feeling of complete trust. Totally engrossed in the moment, they sat there. Tom gently caressed the whale's smooth rostrum. It meant as much to the orca as to the man. Finally, someone cared for her and gave her warmth. Both felt the moment to be an expression of their mutual trust and the start of a friendship that would deepen in time.

Tom finally sat up, looking at the beautiful gentle creature in front of him. Much of the night had gone by and he regretted the prospect of leaving. As he walked along the railing, he saw that the orca followed him, tilted a little to one side to look at him. Her attachment moved him and he found it difficult to walk away from her. He climbed back over the railing and leaned on it while he watched her. After a little while, Tuschka dived and started to swim.

Tom was completely lost in thought when the voice of the guard startled him. "Getting sleepy eh?," he asked. "I don't blame you. By the time I get used to my nightshift, it's over." Tom nodded, a little absentmindedly. He was not in the mood to talk. He just wanted to spend his last hour in tranquility with the orca. The guard sensed that the trainer's mind was elsewhere. Tom did not even notice him leave.

The experience with the orca had touched Tom deeply. He had not had fish to reward her or to attract her attention. She had come to him of her own free will. The little he could offer, his attention and his touch, were clearly important to her. It was obvious there was much more to the orca's natural life than the search for food. That in itself was not surprising for a large dolphin. Nevertheless, it intrigued him why his experience had been so unique. From the first day of his job, he had seen his fellow trainers work with the dolphins. Although exciting, it had seemed so natural to touch and reward them, and to

156

teach them new behaviors. He had quickly taken it for granted that they paid attention to him, albeit not always in ways he wanted. Tom had heard about the gentle nature of other captive orcas, but only now did that knowledge truly come alive for him. Had it been the same when the dolphins arrived? Had his colleagues had similar experiences? Tom realized he had been using man-taught signals from the start. His special time with the orca had been so pure. Her responses had not yet been shaped by man. She had acted upon her natural impulses. That was why she had touched him so much.

When he walked back to his chair for a final recording of her breathing rate, he heard her call behind his back. He turned around and answered it. The orca hovered in front of him and he felt she wanted him to stay near. A few seconds later, lights were turned on and Jeff walked in. "What was that sound? Did the whale make that?" Tom flushed and looked down. He saw the orca dive and swim away. The contact was broken. "Yes," he responded, "she made those sounds."

* * *

A high-pitched sound startled Tuschka as her trainer touched her rostrum. She had heard similar sounds many times over the last few days, albeit from a distance. She inched closer to the man and wondered how he had made the sound. He touched her again, and again there was the sound, together with a fish. Tuschka remained close, watching him. She saw a tiny shaft fall out of his mouth and dangle beneath his head. He kept holding his hand above her. Tuschka rose up slightly, but had no intention to touch his hand. She just wanted to hear that intriguing whistle again. Moments passed. When it did not come, she turned and swam off.

Jeff came in and saw the orca dive. "What was she interested in?," he asked his supervisor. "I blew the whistle twice after I had touched her rostrum. It immediately made her curious and she sat here in front of me for a while, probably hoping to hear it again." The two men watched the orca swim several circles. She had not yet had her ration for that moment. Richard motioned Jeff to sit down and made a warning sign with his index finger to alert him. He tapped the water and waited.

The orca slowed down in her approach. The two men saw her hesitate and then rise to break the surface in front of them. Richard looked her in the eye while he tested her patience. When she patiently waited for a few seconds and let him touch her, he blew the whistle and almost yelled his excitement: "It worked Jeff! Did you see that..? She responded to the tap without seeing the fish first. This is a good start." He quickly grabbed a handful of fish and fed it straight into the orca's open mouth. "Good girl," he said looking her into the eye, "that's just what we wanted you to do!"

Tuschka had experienced small changes every day. Yet there was some pattern to it. They would challenge her in slightly different ways to get a fish and then reward her by throwing several into her mouth or into the water. The inability to take initiative in finding food had unsettled the Tuschka in the first few days, but since she had accepted the dead fish, she had not gone hungry. Yet without companions and the need to hunt, she could do little more than resting and 'traveling' in a very small space. The attention of the people and their little surprises were becoming welcome diversions.

* * *

It was still winter break in the park, and lately, Richard had not been training the dolphins in the performance pool. He had not wanted to expose the orca to too many changes at once, and he also thought it more relaxing for the dolphins to let them get used to the orca's sounds. Richard had mounted a hydrophone in the performance tank to monitor any acoustic activity of the two species. A speaker transmitted the sounds continuously and, if desired, a recorder could be switched on. In the beginning, the buzz of the circulation pump had irritated the employees, but they quickly got used to it.

The trainers had been listening with interest when they heard the orca make her first calls. The dolphins had immediately ceased their conversation. For several days, the orca's sounds had been unsettling for them. Gradually, the orca responded less to the dolphins' voices. It seemed she had become used to hearing her smaller relatives. Yet there was no doubt how the dolphins felt towards the orca. Richard hoped they would eventually trust the whale and become companions for her. Today, he decided to open their gate to the performance tank. That would permit the dolphins to retreat if the sight of the orca were too unsettling. He hoped, however, that the dolphins would realize the orca could not pass through a closed gate.

When Richard and Jeff approached the enclosure, the dolphins greeted them enthusiastically. The system's speaker did not transmit any sound from the orca. As the dolphins heard the hydraulics of the gate, they jostled in front of it. They were six in total: five females and one male, who was the dominant animal in the group. His name was Flash. When the gate was halfway open, the male was the first to slip through, immediately followed by two of the females. The remaining three had just passed the gate when a sharp warning call pierced their ears, almost immediately followed by the ominous voice of an orca. The three scouts doubled back and almost ran into the startled females. The six dolphins huddled together in their own enclosure, as far as possible from the gate. Jeff walked over and asked them to perform a few behaviors to distract them, but they did not respond. He threw them a few fish and motioned them to follow him. The females looked from the trainer to their leader and back.

The male dolphin and one of the females had been there for nearly 10 years. Flash knew every detail of all the tanks and he had known many trainers, but never had he been confronted with an orca. The dolphin hesitated. Jeff understood his favorite's feelings. 'What would win?,' the trainer wondered: 'his fear of the orca or his trust in me?' He knelt down near the tank and was grateful that Flash let himself be touched. In fact, the animal drew the courage from it to overcome his fear. Jeff got up and beckoned him to follow. Slowly, the male dolphin started moving and kept going with the man as he approached the gate. Two females followed close behind. Richard was standing on the main platform watching the behavior of both the orca and the dolphins.

Jeff knelt down beside the gate at the edge of the performance pool and tapped the water gently. Flash warily poked his rostrum past the gate and stopped. He seemed to be persuading himself that there was no orca in the tank. Both Richard and Jeff were a little tense. One call from the orca would definitely spook the male dolphin. The sight of her had frightened him already. Too many fearful experiences would discourage Flash and cause delay. Neither trainer wanted to think about the shows they would have to start within two months.

Jeff walked over to Richard. "He is still wary," Richard concluded before Jeff had said anything. "I'm happy that the orca doesn't vocalize much," Jeff said. "That would've been far more frightening. I think we should leave them for a while. What do you think, shall we keep the gate open?" "Sure," Richard responded. "They'll find out that the orca can't get to them, which should soon give them renewed courage to venture into the main pool." Both men looked at the dolphins, who had all retreated in the holding tank, away from the gate. "Poor guys," Jeff said. "They don't look very happy with that open gate." Richard shrugged his shoulders and nodded. "They'll soon relax."

The two men both had the feeling that getting the dolphins to trust an orca behind the gate was a first step. Their playing together seemed in the remote future. They wondered if the dolphins' fear was pure instinct or based on experiences before they had been taken from the wild. It had been tempting for a moment to close the gate when the three dolphins were in the performance pool, but Jeff knew that such an act would have done more harm than good. The dolphins probably would have learned sooner that the orca behind the other gate posed no threat, but they would have lost much confidence in him as their trainer. It would have meant a setback that would be hard to restore. By leaving the gate open, they had left the dolphins at least the option to retreat.

The other gate in the dolphins' holding tank led to a wide canal that connected with the tank where the orca was kept. The view from that gate had been blocked by a screen shortly before the orca arrived. The trainers had felt that hearing the orca's sounds would not be as frightening for the dolphins as seeing her. Richard and Jeff had discussed two options to acquaint the dolphins with the orca. One was to let them get used to seeing the orca when she came to the gate at the other end of the canal. The other was to give them access to the main pool. Both had chosen the second option. If the sight of the orca behind the gate were very frightening, the dolphins would at least have a retreat from the predator's eyes. With luck, the dolphins would soon realize that the orca could not enter the main pool and pursue them.

In the afternoon, Bob and the trainers called a short meeting. Bob was the research biologist and curator of the park. He did not train the animals, but he did interact with them for research purposes. Bob was especially interested in his animals' cognitive capabilities. He also liked to interact with them for fun and to challenge their creativity.

They discussed the plans and schedules for the upcoming month. There was concern about the start of the season, with the dolphins so reluctant to enter the main pool. "We'll just do the show with the orca," Jeff was joking. "She's fascinated by the whistle!" "Well," Richard said, "that idea isn't so far-fetched. People will certainly find it fascinating to see a Killer Whale. We can explain the response of the dolphins and show how we work with the whale. But we would have to continue such training sessions until we have taught her to change tanks. When she has experienced the extra room, she may not be too eager to go back to the holding tank."

The younger trainers looked at the curator for comment. He did not reject the idea. A thoughtful look betrayed his serious consideration. Then he spoke. "I've talked to the director; we need a name for the whale. We've talked about a public contest, but I don't think that would be appropriate. People in our country don't have as much affinity with orcas as they have elsewhere. Putting it off until after the park's opening, we would have to display, or even train, an animal without a name. The trainers nodded. "I've been thinking about a small contest among the park's employees. We'll think of a suitable reward." The ensuing silence was remarkable. It seemed as if everyone was suddenly trying to think of an appropriate name. Several names passed through each man's mind. Most were immediately rejected while others received some thought. A smile on Jeff's face told the others that he probably had found a name that pleased him. Each of them wondered what names their colleagues would suggest, but they all kept their thoughts to themselves.

15.
A Shy Acquaintance

Tom dreaded the end of his night watch as this would be his last night for a while. He was looking forward to being with the orca again. The young man had the feeling that the orca had come to expect him at night. The previous night, she had come to him when he had approached the railing. She had spyhopped in front of him and greeted him with a call. It had touched him deeply. They had spent a long time together near the gate and she had called to him when he had to leave. That had been a hard moment. Tom had wanted to respond to her, but that would have elicited many questions and rumors among his colleagues. He was not ready for that yet. He felt he would be too emotional about it. For one more night, he wanted to enjoy his secret, dawning friendship with the orca.

The dome was silent when Tom entered. He closed the door quietly and stayed where he was, listening. Poooooh... The orca's strong blow was not only audible, but also visible as a plume of vapor in the cold air. He walked slowly towards his chair, but before he reached it, she spotted him.

The sound of his footsteps had alerted her. She had been expecting him. She had been pacing around, waiting for the arrival of her friendly nocturnal companion. She had been aware of him since that night when he had come to her with his peculiar call. He had been comforting by alleviating her utter loneliness, especially during the first few nights. Tuschka came over without hesitation and spyhopped to take a good look at him.

Tom immediately put down his note pad and came towards her. Her familiar call welcomed him and the confidence in the young orca's voice warmed him. Tom jumped over the railing and bent over the edge of the tank. The orca did not hesitate. Gently, she came close and rose up to touch his hand. As his fingers felt the smooth rostrum of his precious orca, he made a soft call to her. She copied it with stunning perfection. Tom was overjoyed with the prompt and enthusiastic reception by the young whale. The night had barely begun and they had already made contact. The orca nudged his hand and pushed up a little higher. Tom looked her in the eye and caressed her gently. He felt she was enjoying his attention. Playfully, she began to blow little bubbles and turned sideways.

As the orca sank down, he let his hand rest on the water. He saw her make a miniature circle and rise to the surface again. She popped up, just a few feet away, arched high and ran her sleek body against his hand. Tom was amazed. He wondered if she would repeat her behavior and he let his hand rest on the surface. Within seconds, she came round and slid by his hand in another graceful arch. Tom was impressed by the subtlety of her movement: her perfect bow had barely lifted his hand as she glided against it. Only a moment before he would touch her tail flukes, the orca lost contact with him. Tom realized how well the orca knew where his hand was and how much control she had over her movements. He was familiar with such behavior in dolphins, but orcas were much larger and more ferocious predators. Apparently, this master of the sea had not traded subtlety for size and power.

He looked up, realizing that the gate between the holding tank with the dolphins and the main pool was open. The dolphins were near their gate, only venturing into the main pool for a few seconds at a time. Their behavior told Tom they were torn between fear and curiosity. Only a few faint calls were audible over the hydrophone. The orca was silent. Tom walked over to the gate between the holding pool of the orca and the main tank. It had become his favorite spot for interaction with the young whale. The wall was wide and long enough for him to sit comfortably or stretch out, and the lighting was good for them both to see each other. She found him unerringly. Effortlessly she ran her body along his outstretched hand and surprised him even more with a playful squeak.

The dolphins spotted the man as he made himself comfortable near the gate. Although Tom had not worked much with Flash, the male dolphin did know him. His presence was an encouragement for the curious male to venture into the main pool. Creeping closer, Flash noticed the man was interacting with somebody in the other holding tank. One of the females had followed his lead, albeit with hesitation. When she voiced her apprehension, Flash called back to encourage her to stay with him.

As Tom was watching the movements of the orca, the sound of a dolphin blow behind his back suddenly surprised him. The young trainer recognized Flash in the dim light by his characteristic dorsal fin. There was a distinctive notch near its base. Tom had heard from his colleagues how much the sound and sight of the orca still frightened the dolphins. Recently, the orca seldom reacted to their sounds, but seeing the dolphins would definitely be exciting for her. The orca was just beside the gate and still not visible for the dolphin when Tom suddenly got an idea. He jumped up and quickly moved a little away from the gate. He hoped his movement would attract the orca's attention. He lightly tapped the water and watched the black shadow come towards him. He hoped his signal would make her stop in front of him. He quickly glanced over his shoulder and was relieved that Flash and the female were still there. They were close to the wall, almost opposite the gate.

Poooooh, the orca blew as she broke the surface in front of Tom. He was excited that the beautiful animal did exactly what he had been hoping for. He bent over and held his hand out to her. Now that she had begun to trust him, she also had come to appreciate his touch. As Tom gently rubbed her, he took another quick glance at the dolphins. They were still there. Tom did not look at them for very long. He did not want the orca to get the feeling that she had only part of his attention. He moved a little closer to the gate, and kept looking at her as she followed. The young man scooped up some water and splashed her a little. He sensed the wonder in her eyes. "You're a good girl," Tom said in a soft voice. "If you stay with me, the dolphins will get used to you more easily." He gave her another small splash. The orca sank down a little and took Tom by surprise when she sprayed him and squeaked at him at the same time. 'She learns so fast,' he thought. 'She picks up new things so quickly'.

The splashing had come as a playful surprise to Tuschka. She saw her companion move towards the gate and followed, still playing her splashing game with him. Then, she suddenly heard a dolphin call. It was not the sound that surprised her, but the short distance from which it came. She listened and heard another call. It was tempting for Tuschka to call back, but she remained silent. Too often had she experienced a negative response. The water was too dark for her to see the dolphin. She echolocated....

Flash flinched as the vibrations of the orca's sonar clicks reached him. The quality of the sonar differed from that of his own kind. He had heard it before, but this time he had been detected. He was not certain what creature had detected him, but he had not yet forgotten the sound of the orca and the glimpse of her black body. He dared not investigate the source of the sound. The sonar pulses had sent a chill down his spine and he quickly made for his familiar tank.

Sitting near the gate, Tom had seen the orca sink down, quickly followed by Flash's dash for the holding tank. Had the orca called to him? Immediately, Tom realized the speaker had not transmitted a clear call. He wondered whether the light penetrated the water enough for the dolphin to see the orca. Then he realized the two might have been echolocating. Tom had been so absorbed by the splashing game that many sounds over the speaker had escaped his attention, especially those that were common and not very loud.

Tuschka was disappointed. She wanted so much to make contact, but everything she did frightened the dolphins. She turned her attention back to the man. She looked at him and came closer. His odd appearance had become familiar to her and his presence was comforting. Yet, he was a creature of the land. Within her watery domain, she was still alone. Tuschka rose up to be touched by him and called softly. His rubs and caresses partly filled the emptiness inside her, which had flared up with the dolphins' evasive response.

Tom was lying on his belly as he gently stroked the orca. She made a few soft moaning sounds and he felt the sudden change in her mood. Something had made her sad. Less than half a minute ago she had playfully splashed him. It was obvious that the change was related to the event with the dolphins. How wonderful it would be if they could play together, he thought. The fact that it was his last night with her saddened him. He caressed her tenderly and as their eyes met, he felt a longing that he could not satisfy. "How happy I'd be if they would play with you," he said. "Who'll keep you company in the nights to come? I hate to leave you with long lonely nights. I guess I'll have to share our secret with others in hopes that they'll understand and become friends for you too."

Tom had not spoken about his precious moments with the orca, afraid that the head trainer would not approve and would put someone else on watch. That would have been hard not only on him, but even more on the whale, which had been craving for contact. She had left no doubt how much his company meant to her. If he was not to continue, however, someone had to take over from him. It would be heartless to keep it to himself and let her suffer. He tapped the orca gently and sat upright to look at the dolphins. "Perhaps, I can encourage them a little," he said, looking at the orca in front of him.

Tom walked over the gate to the main platform and tapped the water to call the dolphins over. He suddenly realized he had no fish to reward them and wondered if a rub-down would keep them interested. Tom saw the dolphins look at him. He gave them a cue to present at the main platform. It seemed to confuse the dolphins. They had never had training sessions at night.

Flash was wary, and his companions felt it. Yet, whatever it was that had echolocated on him, it had not come after him. He had acted upon his impulses each time he had picked up signs of an orca nearby. But all the rest of the day, until now, that orca had not followed him.

Slowly, it began to dawn on Flash that the danger he feared was not in the main tank, could not get to him. Flash looked at the man, who was still waiting for him to come. Two of the younger dolphins, with which Tom had worked most, had become impatient with their leader. Flash's fearful reactions and sounds had put them on guard initially, but when nothing actually happened, they began to take him less serious. The two young females, Sasha and Lucie, moved towards the gate. Flash quickly blocked their way, but he radiated little confidence. After several seconds, the two tried to go beneath him. This time, Flash let them go and followed them towards the trainer on the platform.

"Great girls, you two," Tom said, in a voice that conveyed his excitement. He bent over to give them several friendly taps as a reward. He regretted that he was not dressed in his wetsuit, otherwise he would have entered the water with the dolphins to convince them there was nothing to fear. He got up and walked closer towards the orca's gate and motioned the dolphins to follow him. Sasha and Lucie showed no fear. Tom hoped they would not be as frightened of the orca as Flash. After another rub-down, Tom knelt down right by the gate and bent over to look for the orca. The whale was down, facing the gate, but not making any sound. 'Wow,' he thought to himself, 'such a young orca and already so much bigger than Lucie and Sasha!' He bent over to lower his hand into the water and moved his fingers gently. The orca noticed it immediately and came up. She greeted him with a soft call. Tom caressed her and started to talk to the orca, hoping his behavior would both interest and reassure the two dolphins. He was full of hope when he noticed that Sasha and Lucie were still close.

Sasha was the first to approach the gate. Lucie was only half her body length behind. Flash was near the middle of the main platform. In the faint light, the two females quickly recognized large pectoral flippers and a pronounced dorsal fin. Backlit as it was, the two young dolphins could not see the striking black and white markings. To them, the animal looked like a huge dolphin, far bigger than their dominant male. Sasha echolocated. It confirmed what she had seen, but within seconds, the dark shape moved down to face them through the gate.

While the man was caressing her and talking to her, Tuschka had not noticed the dolphins' silent approach at the other side of the gate. The vibrating sensation of the dolphin's sonar took her by surprise. She sank down, looking through the gate to see who had been echolocating on her. She felt her heart beat faster as she saw two small dolphins in front of her. In the poor light, she saw their slender gray bodies. A call almost escaped Tuschka, but she kept silent and motionless. She was too afraid to scare them off.

Sasha and Lucie surfaced and looked at their trainer, who was kneeling right beside the gate. Tom beckoned them, but they were just out of reach. He did not want to tap the water and distract the orca. There was silence over the speaker and he felt a mixture of amazement and joy that the orca had not vocalized. Pooooh, the orca surfaced. She was still facing the gate. Tom bent way over and managed to stroke the young whale lightly. "Come, Sasha and Lucie. This is a new friend for you. She's big, but very gentle. You see how nice she is?" Flash had approached too when his curious companions did not retreat with fear. He kept silent, but took in the large shape on the other side of the gate. Taking his time he assured himself that the whale was behind the gate. More experienced, the male dolphin knew what creature it was. He too saw how their trainer rubbed the orca's back. The man's relaxed confidence allayed his tension a little.

Sasha came closer and made a soft tentative call. Tuschka felt an urge to answer it, but she remained silent. Tom listened with full concentration. Sasha made another soft call. Just over a second passed, then Tuschka answered. Her answer had a lower pitch, and was a little hesitant, but she had tried hard to mimic the dolphin's call. Perhaps that would frighten it less. Sasha backed off, but only a little. The sound had a strange quality, but it was obvious that the big creature had responded to her. To encourage the conversation, Tom gave his version of the call, which was much lower in pitch. Tuschka held her breath as she saw the dolphin back away, but was relieved when it stayed. She was full of restrained excitement, careful not to make a move or sound that would scare the dolphin and yet wanting to encourage its hesitant advances.

Tom watched it with wonder. In his perception, the orca's call was remarkably similar. If it had not been for the bubbles escaping the orca's blowhole, he would have been confused. He was overjoyed. This was a beginning! They were making their first contact on his last night. He could not tell what would have happened had he not been there, but he could not escape the strong impression that he had served as a catalyst. It made him feel a lot better, knowing that the next steps would be easier for the dolphins to take.

Tom had noticed Flash right behind the two young females. That was promising. He had not taken the initiative, but had not interfered either. If much of his fear were taken away, the other dolphins would soon follow. Tom was convinced there would be more inquisitive excursions towards the orca during the day. If his hopes would come true, his befriended whale would already enjoy some diversion by the dolphins during the next night.

Tom's knees felt stiff and ached a little as he got to his feet. He tip-toed over the gate and stopped near the fence for the public. He saw the orca and the dolphins watching him, but they did not follow him. The whale was in a spyhop position and he had the feeling she was torn between staying with the dolphins and coming over to him. He waited a few seconds. "I'm not leaving yet," he said to the orca, before he jumped over the fence to get his note pad. Tom realized Richard would ask him what he had been doing all that time without taking any notes, but he felt the breakthrough with the dolphins would amply make up for that. He quickly started writing a summary of what had happened so far.

A call from the orca interrupted him. As he looked up, he saw her with her head resting on the edge of the pool. She had come as close to him as she could get. He felt a lump in his throat, realizing that she did not want him to leave. It touched him deeply that she cared so much for him, but at the same time it troubled him that he had built this relationship with her and then had to leave.

There was not much time left. He quietly climbed over the fence and knelt down in front of her. He took her head in both hands, caressing her gently. Then he bent over to her and whispered: "my beautiful, dearest orca, you have become such a precious friend. If it depended on me, I wouldn't leave you for the nights to come. I'll be around and you'll see me, but I won't be as free to play with you. I wish you could understand. I can only hope we will soon be together again."

Tuschka sensed his mood. She sensed his mixture of sadness and affection. She felt a foreboding of something sad, something that weighed heavily on the man's mind. Not knowing what it was that troubled him, she felt an urge to be

166

close to him. Deep inside she feared another separation, a parting of the ways. Tuschka rose up higher, closer to the man, calling to him with a soft whine.

At that same moment, Tom realized the orca felt as he did. She shared his thoughts and fears. He bent over until his face touched hers. He held her tight and rubbed his cheek against her smooth round rostrum. The tears that stung behind his eyes, burst loose, rolling down over the orca's sleek skin. For a little while, Tom pressed her close. Then a name came to his mind: "I don't know what name they'll give you," he said, "but for me you'll be Gunda, because you're a princess that moves with the grace of a wave."

Regaining his composure, he released his grip and gave her a few gentle taps. "Why am I so sad?," he said to her. "I'm behaving as if I'll never see you again. It may take longer than we both want, but I'll be working with you and once I train you, I'll also play with you." Tuschka felt the change in his mood. It was obvious he had resolved something that concerned them both. Feeling lighter as well, she gave a short, high-pitched call and made an energetic dive. She started circling and threw her head up each time she surfaced, as she would on the high seas: not because she had to contend with breaking waves, but to keep eye contact with the man she had come to respect and love.

Tom saw that the dolphins were milling around in the main tank. They were four in total and it made him feel good to see that they were much more comfortable in the main pool.

Tom heard the door open and looked up to see the guard come in. He was happy that he had had his special moment with the orca. Tom pointed at the main tank. The guard squinted to see what the young trainer meant. When two dolphins came up for air, he nodded with a smile. He too had not seen the gate open since the day before the orca had arrived. The young whale was circling, but she slowed down a bit when she passed the gate, turning her head sideways to peek into the main pool.

The speaker was silent. The light of the new day would soon reveal what the night had been hiding. Tom was happy to see the orca's interest. It had been a very special night. What more could he have wished? He was confident that the curious and gentle orca would foster her contact with the dolphins. Whatever effort the trainers might make to acquaint the dolphins with the orca, with her size and power, she was in control. Only Gunda herself would be able to make them trust her and feel comfortable in her presence. And this night, she had started to do just that.

Tom had left his sparse notes on the table of the trainer's lounge, before taking a long hot shower. He hoped Richard would come in at his regular time to hear his story. He did not want the head trainer to get it from hearsay. If Richard had questions, Tom wanted to be there to answer them and not have his colleagues make speculations.

He gave a sigh of relief when he heard the head trainer's familiar dark voice. "Where's Tom? .. Oh, I see, he left his notes here," he said to the guard, who was sipping some hot coffee. While he picked up the notepad, he murmured to himself. "Unusual for him to leave befo... What!?" Richard's eyes flew over the lines, quickly taking in the essence of the report. As he put it back on the table, he saw a grin on the guard's face. Without asking a question, he turned around and rushed towards the performance area. He stopped in amazement as he saw dolphins surface near the gate of the orca holding tank. He tip-toed closer, so as not to disturb the dolphins in their behavior. There were several soft squeaks over the speaker. He felt a wave of excitement when the orca popped up for a breath, right by the gate. He listened to the sounds. They were not all the same. Some were somewhat lower in pitch and a bit more melodious. 'That must be the orca,' he figured, still amazed at the resemblance to the dolphin calls. He watched for a few minutes, before returning to the trainers' lounge. "Tom?," he yelled as he heard a shower stop. "I'm coming Richard, just a few minutes."

The guard had left and Tom was happy that he had Richard's undivided attention. He began his story by describing the frightened reaction of the male and how Sasha and Lucie had responded to him. "....... I think it must have been encouraging for them to see me touch the orca." Richard's eyes were wide open with surprise. "Touch the orca? It seems you expected her to accept it." Tom understood the head trainer's question. He had indeed expected it, but he felt much more comfortable answering it now that it had proven useful with the dolphins. "That first night, she made a whining sound. She was hovering near the gate towards the corridor. I got up to see if something was wrong, but her breathing seemed normal. She continued that sound and somehow I had the feeling she was crying. It conveyed such a sorrowful and lonely mood. I figured she needed some diversion. So I went over to her and tried to imitate her sounds. Her response was unbelievable. I wasn't very good at copying her, but she was excellent at copying me. It was the orca imitating me that gave me the feeling of contact. That's how it all started. She liked the acoustic contact and the next night, she let me touch her. She has greeted me since on every night watch."

The head trainer looked at him with a questioning frown. Tom heaved a sigh, because he felt that squeaking was one thing, but touching without permission.... "After Gunda ha.." "Gunda?," Richard asked. Tom flushed. The word had slipped from his mouth involuntarily. "Uhh, well.., let me explain. I'd come to understand how much it means for her to have company and I dreaded the end of my night watch. Somehow, she seemed to pick up on my sadness too. She came very close and when I stretched out my hand, she rose up and touched me. I was so touched by her taking the initiative, and it was then that the name Gunda came to my mind. It just fitted her so well."

Richard saw Tom looking down. He understood that the young trainer was trying to hide his emotions. In a flash, he recalled how excited he had been when a dolphin had come to him spontaneously. He was happy too that no other trainer had heard the conversation. Officially, Tom had gone beyond his limits. Yet it was so understandable. With only he and Tom sharing the story, he had the freedom to respond more mildly. He tapped him gently on the shoulder. "Come to my office, he said quietly." Tom saw Richard take the notepad with him, and followed his supervisor. What did he have on his mind? Tom had sensed some understanding, but at the same time he realized that, for the sake of safety and discipline, Richard could not allow much liberty.

The two men sat down. Richard was visibly thinking. He stared at his folded hands in front of him. After a long silence he asked: "did you ever give fish to the orca?" "Oh, no," Tom denied convincingly, "it was all spontaneous behavior. I know I'm not supposed to touch her, but.. I couldn't resist finding out if she wanted it when she drew so close. Later, I was happy that I could use it with the dolphins." Richard nodded. "I'm happy that you did nothing that resembled a training session. I understand that a spontaneous friendship developed between you and the whale." Tom nodded to confirm his head trainer's conclusion. "Normally, one can't forbid someone to befriend an animal, but in case of powerful predators, there are rules for the sake of safety." Tom remained silent. There was nothing he could say against it. "In your case, all went well. Personally, I must admit that what happened between you and the whale is beautiful and I think it was good for the orca as well. Apparently, you have a natural gift of making contact and interacting with her. I'm happy to know this. It's very valuable to have a trainer with such qualities." Tom perked up at Richard's comment.

As his supervisor went on, Tom was both relieved and disappointed at the same time. Fortunately, his violation of the rules had not blurred Richard's realization of the benefits of his relationship with the orca. The head trainer had even expressed his intention to involve him in the orca's training program as soon as possible. But at the same time, Richard had emphasized that for the time being he would only be allowed to interact with the orca under supervision. Overall, it was better than Tom had expected, but one fear remained: if he was not expected to interact with the orca unsupervised, he hoped he would not have to be alone with her. How could he face Gunda and not respond to her? How could he behave so cold and distant? She would never understand. Tom had not dared to ask Richard openly. He could only hope the head trainer would not put him in such an awkward position.

16.
Learning to Perform

In the weeks that followed, Tom worked only with the dolphins. They had become so accustomed to the orca's presence that Tom and his colleagues were preparing for doing shows again. Now, the main obstacle proved to be distraction. Before the orca had arrived, the dolphins were competing for the trainer's attention most of the time. Now, the younger and more playful dolphins had become less patient waiting near the stage. When not given immediate attention, they would go off to interact vocally with the orca. Richard had taken away the screen that had been blocking the view between the holding tank of the dolphins and that of the orca. Richard hoped the dolphins would be less distracted by the orca if they could see her more often during their time in the holding tank.

The performance of the dolphins had stabilized and the preparations for the upcoming season were virtually completed when Richard decided to involve Tom in the orca's training program. Since his night watch, Tom had stayed away from the orca as much as possible and had avoided looking at her. He did not know whether the whale recognized him. He only knew she had not vocalized towards him as she had done during his night watches. He hoped that the time of day, his different clothing, and his ignorant attitude, had kept her from associating him with the person she had come to know during night time. He had been wondering how the orca had felt during the nights after he had left. Tom did not want to think of the possibility that the whale had recognized him, but had lost her interest in him because he had disappointed her.

Tom had been reading the notes that Jeff had written down during his night watch. There was no mention of any vocal or physical contact between Jeff and the whale, but Tom had not written down his interactions either. He was happy, though, that the orca and the dolphins had shown much interest in each other. He hoped she had not missed him that much.

Tuschka had been quick to notice that her night companion had not returned. The first night after Tom left she had come over to the man entering the dome. She had expected to see her friend, but she had immediately noticed the difference in appearance and behavior of the man. She had waited briefly near the fence, and watched him closely. Feeling no recognition, she had turned away and started swimming again. That night, she had listened keenly to every sound near the tank, hoping to see her friend, but he had not come. Tuschka had missed him, but the dolphins on the other side of the gate had prevented her from dwelling too much on her sadness. The remaining females had finally overcome their apprehension. Six dolphins were so new and distracting to Tuschka that she had spent much of her time watching them and talking to them through the gate.

In the nights that followed, Tuschka soon learned that the presence of her human friend was not to be taken for granted. Her expectations of seeing him gradually dwindled. There were moments when she longed for his warmth and gentle touch, but in his absence, she focused her attention more and more on the dolphins. It was a meager surrogate for the void that only her family could truly fill.

* * *

Tom followed Richard towards the main platform. He felt his heart beating as he saw the beautiful animal spyhop to watch them approach. She waited a few seconds before sinking down and resuming swimming rounds. "Well," Richard said, looking at Tom. "Would she remember you?" Tom flushed. He had been avoiding contact with the orca for several weeks, because he was not supposed to interact with her. Now, he was afraid that if the orca was not going to respond, the head trainer would be disappointed. Tom cleared his throat. "It's been a while since my last night watch, but perhaps she'll recognize my voice." "Go ahead," Richard encouraged him. "Do what you feel like." Tom hunkered down near the edge of the platform and cleared his throat again. He was tense and hoped to produce an acceptable call. As the orca surfaced, he called to her, trying to sound as he had done during his night watch. The orca was clearly startled. She did not dive, but spyhopped instead and looked at him.

The two men watched her intently. They did not yet know if the orca had recognized Tom's call as the voice of the man who had talked to her and played with her. Even less were they aware of Tuschka's heart beating fast.

Tom beckoned to her and repeated his call. All doubt was gone when the orca darted over to him without hesitation. A turmoil of emotions overwhelmed Tom as the orca broke the surface in front of him. He was filled with happiness that she had recognized him, but at the same time he felt embarrassed with the situation. How could he acknowledge her when he was not supposed to.... Richard's words flashed through his mind in seconds. 'No unsupervised interaction, but Richard is here.., I ám supervised. Do what you feel like.... what I feel like...'

Tom let go of his inhibitions and bent over, reaching towards her. The young orca came closer to meet his hands. Tom was overjoyed and deeply moved

172

as he took her head in his hands. He rubbed her smooth skin and felt her warm enthusiasm as she returned his touch by rising even more. Tom bent over and lay his cheek against the orca's smooth rostrum. "My Gunda, my precious friend, you've not forgotten me. I've missed you so much." The last of his words melted with Tuschka's soft affectionate call. Tom's eyes became wet as he felt his beloved whale nudge him affectionately. He rubbed her while he held on, cherishing the contact.

Richard had noticed the orca's startled reaction, followed by her resolute response. The orca seemed as happy to see the man as he was to be with her. He watched the two in silent wonder. After a little while, Tom gently sat upright and tapped the whale on her rostrum. For a moment longer she looked at him. Then, with a playful call, she dived. Her subsequent surfacings were close to Tom as if she kept an eye out to see if he was still there. Tom could not believe what had happened. She had not forgotten, she still knew him!

As if coming back to the real world, his eyes met Richard's. The head trainer was obviously fascinated and Tom sensed that it was in a positive way. Richard realized he had definitely made progress training the orca, but he was impressed with the obvious enthusiasm of the orca for his younger colleague, who had never given her a scrap of food. With such a rapport between trainer and whale, much progress could be made. Yet, Richard still had reservations. By experience he knew what could happen if a trainer became too yielding and too giving towards an intelligent and inquisitive animal that would some day challenge his mental strength. It was obvious that Tom had won the orca's sympathy. Would he succeed in keeping her respect?

Tuschka quickly responded when Tom tapped the water. Several dolphins were watching her through the gate, but the young orca did not pay attention to them. She was filled with excitement and expectation upon the return of her human friend. When she came up and stopped in front of him, he blew the whistle and gave her some fish. Tuschka wanted to play with the man and remembered their splashing game of a few weeks back. Playfully, she filled her mouth and splashed Tom a little. The young trainer smiled at her and returned a little splash with his hand. She gave him another one, but he did not continue with the game. Instead, she saw her friend quickly get up and return with a strange object: a long shaft with a round thickened end.

The man grabbed it close to the rounded end and pointed it towards her. Tuschka was curious about the object, but when it almost touched her, she backed away from the unfamiliar thing. Her friend drew it back in a little and beckoned her to come closer. Tuschka kept a watchful eye on the object as she moved over to his hand. She enjoyed his gentle touch, but felt wary as she saw the strange object come closer to her. Her friend radiated confidence. Reassured by his presence and familiar voice, she did not move. She watched intently as the man tapped her rostrum gently and then did the same thing to the rounded end of the shaft. Entrusting herself to the man, Tuschka let it touch her. Before she could realize what it felt like, she heard the whistle and was completely surprised with the sudden reaction of both men. They shouted and clapped their hands. She read their excitement and happily accepted a handful of fish from her friend.

"You did it!" Richard yelled in excitement as he saw that Tom had actually touched the young orca with the target pole. Both trainers were elated with their milestone achievement. They both knew that a dolphin's learning accelerated once it associated touching the target pole with a reward. The key to teaching certain behaviors was to use the animal's motivation to touch the target. "I think it was a good idea Tom," the head trainer said, "to touch the target with your hand in the same way you touch her." The orca was still watching them, wondering what would come next. Tom touched her a few more times with the target. She learned quickly that the object was not frightening. On the contrary, it had brought on only enthusiasm and reward.

After the short training session, Richard talked it over with Tom. Overall, he was very content with the way Tom had worked with the orca, but he had some doubts as to whether his apprentice would be able to keep the sessions highly disciplined. "Tom, I saw that you returned her splashing. Have you done that with her before?," the head trainer asked. Tom nodded and briefly told Richard about their splashing game. "Look, I can imagine that it's tempting to accept her playful invitations, but you should strictly avoid that during a training session. It'll be hard for you in the beginning, especially since playing is the only thing you have done with her so far. But the orca must learn when it's training time and when it's play time. That whale is a very intelligent and powerful animal and she'll do a lot more growing. I can't emphasize enough how important it is to discipline her. When she can get you to respond to her initiatives, she may interrupt training sessions or shows unexpectedly for something she wants to do. Inconvenience is one thing, but in the long run it may result in dangerous situations."

Tom listened in silence. He knew Richard was right, but he dreaded the idea of really being unyielding to the playful young orca. He did not like to disappoint her. "Will you also allow me play time with her then?," Tom asked tentatively. "Sure, you'll have your play time with her. But first, emphasis will be on training. She must learn what to expect from you and, equally important, what not to expect from you when you interact with her as her trainer."

* * *

All employees, Tom more than others, had become impatient to hear which name would finally be chosen for the young female orca. One night, shortly before the park was to open, a small party was held to name the new whale. About 20 names had been submitted and the choice had been difficult. The director first mentioned the names that had come close to being selected. "Freya, the goddess of love, from a Scandinavian myth, was a beautiful suggestion," the director started. "Another one we almost chose was "Regina," because she's the queen of the ocean. But then we heard a special story and a name that came with it. A name that welled up from love and respect. The orca will be named ... Gunda ... one who moves with the grace of the waves." Tom felt a surge of adrenaline when he heard the announcement. He swallowed to hide his true feelings. The director looked in his direction and the head trainer beckoned him to come forward. Tom flushed and cleared his throat when he shook hands with the owner of the park. The announcement had not explicitly revealed his story, but it had revealed the essence of what he felt for the orca. It was wonderful that the name had been announced in association with those feelings.

Tom felt a little uncomfortable to see his colleagues applauding for him. Richard had a camera in his hands and took the floor. "... This camera is only symbolic. For you as winner of the name contest, we have decided to take a picture of you with Gunda and give that to you, enlarged and framed. We have a few alternatives if you don't like the idea." Tom's eyes gleamed. What a great idea it was. The young trainer shook his head to reject the alternatives. He looked into the expectant eyes of the other employees. They expected him to say something. Not really prepared for a speech, Tom kept it short. "I really feel privileged that I may interact with Gunda. Let's toast in hopes that she will thrive at our park!" Everyone applauded and Tom was happy to mingle with his friends again.

Richard had persuaded Tom to submit his name for the contest, but Tom had done so with mixed feelings. The last thing he wanted was that his special name would be used with derision by those who were envious or did not like the name. With the director's introduction and the overall enthusiastic response most of that fear was gone. That night, sleep came slowly. The orca dominated his mind. Memories, wishful dreams, and speculations about the future alternated quickly with each other. When fatigue finally took over, he dozed off with a satisfied feeling. The orca had been named Gunda because the name had come from his heart. It was the only reason that was meaningful for Tom and they had openly acknowledged it.

Tuschka had been excited with the return of her friend, but she was very aware of the change in his attitude. He had started to act more like the other two men who used to interact with her. He touched her much less and he did not play with her as he had done before. In their early games, Tuschka had felt that it was a mutual initiative. Now, the young man seldom responded to her splashes or other invitations to play. He was determined in what he did and there was little that she could do to distract him. But despite his different behavior, Tuschka sensed that he still felt sympathy for her. Something was holding him back from following his feelings. Nevertheless, there were small surprises every day that piqued her curiosity. She still felt excitement when her friend rewarded her. During such moments, his warmth and enthusiasm came to the surface briefly and made her feel closer to him. That was what Tuschka longed for so much. With only two or three training sessions a day, those short precious moments were highlights that she tried hard to evoke.

Although the dolphins distracted the young orca regularly, there were still many painful moments of loneliness. No matter what she felt, there was no one who would swim at her side and comfort her like her caring mother, or play with her like Igor, Annika, or Aleta. Until that tragic night, one of the few things that Tuschka had taken for granted had been the company of her pod and, especially, the endless presence of her patient and loving mother. Now, the dolphins and the trainers were her only contact. It did not matter so much to Tuschka what they wanted her to do as long as they interacted with her and showed that they were pleased with her. Tuschka always spyhopped and called out to her friend in greeting. He always returned her welcome, but he did not always come over to her. Often, he walked by and started to work with the dolphins.

* * *

Tuschka was watching Tom when he called the dolphins to the platform. Suddenly, a strange mixture of sounds filled the dome. Tuschka had heard similar sounds faintly, from a distance, but never so clear and loud. Although it was a strange noise, it was very melodious and rhythmic. Tuschka wondered where it came from and which creature made the sound, but there was no clue. It came from all around her. Hovering at the surface, she listened to it. Just moments later, she heard the familiar sound of the whistle. Rising into a spyhop, she saw the dolphins bow in unison. She could see them pass by the gate and arch upwards in preparation for another bow. The atmosphere was so different! It left Tuschka with puzzled expectation.

Tom glanced sideways and saw Gunda look at him. He realized that the orca had never heard show music before. Although he was not supposed to, he wanted to reassure the astounded whale, and he threw her a fish. The orca had not expected it at all and looked at Tom a little longer before she made a quick turn to grab the fish. Tom had one of the final rehearsals with the dolphins. All went fine. In his heart he wondered what the orca would think of all the people attending the shows and.... what the people would think of her.

The season had started. The park had been advertising with their newest addition and although they had stated that the orca would not yet be performing in the shows, attendance was higher than usual. A close look at the 'killer whale', the fearsome predator of the sea, was for many a reason to pay a visit.

The night had gone by uneventfully and the morning seemed no different from other mornings. Tuschka was circling her pool when faint distance noises penetrated her ears. Underwater, the sounds were barely audible, but she felt the accompanying vibrations through the walls of her tank. She stopped to listen, but she had no clue as to what it could be. Although she had become accustomed to small changes in her training sessions and feeding time, this was something that she could associate with neither. She called to the dolphins. Only two of them were in the main pool.

Sasha and Lucie were the first to come to the gate. Tuschka went over to them, happy they had responded so fast. She sensed some excitement in them, but not a hint of apprehension. The soft high-pitched creaking of the door to the dome caught Tuschka's attention. A rather short, unfamiliar man came in. With the opening of the door, the sounds grew louder. It was like a murmur with an occasional shout. The man came towards the fence, leaned on it and looked at her. She looked at him briefly to see if he was up to something, but when he did nothing, she returned to the gate.

A seasonal guard opened the door and came in. His task was to open and close the dome before and after shows and to see to it that no one fed or bothered the animals. The orca was new for him too and he had come a little earlier than usual to take a good look at her. He immediately saw that she was noticeably larger than the dolphins, but she was smaller than he had expected. It took him a few moments to realize that he was looking at a juvenile and not at an adult orca, like the ones he had read about in books. His eyes followed the perimeter of the holding pool. 'If she grows as big as they say, I wonder how long this pool will suffice...,' he thought to himself. The man forgot his watch as he looked at the beautiful sleek body with its striking black and white markings. Her deeper heavier blow radiated strength. Some shouts and bangs reminded him of his task. He was two minutes late. Several children were impatiently banging the doors. He quickly opened the doors and went to let the people in.

Tuschka was startled when a sudden burst of sound filled the air. In seconds it came closer, rolling at her like a wave. She quickly dived to the more familiar quiet of her watery environment. Sasha and Lucie were still near the gate. They were spyhopping and obviously eager to see what was happening. Still, they showed no fear. When Tuschka came up for a breath, she was again overwhelmed by all the noise. She remained at the surface near the gate, as far away from the fence as possible.

Curiously lifting her head just enough to permit an unobstructed view, Tuschka could barely believe what she saw. People were crowding around her tank and large numbers were streaming in. She had never seen so many at once. She was relieved that they stayed behind the fence and did not climb over as some of her trainers often did. Her eyes scanned the dome. It was a strange sloping land with an ever dark sky, interrupted only by several bright patches of light. Now, people filled those slopes and their numbers were still growing. She looked again at the people against the fence. Their eyes were all directed at her. Some stretched their arms out towards her. Tuschka hung back: this was too overwhelming, too confusing. Suddenly, the melodious sounds of the past few days also filled the dome. When almost instantly the loud murmur grew weaker, Tuschka relaxed a little. There were still lower and higher pitched calls and shouts, but these too gradually lessened.

A different tune started. Tuschka watched as she saw the people leave the fence and disappear into the crowd. With only the guard near her fence, she gathered enough courage to swim a few rounds. Curious, but with apprehension, she surfaced away from the fence for every breath she took. Too preoccupied with all the new experiences, Tuschka had not noticed the trainers who had come in. The sound of the whistle suddenly took her by surprise. She quickly moved over towards the platform and spyhopped to see who it was. She recognized Jeff and Tom. Their attention was fully directed at the dolphins. None of them was near the gate. In this unusual situation, Tuschka felt uncomfortable and lonely. No one seemed to understand her. No one responded to her anxiety. No one even took notice of her. Craving for some contact, Tuschka called towards Tom. She made the same plaintive call that she had made on her first night.

Tom felt goose bumps rise as he heard the sound. He knew like no one else what the young orca felt and how much she needed him. He fought not to look at her, but when he heard her call again, it was too hard for him to ignore her. He failed to resist and looked at her. Then, she addressed him with her special imitation of his own attempts to communicate with her. Never since that first night had Gunda pleaded so strongly for his attention. Jeff noticed Tom's distraction and kicked him discreetly. Tom quickly turned towards the dolphins again. His concentration was gone. He felt miserable having to continue with the show. He fought back his urge to come towards Gunda and managed to finish the show through several more of the young orca's plaintive calls.

When the show came to an end, Richard appeared and tapped Tom's shoulder. The young trainer turned his head and needed no encouragement to follow the instructions of his supervisor. The head trainer took the microphone and addressed the public. "As you will understand, our brand new addition, the young orca Gunda, isn't yet ready to perform in a show. She arrived just a few months ago. She's been adapting very well to her new environment and is making good progress in her training sessions. Trainer Tom is now with her and you are welcome to take a closer look on your way out."

For the many people, still in the dome, Richard went on giving the visitors some more information on the orcas' biology and basic behavior. Tom was grateful for the opportunity to be with his beloved Gunda. Richard had not specified what he was expected to do, but Tom was not even aware of that. The crowds faded from his mind as he knelt down at the edge.

Tuschka saw him come and moved close to him. Instantly, she sensed the different mood he was in. He had not come as her trainer, but as her special friend during those past nights. The brief moment that he had looked at her during the show had given her a spark of hopeful expectation, but it had quickly turned into a painful sting when he had turned his face away from her.

When she felt his touch and caresses, the desolation and hopelessness that Tuschka had felt when her best friend had averted his face, melted away. They were together again. Tom lay his cheek against her smooth rostrum and held her tight against his chest. Tears filled his eyes. They both had missed these precious moments of contact so much. Tuschka made several soft affectionate calls, which Tom could only return with his hugs. His throat was too clogged to produce any decent sound. The young trainer released his hold and sat up a little more. He gently stroked her throat and the side of her face. Tuschka had become oblivious to the crowds as well, who stood watching the two in almost silent wonder. Somehow, they sensed the intimate relationship between the trainer and the new killer whale.

When Tom's hand ran alongside her mouth, Gunda opened it a little, just enough to stick out the tip of her tongue. Tom felt as if she were inviting him to touch it. He ran his hand closer to her chin and then lightly over the tip of her tongue. He stopped briefly and felt its special supple touch. He repeated the same caress and again Gunda offered him her tongue to touch. It was a new special sign of her trust in him. Gunda sank back in the water a little when Tom bent over to touch one of her flippers. The juvenile orca rolled over to her side and offered it to him. He gave her a nice rub-down and went on near the base of her dorsal fin. Gunda delighted in the attention.

When Tom looked up, he suddenly was aware of the people again. He smiled a shy smile at them and then looked back at the orca. He tapped her gently and resolved to keep his friend company until the people had left. When everything was quiet again and Gunda fully relaxed, he got up. "I'll come back to train you soon," he said. Gunda looked at him in a spyhop posture, but she no longer spoke to him with her plaintive calls when he left the platform.

Tom was overjoyed that she bore him no grudges. Their moment together had been so full of affection and friendship. There had been the same precious intimacy that he had experienced with her during his night watches. It gave him hope that she would soon learn that lack of attention from him during a dolphin show was a normal thing that did not mean that he did not care for her.

Tuschka soon got used to the crowds coming in every day. She had also learned that her trainers were difficult to distract and that they dominated the interaction most of the time. The playtime sessions, which had more warmth, spontaneity, and physical contact, were her favorite moments, more precious to her than anything else. It saddened Tuschka when she was ignored, when no one gave her the attention she asked for, but it no longer distressed her with the fear of separation and loss. It did not mean a final rejection. Sooner or later, they would come to her, although it was hard to accept that all interaction was on their terms. When she was still living with her family, the other orcas had not always reacted either in the way Tuschka had wanted. There had been long hours of disciplined foraging without play, but they had always acknowledged her. Tuschka was used to the presence of dominant orcas, telling her what to do. Here, the trainers were the dominant creatures. Yet the difference was not only people versus orcas; there was more to it than Tuschka could define. Deep inside she felt a never-ending restlessness stemming from the fact that these humans did not show the unconditional commitment that she had experienced from her family. For her the loss of that ever-present and self-evident security, acceptance, and warmth was like uprooting the basis of her existence. The moments of playtime hinted at the bond with her family. She clung to those moments, like roots trying to get a hold, but finding quicksand each time.

It was still early in the season with only three shows a day, when Richard called a trainers' meeting. "The management feels that the thrill of just seeing the killer whale will not last long. They want us to involve the orca in the shows." Doubt showed on the faces of his fellow trainers. "Gunda is learning fast," Jeff brought up, but her repertoire does not yet suffice for a show." "She doesn't have to do a full show," the head trainer countered. "I think they will be content if she can do a part." "But even that," Tom remarked, "is quite a ways to go. So far, we have only trained her in between or after shows. Soon, there will be five shows a day, barely leaving any time for training. She hasn't even been acquainted yet with the performance pool. The first thing we need before everything else is to have her smoothly enter and leave that pool on our request."
Richard nodded in confirmation. "Training does not necessarily have to involve show behaviors. If we are short of time, we can do some sort of public training sessions, but she must indeed switch pools easily. I suggest, for now and the days to come, that we work on that after the last show. In case of any difficulties we then have time to get her back into the holding tank for the next day." Richard did not speak it out aloud, but in the worst case they would have to force her back with a net. They all hoped such a distressful measure would not be necessary.

Tuschka hovered close while Jeff unlatched the gate. Although she recognized the sound, she had never heard it so close. She had come to associate it with the dolphins either entering or leaving the adjacent pool. Jeff knelt down near the edge of the platform and kept her stationed while the hydraulics slowly opened the gate. An eerie creak betrayed that it had not been opened for a while. It was strange for Tuschka to see that the way to the other pool was free. She peeked beyond the passage and stared into the blue, wondering if the dolphins would soon come.

Jeff got up and pointed towards the gate. The orca knew this gesture, but until now, only the dolphins had been asked to respond to it. He saw the orca look at him questioningly. He squatted down just beyond the gate and tapped the water gently to call her over. There was no doubt that the orca understood the cue, but some invisible barrier seemed to hold her back. Jeff tapped on the water again to encourage her a little. "Come on, Gunda," he called to her, "this is great for you, lots of room to swim, come.."

So far, her trainers had never put her in danger, and soon Tuschka's inquisitive nature beat her reluctance to leave the relative safety of what she knew. She inched forward, but when she was halfway the passage, she hesitated briefly. It was oppressing to pass through such a narrow opening, even though it was more than wide enough for her to pass through. Tuschka heard the taps on the water and was eager for the reward that lay ahead of her. She inched forward again and echolocated in several directions. Both the echoes and her eyes told her she was about to enter a much larger space. Thinking of the playful dolphins, Tuschka moved forward and touched her trainer's hand. Instantaneously, she heard the approving whistle and gratefully accepted a handful of fish.

Another trainer had joined and both men were applauding and praising her. Tuschka sensed the excitement of the two men and was delighted with what she evidently had achieved. As soon as she had swallowed her big reward, she dived and swam to the center of the pool. The space was amazing. It was not only deeper. It was also much longer and wider. It was great to be able to swim a longer stretch before having to turn again. Tuschka hovered a while near the bottom in the center. In the straight wall, she noticed several squares like the one she knew. They were just dark patches now. She continued on and came by a structure that looked exactly like the gate to her own pool.

It was then that the excited voices of the dolphins caught her attention. Tuschka abruptly turned towards the gate. The dolphins were near the back of the pool and Tuschka sensed the apprehension in their voices. She called her greeting to them, hoping they would return it and come to the gate. To the dolphins, the orca's sudden appearance on the other side of the gate had come as a complete surprise. The sight of the orca was by no means new to them, but until then, it had always been their initiative to go to Tuschka's gate. In fact, part of the dolphins' confidence had stemmed from the fact that they knew that the orca could not come to them. Now, she evidently could.

Flash, the dominant male, was the first to come closer. Tuschka felt him echolocate on her. She stayed still as he approached. Flash had been startled by the sight of the orca near his gate, but he sensed no aggression in the young whale. He called to her and her answer was as friendly and playful as always. Sasha and Lucie came over to join Flash near the gate.

Tuschka heard a tap on the water, but she hesitated briefly before she came over. She had never been called over there before. A good rub down and a few fish were a bigger reward than she had expected. It was a strange training session. They did not demand much of her, other then calling her over in different places. She was by no means aware of her trainers' goal to have her present wherever they wanted. Tuschka enjoyed the extra freedom of movement in the larger tank. She could build up more speed and she found it a game to respond to the taps as fast as she could.

Without exchanging a word the trainers took the hint. They too were excited to see the beautifully streamlined animal move at a higher speed. They had positioned themselves at different points around the tank. Jeff was still on the main platform. In turns, but in an unpredictable order, the men tapped on the water. They saw the orca's immediate and energetic response. Her turns were fast and agile, revealing just a little of what this supreme predator would be capable of when pursuing prey in the open ocean. Jeff wondered if they could speed her up a little more by shortening the intervals between taps. Tuschka's heart beat faster as she sped from one to the next. She knew she was participating in what had become a game. She read the excitement in the men and loved the spontaneity that they radiated.

The young orca's blows were strong and came more frequently. Soon, Richard got the idea of giving the whale a series of taps in a line along the perimeter of the pool. He wanted to see how fast they could make her swim a circle. Taking the challenge to respond as fast as she could, the orca raced along the wall. Before she slowed down, another tap followed. As the whale porpoised right by Jeff, Richard sprinted over for the next tap. He was barely in time. When the young orca flew by, he ran to follow her, but could not keep up. The effect overwhelmed them. With three men, they had not even been fast enough to give her the cues for a full circle. "Wow, what a thrill," Richard yelled as he came trotting after the orca. "She just did a fantastic speed swim. This is so... bweeeeh!" Gunda's fast swim had created such a wake that the water ran over the edge and drenched Richard's legs. Being used to working with dolphins, the head trainer had overlooked the fact that the orca displaced a much larger amount of water.

For an instant the three men looked with amazement, then they burst into laughter. The orca, unaware of her soaking wake, slowed down, waiting for the next tap. None came. She wondered what had happened, why the game had ended so suddenly. She stayed at the surface and floated, catching her breath. Jeff noticed her and beckoned her to come. Not wanting her to think that he was resuming the game, he did not tap the water, but gently moved his fingers just below the surface. She came over and poked her rostrum out of the water

182

in front of him. He tapped her gently on the rostrum and rewarded her with a bunch of fish. "Good girl" he said, "that must've felt good for you, to stretch your muscles a bit. You like this pool don't you? Let's see if you're willing to follow me to your holding pool. Be a good girl and follow me." He got up and kept looking at the orca while he walked towards the gate. He touched the water lightly and without delay, she touched his hand. Jeff rewarded her with another fish and took his familiar spot on the edge of the platform, facing the holding tank. He was happy to see that the young orca followed him without hesitation.

The sound of the hydraulics caught Tuschka's attention. She saw the gate move and obstruct the passage that led to the large pool. She turned to face it and swam closer, but the opening was getting too narrow for her to cross. She watched in disappointment, knowing she could not return to the large space. Tuschka heard a tap on the water and turned reluctantly, feeling that the fun was over. When she poked her face out of the water, both men looked at her. One of them gave her several fish and his voice sounded friendly. Then, she watched them get up and leave.

The session was over. Everything was back to normal again. Tuschka started to swim circles. She had enjoyed the larger space and the game so much that she regretted being back alone in her small holding tank. The situation puzzled her: why had they given her more space and then taken it away from her? Why had they closed the passage to the roomy pool? She swam towards the gate and touched it. She pushed, then pushed a little more, but it did not give. Then, she rested near it, hoping she would soon be able to enter the big pool again.

Richard and Jeff were excited about what had happened. Richard quickly went to change his wet pants. Then he joined Jeff in the trainers' lounge with a big smile on his face. "Wasn't it amazing how she responded to the tapping? Her enthusiasm was so evident, I couldn't resist joining her game. It was so tempting to make her do a fast swim. The water she displaces is spectacular. We should use this in the public sessions. The visitors will love it!" Jeff nodded. He had obviously been impressed in the same way. "But we'd need five of us, at least, to get her to swim the full perimeter of the tank." Richard had realized that too. "Yes, the problem is to teach her to swim along the perimeter towards the next tap. Now, she's taking shortcuts. Perhaps we can use the target pole to create extra taps in between. Gradually, we'll have to take those extra taps out, but that can all be done in a public session."

Jeff was excited about the idea. It had indeed been an awesome sight to see the young powerful orca move with such agility and speed, but Jeff was not so sure that the public sessions could start soon. "Did you see how she turned to look at the gate when Steve closed it? When she entered her own pool again, she didn't know that we'd close the gate. I'm not so sure that she'll follow me in so smoothly the next time." "You're right," Richard acknowledged, "she still has to be trained to switch pools. It's hard to say how much time that'll take. I suggest we start with a public training session after the last show, just like now. The attendance won't be as high, but it's better than nothing. I'll take it up with the management."

Bob came to watch the next day. The young orca needed no encouragement to enter the main pool. Tom had come back and had been listening to the stories with amazement. He was eager to help in teaching Gunda to do a nice fast perimeter swim. The orca was excited at seeing Tom and came over to greet him with a loud call. Tom flushed as he saw the look of surprise in the curator's eyes.

Richard positioned himself on the main platform with a target pole. Jeff and Tom were on the outer perimeter. Jeff had the second target pole and Tom used a paddle. The effect was even better than the day before. The orca swam close to the surface, her relatively tall dorsal fin cutting through the water. She surfaced in a porpoising fashion with water running up her chin. The young streamlined whale moved fast, like a well aimed torpedo. Her wake brought on waves that rapidly built up when she made her second round. The platform was already awash and the crests of the waves ran over the edge of the tank.

Bob was in awe. After one more round the orca came to a stop in front of Richard, Bob was drenched almost to his knees. When he looked at the trainers, he frowned. "You knew this," he said. "You could at least have told me to put boots on." "I'm sorry," Richard said. "We had a similar experience yesterday. We should've told you, but in our excitement, we forgot." They let the orca swim around freely while Richard discussed the idea of doing public sessions after the last show. Bob was in favor. Richard suggested to have some coffee. He did not know what surprises Gunda might hold for them when they asked her to return to her own pool. He had no desire to have the curator around during such unpredictable circumstances.

Jeff's fear proved well founded. Gunda was reluctant to leave the performance pool. When she heard the tap, her initial response was immediate, but she stopped close to the open gate. Jeff tossed a fish in front of her to coax her in. She went half-way, but did not fully enter her pool. It was obvious that she did not want them to close the gate behind her. Jeff motioned Tom to help. He knew his younger colleague had a better rapport with Gunda. Tom was not happy about it. He did not like to be involved in activities that his beloved whale did not like. He felt it was not fair to close the gate behind her back when she came to him trustingly. He came over to Jeff slowly. "I'll give it a try, but don't close the gate immediately if she comes." Jeff looked at him questioningly.

Tom sensed that his fellow trainer knew what he was thinking, but Tom was convinced it would not serve any purpose to close the gate behind the orca. On the contrary, it would have an adverse effect. "She must've been very disappointed when the gate was closed yesterday. That would explain why she's

184

so reluctant to enter the holding tank now. If you do the same thing again, she'll only be discouraged to come back to her own pool." Jeff frowned. It did make sense, but what else could be done, he wondered. "I think we should reward her if she comes and allow her to go back," Tom continued. "We could do this several times and then close the gate. I think she must have many opportunities to enter the main pool, so that she'll learn that closing the gate is only temporary. I'm not sure if this will work out, but I don't believe in closing the gate immediately. Listen Jeff, the last thing you and I want is to have to use the net..." Jeff nodded, agreeing with Tom's plan.

Tom knelt down and looked at his precious orca. He made his typical greeting call to her. Tuschka's heart jumped at the prospect of spontaneous interaction. She cherished such moments with Tom. She hesitated briefly, torn between the possibility that the gate would close and the opportunity to have playtime with her favorite trainer. The choice was not so difficult. The big pool was nice, but warm attention was better. Tom was touched to see that the orca had resolved to come to him. She surfaced in front of him, eager for his gentle touch. She squeaked her happiness to him and pushed up against his hand.

After a brief rub her friend sat upright. She looked at him a little longer. He didn't seem to leave. She had missed him and wanted to play more. She splashed him playfully. Tom splashed back. When Tuschka filled her mouth again, she heard the gate and turned towards it. It had moved only a little. The passage was still wide. Tuschka was surprised. She had not expected the gate to stop closing. She was facing the main pool with her head in the passage. Nothing kept her from going in. It was confusing. Tuschka backed up a little and turned to look at Tom. He was still there. Again, she was faced with the choice of being with Tom or going into the big pool. For the second time, she chose to stay near Tom and turned to come back to him. She was not aware that he had given a signal to close the gate. Tuschka stopped briefly to look back. Then she ignored it and came over to her friend. He welcomed her warmly. His tender caresses quickly made her forget about the gate.

A few minutes later, Tom sat up straight, took the whistle in his hand and asked the orca formally to station. When she touched his hands, he blew the whistle and rewarded her with a fish. "Good girl, Gunda," he said as he motioned Jeff to open the gate again. Tom walked along the perimeter of the holding pool with the orca following him. When he proceeded on past the wall that separated the holding tank from the main one, Tuschka spyhopped to see where he was going. It did not take long for her to find her way through the open gate. Tom tapped the water when he saw her coming. She presented immediately and the young trainer blew the whistle as in any official training session. Upon a signal from Tom, Jeff closed the gate. She watched it but did not leave Tom. "Gunda, just enjoy the tank, I'll be back soon," Tom said to her as he tapped her gently.

Tuschka followed Tom, but found her way blocked by the gate. She hovered near it at the surface, watching the two men, who were standing on the platform at the edge of her own tank. Tuschka felt restless. It was strange that she could not return to her own pool. Although she had spent many boring hours in it, she was unaware of the feeling of security that she had drawn from routine. Now, she missed her familiar retreat.

Within a few minutes, Tom went to the perimeter of the big pool again. He tensed a little when he saw Richard come in. The look on his face left no doubt that the head trainer was puzzled at what he saw. The orca still in the big tank and the gate closed? Jeff briefly explained with a low voice. Richard did not interfere, and watched. While Jeff opened the gate, Tom called the orca over. Without a hint of hesitation, she went through the passage. She barely turned her head upon the sounds of the hydraulics. Then, she spyhopped high in front of Tom and squeaked enthusiastically. Tom felt utterly relieved. He had not only achieved the goal…. He still had Gunda's trust!

Jeff had been watching the two. He had touched and rubbed Gunda too, but he felt he did not have the intimate bond that Tom obviously had. It did not matter to the orca that he had more years of experience; friendship was a spontaneous thing. At least the orca accepted him and worked with him. Perhaps more would come with time.

Richard had quickly been informed about what had happened while he had been away. He was impressed when he saw how smoothly the orca entered her pool. He tapped his younger colleague on the shoulder. "Looks promising, Tom! It's been a while since I last trained a naive dolphin. But that's different. As a gregarious animal, a new one tends to follow the other dolphins. That makes training easier. It's a very valuable opportunity to be able to train a naive orca. It'll put our techniques and insights to the test."

17.
New Playmates in the Water

The public training sessions turned out to be a great success. Attendance was barely less than at the mid-day dolphin show. The orca was learning fast. During the shows with the dolphins the curious young whale often imitated the behaviors of her smaller relatives. She could not often see the cues for the various behaviors, but she felt more part of it all by just trying to do what they did. The trainers had started to exploit the young whale's interest in mimicking the dolphins by giving the same cues to the orca and the dolphins simultaneously.

As Richard had predicted, the fast swim was a great success. Simply because of her size and weight, the young whale could displace more water than dolphins would ever be capable of. Although the orca had learned to do spyhops and pectoral fin waves on command, it was her fast swim that was most spectacular. It came closest to the expectations of a public that wanted to see the physical capabilities of a killer whale.

Tuschka was very aware of the difference between public and non-public training sessions. The music, the yells, and the applauses made it much more lively. She felt that not only the trainer, but also the crowd appreciated what she did. By now, Tuschka felt completely at home in the performance pool and she loved the extra room to swim.

One day, during her fast swim, Tuschka heard the public applaud rhythmically. She picked up the enthusiastic atmosphere and started swimming even faster. She porpoised higher with loud strong blows creating vertical plumes of mist in the damp dome. Tuschka heard the whistle, telling her that she was done, but she was too full of excitement to stop. She dived down a little, then she arched up and kicked her flukes. Her sleek streamlined body pierced the surface, rising fully into the air. Then she turned on her side and hit the water with a splash, larger than any dolphin had ever made.

The public screamed and applauded as the orca came over to Tom. The visitors thought it was planned, but the orca had completely surprised the trainers with her spectacular and unexpected breach. Spontaneously, Tom had rewarded her with the whistle and wished he could ask her to do it again. Yet it would be a while for his Gunda to learn the cue for a full breach in the right spot.

Tom had been working many sessions with Gunda and he had come to feel much more relaxed and comfortable. One reason was that the head trainer was satisfied with the orca's progress, and he had given him more room to follow his insights. But most of all, Tom was relieved that the orca had learned and accepted the difference between training and playtime. His rapport with Gunda had not suffered.

One cloudy morning, Tom entered the dome. The orca greeted him with enthusiasm and rose up against the edge of the platform. Tom imitated her vocalization. He was dressed in his wet suit, which surprised the orca, who was not used to him wearing it during the early morning training session. He sat down beside her and rubbed her gently. "Gunda, I wish I could swim with you. How would you like that? Take it easy," he said as he lowered his feet into the water beside the whale. The orca did not move, but her wide open eyes revealed a mixture of apprehension and curiosity. Tom made the signal for the whale to offer him her pectoral fin. She responded, but kept a little more distance than usual. Tom touched the orca gently with his foot. A slight quiver went through her body and she sank down a little. "Come Gunda, there's nothing to fear," he said while he moved his hand towards the spot where he had touched her. He caressed her lightly, producing a tickling sensation that she liked very much. In response, she rose closer to the surface again. When he felt her relax, he took his hand back and continued with his foot. She kept her position, wanting him to continue his gentle strokes.

Tom was happy that his beloved orca trusted him and it amazed him how quickly she accepted and understood what he wanted. Being one of the younger trainers, he realized that his progress with Gunda depended more on his rapport with the whale than on his experience. Personality was undeniably an important factor. Gunda did not know anything about the experience of her trainers. She followed her natural feelings. Tom felt grateful and privileged that somehow they had clicked with each other from the start.

Suddenly, an idea came to him. Although it was tempting, he felt it would be too big a step to glide into the water with her. He did not expect the orca to intentionally harm him, but she was a powerful animal. He was not so sure that the young whale would know how fragile he was. If she were to investigate him with a little too much enthusiasm, he could easily get injured. Tom got up and lowered himself into the performance pool. Tuschka spyhopped, trying to see what her human friend was doing. She heard some splashes as she saw him disappear behind the edge. Knowing that the sounds came from the big pool, Tuschka approached the gate. She could hear, but not see any movement yet. Then she heard his typical call.

Tom decided he did not want to startle the whale by suddenly showing up right by the edge of the gate. Instead, he wanted to swim into her view from some distance. That would give Gunda time to recognize him in the water. Tom recalled that he and his colleagues had been swimming with the dolphins in the shows. Those moments required full concentration and he could only remember glimpses of the orca watching from behind the gate. Would she have recognized him? He wondered, because it was a setting in which she had never interacted with him before. In a flash, the young trainer remembered his second night when Gunda had not immediately recognized him by his appearance but by his voice. Tom felt his heart beat faster as he stroked to the center of the pool.

Just before swimming into Gunda's view, he made another call to her, wanting to prepare her. He felt goose bumps as the orca's eerie response filled the dome. Full of anticipation, Tom swam towards the gate. He saw the tip of Gunda's black rostrum against the steel structure. A few strokes later, he was facing her from a distance of three yards. A strange vibrating sensation startled him: Gunda was exploring him with her sonar! They watched each other in silence. Tom wondered what the orca was thinking. As he slowly swam towards the gate, he heard a soft call and answered it. He was certain that Gunda had recognized him. Only one foot separated them now. Gunda lay at the surface, her eyes just submerged. Tom sank down again. 'She's big!' he thought as his eyes quickly ran along the contours of her streamlined body. Her eye patch quickly guided them to her dark eye.

Tuschka had recognized her friend's voice, but he had never approached her otherwise than from the edge of the tank. His movements were clumsy, like those of the other humans she had seen. Tuschka did not know what to expect, but she burned with curiosity. She pressed even more against the gate, wanting it to open and let her through. She watched him come closer, but did not want to do anything that might make him change his mind. Tuschka saw him take hold on the steel structure that separated them, and when he sank down a little, their eyes met. It was a unique moment. His face looked different, but she knew it was him. Tuschka pressed her head sideways against the gate to be as close to him with her eye as possible and vocalized affectionately.

Tom was deeply touched. Sharing the watery environment with her made him feel much closer to his precious orca. It touched him to look her in the eye so close and to hear her tender voice. While he came up to breathe she rose a bit too, not to lose eye contact with him. Tom pulled himself up on the gate and rested on it with his chest. With one arm, he reached over to touch Gunda's head. Again, she called to him softly. It felt as if she was begging him to share the tank with her. He slid off the gate and sank down again. He gently ran his fingers along her soft chin and playfully took hold of one of her pecs. The orca kept close to his face. Tom tried to make sounds, but he could barely hear himself through the bubbles he released. The playful orca thought of it as a new game and blew bubbles in response.

Tom imagined how wonderful it would be to swim with the orca. He saw her strong body and knew she would be capable of more than pulling or pushing him through the water. His dear Gunda would carry him with ease and she was by no means full-grown... It was tempting to enter her tank, but he felt he was already pushing the limit of what he was permitted to do.

He moved forward and pressed his face against the gate. The bars were too close together for him to stick his head through them, but the orca's rostrum was pointy enough to fit in between. Tenderly, he kissed her. She opened her mouth a little to explore him with her tongue. Tom was amazed at her response; it was as if his dog was licking him.

Tom finally pulled himself up on the gate and climbed onto the platform. The orca still looked at him. He shared her longing to be together in the water without a gate between them. He listened to her, calling to him while he got up on his feet. She obviously did not want him to leave. It was hard to resist her begging, but Tom knew that if it was up to the whale, he would never leave.

That day, many emotions and thoughts filled the young trainer's mind. He felt the orca was ready to accept him in the water with her. He was certain that she would do him no harm, but how soon would Richard be receptive to that idea? The head trainer would bring up the fact that the orca could be too rough or take him down too long, but somehow Tom was convinced that Gunda would not do such a thing. One part of him was thrilled with the privilege to work with the orca, but another part was saddened by the fact that he was not free to follow his impulses. Tom realized that in some way both he and the orca were held captive. Gunda's mind was free, but she was physically confined. Tom was free to move, but he was not free to follow his mind.

* * *

The season was coming to an end. It was obvious the orca was a great asset to the park. She drew many visitors and was learning fast. Next year, she would have a show of her own. The dolphins seemed to feel very relaxed about the orca. When the young whale was in the main pool, the dolphins were usually at the gate talking to her.

Richard thought the dolphins would make good company for the orca and decided to give them both access to the main pool. He was, however, aware that the dolphins drew much of their confidence from knowing that the orca could not pass the gate. Opening it would be a big step that could be very stressful for the dolphins, but he was confident that the juvenile whale would do them no harm. Tom was happy that Richard had told him about his plans, because he was eager to see how the dolphins would respond. Would they too sense what Richard was so certain about?

Richard, Jeff, Tom, and Bob were all present. Within several minutes, the gate of the orca's tank slowly swung open. She did not hesitate. As soon as the opening was wide enough for her to pass, she glided into the main pool. As expected, she quickly made for the gate of the dolphins, who were already expecting her. The sound of the hydraulics had told them the orca would soon come. Everything looked as usual. They watched the animals socialize near the gate. Gunda had grown visibly since her arrival. In comparison with the dolphins, her larger size was even more striking.

The head trainer knelt down and greeted the animals on both sides of the gate before he grabbed the handle and pushed it away from himself. The dolphins knew that the gate would be opened, but they had not expected it now. The presence of the orca on the other side was unsettling. The men saw the dolphins back away from the gate. Lucie and Sasha hovered closest, while the others swam in a nervous irregular pattern. Tuschka was full of anticipation, but the sound of the hydraulics did not follow and the gate did not move. Richard looked back at Jeff, while he gave the dolphins some more time to relax.

About 15 minutes later, the dolphins had relaxed. Flash and the two young females were back at the gate. When Lucie and Tuschka touched each other's rostrum, they both felt the gate give. They both stopped, but only briefly. When the gate moved again Tuschka moved back a little, wondering if it would open further, but it did not. It closed again when she pressed her head against it. Both Tuschka and Lucie felt the movement. Flash and Sasha noticed it too. Within moments, Tuschka and Lucie had started to play with the gate, making it a game to push it back and forth. Tuschka wanted the gate to open, but it had not yet occurred to her that she could grab it and pull it towards her. Instead, she backed up each time Lucie pushed. As if waiting for the dolphin to push further, Tuschka paused briefly before pushing it back. Gaining more confidence, the dolphin began to push harder and the gate swung back and forth faster. To encourage Lucie to push more, Tuschka changed her strategy. Each time when the dolphin pushed, she pushed it back only a little and step by step, the gate opened further.

When the gate was open wide enough for a dolphin body to pass, Tuschka's attention was suddenly drawn to the passage. She moved sideways, and poked her rostrum into the opening. At that moment, it struck them both that they were looking at each other with no structure to separate them. Lucie froze at the sight of the huge black orca facing her. Tuschka noticed the sudden change in the dolphin's behavior. Not wanting to upset Lucie, she backed up a little. Then she hovered, calling to the dolphin, begging her to come close again.

The men watched in fascination at the orca trying to manipulate the situation. They could not have thought of a more gradual introduction of the whale. The trainers were excited with what they saw. It was a great step that the two species, one of which was known to feed sometimes upon the other, were looking at each other through an open gate. It pleased him that the orca was patient and gentle. She showed no sign of threat, nor careless curiosity. He left to get two buckets of fish, hoping he would manage to feed both the dolphins and the orca at the main platform. Gunda needed no encouragement. She was already spyhopping in front of Tom, eager for his attention. Jeff positioned himself very close to the gate and tried to entice the dolphins into the tank.

Warily, Flash rounded the corner and accepted a fish. He could see the large orca, just three yards away from him. All his muscles were tense, ready for a retreat into his own pool. The fact that the orca's attention was not focused on him, and the presence of his familiar trainer boosted his courage. Sasha, Lucie and another female followed the example of the dominant male. Tuschka noticed the dolphins from the corner of her eye. She had never shared a tank with them. Her heart beat fast. No matter how tempting it was to play with them, she knew that fear did not make good companions, let alone friends. There was no other way than patiently waiting until they were ready for it. The warm and gentle caresses of her favorite trainer made it easier for Tuschka to stay where she was.

Both trainers had been so engrossed in what they were doing that the voice of their head trainer came as a surprise. "Looks promising," Richard said. He watched until the fish were gone. The feed had been deliberately prolonged to expose the dolphins and the orca to each other for as long as possible. When the two men got back on their feet, they saw the orca turn to face the dolphins. They stood their ground, but only until she began swimming towards them. Seeing their apprehension, the attentive whale swung a little wide and passed by. The three men decided to give the dolphins an opportunity to relax by closing the gate, but they left it unlatched.

Tuschka was beside herself with joy as she gently nudged Lucie's pec. The young female dolphin was the first to permit the orca such intimacy. For most of the day, the dolphins had been swimming circles in the main tank, but not within touching range of the orca. It was after the late afternoon feed, that Lucie and Tuschka finally made contact. The touch was more than just a touch: it had been a tentative step in trust on the dolphin's part and a sign from the orca that she would not abuse that trust. With Tuschka's gentle response, all apprehension left the young dolphin. They started to circle in graceful turns, gliding under and over one another, and touching each other subtly.

Tuschka was overjoyed. Since being taken from her family she had not enjoyed the company of a playmate, who had so much in common with her. The dolphin was a lot smaller, but she had the same type of body, possessed an agility and speed that matched her own, and communicated in similar ways. For

Lucie it was not the craving for company that had motivated her to interact with the orca, but the fascination for something new. The dolphin had been young when she arrived at the park. She had not experienced an orca attack. The apprehension and warnings of Flash had initially made her cautious, but as the whale's behavior did not justify his anxiety, his wariness made less impression on her.

Flash watched from some distance. Lucie had ignored his first call to move away from the orca. The scene confused him. What he saw did not conform to his view on orcas. He was not yet ready to believe that Tuschka was not to be feared. He approached, called sharply to Lucie and intercepted her to bring her back to his 'pod'. Lucie was reluctant, but followed her leader's command. Tuschka was disappointed and followed behind. As the dolphins retreated into their holding tank, the young orca did not follow them in. Something told her that it was their territory, which she was not expected to enter. Lucie kept an eye on Tuschka and called to her several times. Although the dolphins had retreated, it was not the same. One of them, at least, had trusted her and wanted contact with her. She watched as they made small circles with the dominant male on the outside of the group. After a few minutes, Tuschka went to her own pool to look into the corridor, but it was a little while before Lucie managed to break away to chat with her near the gate.

The contact between Tuschka and the dolphins progressed rapidly after the first contact with Lucie. The moments of playtime with her agile small grey friends had contributed much to Tuschka's quality of life. It had brought back some sense of the companionship and togetherness that she had been deprived of for so long. Although the trainers provided her with a welcome mental challenge, Tuschka no longer depended solely on them for company. Yet the decision to share the main tank and play together was not hers to make, nor the dolphins'. It depended on the men. They decided when the gates were opened and closed. Tuschka did not like to be separated, but she was often rewarded with fish, a rub-down, a training session, or playtime, when she returned to her own pool. If she did not cooperate, however, they put the dolphins in their holding tank and left her by herself without any attention. That option was worse. Besides, she had discovered that the separations were temporary. Sooner or later, they would be together again.

The trainers had experienced some difficulties in getting the orca back into her tank, especially in the beginning when it was so new and exciting for the young whale to interact with the dolphins. When the separations went smoothly, they started to have part of the training sessions with the orca and the dolphins together. The effect was undeniable. Gunda was an eager and fast learner who had been trying to imitate the dolphins with all she could see from her bad vantage point in her own tank. Now that she shared the tank with them, her progress was unbelievably fast. The orca's inclination to join in her companions' behavior, combined with her observant nature and intelligence, made her quick to associate the trainers' cues with the proper behaviors. In intermediate sessions with the orca alone, the trainers would repeat a similar program to see how much the orca had retained. It was amazing. She would not immediately have the timing, positioning, and perfection of the dolphins, but she did know the essence. She had learned to spin around her axis, both horizontally and vertically, to do bows, tail slaps and, even more surprising, to come out on the main platform. In the private sessions, the trainers perfected on newly learned behaviors and on teaching her to read from the cues where in the tank she was supposed to perform them. Before the winter was over, Richard decided Gunda was ready to start her own shows.

Since he had been in the water near Gunda, Tom had been looking forward to entering the water with her. He had been hoping the head trainer would suggest it, but it seemed he had other priorities. It was tempting to proceed with it on his own, but he felt Richard would not appreciate it if he took that liberty. After having gained so much of the head trainer's confidence, he did not want to spoil it, but about a month prior to the opening of the new season, Tom brought it up. He told him how he had interacted with the orca from the other side of the gate. "I think she's ready for it," Tom said. Richard gave him a thoughtful look.

The responsibility for his fellow trainers weighed heavily on him. The orca was far bigger and more powerful than the dolphins. After seeing how gentle and patient the orca had been when first introduced to the dolphins, he felt much more positive about it. Yet a dolphin was strong and agile compared to a man. He wondered if the orca would know her own strength and control it appropriately when dealing with humans. Would she take Tom down to play with him, or would she understand that he would need to breathe much more frequently?

"Dolphins could do similar things if they wanted to, but they don't," Tom said. "The orca will probably respond in a similar way," the head trainer commented. "It's just that she's so much bigger. It's a matter of scale. It would indeed be exciting to work such a thing into the shows. It's probably good to start swimming sessions early if we plan to start them at all. She's not yet full-grown and a young mind is more flexible." Richard sighed. His face showed he had resolved the matter. "We'll take it slowly, step by step. You should have a small tank of air with you, for emergencies." Tom was thrilled. He realized that it would not be part of the show in the upcoming season, but the prospect of working with Gunda in the water filled him with eager anticipation and joy.

As if wanting to trigger the orca's memory of their special moment near the gate, Tom slid into the main pool. The young whale came over to the gate immediately. He exchanged some calls with her and dived a few times to make eye contact under water. He touched her rostrum with his nose and caressed her gently with his hand. When he felt the warm intimate contact with her, he pulled himself up on the gate and let his legs dangle down from it into the orca's tank. He saw her carefully back up a little to give him room. Then she nudged his legs lightly and spyhopped to look at him in expectation. Tom encouraged her to rise a little higher, grabbed her head with both hands and pressed his cheek against it. 'My Gunda, this is a big moment for you and me. I'll be in your domain, at your mercy. If you'll be as gentle with me as you have been so far, it'll be all right,' he told her in thought.

Tom's heart pounded as he slowly lowered his body into the water. The orca watched patiently, just two feet in front of him. He took several deep breaths as he looked at the huge animal in front of him. It was as if she grew with each foot he lowered himself.

Tuschka sensed his apprehension. The situation was entirely new for her too. The tension in the man brought some distance between them. They both felt it. Tom held on to one of the steel bars of the gate. He tried to make his typical call to her, but it got stuck in his throat. He cleared his throat and tried again. It was not good, but better. The orca was quick to pick up on his intention. From the very beginning, they had made contact by voice. The young orca answered, soft, with a little upsweep, as if she phrased a small question. With the orca's response a feeling of relief washed over Tom. He reached out to touch her. She nudged him in acknowledgement. Tom's heartbeat accelerated again, but this time in pure exhilaration at being so close to her. In a moment the warm intimacy had returned. He felt that, especially in new situations, his imitation of her voice would not fail to regain her recognition and trust.

Tom had let go of his grip on the gate and was caressing the orca with both hands. She was so gentle in her movements that he forgot about her sheer strength and what she could do with him if she wanted. While he rubbed her back, Tom moved along her flank towards her dorsal fin. He had already learned that the base of her dorsal fin was one of her favorite spots to be rubbed. Perhaps it was one of the spots that she could not easily scratch on something in her tank. Gunda was already used to having her fin touched, but he had never really grabbed it very firmly. He wondered if she would drag him along if he were to take a hold on it. He folded his fingers along the think round front edge and pulled a little.

Tuschka felt the tug and backed up a little, turning at the same time to see what her friend was doing. She saw the man vertically in the water against her flank and felt the drag of his weight on her fin. It was a strange feeling that slightly hindered her otherwise free movement. Tuschka wriggled a little and felt his hands slip away. She turned around and nudged his shoulder. Tom smiled while he tapped her gently. Then he started swimming, wondering whether she would follow him.

Tuschka watched. For the first time she had a good view of his way of swimming. It did not seem very efficient to her. It was slow and clumsy. She watched the man flailing and kicking with his long thin extremities. It gave her the feeling that he was struggling to stay near the surface and trying to make some progress at the same time. Tuschka moved closer and nudged his left thigh. The man quickly paused in surprise and looked back. Curious about her intentions, Tom resumed swimming. It was a few moments before he felt the orca nudge him again. He tried to continue as if nothing had happened. To his delight, the nudge became a gentle push. He had already more speed than he could ever achieve on his own.

While the orca pushed him between his legs, he let the orca take the initiative and only moved his arms a little to keep his balance. In his excitement, Tom let out a squeak. Tuschka answered without delay. She sensed that the man liked what she was doing and began to move a little faster. Tom hesitated for a moment to see if he should continue. He was not sure if he could keep it under control. They were approaching a sharp corner in the tank. Tom was about to roll away to avoid a potential crash into the wall when he felt himself being pushed away from the corner in a nice round curve. The orca was steering him! Tom was thrilled. They moved naturally. It felt as if they were one. He wished the exciting moment would last.

After three full rounds in the orca's small holding tank, he slid off the orca's rostrum. She stopped right by him. Tom wrapped his arms around her and pressed her against his chest. He lay his cheek on her smooth melon and felt himself overwhelmed with love, warmth, and gratitude. "You're so wonderful Gunda," he whispered. Then, he made several strokes towards the platform. She followed and pushed him along.

Tom rewarded her with a good portion of fish. Both he and Richard were kneeling down at the edge. The head trainer was visibly pleased with what he had seen. The two men got up to work out a training plan for water work with the whale. Tom looked back and was heavyhearted as he saw Gunda looking at him with her chin resting on the edge. She called softly, making clear how much she regretted he was leaving.

That night, the wonderful experience with Gunda kept Tom awake till late. Hidden behind the orca's gentle push was intelligence and a complete mastery of enormous physical strength. Being trained to swim with dolphins, Tom had learned that he could lead the way by using his arms to swerve left or right. He did not have to follow the perimeter of the tank, but could also make turns in the middle of the pool. Tom was not sure what movements he had made when they first approached the sharp corner of the tank. Whatever he had done or not done, the orca had known what to do. From that moment on, he no longer feared injuries due to lack of subtlety on Gunda's part. For Tom, a long awaited dream had come true. Since his first contact with the orca, he had been longing to deepen his friendship with her and to know her intimately. Swimming with the beautiful gentle orca, and being pushed and carried by her in play, was the ultimate fulfillment of that dream.

Tuschka's shows became a great success. She did not yet have as rich a repertoire as the dolphins, but people were in awe at seeing the supreme predator of the sea interact with humans as a gentle friend. Her speed swim betrayed her strength and her careful handling of her trainer bespoke a subtlety that amazed the spectators. Few of them had ever thought that the voracious creature harbored such refined qualities. At the end of most performances, the orca slid gracefully upon the platform to show her glossy streamlined body with its striking black-and-white coloration. Many of the visitors marveled at what special gifts the trainers had that enabled them to tame this queen of the sea. They did not use a whip, and they put themselves in potentially dangerous situations many times.

18.
A Friend is Missing

Life was changing for Tuschka, because there were fewer and fewer challenges. During the first two years of her captive life, the painful loss of her family had been softened by the many new experiences that fed her curiosity: the interaction with humans, the training sessions, the challenge of understanding what they wanted to teach her, and her acceptance among the dolphins. Since then, time had passed by with many shows and relatively few training sessions, which were mere rehearsals rather than challenging learning experiences. At the beginning of each season, the music and the visitors were a welcome distraction after the quiet winter time, but soon the excitement wore off. Although there was more activity, it was very predictable. With the little time in between shows, the trainers often did not even bother to open the gate and let her play with the dolphins. The more shows there were, the less playtime Tuschka had with her trainers, especially in the peak season when they ran four to five shows with the whale and with the dolphins.

Yet, there was more than just the repetitive character of her activities that sapped Tuschka's motivation. She sensed a change in most of her trainers as soon as the first few weeks of the season had passed. For every behavior that she performed correctly, they rewarded her with fish or a rub-down, but they rarely put their heart in it. Tuschka, somehow, sensed that there was less contact. They rarely watched her with that eager hope that she would grasp what they wanted from her, nor was there the enthusiasm and joy when she got it right. It began to dawn on Tuschka why their rewards often were totally predictable, with little or no feeling. They simply took her performance for granted.

One day in early fall when Tuschka was circling her tank, she heard the distant noise of the crowds waiting to enter the dome. As usual, the people would line up against the fence in several rows to look at her. Some would stay longer than others, some shouted and pointed, while others stood in quiet awe of her. Tuschka had taken an interest in observing them, to watch the differences in their behavior, reflecting bits and pieces of their personalities and feelings. Tuschka took a special interest in the young people who were often lifted up and carried by the adults. She had noticed that they acted much more spontaneously and naturally than their parents. Fear, joy, curiosity, amazement: all radiated from their little faces and the sounds and movements they made.

These moods and feelings were not strange to Tuschka. Among her kind too, the young were uninhibited.

A little squirt of water startled Tuschka. She stopped and swung around to see where it had come from. There it was again. A small boy had some green object in his hand from which the little squirts came. She spyhopped to face the boy and opened her mouth. When he squirted water in her mouth, Tuschka squeaked with delight. Assuming the youngster wanted to play with her, she took some water in her mouth and delicately squirted back at the boy. The well-aimed spray did not have the effect Tuschka had intended. Instead, he gave a cry and turned his face away. His mother frowned and they quickly vanished into the crowds. Tuschka was disappointed: the response itself was not uncommon for her, but this child had seemed a playful exception.

She swam several more circles and noticed a man shouting and waving at her. A few moments later, he started to hit the fence with some hard object. It made an unpleasant banging sound. When she stopped in front of him, he pointed at her with the object, leaning over as if attempting to touch her. In an instant she filled her mouth and gave the man a good-sized shower. Before he had time to wipe his face, he received another one. Shouting something at the whale, he quickly disappeared in the crowd. This time, Tuschka felt she had had a victory. The man had used an obtrusive, somewhat aggressive way of asking her attention and she had been successful in making him leave.

Tuschka had learned long ago that most humans did not like to get wet, and squirting was an effective way to repel those that annoyed her. Similarly, it had been obvious from the start that spyhops and squeaks were most appreciated by the crowd. Although the visitors' response was quite predictable from day to day, there were little unexpected events that lifted Tuschka's spirits in between dull daily shows.

One afternoon, in an indifferent mood, Tuschka had refrained from doing certain behaviors. Her trainer had tapped the water many times, had come over to her with a fish, and had even rubbed her, obviously intending to make her willing to respond to his cues. She liked the special attention. His pleading had melted her cool indifference and succeeded in kindling some of her enthusiasm. When she finally cooperated, Tuschka felt the strong change in the man's mood. From being impatient and nervous, he suddenly felt relieved, and made an effort to reward her well. Yet some tension remained: a tension that pleased Tuschka especially, because the man obviously no longer took for granted what she would do...

The experience left a seed of awakening in Tuschka. After several similar events, there was a slowly growing awareness that she could make choices that differed from what her human trainers wanted. It became a challenge for

Tuschka to see how her trainers would respond to her tricks. She began to discover that she could influence them and sometimes even make them yield to her wishes. They were only in command insofar as she allowed them. In their attempts to win the orca's cooperation, the trainers had become more attentive to her circumstances. They gave her more time with Lucie or other dolphins in the large tank. Tuschka would often respond with a good energetic show afterwards. It was her way to communicate to her trainers when she was happy and satisfied, and in doing so she was in fact manipulating them: rewarding them when they gave her attention, playtime, and other types of diversion.

But the initial success of her mental game was short-lived. Richard recognized the nature of the orca's behavior and was aware that if he did not call a halt to it, she, instead of the trainers, would soon be controlling the situation. It would not only ruin the shows, but also become potentially dangerous. Richard instructed his trainers and initiated new training sessions under his guidance. The pattern could be broken only if they did not yield to the whale's whims. If she refused to cooperate, they were expected to walk away from her and try later in case she had changed her mind. The latter was important: the orca should always be given a second chance to restore contact.

The change in the trainer's attitude did not go unnoticed by Tuschka. Her stubbornness was rarely answered with food or affection. Often, they ignored her for shorter or longer periods of time. She did not like being ignored. It was a reaction that brought up the fear of separation from deep within. Yet her human caretakers were more alert when they interacted with her, and if she performed well, they put more heart into their rewards. Tuschka's behavior was driven by a deep need for acknowledgement, respect, and even more, a warm caring friendship. Anything was better than indifference and lack of concern, even adverse reactions. Her struggle against indifference required a delicate balance between cooperation and opposition.

Of all trainers, Tom was still Tuschka's favorite. Although Bob was still curator, several trainers had come and gone. One had changed positions with one of the sea lion trainers, Steve had left the park, and two new ones had been hired. Initially, the exposure to new trainers had aroused Tuschka's curiosity. She had been eager to explore their personalities. They were all different: some were easier to manipulate than others, but even those who stood their ground were not all the same. With none of them did she have the intimate relationship she had with Tom. The others did not have that subtle understanding and tender warmth, nor was she so certain of their commitment. Some had disappeared and those experiences made Tuschka focus even more on whom she trusted most. Lucie was her best friend among the dolphins, but they both knew they depended on the decisions of man for their time together. Tom had Tuschka's complete trust, because she knew that he cared for her beyond fish and rewards.

His feelings came from the heart, even though he did not always let them flow as freely as they both wished.

* * *

Tuschka felt restless and sad. She missed the positive reinforcement of her favorite trainer, who had no equal in understanding her. It had been several weeks since he had last come to her. For the past five years, he had been away several times for longer than just a few days, but he had always returned. But now, after a much longer time, she began to feel restless. A fear crept into her mind that he might not return, a fear for another parting of the ways with one who had become her closest friend.

The remaining trainers noticed that the orca had less appetite. She performed in the shows, but with visibly less interest. Bob had called in a vet, but blood samples had revealed no sign of infection. They kept the whale under closer watch and had asked the guard to take respiration rates on Gunda twice a night for 15 minutes. In the following weeks there was little change, either for the worse, or for the better.

Not only did the orca miss her friend; the young trainer equally missed his beloved whale. He looked at the picture Richard had taken of them at one of their precious moments together. The scene filled him with worry and longing. Two months ago, Tom had been hit by a medium fever and other signs of influenza, but about a week later, he had suddenly begun to lose muscle control in his upper legs. Within a day, the disease had paralyzed most of his legs and was advancing upwards. He had been admitted to intensive care, where he had been able to do little more than breathe and mumble some words.

Tom had been very frightened when the physicians explained the diagnosis to him and revealed that he should be prepared for artificial ventilation in case the disease affected the muscles of his rib cage and diaphragm. He was relieved when his worst fears were not realized, but he was filled with sadness when the physicians described the general course of his disease and the average prognosis. Tom had been struck by the rare syndrome of Guillain-Barré, which is often preceded by a viral disease. It is believed to be some auto-immune response, which affects the spinal roots and peripheral nerves. In the most fortunate case, Tom would fully recover within two months, but in the worst case, recuperation would not be complete and would take one to two years. After about three weeks, he had begun to experience improvement, but it was slow. He was happy to be able to use his hands again and to talk better. It was clear to Tom that it would take a long time, if ever, before he could work with his dear Gunda again.

Richard and his colleagues considered the possibility that Tuschka's depression was attributable to Tom's long absence. Yet there was no way for

201

them to test that hypothesis. The temptation to pamper the orca was strong, but Richard feared that if his trainers gave in too much, she might become difficult to control. To compensate her loss somewhat, he decided to give Gunda more playtime with the dolphins in between shows, and on some nights he gave her Lucie as company. Richard and the others had not told Tom about the change in Tuschka's mood; it would only make things more difficult for the dedicated trainer. The orca had touched him so deeply that she had come to play a large part in his life.

As soon as it became clear that Tom would not be back for at least several months, a young woman had been hired to fill the gap. Her name was Sheila. During her first visit to the park, the orca had both impressed and touched her and many visits had followed. She had no former training with cetaceans, but she had been educated in animal care and husbandry and had some experience working in a zoo. Since the orca was fully trained, Richard expected the young woman would quickly be ready to help run shows. The dolphins quickly accepted food from her and responded to her cues as long as she worked with one of the more familiar trainers. The girl had been looking at the orca with interest. The large, beautiful creature intrigued her. She had heard her colleagues talk about the changes in the orca's behavior. Although she had nothing with which to compare Gunda's behavior, the explanations sounded plausible.

When winter break was approaching, Richard decided to introduce Sheila to Gunda. Sheila followed Richard towards the edge of Gunda's tank. The head trainer put the bucket down and tapped the water to call the whale over. The response was slow, but she did come. Almost sluggishly she opened her mouth to accept a fish. Richard frowned slightly as he looked at Sheila. The young woman had no difficulty in picking up the message: working with a new trainer seemed not to bring the diversion which the head trainer had hoped for. In the silent dome, the orca was not eager for a training session, nor interested in a visitor.

Richard asked Sheila to kneel down and offer Gunda a fish. The orca did not raise her head to accept the fish. He bent over and rubbed Gunda gently. "Come, young lady, we're here to divert you a little. Look, who's here for you. You'll see her a lot more, from now on." His friendly voice lifted the whale's spirits a little and she poked her rostrum out of the water into Richard's direction. He blew his whistle and nodded to encourage her. When he felt eye contact with the orca, he gave her a cue to roll over and offer him her pectoral fin. Gunda responded and while he gave her a rub-down he invited Sheila to touch her flipper gently. The orca did not resist.

The head trainer continued with several small behaviors and, as he had hoped, they seemed to work as a mental warming up for the whale. Sheila tried to give her another fish, but without success. Richard continued the training session with several bows and even managed to have her do a full breach. The young woman was in awe when she saw the powerful, streamlined body totally clear the water and arch in the air. They stayed just out of the splash as the orca crashed back on the opposite side of the tank. Each time, Sheila blew the whistle, but only from Richard would Gunda accept the rewards. She had seen many shows before, but now she looked at them with different eyes. Would the beautiful orca some day do these things for her? It was obvious for both Richard and herself that it would not be the same as with the dolphins. They were now taking most cues from her without the assistance of another trainer. That had taken only several weeks.

"She's not herself," Richard said quietly as he emptied the last of the bucket into Gunda's mouth. "It normally takes a bit longer to introduce a new trainer to the orca than to the dolphins, but under the present circumstances, I simply don't know what to expect. As a matter of fact, it puzzles me that we don't find any pathology. A mental cause is becoming more and more likely, but it doesn't seem appropriate for a wild animal to let emotions rule its life." Sheila looked at Richard with questioning eyes. "They're very intelligent and social animals. Who knows what they experience in the wild. We tend to relate all behavior to the necessity of survival. There may be more." Richard's look told to Sheila he did not reject her suggestion, but he did not wholeheartedly accept it either.

Tuschka was quick to understand that the new woman was not a visitor, but one who intended to become her trainer. Tom's disappearance not only left an aching emptiness, it meant the loss of one she had come to trust like no other. The attachment to the young man was so strong that part of her spirit seemed to have gone with him. Tuschka's confidence was severely shaken. She had been drained of the resilience to begin a new relationship. Many emotions disturbed Tuschka at the same time: she was craving for friendship, yet skeptical and wary of another loss. It was a confusing mixture of feelings and without knowing it herself, the latter emotions dominated, making her unreceptive to a new friendship.

Sheila was making slow progress in her training sessions. Richard tried to stand back as much as possible. The young woman also worked with some other trainers, but that was not as effective. Only in Richard's presence would Gunda let herself be touched. They both wondered how they could keep Gunda from sinking deeper in her dull disinterested mood.

Late one afternoon, Sheila was watching the orca through the viewing window. Lucie stayed close to her as the two circled round. She noticed the slower rhythm of the whale's fluke strokes and sensed the power they held. The orca's head moved slightly up and down to match the movement of her tail. In the twilight, she was barely more than a black shadow, the white patches hardly visible. As the light faded, the two looked like a mother and calf. It was a joy to watch the graceful silent movements that were rapidly fading into the darkness.

The stories about the orca passed through her mind. She sensed that the indifferent behavior had nothing to do with her as a person, but was a state of mind that could be broken only if the right chord were struck. Although Gunda responded much better to the head trainer, it was obvious from his comments that the interaction was devoid of her former engagement. Sheila wondered how long the orca would keep missing her former trainer and she felt a desire to learn about the special relationship that Gunda obviously had shared with him. She decided to soon visit Tom in the hospital.

* * *

When she entered the department of neurology, her heart beat faster. She was so eager to meet this obviously special person, but she did not know how to start the conversation without immediately making him worry about the mental condition of his beloved whale.

There were four patients in the room. In an instant Sheila spotted a framed picture of Gunda in the embrace of a young man. She swallowed. What a special and tender contact. As the picture held her eyes, the young woman did not notice that the man in the adjacent bed woke up. The lifting of his eyelids had been his only movement. She was startled he addressed her. She sucked in a breath of air and felt her cheeks flush as if she had been intruding in a private moment. For a moment, they looked at each other. Tom did not know that she had come for him. She was an unknown woman who clearly had been touched by the unusual picture. Her reaction warmed him. The precious moment obviously had meaning to the girl.

Sheila cleared her throat and spoke: "Are you Tom Kirkman?," she asked with a light questioning look. "Yes," he nodded and motioned her closer. "What an exceptionally precious picture of you and Gunda," she remarked. He seemed to perk up. "So you must be the new trainer," he said and managed a slight smile. "How's my girl doing?" was his first question. Sheila felt blood rise to her cheeks again. "Her blood work is fine and .. uh .. we train her several times a day."

Sheila felt him waiting for more. His eyes seemed to look right through her. She knew he had already read the message that she had so clumsily tried to hide, but he did not embarrass her further by pressing for more. Tom knew the young woman could not possibly have had the time to get to know his Gunda well, but he also realized that her more experienced colleagues had all but been raving about the orca's behavior. He felt some relief that Gunda seemed not yet to have taken to someone else, but at the same time he despised his own selfishness, knowing that if no one filled the gap that he had left, it would be at the cost of Gunda's wellbeing. One part of him was eager to hear all about his dear orca, but the other part wanted to hide in the soothing ignorance, that left room for his wishful dreams.

Tom motioned Sheila to take the chair just behind her. She took her coat off and sat down. The short pause helped them both to prepare for the conversation that somehow was bound to follow. Tom decided to leave the initiative to the young woman. Sheila changed the subject and inquired about his health. It soon became clear to the young woman that his recovery would take many more months, and that it remained questionable even then whether he could take up his job as a trainer again. "It must be very hard for you," she said with empathy. "Such a disease would be hard on everybody, but you've been cut off from a special friend." "To whom I can't explain," Tom completed. Sheila nodded. The ill trainer broke the ice. "Are you already working with Gunda?" Sheila explained how Richard had introduced her to the whale, and that Gunda had just begun to accept some cues as long as she was in the company of a more familiar trainer. The stories about Gunda's overall behavior left no doubt about her depressed mood.

"I've understood that you have a very special and intimate relationship with her," Sheila said. "That picture tells it without words. They are all sayi..." She suddenly stopped, knowing that Tom would be with the orca if he could, but he encouraged her to continue. "Although it isn't expressed very openly, most of the staff believe Gunda will change as soon as you return, but unfortunately no one knows when that'll be. I've been thinking that perhaps I can .." Sheila stopped abruptly and blushed. "I suddenly don't understand how I could've been so naive to think that ..eh.. I could help Gunda a little by learning from you." "That's not so farfetched," Tom said. "But your fellow trainers also know the orca well," Sheila went on, "and they've seen you interact with her. If they don't succeed in bringing her out of this depression what difference could I make?" "It's not experience, reasoning, or knowledge, that is most important, although it's a help. What counts most of all is your heart. That makes all the difference ... " "That is indeed what I have been thinking all along," Sheila interrupted, "if I could only reach her."

Tom tried to shift position, but with little success. Sheila helped to prop him up and raised the head section of his bed. Then, he picked up the conversation. "It seems Gunda's sadness or frustration is making her less receptive. Unconsciously, she may fear another loss, at the same time depriving herself of the friendship and love that she needs so much." Sheila took a deep breath. "You reached her when she was brought in from the wild. That must have been a far more traumatic experience. Is there any advice you can give me?" "She was very young then, and younger animals are more eager to try new things," Tom said. "I understand," Sheila interjected tenaciously, "but perhaps I can reach her by doing things that you did..." Tom frowned. It was the question he had expected all along, but did not want to answer. For Sheila to befriend Gunda would be one thing, a very important thing for the whale's sake, but he could not bear the thought that she would follow in his footsteps. His ways with

205

Gunda were a special intimate secret that only the two of them shared.

The silence and the expression on his face told Sheila that her question was hard on him. She did not want to make him uncomfortable, yet she wanted to help the whale. "You must find your own way," Tom finally started. "If what you dó is all that counts, all trainers would have the same response. Trying to copy what someone else does can never communicate your own spontaneous feelings." Sheila nodded in silence. His words sounded wise and thoughtful, and there was nothing she could say against them.

Tom refrained from saying that a truly intimate relationship was not given to all and that many never went beyond a good working relationship. Yet he was subtle enough to sense that the girl did have the potential for a special relationship and he also realized he would never forgive himself for keeping from Gunda any help that he could give her. "I'm always supervised...," Sheila said. That was indeed a problem. Tom was very aware that his early night watches had played a crucial part in building his relationship with the orca. It would be hard to break Gunda's shield under the given circumstances. "That's a big handicap Sheila, but time and patience will be rewarded. I can give you this advice: if you can't do what you want, either because Richard or Gunda will not let you, then tell her what you feel," and he stressed the word 'tell'. "She's a very acoustic creature....." He spoke these words slowly to emphasize their meaning, and Sheila understood. She knew that the secret lay in sound, but the challenge remained hers to find a way to reach Gunda's heart: her unique way.

"May I have a closer look at the picture?," Sheila asked. "Sure," Tom replied, "go ahead." She picked up the photo and smiled, but in a different way. The young woman no longer looked at it with an undercurrent of sadness about something that she would never experience. She looked at it with the glow of hope and anticipation that something similar was in store for her some day. Sheila thanked Tom for sharing his thoughts and advice while she picked up her coat to leave. "Wait," Tom asked at the last moment. "Thank you, for caring about Gunda." Tears welled up in his eyes, but he managed to swallow them back. "I'm still struggling too much with my own feelings. She shouldn't suffer. She needs you. I hope you'll come back and tell me how it goes." Sheila smiled at him. "Gunda will never forget you." Then she turned and walked out of the ward. Her last words stayed on his mind. Would it truly be so? He had not allowed himself to think about it much, fearing the heartbreaking reality of being forgotten. Now, he felt a spark of hope. As soon as he could leave this ward, he would go out of his way to see her.

19.
Comfort from a New Friend

Lately, Richard had not spent much playtime with the orca. The few times he had tried, her lack of interest had discouraged him. He hoped the dolphins would help to divert Gunda's mind so he gave them a lot of time together in the main tank. He hoped that by the time the animals needed to be prepared for next spring, everything would have returned to normal.

Sheila knew that playtime normally had its place in each animal's repertoire and she longed to give it a try with Gunda. Yet she pondered how to bring the topic up. If the head trainer was discouraged, how could she be so arrogant or so naive as to think the orca would want any part of her? At the same time, she kept thinking of any strategy that she might use to get the orca's attention. If she could just sit at the edge of the pool and talk to the whale.

After weighing the pros and cons for several days, Sheila approached Richard with the suggestion that the orca might be more receptive to her if she interacted with the animal not just as a trainer. Sheila explained to him that, until now, Gunda always had to do what she asked her and that she wondered if it would make a difference if she showed some spontaneous interest in what the orca did.

To Sheila's relief, the head trainer did not immediately reject her proposal, but he frowned and took a long time to respond. "I wonder if the orca will do anything at all for you to react to," he said with dull eyes. Isn't it simply that you want to pamper the whale in an attempt to win her sympathy?" "There's certainly truth in that," Sheila said thoughtfully, "but is playtime much else? If it is, I would like to learn. I haven't had an opportunity to participate in playtime sessions." Richard nodded. "In a sense you are right about that, but things are not so simple. As you know, we try to stimulate positive behavior and to ignore undesired, in this case indifferent, behavior. Not long before you started here, Gunda was challenging us in the sense that she was trying to find out how far we would go in our attempts to get her to respond to our cues. It soon got out of hand, so we started to ignore that behavior. The risk of playtime with us is that it may encourage her to persist in her present behavior. To compensate for that I give her playtime with the dolphins instead."

Sheila understood her supervisor's logic, but she was not convinced. If sadness caused the whale's behavior, then ignorance was not the way to lift her spirits. After her conversation with Tom, the young woman was even more convinced that challenging the trainers would not be the first thing on the orca's mind, once contact was re-established. On the contrary! The orca would foster the regained contact and give in to her need for friendship and affection.

The young woman took a deep breath to gather courage for her daring response. "Richard, I don't think Gunda would be so stubborn in her challenging behavior that she would push it to a point where the contact is broken. That's not the way of her kind. I recall she was doing relatively well until after Tom got ill. The sequence of events makes me think she may be blocked by lack of confidence and fear of, who knows, another such loss." Sheila realized her endless reflections had made her quick in phrasing her thoughts, yet the head trainer might interpret it as arrogance. She quickly decided to boost her credibility by mentioning that she had talked to Tom. No one used to read Gunda's mind better than he. "I wouldn't have thought of all this if I'd not talked with Tom."

"Hmm," was all Richard said. Sheila did not know what he was thinking and how he felt about her taking the initiative to discuss these things with Tom. She suddenly blushed and realized how the other trainers had been trying to spare Tom by refraining from mentioning the problems with the orca. It was clear now that she had shared it all with their sick colleague.

At the same time, many thoughts raced through the head trainer's mind. So Tom knew about the situation. Had he advised her? Why had he not contacted him if he was concerned about Gunda? Yet it was equally strange that he had not asked Tom's opinion. Richard painfully had to admit to himself that hiding the information from Tom had not only been to spare the ill trainer: he had also considered it a weakness to take a younger trainer's advice. This newly hired woman was free of all these thoughts. Richard realized how plausible Sheila's remarks were. Even worse, he would have thought of them himself had he not let his pride cloud his reasoning. He did, indeed, feel uncomfortable approaching the orca with true spontaneity. He would feel embarrassed if she did not respond well. The orca had confronted him with the fact that he was not as self-confident as the dolphins had given him to believe.

Then his resolve washed over him. It was his task to see to the well-being and training of all the animals entrusted to him. That task did not require him to excel at everything, but to have insight and make wise decisions. At last, the head trainer looked up at Sheila's slightly shamed, questioning eyes. "I'll give your proposal the benefit of the doubt," he said. "We'll try playtime sessions with her, and why shouldn't you participate? If spontaneity can break this pattern of indifference, the renewed rapport will be a new starting-point. But, I can't emphasize enough that you should keep training and play strictly separated".

Sheila was both relieved and excited at Richard's decision. On purpose, she took the liberty not to plan all her playtime with the whale. Sheila tried to pick quiet moments when no other people were working in the dome.

210

In the morning, Sheila came to the edge of the platform, alongside the whale's tank. Gunda was hovering near the gate to the corridor. She barely stirred when the young woman lowered herself to sit down. It was an unusual situation for both of them, but that in itself seemed no trigger for the orca to come over.

Tuschka was watching the dolphins when the female trainer came to sit down. With the keen senses of a hunter, nothing escaped her consciousness. She had been observed before, though not often by this woman. Her attention went back to the dolphins, who were simply circling their tank. Then, suddenly, a melodious humming sound caught Tuschka by surprise. She did not move, but listened intently. It was the woman, who was making the sounds. They bore a faint resemblance to the type of sounds that accompanied the shows, but those sounds had not come from humans: they filled the dome out of nowhere and vanished as abruptly as they had come. After a few minutes, the song was interrupted by a soft voice. Tuschka had heard the woman speak to others of her kind. Her voice used to be higher pitched and a bit sharper than those of the men who interacted with her. But now, the sharp aspect was not present. There was a hint of warmth in the softness of her tone.

Sheila moved her fingers in the water and saw the orca looking at her. Then, she cupped her hand and sprayed a little water at the whale. "Come Gunda, play a little with me," Sheila beckoned, as she splashed another handful of water towards the whale. "You don't know what to expect from me eh? You don't know what to expect from any of us, do you? We come, make friends with you and suddenly disappear. I hope I won't be forced to do the same. Parting of the ways is hard, but loneliness is worse. If you don't make a new friend after losing one, you'll suffer more than you need to." As Sheila spoke her thoughts, she was filled with compassion for the broken orca, whose life was ruled by the habits and whims of man. Tom understood that, was aware of that.

Tuschka felt the sincerity and concern in the woman's voice. It stirred feelings deep inside her, but something still blocked their release. She heard the melodious humming sound again and was drawn to it. It was barely worth calling it a response, but Sheila saw Gunda move her head slightly in her direction. Although the orca did not come away from the gate, the young trainer took the sign as a subtle beginning of contact.

Sheila had quietly hoped that perhaps that first personal approach to the orca would have some positive effect on her training sessions, but she could not observe any change. She also experienced for the first time how difficult it was to adhere to Richard's strong advice to keep playtime and training separate. What would the orca think of people with 'two faces'? How credible would her spontaneity be to Gunda? Sheila was aware that it had been the way of Gunda's trainers since her capture. How hard must it have been for Tom to start training sessions, knowing that, at least in the beginning, the orca would not understand his detached, unyielding attitude. Yet, Tom had been Gunda's closest friend. The picture of the man embracing the whale stood vividly in her memory. Sheila did not give up. She found more moments to have private time with the orca, and her attention slowly melted the thin layer of bitterness with which Tuschka unknowingly tried to protect herself against new wounds of loss.

One afternoon, Sheila came in with a bucket of fish to feed Gunda. To the young woman's amazement, the orca needed no encouragement to come over and feed. In between her mouthfuls of fish Gunda swam circles with obviously more vigor and seemed to look at her when she surfaced near the opposite wall of her tank. When the fish were nearly gone, Sheila began to walk the perimeter of the tank, dropping a fish into the water every few yards. To her great delight, she found the whale following at her heels as she made another circle around the tank. For the first time, Sheila regretted the bucket was empty. Back on stage, she dipped it to fill it half with water and playfully dumped it close to the whale, who seemed to be expecting more fish. "Next time, I'll run more circles with you when I feed you," she said with a smile.

Gunda spyhopped in front of her. Sheila was surprised at the orca's eager attention. Not knowing what was motivating the whale, she thought of something she could do to keep her interested. She bent over and splashed Gunda, then ran a few yards ahead and made another splash. Gunda followed! Sheila was elated and let out a whoop of delight as she felt herself being splashed in return. There was contact... they were playing together!

After two more circles of their splashing game, Sheila stopped near the edge of the stage. Gunda stopped close by, looking up at her. Sheila knelt down. "That was wonderful Gunda! Doesn't it feel better to play with a friend than to lie lonely near the gate?" Her face was not so far from the orca in front of her. Sheila felt a closeness that she had not experienced before. Gunda made a soft call and the young woman knew that the orca was talking to her in her own way. Then Gunda approached the concrete edge and lifted her chin towards her. There was only one feeling that filled Sheila's mind: 'Gunda accepts me, she wants to make friends with me'. As she brought her hands closer in hopes of touching the beautiful orca, Sheila felt the little nudge of the whale's smooth chin in her hands.

The orca's gentle gesture touched Sheila deeply. In a mysterious way, she experienced a sharing of minds. She was overwhelmed by the tenderness and warmth the orca radiated. The invisible barrier that had kept her at a distance was gone. Sheila knew in her heart that in fact Gunda had taken it away. She ran her hands tenderly along her soft throat and then over her smooth glossy rostrum.

Tuschka sensed the sincerity in the young woman's caressing and voiced her affection in response. They both savored the precious moment. For the first time since Tom had disappeared, Tuschka felt joy and warmth spark in her heart again. The private moments with Sheila had brought Tuschka's longing for friendship and affection closer to the surface. Now it suddenly flowed freely, like a waterfall released from the frozen grip of winter ice. Sheila would never forget the special moment. It was etched in her memory, especially that first subtle nudge with which Gunda had acknowledged their friendship.

Since their special time together, Gunda responded incomparably better in her training sessions. The orca tried to entice Sheila into play and sometimes she had a hard time resisting, but Gunda's spirit was back! Richard and the other two trainers noticed it too. Their rapport with the whale was not as strong as Sheila's, but Gunda responded a lot better to most of their cues.

* * *

After their first unforgettable moment of mutual contact and acceptance, Sheila had felt an urge to visit Tom and tell him, but mixed feelings had kept her from acting solely upon her impulses. On the one hand, he would be happy for the whale, but on the other it was likely he would miss Gunda even more and would worry that she was taking his place in the whale's heart. Sheila had decided to wait a while, hoping to find a good way to tell him about Gunda.

Although everyone was happy with the dramatic improvement in Gunda's behavior, it was undeniable that the orca was not the same as before. There were stronger fluctuations in her mood, which was most apparent to those who did not have a very strong bond with her. Some days, she seemed not very interested and other days she was full of energy. On her down days she would cooperate fairly well with her favorite trainers, but others had a hard time getting her to respond. It seemed as if the orca valued some bonds more than others and invested in them accordingly.

Sheila was excited about the friendship that had developed between her and the orca. Her relative success in the shows was a welcome side-effect, but it was not what she found most important. As their bond grew, a whole world opened to her; it was like a journey of discoveries into the orca's mind with Gunda being the leader. Especially during their moments of spontaneous contact, Gunda gave herself more and more. Sheila learned of the orca's endless creativity, her surprising intelligence, and fast learning, but also of her little tricks to lead her up the garden path or to manipulate her to yield to her wishes. In fact, the orca read her better then she could read the orca.

Over the past weeks, Sheila increasingly felt that Gunda could not continue to lead her further on their journey together, unless she took away the last barrier. Only if she entered the orca's domain, could Gunda show more of herself. The head trainer had been more receptive to Sheila's request than she had dared to hope. Although she was a novice compared to others who worked with the whale, her remarkable rapport with Gunda was considered ample compensation for her relative lack of experience. They discussed the possible responses of Gunda and how to act on them. In the past, the orca had shown her annoyance with newcomers in the water a few times: she had tail lobbed relatively close, pulled them under briefly, or even bruised them. None of these cases had led to severe injuries, but it had ended the former practice of having trainers enter the water with the orca before they had a good working relationship with the maturing whale.

Sheila's heartbeat was fast as she appeared on the platform in her brand new wetsuit. Richard gave her an encouraging nod. She immediately noticed Gunda's hesitant greeting. The orca was clearly not used to seeing her friend in this attire. Sheila knelt down at the edge of the platform. The orca came over and quickly accepted a handful of fish. Yet it was different. Sheila was tense and she knew that Gunda was aware of it. The fact that no one had entered the water with Gunda in a long time did not make things easier for Sheila. She tried to entice Gunda in a splashing game to divert her attention, but the orca was not eager to participate. She followed her trainer's every move. Sheila realized tension would only build if she continued her fruitless attempts to create a relaxed and normal atmosphere, but what would happen when she entered the water? The orca seemed to measure her in uncertain expectation. Sheila felt her self-confidence ebb away and cast a glance at Richard. Nothing in his attitude hinted at a warning. 'Of course you are curious', Sheila reassured herself when she addressed the orca in thought. If she was going to swim with her dear friend, she had to do it now.

Slowly Sheila slid into the water. She saw the orca back off and lost eye contact. It was unsettling. She gave a light tap on the water, but instead of coming over, the orca submerged and sank down. What was she up to? Without contact her precious Gunda had turned into a distant whale she could not read, an animal she could no longer predict. The young woman felt a sudden urge to leave the water, but suppressed it. On the one hand she tried to convince herself that Gunda needed time to realize who she was, and on the other she was afraid to trigger an adverse reaction with the sudden splashing of climbing out.

As Sheila drifted motionless, she saw the whale glide under her as a big black shadow. Her heart pounded in her chest. She had no way of knowing what the orca's next move would be. Sheila turned her head away, too afraid to look. She envisioned the top predator of the ocean rising up underneath her with jaws agape to grab her around the waist. The tension was unbearable. Sheila trembled in terror as time seemed to come to a halt.

A blow close by startled Sheila. Slow and hesitant, she turned her head toward the sound. The orca had surfaced just two yards away from her. As the whale slightly lifted her head, their eyes met… As mysteriously as the contact had been lost, it returned. Gunda slowly glided over and gave Sheila a gentle and reassuring nudge. Then, before Sheila had come to herself, Gunda rolled over, and in an instant the young woman felt herself being lifted on the orca's broad chest. There she lay, between Gunda's pecs, her cheek on her soft throat, and her arms lying down in a large embrace on both sides of her beloved orca. Sheila was overwhelmed with emotions. What had been agonizing fear moments ago, was now complete trust. She wrapped her arms around the orca, changing her passive embrace into an active hug, and felt Gunda's gentle nudge against her cheek. As Gunda gently carried her, Sheila was aware of every subtle movement. She felt the tranquil undulations of the orca's flukes and cherished their precious closeness. She caressed Gunda while her tears ran down her cheeks. She was endeared to feel how Gunda acknowledged her every caress with a little nudge by lifting her chin in response. There was no doubt that the orca enjoyed every moment of it. It was as if she shared her wish to let the moment last. Sheila experienced a sharing of minds, a closeness stronger than ever before. She could barely comprehend that this top predator of the ocean was carrying her so gently, and communicating such unlimited trust.

Not far from the platform Gunda slowly turned upright and rose in a spyhop before her trainer. As Sheila took a hold on Gunda's pecs, the orca began to spin around, pulling Sheila along as in a big waltz. Sheila squealed in delight. She marveled at the orca's strength and grace. Gunda came to a stop and leveled herself. Sheila stroked her back and held on to her dorsal fin as the orca carried her to the platform. Speechless, she climbed back on stage and pressed her friend close, unable to answer Gunda's soft squeak.

Sheila was deeply touched. She realized that her initial apprehension had alienated herself from Gunda. It was a state of mind which Gunda had not experienced in her before. Sheila figured the orca had felt a similar distance and had needed time to read her. Whatever had been on the orca's mind during those tantalizing minutes of broken contact, she had recognized her vulnerable position and fear. She had entered Gunda's domain…, she had put herself at the orca's mercy, and Gunda had done far more than just accept her. The orca had taken the initiative to restore the contact and had made the most convincing and tender gesture to reassure her of her friendship.

Sheila slowly released her grip and ran her hands along Gunda's jaws as she slid back down. When she tilted her head, their eyes met and held. For Sheila it was a mutual acknowledgement of their reinforced bond.

* * *

It was not long before the new season that Sheila went to see Tom. He had recovered sufficiently to be transferred to a rehabilitation clinic. She found him reading in a wheelchair near one of the windows of a room that he shared with two others. Sheila was happy to find him alone. She had already seen the precious picture of him and Gunda on his bedside table, before he noticed her. A smile came over his face as he invited her to sit down. "It's good to see you in a chair Tom," she said, "and even more to see you smile!" She asked him how he had been doing and if there was still progress in his recovery. He had almost normal use of his arms, but his legs were still weak. Also, his sense of balance was still insufficient for him to walk with crutches. "They think, I'll be able to walk again, but I may not regain my former strength and stability. I'm training as much as I can. It's going slow, but I'm still hopeful."

Soon the conversation turned to the orca. Tom seemed less emotional or more in control of his emotions than the previous time, which made it easier for Sheila to speak openly. ".... Gunda is doing incomparably better now, although her mood is a little more variable than it seems to have been in the past. I don't know if it's the behaviors, the style of training, or some of us that fail to keep her interested sometimes." Sheila gave Tom some examples to illustrate Gunda's behavior. "How about you and Gunda?" he asked. The corners of Sheila's mouth lifted in a shy smile, which already told Tom that the young woman had made contact with his beloved orca. "I think she has two special friends now," she said empathically to the man in the wheelchair. "I would be very happy if this is so," he said, thinking of his own relationship with the orca. "Tell me how it went."

Sheila told Tom her story of Gunda's initial lack of interest and how she had started to talk to the whale and sing songs for her when she was floating near the gate. Tom listened intently as Sheila continued. "....and then, I'll never forget that moment. She came close and rose up as if inviting me to touch her. As I turned the palms of my hands up to cup her chin, she took the initiative and nudged my hands. It was so special. In that moment, she opened some unseen door and our minds made contact. She expressed her trust and accepted me as a friend. From that moment on everything was different." The former trainer smiled. No one understood better than he how meaningful that first touch was. It was the tangible beginning of a special friendship.

Sheila told Tom of Gunda's games and tricks and how the orca seemed to always be ahead of her as they explored each other's minds. "I increasingly felt the desire to swim with her and was so thrilled when Richard gave me permission. When I entered the water with her for the first time, she seemed confused and dived. I was so afraid. But then, after a reassuring nudge, she rolled over and carried me on her chest between her pecs. It was so touching, such an indescribable gesture to tell me I could fully trust her. It was as if she said 'come with me, it's all right'…"

216

Tom was touched by the story and as they looked at each other, they both felt recognition. In unison, their eyes turned towards the picture on Tom's bedside table. It was an experience that they shared and yet it was unique for each of them. Tom was happy for Gunda and for Sheila. Yet he was also relieved that the woman had not tried to mimic him, but had approached the whale in her own spontaneous way. It was a soothing thought that the woman had lifted Gunda's spirits, but had not taken his place. They talked some more about possible explanations for the changes in Gunda's behavior. When Sheila mentioned Gunda's subtle sense for sincerity and respect, it dawned on Tom that some changes in that direction had already begun to take place shortly before he had fallen ill. Finally, they both agreed that maturation probably played some part.

20.
Adolescence

The subsequent show season was not as great a success as it had been in the previous years. It was not only the orca's unpredictable behavior, but also the frequent cancellation of water work with the trainers that left the public less excited. Already after the first several weeks, boredom had seemed to set in. During some shows, the orca refused to enter the main tank, or she would spend most of the time resting on her back near the gate. Doing shows with the orca became increasingly stressful and it seemed that the more nervous a trainer became, the less the orca was under control. Sheila and Richard had the best results and did the majority of the shows. When Gunda was in a cooperative mood, or when logistics did not permit otherwise, others did the orca show. When nothing seemed to attract Gunda's attention, it often helped to let Lucie perform with her. But that stimulation was a last resort, and used as little as possible. Sheila and Richard sensed there was more to the problem than simply boredom.

As Sheila walked passed the whale tank to work with the dolphins, it was hard for her to ignore the soft moaning calls of Gunda, who was reaching over the edge to get attention. For the second time in three months, the orca was over affectionate. Like then, besides cooperating well, she was interested in physical contact more than anything else. Sheila wondered what was causing the orca to be so much more in need of affection and warmth. Would wild orcas have similar variations in their moods and needs? Did Gunda really need the extra attention, or was the intelligent creature trying to manipulate her? Sheila found it difficult to decide how much she should yield to the orca's pleading behavior. She knew that in the wild Gunda's family would understand her unerringly. Her love for the orca made Sheila worry more about Gunda's wellbeing than her own control over the animal. Over the past several days, Gunda followed her as much as her enclosure permitted, and her calls carried a pleading, plaintive quality. Whenever possible within her relatively tight schedule, Sheila come to the orca and try to satisfy some of her insatiable need for attention and physical contact.

It was already evening when Sheila came to Gunda to say good-bye for the day. Still dressed in her wetsuit, she sat down and was warmed as Gunda rested her head on her lap. Sheila hummed a tune and gently ran her hands along Gunda's gums and smooth melon. The orca rolled over to her side and offered her flipper to be scratched. As if guiding the woman to where she wanted to be caressed most, she moved a little forward, keeping contact with Sheila's hand as it ran along her flank. Sheila flushed a little when the orca rolled over on her back and stopped when her hand was resting on her mammary slits. She felt the whale pressing up against her hand, asking her to fondle the spot. Gunda had started this behavior a few days ago and Sheila had quit her caressing several times in hopes to discourage the behavior, but Gunda remained persistent. It was a sensual need with which Sheila felt uncomfortable; she clearly did not feel at ease to even attempt to satisfy it. Yet she could not bring herself to walk away from her beloved whale every time she offered her genital area, knowing deep inside that the orca could not be blamed for it. A few gentle taps were as much as Sheila could bring herself to give.

As Sheila looked at the mammary slits, it suddenly struck her that they were swollen and more pink than normal. Gunda pressed up at her again, wanting her to continue touching and stroking her. She saw the orca lift her chin a little as if trying to see what was distracting her friend. Absorbed in the implications of what she had observed, Sheila stroked Gunda lightly. Instantly, the orca relaxed, let her head rest in the water again and held steady, savoring the caress. As Sheila's hand quietly came to a rest on the orca, another nudge brought her attention back to the whale. She saw her lift her chin again. It suddenly struck Sheila that Gunda had not been taking a breath for a while. Aware that she had been lost in thought for some moments, she wondered how long Gunda had been holding her breath. She tapped the orca lightly, intending to signal her that she was done, but upon her touch Gunda relaxed her head again, lifting her belly up for Sheila to continue.

Sheila was familiar with this behavior. Especially when she was rubbing the underside of Gunda's peduncle, the orca would also hold her breath and stay up-side-down to savor the moment. It was her way to express her appreciation and a request for more. It was obvious that Gunda was pushing herself to hold her breath in hopes that she would continue. In some way, Sheila found herself curious as to how long Gunda would resist her need for air when she continued to satisfy her, but she had not timed it.

As Gunda lifted her chin again, Sheila felt her tense. She rested her hand on the orca's belly, just moving her thumb to caress her. Gunda pushed her belly up in response, but she did not fully relax as before. Then, Sheila lay her hand on the orca's upturned chin, pulling on it to make her turn over. Gunda followed smoothly and exhaled explosively. She took several deep breaths in succession, indicating that she had indeed made an effort to hold her breath. Sheila held Gunda's head against her chest and felt overwhelmed with compassion. "Poor girl, you're growing into adulthood. You're longing for a male orca, but I can't give you what he can give you. You need a companion." Sheila held her and felt tears well up in her eyes as she felt the orca nudge her cheek. It was obvious that Gunda's need stemmed simply from the fact that nature took its course and was trying to find its fulfillment in an environment that deprived Gunda of male companions and much more..... As Sheila let go, Gunda followed her along the edge of the pool. Just before leaving the platform, she looked back, feeling helpless as the orca's soft pleading voice filled the dome.

Richard showed little concern when Sheila told him about Gunda's behavior of the past few days. He too had noticed the orca's increased need for physical contact, but he had not been aware of any sexual component in her affection. "You'd expect her to prefer me over you for such games," he joked. But when Sheila mentioned the pink swelling of the genital area, his face turned into a serious expression. Suddenly, a light went on: "Perhaps that explains her mood swings!" They both had been thinking for a while that boredom was not the only explanation for the orca's behavior. Sheila had already come to the conclusion the head trainer had just made. She nodded, but said nothing. She believed that Gunda took more to her than to Richard, making it easier for her to read her needs. Sheila was happy that the head trainer had picked up the message so quickly. The decision to test the whale's hormone levels was quickly made, but she wondered what effect, if any, the results would have if they supported their hypothesis.

Tuschka felt a stronger longing to be with the dolphins than usual. Although she had Lucie's company fairly often, she was only rarely allowed playtime with the entire group. As soon as the gate between them had been opened, Tuschka joined them gracefully, gliding and rolling with them, and brushing against their sleek bodies. She felt a strange attraction to Flash, but he was not used to interacting with the orca. He too felt attracted in some way, but was confused and uncomfortable when the large female huddled around him, obviously seeking more physical contact than ever before. He snapped at Tuschka a few times, which discouraged her and made her seek physical contact with her female companions. They were far more accepting of her affection.

Tuschka ran her belly along the tip of Sacha's dorsal fin and savored the special sensation it gave her. When the dolphin made a sideways roll, Tuschka lost contact, but quickly found another female willing to let her glide against her flipper. The movements of the large whale blended gracefully with those of the much smaller dolphins.

Being surrounded by so many companions, Tuschka's excitement built and the gentle rubbing and caressing occasionally burst into short chasing games. Although the dolphins were agile and liked the sudden bursts of speed and chases, it made them uncomfortable when Tuschka really put her heart into it. Tuschka was many times their weight, but no less maneuverable. Having the orca at their heels for more than a few seconds stirred up a feeling of fear from deep within. Several times, Tuschka immediately broke off upon a distress call, but it was apparent from the dolphins' evasive behavior that she had pushed it too far. Lucie was more trusting than the other dolphins, but she also had her limits. Not wanting to lose her smaller friend, Tuschka quickly refrained from the chasing and tried to reassure Lucie with gentle nudges and rubs.

When evening fell, Tuschka was reluctant to separate from the dolphins. As soon as she had heard the gate open, she avoided looking at the man standing near the edge of the platform. She knew exactly what he was going to ask her when she heard his tap on the water. He would reward her when she heeded his request, but staying with the dolphins was far more exciting than the prospect of a long lonely night. Although Tuschka did not respond to the man's tapping on the water, she wished he would just leave them be. As long as he was there, she was not sure what he was going to do to pursue his goal.

Another hissing sound preceded the opening of the gate to the dolphin tank. Tuschka was in no doubt about the man's intentions. Flash and several other dolphins went into their holding pool without hesitation. The orca poked her head into the passage, but did not go in. In protest, she grabbed the gate and pushed it wide open. She knew they would not close it as long as she was in the way. In the corner of her eye Tuschka saw Lucie heading for the passage. In an instant the orca swung around, just in time to block Lucie's way in. Startled, the dolphin backed up a little. When she made another attempt, Tuschka interfered again and resolutely nudged her away from the gate. The much smaller dolphin understood the message of her big friend. She was uncomfortable not obeying the trainer, but it was obvious that Tuschka left her no other option than to follow her. The orca swung away from the gate and started to circle the tank with Lucie on the inside of the circle. It was a strange sight to see the two swim together as if they were mother and calf.

The gate to the dolphin enclosure slapped shut. After two more rounds, Tuschka saw the man leave. She relaxed, knowing that she had succeeded in keeping at least Lucie with her. Without an immediate threat of separation, Tuschka slowed down and nudged Lucie gently, showing appreciation for her company. The dolphin's tension subsided as well and the orca found her more receptive to physical contact. Tuschka ran her belly against Lucie's dorsal fin. She had a special sensation when the fin tip touched her genital area and hovered over the dolphin to keep her position. Lucie rolled away a few times, but Tuschka did not immediately give up. She quickly perfected the technique so that she did not exert pressure on the dolphin's fin and moved her flukes to match Lucie's. Lucie became more accepting as she discovered that the orca remained gentle with her.

Sheila started to pay more attention to Gunda's behavior in the subsequent several days. She had noticed the peculiar swimming pattern of the two and had observed it accurately through the viewing window. Blood tests had confirmed that the orca had reached sexual maturity and was in estrus. It made her feel sad that Gunda had no natural way to satisfy her needs. Yet as long as the dolphin did not show adverse reactions or signs of stress under the orca's behavior, she would not interfere with it.

With the passing of Gunda's cycle, her behavior became less predictable again. Sometimes, Gunda did not leave her holding tank until late in the show, or she would suddenly stop and roll over on her back to rest in the passage to her tank. Doing shows with the orca was often stressful. It was one thing to stand your ground during a training session, but it was another to do it with a dome full of spectators. Richard still hoped everything would eventually return to normal, but as long as the whale was not completely reliable in her behavior, he felt uncomfortable about water work. To his and the park owner's great regret, the water work was dropped as a regular part of the show.

Despite her mood swings, the orca was very much loved among those who worked with her. When she was cooperative and interested, her gentle and warm nature melted everyone's heart. It was commonly felt that the absence of companions of her own kind was becoming an increasing problem. Deep in their hearts, Richard and his colleagues did not blame it on the whale when she was unwilling to do the show routines. If it was not for the public demand, they would not press so hard on Gunda in an attempt to make her do what they wanted. It was undeniable that it had a positive effect on Gunda when she was given more playtime and affection, but she seemed to become ever more pronounced and persistent in communicating what she liked and disliked.

* * *

Tuschka had sensed Jeff's nervousness when he had entered the platform to do the show. She was not excited about yet another performance, and the man's uncertainty incited her to challenge him, to explore how he would respond if she did not meet his expectations. She knew exactly what she was expected to do when he gave her the cue for the perimeter bows, but she skipped the last bow on purpose. Tuschka knew she did not deserve a reward, but she was disappointed and somewhat irritated when she could not elicit a more exciting response from her trainer than simply repeating his cue. As he was waiting for her to come around, she suddenly came up high out of the water, and jerked her head into his direction with jaws agape. It satisfied her to see him jump back, to see his respect and fear for her. She knew she had shaken his confidence.

Jeff's heart beat in his throat as the orca suddenly lunged at him with open mouth. A sigh went through the public. He wanted to run away from the scene, but a thousand eyes were watching him. The situation was out of control. He watched the orca circling the tank. She radiated tension and irritation. To persist with the cue was obviously more than the orca would tolerate. The menacing lunge had been a warning message. He felt no desire to force his dominance on the whale. 'Dominance'....., the word had no more meaning than the whale was willing to concede.

As a last resort to avoid total disgrace in front of the public, Jeff opened the gate to let Lucie join Gunda in the main tank. The swimming pattern of the two animals revealed that the tension was subsiding. He tapped the water, trembling inside as he watched who would come over to respond. Lucie was the first, but within a few seconds Gunda spyhopped next to her. Jeff almost avoided eye contact with the orca as if he did not want her to think that he was asking yet another behavior from her. He made small movements with his index fingers, asking them to sing. They both responded. The high shrill voice of the dolphin mixed with the lower, more musical voice of the whale. Relieved, Jeff grabbed some fish and rewarded them both. Fortunately, they performed the next several small behaviors without resistance. With the applause from the public, he regained some confidence. At last he asked a backwards bow. Both Gunda and Lucie responded, though the orca did not put her heart into it. He did not end the show with Gunda on the platform to show herself in full splendor with head and tail lifted: that was more than Jeff felt comfortable asking the whale.

Tuschka found it a challenge to explore her trainers' mental strength and creativity. She knew exactly who was easy to manipulate and who was not. Total rigidity frustrated her because it communicated indifference to what she wanted or felt. Getting trainers to yield to her whims had initially excited her. For a while it was fun to confuse them and get rewards for behaviors that were only partly correct, but if they rewarded her too easily, she soon lost her interest. Such rewards were not an expression of true appreciation, but of uncertainty and lack of understanding.

Tuschka's behavior stemmed from a deeply rooted need for contact, for mutual perception and response. Without that contact, the world around her was bleak and unmotivating. But if it was there, it sparked her interest, making her more cooperative and playful. She loved and respected those who knew when she was simply testing their patience, when she wanted to play, or when she needed comfort. It was the way they looked at her, made their signals, withheld or gave rewards, and above all, their spontaneity, that told Tuschka who truly cared for her.

The incident with Jeff had not been the first. He and others had experienced several other occasions when the orca's behavior had hinted at aggression. It did not contribute to the confidence of the trainers. Sheila had not yet experienced it, and it was silently understood that she was closest to Gunda. Her shows were not always smooth either, but overall she was most successful. There were often lengthy discussions about how to act when the whale was cross.

..."I too feel unhappy about such situations," Sheila said, "but if I can't make her change her mind easily, I accept it as it is. It's an animal with ups and downs, just like us, and she'll act as she feels. You can't expect Gunda to feel responsible for a good show." There was little response. It was not the first time the young woman said these things. And it was difficult enough that their least experienced colleague was the most successful. "Besides," Sheila continued, "if you keep trying to make her do something without success, you'll become more tense and frustrated. That's a sign of mental weakness." Richard nodded. "That's certainly a good point. No matter what the challenge or situation is, this strong-willed orca must know that we eventually are above such things."

Sheila was silent. Avoiding a display of mental weakness was an important strategy when interacting with cetaceans, but there was another, more important factor, that made it easier for Sheila to accept Gunda's 'downs' and moments of poor cooperation. It was something that she did not speak of openly, except during her conversations with Tom. Gunda's wellbeing was more important to Sheila than anything else. Somehow, she felt that the orca knew this and was, therefore, more accepting of what she did. Sheila worried most about how much longer she would be able to reconcile the needs of the whale with the goals of the management. She expected the problems only to increase with Gunda's further maturation into adulthood. The whale was already close to 16 feet long, far too big for her small enclosure, and she had recently taken dominance over Flash....

The change had come suddenly. Whenever Flash had wanted the orca to back off, he told her so in his usual way. Over the years, the submissive behavior of the whale had made him confident in his role, despite her size.

Now, he did not want to compete with Tuschka for Lucie's attention. The young female dolphin was receptive and he felt strongly attracted to her. When the orca was reluctant to leave Lucie's side, he bumped her in her belly with his pointed rostrum. The bold unpleasant nudge suddenly triggered a self-awareness that had been awakening in the maturing orca. As Tuschka kicked her flukes to get out of the way, a strong feeling of rebellion came over her. She turned and looked at the dolphin for a second as if measuring his physical strength. It did not take long for Tuschka to resolve who was superior. She bolted towards him, so quickly that Flash barely managed to escape her. But that was not enough to satisfy Tuschka. She was in hot pursuit of the dolphin and proved to be faster and more agile than he had ever imagined.

It was no playful game. The large docile female had suddenly turned into the fierce predator that he vaguely remembered from his younger days. She chased him into every corner of the tank, leaving him no other escape than to jump out of the water over her back. At one moment, the orca swung her flukes underneath him and flung him to the other side of the tank. Seeking refuge in his own tank was no option. It would be a trap with no room to maneuver. The chase lasted les than two minutes, but seemed an eternity for the frightened dolphin. When Tuschka pinned him in another corner, his heart almost stopped. If she wanted to kill him, this was her opportunity. Tuschka read his mind. Then, as abruptly as she had started her pursuit, she turned away from him. Flash's capitulation had been Tuschka's goal. From now on, the dolphin would no longer interfere with her actions.

Flash lay catching his breath, frozen, frightened that any movement might set the orca off again. The other females, including Lucie, had retreated to their own holding tank as soon as the chase had begun. They timidly huddled together, as far as possible from the gate. The message had not been lost on them. Tuschka circled the tank twice, than called for Lucie as she passed the gate to the dolphin tank. The outburst of aggression in her orca companion had confused and frightened her, but she dared not resist the invitation. Timidly, she approached the gate and joined Tuschka as she swam by. The orca was still tense, but she gradually relaxed and nudged Lucie to reassure her. As the two left to rest in Tuschka's holding tank, Flash came away from the corner where the orca had left him and quietly joined his intimidated congeners.

* * *

There were periods when Gunda performed excellently with virtually no problems, and during such times hopes flared up that the good old days were returning. But then, suddenly, the orca would remind them that the problems had only slumbered and were taking a turn for the worse. Although Richard had explained and discussed the problems several times with the management, they had not seriously given the matter a thought until Gunda's appetite began to show temporary dips. The general belief was that the whale needed more room and probably a companion. Yet there was no way that the park could accommodate another orca in the present tank system, let alone a male. Possibilities for expansion were investigated, but nothing seemed financially feasible. They doubted that a second whale would bring in the extra cash flow that was needed to cover its needs.

It was with reluctance that the discussion went in the direction of an alternative way to give Gunda company. With permits for new captures from the wild becoming hard to obtain, several oceanaria would be interested in obtaining an orca from another park. Whereas a second whale might not bring in much extra cash, however, what would happen when the only, now famous, orca left? Somehow, it was the general opinion that the orca should not be sold, leaving the option open to take her back when the situation looked more promising. Hence, it was decided to look into the possibilities of a breeding loan. Sheila dreaded the thought of parting with her beloved orca, but she knew it was in the whale's best interest to have the companionship of others of her own kind.

Sheila visited Tom soon after Gunda's sexual maturation had started the discussion about her future. Although the recovering trainer had no experience with the behavior of mature female orcas, it seemed plausible to him that Gunda's mood swings were in some way related to the hormonal changes that had taken place. The incident with Flash had come unexpectedly, but it fitted into the picture. He understood that Flash was avoiding coming close to the big whale since then. Although Tom was happy that Gunda had Lucie's companionship most of the time, he regretted there was not a more natural companion for the orca to satisfy her needs. "She may get one sometime soon," Sheila said. Tom looked at her with questioning eyes. "Are they going to expand?! How can they afford that? I assume they aren't considering cramping another whale in that tank." Sheila shook her head. "No, they'll do neither. They are considering moving her to another park, on a breeding loan."

Tom's mouth fell open, in both shock and amazement. For a moment, he was speechless. There was a sudden turmoil of thoughts in his mind. Transfer was an option that indeed offered perspective for the orca, but it was something he had not expected the management to consider. Besides that, it shattered his visions of returning and working with her again. He tried to think what the management's main motivation might be.

His face changed into a frown. "Is Gunda performing so poorly, or is it really for her sake?" "I think it's a mixture of things," Sheila said. "There are periods when she's performing quite well, but a few times Gunda has challenged some of us in an aggressive way. Only Richard and I feel confident enough to work with her regularly. Others, especially Jeff, only work with her during her better periods. I think the management now sees that the circumstances are no longer suitable for a lone mature female orca, but I'm certain that the past incidents have facilitated the decision to do something." The thought was sobering. Gunda needed a change, but it was unlikely that he would take part in it.

Tom had been at home since several weeks and was working hard to build up muscular control. He was able to walk without crutches, but he tired quickly and he was unable to run without tripping. While still at the hospital, it had been his intention to visit Gunda as soon as he would be in a wheelchair. But as his condition improved, he kept postponing it. On the one hand, he longed to see his precious friend, but on the other he feared she might not recognize him. Being physically impaired would not be a help. As long as he did not go, he could foster his visions of their reunion. He kept telling himself that the closer he came to recovery, the better he would trigger Gunda's memory.

Recently, Tom had been in touch with the management. They had not mentioned any plans for the orca, but they had told him that they would consider taking him back as a dolphin trainer if he were able to swim. It was the next step that he had planned to work on. Being back at the park would have given him the opportunity to reacquaint himself with Gunda. If all went well, he might some day have become her trainer again. But now, those hopes vanished. If he wanted to see his friend again, there was not much time to lose. He had to face the confrontation with his fears and hopes. The thought of Gunda not recognizing him almost choked him, but to live without knowing was worse. What a joy it would be if she did. It was unacceptable to pass up that chance because he lacked the courage to face another outcome.

It was the first week after the summer evening shows had ended. Gunda had been doing well during the past several days, and Tom and Sheila had decided that if they did not want to press their luck, this was a good opportunity for Tom to visit Gunda. The management had turned a blind eye to the idea, but had insisted that they be careful and keep it quiet, since insurance did not cover any injuries for an employee visiting the park while on sick leave.

Tom had not slept well the night before. Numerous different versions of their reunion had run through his mind. He had been thinking of strategies he would use if Gunda were slow to recognize him. In particular, he had been practicing his calls, hoping they were still the same. Although he was gaining confidence, one thing bothered him. If Gunda would recognize him, as he was hoping, would she bear him any grudge because he had stayed away for so long? Almost a year had passed since their last time together... The question revived a remembrance from long ago. He had not interacted with her for quite a while after his night watch either. She had not borne him any grudge then....

Tom's heart beat fast. He felt it throb in his throat as he stood behind the door to the platform. "Would you mind if I go by myself first?" he asked Sheila. "Then I'll really know how she responds to me." She nodded. "I understand, but if it doesn't bother you, I'll peak through a chink." Tom did not wear a wetsuit, but he had put on the clothing that he had worn during many training sessions. He opened the door and walked over to the edge of Gunda's tank. He tried hard to walk as steadily as possible, but his physical condition did not permit the supple athletic gait he had had prior to his illness.

Tuschka had heard footsteps, but it was not immediately clear to her who was coming. She came up and looked in the direction of the wall at the back of the platform, but there was no one yet. Moments later, she saw at a glance that it was not Sheila who was coming towards her. A little disappointed, she continued her circle. At the end of the day, Sheila often came to play with her, but the other trainers rarely interacted with her after the last show. The person did not carry a bucket either, so she did not expect anything exciting to happen.

As she arched up for another breath near the edge of the tank, she saw him standing close. Through the restless surface of the water, she could not immediately make out who it was, nor did she know what he was up to. When she surfaced, her first sight of the man confused her. There was something very familiar in his appearance. In a strange way, she felt sympathy for the figure looking down at her. Tuschka drifted at the surface and saw the man kneel down slowly. Judging from his stiff and somewhat trembling movements it obviously caused him difficulty.

As Tom saw his precious whale looking at him, he wanted to take her in his arms and tell her how much he had longed to be with her, but he did not have the strength to bend over and reach for her. As he beckoned her to come closer, he spoke to her. "My Gunda," he said with a voice that revealed emotion. "How are you my girl? I've missed you so much!"

The voice, the tenderness, the face, it suddenly all fell into place for Tuschka. It revived memories of long ago. As if wanting a final confirmation, she greeted the man in the way she had greeted him for so many years. His answer was a little hoarse and dim, but it was prompt and sincere. It left Tuschka no doubt that her friend had returned. Overwhelmed with joy, she squeaked her delight, came over to the edge, and rose up into his outstretched arms.

Sheila, deeply moved, blinked away a tear. It was as if she experienced the moment herself. Not only did she know how special intimate moments with Gunda were; she had also come to share the fears and hopes of the man who had been the first to befriend the orca.

Tom was overjoyed when he felt his dear friend touch his hands. She was big and strong and he felt her body rise up to fill his arms. He felt the sheer strength in her and yet her subtle control of it. He lay his cheek on her rostrum and felt tears brimming. He let his emotions flow freely and with them the awareness of his condition faded away. They were together again... just as in the old days. The time they had been separated shriveled to a mere moment. But the disease had struck Tom, no matter how small that moment seemed.

Totally absorbed by the intimate reunion, Tom was unaware that Gunda supported him in his embrace. Then, as his friend slowly sank down, he was painfully reminded of his weakened physical condition. Unable to sit back up, he lost balance and fell in, still holding on to Gunda's rostrum. Sheila was startled as she saw it happen. She ran onto the platform to quickly grab a pole and a floating device for Tom to hold on to.

When Tom's body hit the water, his hand slipped away from the whale. He panicked for a moment, afraid to lose control of the situation. Tom's clothes made him heavy, totally unlike the buoyancy he used to experience in his wetsuit. Managing to stay at the surface, but tiring fast, he reached for the orca, who was still very close to him. As he saw her head go down, Tom quickly looked towards the edge of the tank where Sheila hurried towards him with a pole and a life ring.

Tuschka was surprised with the way her friend entered the water. In an instant, she noticed the startled reaction of the man. It took only a second for her to see that he was tense and struggling to stay at the surface. He was in too much trouble to play the games they had shared in the past.

Just as he tried to grab the ring that Sheila threw in, he felt himself being lifted. In an instant, he found himself lying diagonally over the orca's broad back. He embraced her as he strained to pull up one leg and place it on the other side of the whale's dorsal fin. She stayed at the surface, carrying him stably and carefully. A warm feeling of relief and complete trust overwhelmed him. It did not unsettle him in the least to see that Gunda was taking him around the tank. He saw Sheila's frightened face relax as he smiled at her. "My Gunda," he said, still breathing heavily. "You're so precious. I'm still too weak to swim and you understand," he whispered. "You've helped where I failed. I'm so happy to be with you… like this." He felt her gentle, rhythmic movements and lay his head on her sleek skin, savoring the precious moment. He was so totally absorbed by it that there was no past, no future, only now. A deep contentment and gratitude filled him and he entrusted himself completely to his dear friend.

Her strong blow parted his wet hair. Tuschka felt her friend relax on her back. With his trust, the intimacy returned that she had shared with him in the past. She knew he depended on her, and feeling that he was comfortable while she carried him, she did not want to part with him. Gliding along the perimeter of her tank, Tuschka relished his gentle rubs that emphasized what she already knew: their bond was as strong as always.

Tom did not know how long Gunda had been carrying him around when she brought him over to the spot where Sheila was waiting. He grabbed the edge, but did not have the strength to pull himself up on it. Sheila grabbed him by his upper arms to help. Tuschka immediately understood her friend's inability to climb out. She poked her head beneath his legs and lifted him up, pushing forward to place him on the platform.

Soaked, but deeply moved, Tom sat up with his legs still hanging over the edge. Gunda hovered close to him and squeaked softly. He tried to answer her, but his voice failed him. He opened his hands to let Gunda rest her chin on his palms. As he rubbed her gums, she opened her mouth and offered her tongue. Tom tapped it gently. "You wonderful girl," he said softly. He swallowed, trying to hide the sadness that threatened to overshadow his joy. But Tuschka read him unerringly. She sensed his mood grow heavy with sadness and with it a fear that hinted at a parting of the ways. She let out a plaintive cry as she nudged his belly and pressed her head in his lap. Tom bent over and kissed her rostrum, tenderly touching the tip of her probing tongue. He could not help his tears flowing down his cheeks, onto his beloved orca's sleek skin. "My Gunda," he said, pressing his head against her and holding her tight. 'I will see you again', he told her in thought. 'You'll have a better life soon with other friends of your own kind. When I see you then, we'll both be happy.' Tuschka did not move as her friend held her close. Then she felt him loosen his grip and watched as her female trainer helped him up. She cried softly as she saw him look back at her, just before they both left the platform.

21.
The Move

Although Sheila had been expecting it, the announcement struck hard. After six years, this would be Gunda's last season at the park. Soon after the shows ended in September, Gunda would be transferred to Ocean Adventure, a big park overseas where she would be introduced to three other orcas: a male and a female with a two-year-old calf. Although Sheila dreaded the moment of parting with her precious Gunda, she knew that the new circumstances were far better for the orca. In the relatively short time that she had worked with her, the bond with Gunda had grown strong. Sheila had come to appreciate the orca's intelligence, wit, and subtle perception. She felt deep inside that only the open ocean and the company of her own family could offer Gunda the full and rich life that suited her magnificent species. To be united with others of her own kind was a small, but important step in that direction. Although it would be hard to part with her friend, Sheila drew comfort from knowing that what Gunda would gain was more than worth it. That joy would soothe the wound of loss.

* * *

Music filled the dome and people were streaming in. Nothing was different, and yet Tuschka sensed that it was. People swarmed around her tank in thick rows and seemed reluctant to move on. She circled by, occasionally spyhopping in front of them, amused by the way they tried to get her attention. Passing by the corridor, she saw Lucie behind it and stopped to squeak with her briefly. Tuschka frequently raised her head, wondering why it took longer than usual for the trainers to appear on the platform. Music and numerous voices filled her ears each time she came up.

As soon as Richard and Sheila entered the platform, the orca called loudly in greeting. Her strong crystal clear voice was amplified by the dome's acoustic properties. It was a familiar sound. Since the orca's first performance, her voice had resounded at every show. Tuschka was happy to see Sheila coming over. Her friend tapped her gently on her rostrum. Yet she was a little tense with restrained emotion. Somehow, something was very important. The big crowd, the extra excitement from the visitors before she had even begun her show, the look in her trainer's eyes, it all radiated to Tuschka that they had high expectations of her. She felt she would shine if she performed well.

And she did. The dome was packed. Not a single seat was free. The orca smoothly entered the show pool as the gate swung open. Sheila felt it at once and was grateful: Gunda had picked it up.

Tuschka knew this show was important. It had to be good and she was going to be good. Alert to her trainer's signal, Tuschka already picked up her cue as she glided by the platform. She gracefully dived and burst through the surface in a majestic bow. The applause and yells from the public, and Sheila's response, left Tuschka no doubt that she was the star. It was a show in which she excelled.

Even Sheila and Richard had known few performances like this one. Her speed, agility, grace, and power, captivated the audience and were awe inspiring. A beautiful high backwards somersault concluded the dazzling performance.

Tuschka came out on the platform to show herself in full splendor, head and tail lifted high. She was flabbergasted to see all her trainers come to her with a big tray full of little lights. When they knelt down around her, they blew and made the little lights disappear. She could see a large number of fish on the platter and gratefully accepted them from their hands. Her friend pointed her back and asked her to come on the platform again. Tuschka loved the attention and slid back to come out again, and again, and again. Each time, the visitors applauded and yelled, and each time she received fish and rubs.

Sheila had wished to swim with Gunda, because it would have shown the orca's fine qualities in her special bond with humans. But in another way she felt that it was good as it was. She had not wanted to distract attention from the whale. As magnificent as Gunda was, she needed no trainer to substantiate that. She deserved pure and undivided appreciation. Besides, Sheila realized, to swim with Gunda under more than a thousand watching eyes would never have been the intimate experience they were used to sharing. And so it should remain.

Tuschka saw her friend bend over to come close to her and felt how the woman's hands held the sides of her mouth. She was aware that her human friend was filled with emotion and she wanted to respond with affection. Sheila was very aware of Gunda's gentle and meaningful nudge against her cheek. Although she swallowed to hold back her tears, Sheila's eyes became wet. It had been their last show together. But now was not the moment to let her emotions flow freely, nor to prolong her intimate moment with her friend. She sat upright and let her colleagues rub and pet the orca.

It took a long time for all the people to leave the dome. Tuschka was still enjoying all the attention on the platform. When her trainers started to leave, she finally slid back. Content and still excited, she had not the faintest notion of what lay ahead.

Tuschka knew the show season was over, and yet it was different. Since her last show, there were fewer training sessions and relatively more playtime. Although she liked the attention, she felt a difference in her trainers' mood. They showed special interest and put more heart into their time with her, but it was with an undefined undercurrent of sadness. Tuschka felt a hint of trepidation. She had been confined to her own tank for the past three days, which was unusual during winter breaks when there were no shows.

The next morning, footsteps in the dome attracted Tuschka's attention. She kept her position near the gate and recognized one of her trainers, together with two other men. They started to pull, push, and bang at the fence. Tuschka saw it being taken apart and carried away in pieces. While she watched questioningly, a slight tap below the water caught her attention. She dived quickly and saw the familiar presence of Sheila at the viewing window. The sight of her human friend was comforting and helped her to briefly forget all the strange things that were happening. Tuschka called tenderly to her trainer and glided gently with her belly along the glass.

It warmed Sheila to see that her presence somewhat calmed Gunda. She understood how confusing the events had to be for the young adult female and wished she could give Gunda more mental support. Sheila tried to hide her emotions, lest she add to Gunda's confusion. But it was unmistakable that Gunda was sensing something.

Until two weeks ago, it had not been clear who would accompany the orca during her transfer and for the first several weeks in her new environment. Being the head trainer, and having worked with Gunda since her arrival, everyone had been expecting Richard to go, but they all knew that Sheila was closest to Gunda and that no one could offer the orca more mental support than she. The arrival of new animals in exchange for the orca had helped staff make the decision. Richard would supervise the new arrivals and Sheila would accompany Gunda.

Sheila was grateful for the opportunity to accompany her precious friend through the ordeal. She knew she would have to part with her beloved whale at some point, but not the day after tomorrow, when Gunda would be leaving the park. It was comforting to know that she could go with Gunda and stay with her until she was doing at least reasonably well. Sheila savored her last quiet moments with Gunda, but it was not as emotionally laden as it would have been otherwise. She was grateful for her relative stable mood, since she felt that Gunda needed a strong and reassuring presence at her side in the days to come.

* * *

A mixture of voices, footsteps, and rumbling vibrations disturbed the quiet morning. It made Tuschka restless and apprehensive. Several people were carrying away many of the small objects, that had been lining the sloping wall in front of her. A while later, the dark dome with its many small lights started to give way to a patch of blinding light. Tuschka rolled over on her side to look up at the strange changes above her. As her eyes became adjusted to the light, faint memories returned of times when she swam under a sky, bright with day and dark with night.

With her mind drifting off, she almost hit the edge of the platform. It brought her back to the reality of her small tank and the absence of companions. The many people, shouting and walking back and forth, stirred memories deep inside. She swam over to the gate, calling for Lucie. The dolphin huddled close to her companions. They too, were confused by the bright light and the sounds around them. After several minutes, Lucie came over. Their rostrums touched lightly as if they tried to find reassurance in each other's presence.

Something splashed in the water behind Tuschka and she turned around to investigate. She had not seen anything like it in a long time, and yet it seemed familiar. The large wire mesh object was flexible and started to unfold, gradually occupying more space in her tank. Instinctively, Tuschka moved a little away from it, watching it expand and come closer to her. Several people lined up at the edge of her pool in the spot where the fence had been. Some of them were just watching her, while others were gesticulating and shouting. Tuschka knew at least half of the humans in front of her, but they acted very differently from what she was used to. Then, she became aware of sounds on the platform and noticed that several people had gathered there too. She recognized one of her male trainers. He looked back and forth between her and the people on the other side of her tank. Although most of the people directed their attention at each other, Tuschka felt she was the center of the commotion. It was all very confusing.

Something touched her right flipper. Instinctively she pulled away, but there was no where to go. The wire mesh was being pulled underneath her. People were almost all around her tank, holding on to it and pulling it up against her belly. Suddenly, she stiffened with panic. Memories of days long gone flashed through her mind. Something terrible was happening...restraint...separation... In a reflex, she shrieked for her mother. Something ominous was imminent. Just as then, panic and desperation took every bit of resistance out of her and left her in a motionless cramp. Tarka did not answer, but there was an answer....

Sheila had heard Gunda's heartrending squeal. The orca's voice gave her a chill. It was so loud, full of despair and desolation. Although many people lined the tank, Sheila quickly found an opening to squeeze herself in. She was not supposed to help with the actual loading process, but concern had urged her to come close. Only six feet separated her from her dear orca, but the panicking whale had not yet noticed her. Sheila saw the tense muscles in the orca's body and the unnaturally lifted flukes. With a high-pitched voice, she imitated one of the calls that she had shared with Gunda in happier times. Although Sheila sympathized with the orca for what she had to endure, she had the strength to show no sign of it. For Gunda she had to be strong, to be reassuring. In the days to come, she would be the only one to whom Gunda could relate, the only source from which the orca could draw confidence.

The call struck Tuschka. Her friend was near! It took only a second to meet the eyes of her favorite trainer. The one she trusted most. She was talking to her now with her warm reassuring voice. It brought Tuschka back to her senses. The situation was far from familiar and she had no idea what all these people were up to, but her human friend radiated reassurance and comfort. As comfortable as Sheila seemed with the situation, it could not be as bad as she had feared. In the presence of her human friend, Tuschka slowly relaxed.

Sheila noticed the orca lower her flukes and the tense bundle of muscles in her flank smooth out, but the whale did not look away from her. Sheila made several more playful squeaks and was filled with relief and joy when Gunda answered them in a voice that no longer reflected panic. The young trainer knew she was essential for the whole procedure. Reducing the orca's stress was not only mentally beneficial to the whale, but also reduced the risk of the orca flailing in panic and injuring herself.

With the orca much more relaxed, it was relatively easy to maneuver the carrying sling around her. Sheila's presence was silently accepted. She feared the whale's reaction when the white canvas blocked her view and kept on talking and squeaking to maintain acoustic contact. At the same time, the orca became much more talkative, obviously wanting to assure herself that her friend was near.

As Tuschka felt herself being lifted, memories of her youth plagued her and caused fleeting moments of panic, but the voice of her friend was right next to her and she clung to it for reassurance. Every call, every whimper found an answer. As uncomfortable and helpless as she was, Tuschka entrusted herself fully to her human friend. Just as in her early days, she surrendered, making no attempt to struggle free. She did not know what she could do for the better, nor did she want to make it worse. Yet, she was not as desperate and desolate as she had been before. The unmistakable voice of her friend, almost lost in the turmoil, was just enough to fight panic and feed a spark of hope.

Sheila rested her hand on the orca and stayed with her as the container was lifted onto the plane. She checked whether there was still enough ice in the water to keep Gunda cool. Her breathing was strong. It was an ordeal for her beloved whale and she wished it would be over with fast. Sheila was amazed at Gunda's seemingly unlimited trust and felt deeply touched by the power that lay in their strong bond. It was all that the poor whale could draw her strength from now.

Sheila had never questioned the orca's sensitive and intelligent nature, but she had not realized how far an orca would go along purely on trust. Apparently the essential source of the orca's self confidence and mental strength was not physical supremacy, but trust. Then, it suddenly struck her. This was why the top predator of the ocean did not fight for dominance and lived a life that radiated discipline and peace. The orcas in a pod had to cooperate and rely on each other for their survival. Rivalry would not serve that purpose. Compliance with the leader, with the rules in the pod, came naturally as trust was built in childhood.

A group of people watched the plane taxiing away, listening to the orca's eerie voice for the last time. It was drowned as the plane built up speed and finally took to the air.

22.
Voices from her Own Kind

Tuschka felt uncomfortable and stiff. The edges of her support sling hurt in front of her pectoral fins. Most of the way she had been calling out for attention, for reassurance, for someone to end her miserable situation. It seemed to take forever. Her friend was still there, but she had not been able to help. Tuschka fought despair.

Her hope flared up when her flukes touched water. Impatiently, she began to move them up and down. Within seconds, the cool water touched her belly and started to carry her weight. Was she finally back in her tank? The canvas fell away. Tuschka almost rolled to her side, but managed to upright herself, encouraged by pushing hands. Bright lights stung her eyes. She wriggled briefly to loosen her stiff muscles. Then, with a strong thrust of her tail flukes, she glided forward between and beyond the people who had been lining her on both sides.

Tuschka realized instantly that she was not in her own tank. Not only her eyes and echolocation told her so. Most startling were the sounds she heard. She did not recognize the voices, nor did she grasp much of their meaning, but they unmistakably came from what had to be her own kind. Tuschka was confused. She was not in the open ocean. Yet she heard other orcas, although they were not from her family or a pod she knew. Where were they? Did they mean friends or danger? In the absence of anything familiar, and with nothing to fall back upon, Tuschka did not want to stop swimming, lest something bad come to her. She looked around in the faintly lit pool with eyes wide open. She stayed away from the walls and what seemed to be gates. She swam in circles, frightened and feeling desperately alone. A shiver went through Tuschka as something splashed the water close by. She only wanted to get away from it and stayed down, speeding by. When she surfaced, Tuschka suddenly heard her trainer's familiar voice. She needed no encouragement to come over.

Sheila saw the sudden response in the restless whale. The orca made her approach under water. She saw her slow down, just before her rostrum broke the surface. Sheila had selected a relatively quiet corner, away from the bright lights and the many people. The orca took several breaths in succession and made small restless movements with her head. The girl sensed the tension in the whale. She stroked her gently and tried to calm her. "My Gunda, you're such a brave and good girl. The worst is over now. You can swim again and relax and soon you'll make friends with others of your own kind. That's what you've been missing for so many years."

Sheila had brought a small bucket with fish to see if Gunda would accept any, but the orca refused. She quickly gave up, not wanting to stress her any further. Then, she heard someone calling her and felt annoyed that they did not respect her quiet time with Gunda a little longer. She bent over to the orca and took her chin in both hands. "I'll be back, Gunda, it's all right." A soft plaintive call made it even harder for Sheila to get up and walk away. She knew all too well that it welled up from a heart in need of reassurance and comfort. Tuschka rose up higher and followed her trainer for a few feet. Then she stopped and watched her go, not wanting to come closer to the many unfamiliar people.

"What do you think?," Brian, the head trainer of the new park asked. "She's disoriented and tired as far as I can see. She didn't accept food," Sheila responded, "but that doesn't surprise me much after such a strenuous trip." One of the veterinarians stepped forward and greeted Sheila. "After a quiet night, she'll feel a lot better tomorrow. As soon as she lets us we'll take some blood samples for a medical check-up. Fine whale. We are happy to have her." The young woman only nodded, realizing that the night would not make the orca feel better unless she stayed with her.

Sheila was not in the mood to talk much and wanted to go back to Gunda when two other men came over and offered to take her to her hotel. She did not want to leave Gunda in this unfamiliar environment and suggested staying with the orca through her first night. "We'll look after her," a young woman of her own age assured her. "We know how she feels. You must be tired. It'll do you good to rest. You can entrust Gunda to us." Sheila suddenly felt how tired she was. The thought of a bed was tempting. She looked back to see if Gunda was still waiting for her. There was nothing visible but water. Several blows came from the other tanks. An adult female with her juvenile calf were circling in an adjacent pool, while the big adult male lay at the gate facing Gunda's tank. He seemed very interested in the new arrival. Sheila wondered if he was vocalizing to Gunda and what Gunda would think of seeing such a large individual of her own kind. Then, she heard Gunda blow and watched her sturdy straight fin go down. She was swimming circles without using the entire pool. It was obvious that she was not yet ready to face the big male behind the gate.

Sheila followed the two men in silence and stepped into the park vehicle. Before they had reached the gate, Sheila's heart almost stopped as the orca's scream rent their ears. The men looked at each other questioningly and then turned around to see their passenger's shocked face. "Is that your whale?" they asked in disbelief. "I must go back," Sheila said. One of the men grabbed his phone. The person at the other end was not easy for her to understand, but it was obvious that it had to be somebody at the whale stadium. "She's swimming an..." another cry interrupted his sentence. "She's swimming circles and looks fine otherwise," the man with the

238

phone said. "There are a vet and two trainers with your whale. If they need you, they'll let you know."

For Sheila, the message was clear: they were not intending to take her back to Gunda. In a different way, she was alone too in this huge park. She fought the urge to protest. Who would listen to a young female trainer? It was true that they were experienced in moving orcas around. They had to know what to do. Yet Sheila had never heard Gunda cry like that. Sheila managed to maintain her composure until she was by herself in her room. Another cry from Gunda set her tears loose. 'I've come all the way to be with you, to comfort you, and now that you need me most I'm not with you', she thought by herself. Gunda's cries kept Sheila awake for a long time until, at last, she drifted into fitful dreams.

Although it was night, there were several spots lighting the pool. Tuschka swam in restless circles, calling out loud almost continuously. She was looking for her buddy, frequently raising her head near the corner where they had last been together. Long eerie calls came from behind a gate. Not knowing what to expect, and with no one to reassure her, Tuschka had no desire to explore. Her otherwise inquisitive nature was dominated by fear and she stayed away from anything that might bring more confrontations. With her scream like calls Tuschka did not only plead for attention. She also voiced her protest and frustration with the situation, at the same time trying to drown out the unsettling noises around her. But perhaps more than that, she fought her loneliness with the sound of her own voice.

Two trainers and a guard were watching the new orca as she circled, as much intrigued as annoyed by her distress calls. Neither trainer made an attempt to attract the orca's attention. They were junior trainers, expected to do nothing more than observe the new whale's behavior and time her respirations.

Dawn rapidly progressed into bright daylight. It was an experience for Tuschka that roused faint memories of the past. In a strange way, it lifted her spirits and made her more aware of her environment. During the past night, Tuschka had caught a glimpse of the large whale behind the gate. Now, she eyed him again from a distance. After having been with dolphins for so many years, she was struck by his size. She recognized the striking pattern of black and white that she had not seen in so many years. He was a male orca. Tuschka inched a little forward along the wall opposite the gate where he was watching her. Now, she saw more of him. His fin was bent over, the majority of it hanging down in a sideways arc. The size of the fin and the curled ends of his flukes revealed that he was well into puberty, but not yet full grown. He called to her in sounds she did not understand, but they conveyed no threat. He obviously wanted her attention. She sensed he was begging her to come over. The male orca's seemingly friendly interest diverted her attention away from her loneliness. Although a desire to interact was awakening, apprehension still held her back.

A feeling of relief and joy filled Sheila as Gunda greeted her loudly and started squeaking back and forth with her. As she rested her hand on Gunda's smooth head, she immediately felt that the orca was more relaxed than last night. Sheila needed to encourage her, but Gunda did accept a few fish from her hand. Janet, dressed in a wetsuit, knelt down beside her. The orca backed a few inches away, but not for long. Janet remained calm and unobtrusive, and saw the whale come close again upon Sheila's beckoning. She listened as Sheila imitated Gunda's short high-pitched calls. "Try to talk to her," Sheila encouraged her colleague from the new park. "That's the best way to make contact with her." Janet smiled shyly. "My voice is not so high. I doubt that I can produce anything that comes close to what you do." "That doesn't matter," Sheila interjected. "It's the attempt that counts. Gunda will understand that you're trying to talk to her." A little shy and in a soft voice Janet tried to imitate the sounds that Sheila made. Her calls were lower and not the best copies, but both trainers were aware that Gunda had looked at Janet when she tried.

As Janet and Sheila stood up, they saw the orca rise a little higher. She did not want Sheila to leave. Sheila felt a stab of remorse when she heard Gunda emit a loud imploring call. When she looked back and saw the orca following her, she stopped and considered going back to the whale, but Janet motioned her not to give in to the orca's plea. Sheila gritted her teeth as she heard the wailing orca behind her.

The sound dulled as Janet closed the door of the trainers lounge. "I know it's hard for you b.." "I understand," Sheila said with a nod. She knew that Gunda would not look at others as long as she could get attention from her. At least not now. Eventually, she would, but there was not enough time to wait for her spontaneous interest. Within a few weeks, Gunda had to trust some of her new trainers enough to accept food from them and have some interaction with them. That process could only be speeded up by letting Gunda face her loneliness, thus making her more receptive to other sources of comfort. It was a hard way, on Gunda as well as herself. If it worked well, Gunda would suffer more intensely, but for a much shorter time, provided.... she had the mental resilience to overcome another parting of the ways.

Janet took Sheila out of her contemplations as she put a cup of coffee in front of her. "You had a short night. This will make you feel better." Sheila picked up the cup and looked out of the window in the direction of Gunda's tank. "She has to focus her attention more on you. To achieve that, I have to fade out..." Sheila looked down, trying to hide her emotions. "I have to prepare for the show now," Janet said. "After that, we'll go to Gunda again." She smiled empathetically at Sheila and went out.

Sheila could see Gunda well through the window, but she was happy that the orca apparently did not see her. Reflections of the sky in the glass would probably make it hard for the whales to see inside. That was a good thing. It gave the trainers more privacy from the animals they worked with. After what had happened a few minutes ago, Sheila realized the strange paradox in her mission. She had come to ease what she had never wanted Gunda to endure: another parting of the ways. It had not been her choice to part with her beloved whale. She felt forced to disappoint Gunda and be unworthy of her trust. It was the mildest way for Gunda, but hard on her. Parting was one thing, but ..oh... if she could only part as a friend...

* * *

"Eeeeeeuuee," the orca greeted. "eeeeuuuup," Sheila and Janet imitated. "She's talking to us!," Janet said with a smile. Tuschka did not take a special interest in the new trainer, but she was craving attention of her friend. After the long trip and having gone nearly two days without food, Tuschka was quite hungry. The mental and physical stress of the transfer had suppressed her appetite, but she felt it now. She eyed the new woman briefly, then focused on her friend again. Both women offered her fish, but Sheila was so relaxed that Tuschka accepted it from both of them. Tuschka saw the warm nods of approval on her trainer's face and felt reassured that all was well.

Janet tossed a few fish in the orca's mouth and was excited when the whale accepted them. "Good girl, Gunda," Sheila said as she laid her hands on both sides of the orca's head. Then, she gave her a gentle kiss on the rostrum. "I'll try and see if she is willing to take some cues," she said to Janet.

Sheila sensed that she had to start with small behaviors. It would be too much to ask Gunda to race along the perimeter of the unfamiliar tank in a fast swim or to build up speed for a series of bows. The training session was meant not only to divert Gunda, but also to convey information about the orca's background. Without any knowledge about the cues that Gunda had learned in her previous facility, the new staff would have to give the orca extensive training. Having insight in her capabilities and the associated signals would make it possible to gradually acquaint her with new cues for the same behaviors.

Janet watched Sheila closely, eager to register what was going to happen. Sheila gave Gunda a cue to vocalize and asked her to rise in a spyhop and wave her flippers. The orca's responses were prompt and correct. It occurred to Janet that Sheila's whistle sounded a little different than hers. She tapped Sheila on the shoulder and suggested that it might be a good idea if they both blew their whistles to reward the whale.

The sound of the second whistle seemed to make little impression on the orca. Sheila understood that Gunda was not yet into working with a new trainer. Sheila did not look at Janet, while she was explaining more about Gunda's personality. Sheila was very aware that Gunda did not like others to distract her attention away from her. Gunda wanted her full attention. She had always demanded respect, but now in the unfamiliar environment, reassurance seemed to be her primary need. Even when she was talking to Janet, Sheila kept eye contact with Gunda, making her feel that she remained the primary focus of her attention.

After several more short cues, Sheila splashed Gunda playfully and started to walk along the edge of the pool. The orca followed her, but did not engage in the game. Sheila was not surprised that Gunda was not yet into playing, but she did not expect her to suddenly hesitate and stop. 'Strange. The orca had followed on her heel every time she had left'. Sheila tried to reverse direction again. After just a few steps the same thing happened. The whale was holding back for something. Sheila's eyes scanned the tank. There was nothing in it. Nothing seemed different from the days before. Then she suddenly understood and looked at the large male, facing the gate. Gunda had not been near that gate since her arrival. She obviously did not feel comfortable going near him. Sheila realized it was too optimistic to think that Gunda would enthusiastically jump at the opportunity to interact with her own kind. The orcas' social bonds were strong, but this was not her family. Another factor could be his size and rank. There probably was a hierarchy among the other orcas. Gunda would certainly have to start at the bottom.

Sheila knelt down at a spot where Gunda felt sufficiently relaxed to hover. She looked at Janet and nodded towards the male. "Would he be vocalizing? What do you think he might be communicating to her: friendly interest, or some sort of territorial hostility?" Janet's eyes showed a little surprise. "Durak is very submissive towards the dominant female." "But Gunda isn't dominant here," Sheila interrupted. "We've had females in the past," Janet continued. He's never shown any aggression towards them, but there seems to be no end to his libido. His sexual advances are not always appreciated. Therefore, we keep him separate much of the time." "Are you suggesting similar interests in Gunda?" "It wouldn't surprise me," Janet said with a smile. Sheila paused for a moment. "Can you tell his mood when he vocalizes?" "Probably," Janet nodded. "It might be that he only calls to her when he sees her," Janet said. After several more minutes, Sheila bent over and pressed her cheek against Gunda's rostrum. She savored the moment. She was such a precious friend.

Night had fallen. Tuschka was not happy with it. For many hours to come, no one would come to her. "Eeeeeuò," "eeeeuò." It was the voice of the big male. His voice painfully reminded her how strange everything was. In the past few days, Tuschka had quickly come to recognize the voices of the other three whales. She had noticed that the female and her calf were very close to each other, but they barely responded to the calls of the male. Tuschka did not see much of the mother and her calf. They rarely looked at her. She felt a mixture of feelings towards them. She longed for the closeness they shared, but at the same time, their distant attitude, combined with the obvious dominance of the mother, was unsettling.

The male orca had been vocalizing often in response to Tuschka's calls, although she had not been talking to him. She had been calling loudly for her human friend, voicing her need for comfort and reassurance, but to no avail. Now, as Tuschka was learning that the night would bring her no solace, her feelings of uncertainty began to make room for a hesitant curiosity.

"Eeeeeuò." The male orca caught her attention again. The big whale had been at the gate almost continuously. His interest in her was apparent. It seemed that he even knew when she moved, often calling when she started swimming. He was big and strong, but he could not get to her and do her harm. In the absence of caring people, the voice of the male began to take on a different meaning. He was interested in her and she wanted contact. Tuschka was not familiar with his call, but instinctively she began to swim, wanting to hear him. As he sounded, she listened intently, probing the intonation in an attempt to read his mood and intentions. She sensed a questioning in it without threat, but a look at his movements would tell more than sound alone.

Concealed in the dark water, she slowly approached, drifting along the wall opposite the gate. He echolocated. Tuschka felt the pulses touch her and knew that he had detected her. He called again. It was a soft call, almost tender. Tuschka sensed that the big orca wanted to make contact. It roused a deep longing in her. It was as if his voice echoed a desire that she had not yet allowed to surface. Although her lack of insight in his personality made her hesitant, Tuschka could not resist the temptation to explore his reaction to a response from her. She ventured a little closer. The spotlight near the gate penetrated the water enough for her to see his contours and the lighter shading of his white chin. He was facing her with his rostrum pointed towards the gate. She gave a soft short greeting. His response was immediate. His call was a bit different from the previous one. Was he acknowledging her? Again, Tuschka made her greeting. His response struck her: he had not copied her call exactly, but it was too similar to be coincidence. She no longer doubted the benign intentions of the whale on the other side of the gate. There was no threat, no sign of aggression in him. He exhaled with a heavy, explosive blow. Tuschka saw how he moved his head a little sideways, revealing his white eye patch. He repeated the greeting, followed by his initial longer wail.

Still cautious, Tuschka glided towards him. She stopped just a few feet in front of him. He rose in a small spyhop and Tuschka saw the spotlight reflect on his glossy chin. She noticed the movements of his wide pecs as he sank down and steadied himself again. His presence stirred faint memories in her. Somehow, he radiated reassurance. They exchanged a few more squeaks, until at last they were almost touching. Tuschka was grateful for his company. She drew comfort from knowing that she was no longer alone.

Sheila found Gunda waiting in her usual corner of the tank, where she was nearest to the trainer's lounge. She had been excited about the story of the night watch, who had reported the interaction between Durak and Gunda. She was relieved that Gunda had found a companion, especially during the lonely nights. It was no secret that the management felt relieved too, not so much because of their empathy with a lonely whale, but more because the newcomer had almost ceased to make the loud distress calls that had been causing many people in the park's vicinity sleepless nights. Several people had called in with complaints of sirens going off in the park at night, only to find out that it was a whale whose voice they could not control. The past night had been a dramatic improvement.

Gunda was acclimatizing to her new environment. She was eating well and was responsive in training sessions. Now Sheila had to face the more difficult part of her mission. She had to fade out, making sure that her orca would be okay in the hands of her future trainers. The day before, Janet had done most of the interactions, with Sheila joining in the rewards. From now on, she would keep as low a profile as possible to let Janet try on her own.

It did not work out as Sheila had hoped. The more she tried to step back, the more the orca pleaded for her attention. Sheila felt heavy with dread. She felt it was bound to happen again. How could she resist Gunda's pleading? Would she really have to push it to a point where Gunda would be so severely disappointed and her feelings so much hurt that she wanted no part of her any more? It could not be! Apart from the fact that Sheila could not bring herself to such an act, she felt it would only have an adverse effect. Gunda might well lose her faith in people, especially if one she trusted fully let her down.

A resolve washed over her. Fading out by a step-wise increase of distance was not the way to do it. Sheila realized that she had to fade out by interacting with Gunda less often, but the quality of their time together need not be less! A spark of hope lifted Sheila's spirit. Perhaps, she could leave Gunda as a friend in the comfort that she would not be alone.

Sheila was heavyhearted when the sun began to set. Durak was put in the performance pool, which was not adjacent to Gunda's tank. The desire to give Gunda comfort was strong, especially now that she would only have Durak's voice to accompany her in the long night. Sheila was counting the days and the opportunities she would still have to be with her beloved orca. How much she longed to be with Gunda now; just the two of them in this night. To swim with her and caress her, to feel the orca's gentle nudges and to be carried on her chest. Soon it would be an experience of the past. Even though Gunda would be grateful for that and savor such a time together, it would not be in her best interest. Not right now, not until she allowed herself a bond with someone else as well. She thought of Tom. She was going through a similar struggle.

As she was leaving the park, Sheila listened to the blows of the whales, noticing the difference between the male, the females, and the juvenile. Gunda was lonely now, but her loneliness would be the key to its own solution: it would help to make her more receptive to someone who sincerely tried to make contact. It had already worked with the male!

It happened as Sheila had hoped. Tuschka had been lonely during the night and was craving diversion. At dawn, she was pacing around in restless circles, lifting her

244

head upon every series of footsteps that came in her direction. When she noticed the approach of the new trainer, she had an initial upwelling of protest and a desire to turn away. Yet she had a raving appetite.

A squeak from the woman surprised her. Then she tried a few more. Her intentions seemed sincere. Tuschka's playful nature made it irresistible for her not to teach this human a lesson in making proper orca calls. She squeaked back. The woman voiced her delight and clapped her hands. The sudden outbreak of enthusiasm took Tuschka by surprise, but in a positive way. She returned another squeak and saw the delight in the trainer's eyes. The woman tried again. It was obviously an improvement, but there was still reason to work on it a little more.

Sheila was watching it all from the trainers' lounge and was endeared by the first contact between the two. Janet was obviously filled with delight. She had made contact with Gunda. All by herself! The orca was taking food from her hand now. Even more so, she talked to her! Sheila was happy for Gunda, but she could not help feeling a pang of regret. She wished she could put the clock back. Gunda's future lay with Janet and others now. What would soon be a precious memory for her was just beginning for Janet. Sheila knew that the sad part of her feelings were mostly because of herself. She showed no sign of them as Janet returned. Janet gave Sheila a warm hug. "We played, we squeaked!" she said in a voice full of enthusiasm. "Gunda is accepting me. It is going to work!"

* * *

Tuschka noticed a change in the attitude of the juvenile orca. Although she still spent the majority of her time with her mother, she sometimes peeked through the gate. She would barely make a stop, but it was not lost on Tuschka that the young whale was curious. It mostly happened when her mother was interacting with the trainers. As it seemed, the youngster would try to sneak away, but that never lasted long. The observant, dedicated mother usually called her back within minutes. The juvenile was much smaller than her mother. She revived recollections of Aleta. She made occasional vocalizations while peeking through the gate. Although the sounds differed from those of Tuschka's own family, they sounded more familiar than the calls of the big male.

Tuschka had been at the new facility for almost two weeks and in that time she had learned much about the vocal repertoires of her congeners in the other tanks. Although she had not interacted with the mother and her offspring yet, Tuschka had picked up that the calf shared all her mother's calls, but also some of the male. Tuschka was curious about the calf, but she held back. It was obvious that the mother did not want her offspring to freely interact with her, and the mother was obviously dominant. Even though Tuschka had never known her as family, she radiated an authority that would not tolerate opposition. The mother whale could not enter Tuschka's enclosure, but Tuschka felt that she was the leader. In her own pod, Tuschka had felt only respect for Furka or the matriarchs from other pods, but never fear. Yet this leading female made her feel uneasy and indecisive about how to respond to her curious calf.

When Tuschka made a hesitant greeting call to the juvenile orca, her mother glided by and took her baby away from the gate. The pair started circling and the big body of the mother barely permitted a glimpse of the calf each time they passed by. Tuschka turned away, strangely relieved that she was not in the same pool as that dominant female. She had longed for company so much, but she discovered that being close to her own kind did not automatically bring the warmth and comfort she had known in her family. In the first few days she had also felt wary of the male, but that had changed. He had shown a warm interest in her. He obviously wanted to interact with her. She had not only started to feel more comfortable in his presence; she would even welcome his company.

* * *

Since that first moment when Janet had truly made contact with the new whale, her sessions with Gunda became more and more rewarding. Initially, there had been more play than training sessions, but Janet strictly separated the two. She had kept the training sessions short until she discovered that Gunda's attention span increased. It was clear to Sheila that Janet was quickly learning to read Gunda. She was an experienced trainer. Previous work with several orcas had given her enough confidence to not feel intimidated by the initial aversive attitude of a new whale. Janet had even successfully used the orca's beginning receptiveness to introduce a male colleague. As a start, Gunda had to accept at least two trainers to make sure that she could be properly trained and cared for every day of the week.

Sheila was amused when she saw the young man struggle to attract Gunda's attention by attempting to squeak with her. No matter how hard he tried, he did not come anywhere near the proper pitch. Yet the intention seemed to reach Gunda. Sheila even could not escape the thought that the orca was amused by it herself, since she always seemed to tease him by demonstrating what he would never master. At times, Sheila, Janet and several other girls could not suppress their laughter when the walls of the food preparation room or the shower echoed the attempts of the men imitating Gunda-calls. Sometimes, the orca seemed to respond to the distant sounds, which elicited shouts of victory and accomplishment. It was widely believed that the new whale would not pay any attention if one did not attempt to address her in her own language.

Sheila had interacted with Gunda a few times since she had started to work well with Janet and to some extent with Mark. Gunda was obviously most excited when she had an opportunity to interact with her old friend. Although Sheila longed for playtime more than anything else, she also did some training to avoid too much reinforcement of Gunda's preference for her.

23.
Durak

Three weeks had gone by and time had almost come for Sheila to part with her beloved orca. For a few days, Sheila had been pondering how she would say goodbye to Gunda. It was probably best to leave quietly without anything that might deviate from the normal routine. Yet Sheila felt a strong desire to have one last intimate time together, but could she hide her emotions? As sensitive as she was, Gunda would quickly notice if she felt heavyhearted. That would be enough to trouble the orca. But for how long? She did have someone now, who had gained enough of her trust to comfort and divert her. Would Gunda suffer more or think worse of her if she left after an intimate session than after leaving without it? Gunda would enjoy such time together and it would be such a precious memory to take home. Perhaps it would be possible to delight fully in their play without thinking of what was to come. It was such a difficult trade-off, such a difficult decision to make!

Sheila realized that if she wanted to share time with Gunda before she left, she had to discuss it with Janet. At this new park, there was always a spotter required when a trainer interacted with a whale. Janet was more than just qualified to do that job, and Sheila wanted her more than anyone else. Janet was closest to her. With her understanding of their strong bond, Janet would give her more freedom to interact with Gunda than anyone else.

Janet needed few words to understand Sheila's thoughts. "I was prepared for it," she said. "I've already arranged for an evening shift tonight. Brian agreed to give you a playtime session with Gunda, but he insisted that I watch you very well..." "Oh, Janet, thank you so much! It was so difficult for me to bring it up. I'm afraid it is selfish." Sheila explained some of the pros and cons that had burdened her mind. "I think Gunda will be alright. We will give her extra attention and we will put Durak next to her pool for the night. If they show signs of wanting to be together, we will open the gate in the morning. That'll certainly divert her!" It was more than Sheila had hoped for. The resolve was complete. Tonight she would be together with Gunda and she would not think of sad things. "It's good that you brought it up," Janet said. "I might have done it otherwise, but I wanted to give you time to resolve how you wanted to part with your dear Gunda."

Quiet had returned to the stadium. Apart from the distant roar of traffic, only the orcas' blows sounded in the night. Janet had already seated herself near the

249

edge of the pool. Gunda had followed her as she walked by, but after a brief greeting it was obvious to the orca that her trainer was not going to interact with her. She started circling the tank, looking at Janet a few more times.

Sheila appeared in a wetsuit. She knew the trainers of the park did not yet have permission to swim with their new whale. Although acquainting the orca with the presence of trainers in the water was an early topic in the training program, a free swim hadn't been given a green light. Water interaction with the orcas was only done by experienced trainers after they had learned about the personality traits and responses of the whale involved. Janet knew that Sheila and Gunda had amply passed through that process, but she also was well aware that her position was in jeopardy if she bent the rules.

Tuschka had not been expecting to see her friend and it was not until her favorite trainer was close to the edge of the tank that she saw her. She saw her kneel down in the shallow water on the wide ledge in front of her. Tuschka immediately sensed that Sheila had come as the friend she loved so much. Excitement and joy filled her and banished the confusing moments of the recent past. She voiced a loud greeting and spyhopped high.

The enthusiastic welcome elicited a surge of adrenaline through Sheila's veins. As Gunda rose up to her, she laid her hands on the orca's smooth skin and caressed her tenderly. The orca responded with a soft squeak. Sheila imitated it and soon they were making playful calls back and forth. She kissed Gunda on the rostrum and was touched by the gentle nudge that the orca gave in return. The orca's uninhibited and enthusiastic response filled Sheila with confidence and took away all the worries that had burdened her. They were together again.

Janet watched it all with great interest. To see the orca interact with her favorite trainer told her much about the whale's preferences and personality. It was clear that Gunda was a sensitive whale, who responded to subtle touches and sounds. The strong rapport between the two touched her and made her forget why she was there in the first place. As if waking up from a dream, she was suddenly alerted by seeing Sheila's lower legs hanging down in the tank. She almost felt an urge to warn Sheila that she could not enter the water, but the intimacy of the moment held her back.

Sheila had her knees a little apart and felt moved when her beloved orca glided forward, resting her head in her lap. She caressed her tenderly and rested her hands on the smooth natural depression between her melon and rostrum. The orca was overjoyed to have such spontaneous and affectionate playtime with her friend. Yet land and water were still separating them. Although that was the case most of the time, it was the intimacy of the moment that filled Tuschka with the desire to interact with no barriers. Only if her companion shared her domain would they truly be together. She lifted her head, slightly pulling against her trainer's loose grip, but her friend seemed not to take her hint. Then, she came forward again and

250

nudged her encouragingly. Curious about the orca's intentions, Sheila rested her hands again on the same spot and felt the pull when she lifted her head.

The message left no more doubt: Gunda wanted to swim with her! The rules of the park, however, denied it. She looked at Gunda and felt her pull. There was no doubt that she shared the orca's desire just as much. Sheila even wondered if Gunda had read her mind. But what should she do? The decision had to be made quickly. Either she would disappoint Gunda and disrupt their closeness or risk interference from Janet. It took Sheila only a second to make up her mind. This was their last precious time together. She could not bring herself to refrain from what she and Gunda wanted so much. How could she refuse such an obvious request? She had to take her chances. She quickly looked into Janet's direction and tilted her head as if telling her that she had no choice. Her heart beat fast as she saw Janet sit up straight, but her spotter did not speak.

Tuschka noticed that something was directing her friend's attention away from her and she pulled to win it back. Sheila did not resist... and slid off the edge into the water. She held on to the strong whale and was once more impressed by the physical control that enabled her to be so gentle. Sheila let her hands glide down in a full embrace and pressed her cheek against the soft underside of the orca's chin. Tuschka immediately knew what her friend wanted when she felt two hands take hold on her flippers, and she began to spin around. Sheila loved this dance. She felt herself being pulled along, in rhythmic undulating movements. Sheila completely lost herself in her dear orca. She was oblivious to her surroundings, including Janet. She squealed her delight in a duet with the whale.

The orca slowly came to a stop. For a moment, they were face to face. Sheila felt Gunda's soft tongue touch her and returned the tender gesture. Then, in one graceful movement, the orca rolled over, glided underneath her, and lifted her gently upon her chest. Sheila was deeply moved. She felt the same emotions as that first time when Gunda had accepted her as a friend in her domain. She knew it was the orca's special token of affection for her. Lying between Gunda's large pecs, she stretched her arms to embrace the orca and pressed her cheek against her soft underside. She gave little kisses that made small squeaky sounds on the orca's smooth skin. Sheila let her emotions flow freely and felt warm tears well up in her eyes and roll down onto Gunda's chest. As the orca gently carried her, Sheila caressed her lovingly, enjoying the soft undulations of her flukes.

Tuschka was as engrossed in their being together as her friend and relished the intimate moment. Wanting it to last, she held her breath and kept going round, gliding along, feeling every subtle touch and caress of her companion. As a finger playfully touched her rostrum, she touched it with her tongue. When a hand gently stroked her flipper, she subtly moved it in acknowledgement.

Sheila was as aware of the orca's delicate responses as Tuschka was of hers. She felt a sharing of minds, the utmost closeness. She moved a little forward to press her cheek against her chin and was filled with endearment when Gunda lifted her chin and nudged her gently in return. It was the warm response Sheila loved so much. Tuschka felt the emotions in her friend and lifted her chin once more to tell her she understood. As Tuschka carried her friend a little longer, she felt a growing need for air. Slowly she sank down, feeling the water take over the weight of her friend. Then she rose in a small spyhop and took several deep breaths.

Sheila watched as she saw Gunda come into a horizontal resting position. She stroked her in gratefulness as the orca caught up on her breath. She did not know how long Gunda had carried her, but it was obvious that the orca had stretched it. Sheila had been too engrossed and too deeply moved to be aware of time. A playful push waved her concern away. Turning towards the edge of the tank, she let herself be pushed to the spot where they had started.

As she climbed out of the pool, she was suddenly aware of Janet, who was still watching her in silence. Then, she looked at her beloved orca, who was facing her with her head a little raised. Their eyes met. The reality of the moment struck her now. She had to part with her special friend. But she did not want to spoil the unforgettable time together with a heavy mood. She swallowed the emotion away before it had a chance to develop.

Tuschka noticed a moment of absentmindedness in her friend, but her attention came back quickly without alerting her that something might be wrong. Her friend was moved, but that was a beautiful thing that they had been sharing together. As Tuschka felt a warm hug of the woman's arms around her, she felt only happiness. She listened as her friend spoke to her. "My precious, lovely Gunda. I will always cherish in my heart what you just gave me. I'll be with you in thought until we are together again some day." Sheila pressed her close and Tuschka felt the intensity of the hug. Then, as her human friend released her grip, she noticed her wet eyes and an emotion that she could not tell as poignancy or sadness.

Sheila let one hand rest briefly on Gunda's rostrum, feeling her smooth skin for the last time and once more a gentle nudge. Then she got to her feet and stepped over the edge to walk away. Gunda's soft squeak sounded gentle and satisfied as a good-bye for the night..

Janet joined Sheila in silence. They were both full of what had happened, but in different ways. Janet had so much she wanted to say and Sheila wanted only to be alone with her thoughts. Janet sensed it and respected it. Sheila finally gave Janet a meaningful look. "Thank you so much. This meant so much to me..," Janet nodded. "I could see that and I'm touched. Not knowing what was going to happen I felt a little concern at first, but I realized that the rules are to protect us from the risks of the unknown. What you were doing wasn't unknown to you. Truly, Sheila, it was a privilege to witness what you and Gunda shared. I hope we'll be worthy of Gunda's friendship. You can trust me that we'll do all we can to have her thrive." The two girls hugged each other warmly. Sheila blinked back her tears. "Come," Janet said, "get yourself dressed and I'll accompany you to your hotel."

Janet and Sheila arrived early the next morning. They were happy to find Gunda at the gate with Durak, and they slipped unseen into the trainers' lounge. After her precious playtime with Gunda, Sheila had prepared herself to leave quietly without showing herself to the orca. There was a chance that she would not be able to completely hide her emotions and would confuse Gunda. Besides that, she knew that daytime would afford no more than a bleak reflection of what they had just shared. Yet, Sheila did not want to miss the orca's response in case the gate that separated her from Durak were indeed opened. She watched as Janet went outside to follow the head trainer and two other colleagues toward the gate.

Tuschka had not hesitated to come over when the big male appeared on the other side of the gate. He had become a familiar presence for her and despite his different calls, he radiated gentleness. The large orca revived faint memories of the past, memories that evoked feelings of reassurance and security. As usual, they had started to exchange squeaks as if teaching one another, but soon after, they were content just to hover close together.

Both whales looked up as the small group of trainers approached. They eyed them warily, expecting them to bring an end to their time at the gate. Tuschka watched in silence. She had noticed Janet among them, but all her attention was directed at her human companions. They made their typical guttural sounds and many gestures. A tap on the water in the other tank alerted Tuschka. Just as the big male backed up and turned, she heard a similar sound in her own pool. As usual, Tuschka left the gate and came over to her trainer. She spyhopped high to look for her favorite friend, but she was not there. Although Tuschka was a little disappointed, Sheila's absence no longer disturbed her. It had become more rule than exception that the new girl came by herself, and since Tuschka had shared play time with her she had found that the new trainer was gentle and sincere.

After Tuschka had swallowed a handful of fish, a hissing noise sounded nearby. It was a sound that Tuschka had heard many times. The sound seemed a little closer than usual, but it was a slight creek in the gate to her left that drew her attention. She watched in amazement as the heavy steel structure slowly opened until it lay against the wall of her tank. Tuschka did not move, nor did she take her eyes away from the spot where the gate had been. The subtle sounds of something moving through the water made her heart beat faster. She inched closer to her trainer, seeking reassurance from her.

The black form of the big male startled Tuschka as he glided into her tank. Nervously, she backed up further alongside the wall, but the hand and the voice of her trainer steadied her. In full view from the side, the orca looked even bigger than she had thought. Her heart pounded when their eyes met, but he did not come to her. Instead, he stopped and turned to face his trainer. Tuschka quickly surveyed the confines of her tank. There was no refuge if the powerful orca chose to approach her. Uncertain and a little fearful, Tuschka looked up at her trainer.

She found her looking towards the male orca, but soon her attention was back. Her voice was soft and gentle, but Tuschka sensed a slight undercurrent of tension. There was something that was even beyond the control of her trainer. Tuschka looked at the big orca again and felt a mixture of surprise and relief when she saw him leave her tank. Yells and cheers of approval came from her own trainer as well as from the man in the adjacent tank. She wondered why. The reward boosted her confidence.

Tuschka was on guard when the big orca entered the tank again, but she was not as frightened as the first time. The large whale stopped in front of his trainer, but after his reward, the man took only a step back. Tuschka watched the male orca turn. His eyes found hers. She felt her heart beat again. What was he up to? She waited motionless. From her posture, the big male read Tuschka's mind unerringly. She was confused and afraid of him. It was in sharp contrast with her relaxed mood of a little while ago when they had enjoyed each others presence near the gate. He saw her stiffen as he inched towards her. He stopped and called softly as he had done so many times before, to tell her that she need not fear him. The tender call stirred something in Tuschka. It was one she had come to know well. It conveyed gentleness and patience. She looked him in the eye as if seeking confirmation of what she was hoping.

He called to her again, mild and friendly. Tuschka took him in again. He was big and powerful, but there was no aggression in him. Nothing hinted at something to fear. On the contrary. With no physical barrier to keep him from approaching her, Tuschka realized that the large bull was controlling himself for her sake. He was aware of how she felt and was attempting to reassure her. His consideration touched her and, with the growing belief that he would be patient with her, the tension in her muscles ebbed. The large orca saw the subtle changes in the posture of the beautiful young female. Still, he waited. Tuschka turned a little in his direction and made a tentative call to him. He acknowledged her promptly with a call that was almost a copy of her own. It struck her as much as it had the first time, and from one moment to the other, Tuschka felt contact with him. Her initial fright gave way to excitement and a desire to be close to him.

Before Tuschka realized that the time was right, the big male started to move, and came gliding towards her. But the time was right: the mental change in her had told him so. He called to her softly. Tuschka watched him in wonder. The situation was new and yet, vaguely familiar. She was still hovering at the surface near her trainer, but her attention was fully focused on the large visitor in her tank. He slowed down when he was about eight feet away from her. Then, he veered slightly and looked at her as he slowly glided by. Tuschka looked at the strange dorsal fin. It was a big fin, but it had somehow collapsed and was hanging down in a big curl with its tip close to his back. Otherwise, he looked like a male in his prime with curled flukes and broad pecs. He made a short circle and called to her again. Tuschka saw how he looked back at her when he glided by, inviting her to follow.

She briefly looked at her trainer. She was still there, but she was not asking her to do anything. When their eyes met, she pointed at the other orca. Tuschka saw him come around again and heard his pleading call. He could have forced her, but he did not. Still, he was being patient, waiting for her to join his side. The temptation to go to him and swim with him was almost irresistible. Yet, something still made her hesitate. Somewhere, deep inside, she was looking for approval, for reassurance that it would be the right thing. The scene evoked memories of long gone days in which her family was always with her, protecting her and guiding her. The pain of loss gnawed itself to the surface. Her loving and caring mother was not there to reassure her. A wave of depression and indecisiveness swept over Tuschka.

Durak sensed the sudden change in her mood. He noticed how she turned inside and became filled with sadness. He glided by closer, calling to her softly. He grazed her flank tenderly with his flipper to divert her attention and to lift her spirits. Tuschka felt the subtle touch and with it the painful memories faded. She was not alone.... Right here was one of her own kind, who cared for her, who wanted to accompany her. When she heard his voice again she answered him, but not only with sound. She waved her flukes and moved away from the wall. When he came by, she slipped at his side, feeling the pull of his wake.

They swam together in silence, but very much aware of each other's presence. It was comforting in a way that Tuschka had not experienced in a long time. Even the enjoyable hours with Lucie and the other dolphins had not given her a similar satisfaction. Her companion was a wonderful combination of physical strength and gentleness. As they swam along, his closeness filled her with a warmth that was covering the pains of the past. They occasionally touched each other. It was the delicate beginning of exploring each other and gaining mutual trust. When they came to a rest, their heads were close together, but not yet touching.

Durak was thrilled with the new female. She was young, but mature. He noticed her broad-based erect dorsal fin, which was in contrast to that of the dominant female in the other tank. But it was her perfectly smooth skin that both amazed and puzzled him. The skin told much about an orca's rank. Females of high rank had few rake marks, because few orcas would dispute them. This female had none?! Yet she was a little timid and young to be of high rank. Whatever explanation there was for her exceptionally smooth skin, it made him cautious. If she was used to being treated with great respect, he had better be careful with his advances. Durak knew she was a newcomer. Her rank was still to be established, but the fact that she was female made it likely to become higher than his own.

Two taps on the water abruptly interrupted their pleasant reverie. They were both reluctant to separate, but their respective trainers happened to be close together. Tuschka was the first to come over and was pleased with her warm reward. It was more than she had expected for just coming over. Another tap close by was meant for her male companion. Tuschka noticed that he approached the man near the edge with great reluctance. His trainer pointed in the direction of the channel. Did he want her companion to leave the tank?

Durak called to her to follow him as he glided by behind her. Tuschka was about to turn when a touch on her rostrum brought her attention back to the woman in front of her. It was obvious that she was expected to stay. Keeping her position, she looked at the big male. He was looking back at her and hovering in the channel that was otherwise behind the gate. It looked narrow with the great orca filling most of it. She felt no desire to follow him into that narrow passage. It took a little while until the big whale finally moved forward into the other tank. As Tuschka saw him disappear from the channel, a hissing sound announced the closing of the gate. She regretted that her companion had left, and waited near the gate for a little while. Perhaps her friendly companion would return and sit with her at the gate as they had done before. But he did not return. She wasn't aware that the trainers had led him into a tank not adjacent to hers, lest she distract him too much.

Time was pressing for Sheila to leave. Seeing Gunda's attention still focused on what might happen behind the gate, she quickly stepped outside and slipped away unseen. Janet had followed her. From a higher vantage point, used by cameramen during the show, Sheila watched her special friend for a few more moments. 'Just one more blow', she thought, wanting to hear the strong sound of Gunda's exhalation once more and etch it in her memory. "Poooohhup." It sounded strong and healthy. Sheila saw the large white eye patch as the orca bobbed up her head. Her eyes followed the sleek skin of her back and took in the firm erect dorsal fin. 'You are such a beauty', Sheila almost whispered in thought, 'physically and mentally. I will miss you, my dear Gunda.'

She was tempted to walk up to her precious whale for a last brief good-bye, but she kept to her decision. It was comforting to know that Gunda would not be lonely. She was making new friends. Janet, and soon other trainers would work and play with her. But most important of all, she had begun to enjoy friendship with her own kind again. Sheila's eyes were wet, but the wonderful memory of the previous night would comfort her as would her resolve to see her beloved Gunda again some day.

24.
Shachi's Pod

"Wow," Janet exclaimed and clapped her hands. "Eeeoee," Mark squeaked, trying to express his excitement over the orca's excellent response. "Those bows were beautiful and so high! She only needs to learn the proper positions in the performance pool and she's ready to do a part of the show." Janet smiled at her colleague's enthusiasm. "It's true that she knows quite a bit for the time she's been here: bows, a fast swim, barrel rolls, and pec waves. Her tail wave needs some polishing, but it's a good start. We should begin to acquaint her with the other pools. I'll ask Brian what he thinks... "

Gunda surprised her mid-sentence, suddenly breaking the surface in front of her and rising shoulder high. The orca had obviously picked up upon her trainers' enthusiastic approval. Janet playfully laid her hand on Gunda's rostrum as she sank down again. "You're such a good girl, and so clever. You will be a star performer some day!" She gave the orca a big batch of fish and sent her on a fast swim. The waves that the whale was creating were rolling over the edge. Janet blew her whistle to bridge the orca and saw her slow down. Before Gunda had stopped, Janet gave her a cue for a pec wave. She picked it up on the swim and rolled over instantly. The orca's alertness was amazing. It was not surprising that orcas, as top predators of the ocean, were capable of fast reactions, but the prompt response reflected how well motivated Gunda was and how confident already with the cue.

Although the orca was eager to work, Janet stopped the training session only a few minutes later and rewarded Gunda with a chasing game around the perimeter of the tank. Janet would accelerate, then suddenly stop, make unexpected turns, and run again. The orca was quick to follow her, splashing about and turning the water white with her fast maneuvers. Gunda was just in the right mood for the energetic game and it would leave her with a good feeling after the session. Janet was careful not to ask the orca's attention for too long and risk losing it. It was tempting to work a little longer when all went so well, but experience had taught her that the rewards and the overall reinforcement would lose strength as soon as the orca's interest began to wane.

Just as Mark and Janet entered the trainers' lounge, Gunda was still squealing exuberantly and pacing around the tank, lifting her head high upon each surfacing as if making sure that they had really left. Her frequent blows told them that the session had given Gunda a good work-out.

It did not come as a surprise to head trainer Brian, when Janet suggested familiarizing Gunda with the other tanks. He had kept an eye on the newcomer's progress and agreed that the orca was close to mastering all the behaviors that were necessary to do the opening of a show. "You may want to start with the left holding tank," he said. "I suggest you put Shachi and Kiki in the front pool and Durak in the right holding tank after the noon show. That'll give you a nice window of time.

Tuschka was stationing in front of her female trainer when the hissing sound to her left announced the opening of a gate close by. When she saw that it was the gate to the tank of the big male, she waited with eager anticipation for him to appear. But he did not. Disappointed, Tuschka looked up at her trainer again. She saw her stand up and point her arm to the left. She started swimming in the indicated direction, but she tensed as the tap on the water sounded mid-channel. She had no desire to enter the narrow unfamiliar passage. She saw her trainer kneel down, right at the entrance of the channel and tap the water lightly. Tuschka crept forward, stopping a yard short of her. She understood that it meant a great deal to her trainer, but at the same time, she noticed a difference in her attitude. Her encouragement had much of a plea as if she had somehow expected her to hesitate.

Tuschka had expected a training session, but now things took a turn that made her uncomfortable. She looked into the narrow passage. She could not easily turn around in it. Without the option of a fast retreat once she swam into it, she held back. Until now restraint had meant loss and change. She had just begun to make new friends and to feel comfortable in her new enclosure. She was not ready to go through yet another change. A feeling of frustration came over Tuschka: she felt too uneasy to cooperate. She called loudly, voicing her discomfort.

Janet saw the orca's apprehension. For her too, it was a difficult situation. She had dealt with newcomers before, but the few that had arrived since her employment had all had the same training background. Although Janet had asked Sheila many things about Gunda's past, each day brought new questions. She wished she could fall back upon the orca's former trainer, but those days were over. Had Gunda always been in one tank? No, that could not be. She had to make room for the dolphin shows. Could it be a difference in the type of gates or passage ways, or was it simply a trait of this orca to resist something new? Whatever the answer was, she could not reward the whale for what she failed to do, and yet Gunda deserved better. Janet sensed that the step she had hoped the orca would make was too big. She came a foot closer to Gunda and motioned Mark to join her. Then, she gave another tap on the water.

Tuschka poked her head into the passage. Besides being narrow, it was also shallow, but the narrow part was not long. One of the walls was short and beyond it seemed to be a larger space, but Tuschka did not know what lay ahead and she stayed where she was. Knowing that her trainer was not satisfied with her behavior, she waited in hopes that the woman would change her mind and ask her to do something she would feel comfortable with.

Tuschka was only a foot away from the two trainers. She inched closer to them, observant of every movement near her. As soon as she touched her trainer's hand, the girl let out a whoop of approval, rubbed her briefly, and gave her a large handful of fish. Tuschka accepted it, still tense and wondering what would be next. But instead of another request that would call upon her courage, she was led away from the gate. As it fell shut her apprehension quickly faded and she vented her relief with an exuberant response to the cues that followed.

Janet noticed that the orca was expressing her gratitude. It endeared her, but it made her more reluctant to subject Gunda to the same request again. Now, she brooded even more on a strategy that Gunda would find less aversive.

As the gate opened, Tuschka watched her trainer warily. Would she ask her to enter the channel again? Excitement filled her as, instead, her big male companion glided into view. They had not seen each other for two days. Tuschka saw him approach and was eager to join him. She watched her trainer get up and walk away. As Durak swam by, he tilted his head sideways, inviting the young female to come to his side. While they glided together, Tuschka experienced again how wonderful it was to have a companion of her own kind. To see him and to communicate with him had already meant much, but also sharing physical contact made it so much richer. His skin felt soft, but Tuschka saw the numerous scars on his flanks and peduncle. Most were minor, but some indicated he had received several severe rakes in the past. She remembered similar scars on companions in her younger days, but only vaguely did she recall what had happened. Above the big male's eye patch was a fairly fresh gash with some frayed pink flesh. It puzzled her. Who would dare to challenge such a strong and powerful animal?

Brian had joined Janet. Together with two other trainers they were observing the pair. "They found each other a lot more quickly than I'd expected," Brian said. "Their geographic origins lie so far apart." The gate was still open. The trainers had decided to let the two orcas enjoy some undisturbed time together. There was a chance Gunda would follow Durak if he decided to go into the holding tank. That would take most of her fear away to enter the other tank also on request. But the male orca had not shown any intention of leaving the big back pool yet. That in itself was not surprising: the back pool was both larger and deeper than the holding tanks that lay between it and the performance pool. As a next step, the trainers had planned to give Durak a cue to leave the back tank, but it made no sense to try that right away. The male, who was most of the time by himself, would not be very willing to leave immediately what he had just been given: a beautiful companion and more room to swim.

The afternoon wore on and still Durak had not left the tank. Brian stepped forward and slapped the water hard. The head trainer was standing fairly close to the gate. Janet was not so happy with it. Gunda would not like it much and if the female would not station, it was unlikely that Durak would. Both orcas slowed down and as the big male approached, Gunda fell behind. The head trainer had worked with the male more than any other trainer. He gave his cue and walked over to the other pool. His behavior was resolute; as if he did not even consider that the male might have other plans. Durak looked at his female companion. She had not been given the same signal. The prospect of being separated did not appeal to him. He heard another slap on the water in the adjacent tank. He hesitated only briefly, then turned away from the open passage and nudged Tuschka gently to join him. A little confused, Tuschka followed.

"Don't count on him for the evening show," Brian yelled at Janet. "Shachi will have to do the wet parts again." The head trainer was disappointed, but not really surprised. Few trainers had worked with the male since he had arrived about a year ago. At that time, he had not been more than a distrustful whale, barely responding to anything but food. With his past, it was no wonder. Twelve years ago, he had been taken from a small pod that roamed the temperate ranges of an ocean far away from Gunda's home waters. In his new home he had been introduced to four other orcas. The three females and a juvenile had not been very friendly to him. When they were together, there was little he could do without being chased or raked. It had made him timid in their company, but when alone his pent-up aggression had sometimes surfaced. Training had become increasingly difficult with his unpredictable temper. Soon, they had given up on using him for shows. Kept in a tiny back pool, serving no other purpose than breeding, he had been grinding his teeth away on the concrete walls.

Ocean Adventure had purchased him primarily for the same reason, but they saw it as a challenge to gain the whale's trust and turn him into a performer again. Brian had decided to expose him to a few trainers only and to start with just feeding him. The trainers understood that the first brittle trust could be gained only through consistent feeding, irrespective of his actions. Brian vividly remembered the days when Durak first started to follow him along the side of the tank. Although he knew it was mainly interest in food, it was a basis for contact. At least the orca had come to associate him with feeding, something positive. But ever since his arrival, the moments of bad temper, of upwelling frustration, kept recurring with unpredictable intervals. Those moments were frightening displays. The large orca would scream loudly, and at the same time, he would pace around the tank and bob his head up and down. In the worst cases, he rammed gates and walls until he bled. The displays filled every onlooker with horror. The bouts were usually short, and only after he had calmed down would someone approach him.

Brian and his colleagues had been careful with the introduction of training sessions. Although many bursts of aggression still came without obvious reason, it was apparent that Durak was more touchy than any other whale, when it came to disapproval of his behavior. The slightest rejection, like breaking contact by

262

averting the eyes, could set him off. The positive thing about it was that it meant much to Durak to have contact with his trainers, but it called for creativity to make every session as positive as possible without reinforcing undesired behavior. There was always an undercurrent of tension, of suppressed fear for an adverse response.

Over the last several months, training had suddenly taken a turn for the better. Craving for a caring friend, but with a confidence too much shaken in the past, Durak struggled to find the way towards harmony and trust. Little, fleeting moments of rapport filled Brian and his fellow trainers with a tremendous feeling of joy and accomplishment. For the orca, the moments began to soften his scarred heart.

Durak felt almost in heaven with the new female. She was beautiful and at the same time so gentle. Her behavior was so different from that of the other adult female. She had the appearance of a dominant animal, but she did not act like one. He wondered if she would change when she gained more confidence in her new environment. He took in her figure. She was muscular and streamlined, but with limited fat reserves. The grace of her movements excited him. He kicked his flukes and accelerated.

The sudden change in his behavior surprised Tuschka. She saw him slow down, look back at her and speed up again. This time, she read his intent and caught up with him in an instant. She stayed at his side only for a few moments, then played the same trick on him. As Durak saw her dash forward he kicked his mighty flukes to follow her, but it was not easy to catch up. She was fast and agile! When he seemed to gain on her, she accelerated again or prevented him from closing in by taking a sharp turn. Despite his physical strength, Tuschka felt within moments that she could easily outmaneuver the big male. But Durak did not give up easily. His wild pursuit, combined with his bulk, sent waves rolling over the edges and into the adjacent tanks. The big male was pumping his flukes and breathing fast and deep. The excited squeals of both whales filled the tank and echoed back from the walls.

Unexpectedly, Durak did not turn when he approached the gate, but sped straight through the channel into the holding tank. Tuschka had only a split second to realize her position and barely managed to clear the wall when she forcefully veered away. She had almost come to a stop and was turning to look for her companion when the male orca suddenly reappeared. Tuschka resumed the game and sped away, but cut off the corner near the gate.

A sharp call pierced the water. Neither of the two had made it. Tuschka had heard it a few times before and knew it had come from the adult female. Although she had never felt addressed by it, she did so now. It suddenly triggered memories of past moments when someone called a halt to her activities, especially when she was exuberant. And she was exuberant now, indulging in unrestrained play.

Tuschka slowed down and looked at the male. The change in his behavior was sudden and confirmed what she had sensed. He had obviously felt addressed. Tuschka and Durak glided side by side, catching up on their breath. As they came to the corner near the gate, Durak did not turn. Tuschka sensed his intent and, being blocked by his body, she quickly passed underneath him. Durak went on and stopped at the other end of the short passage. Tuschka heard his calls and came around to see what was happening. She stopped at a safe distance opposite him and waited. They both waited. It was obvious that her companion wanted her to join him, but she still felt uncomfortable entering the passage into an unfamiliar enclosure.

After a little longer, Durak came forward and nudged her gently. Then he backed up slowly, calling for her to follow. His body filled most of the passage; it was obvious that he could not move much in it. Yet he seemed comfortable. Tuschka came forward a little, but her courage ebbed quickly. Nervously, she backed up. Durak came forward and tried again. This time, he backed up just a little and waited for her. His voice was gentle and supplicative, imploring her to come, but to no avail. Convinced that this strategy was not going to work, he entered the big back pool, made a circle around his female friend, and went back through the channel. He made several passes back and forth, hoping it would make her less wary about it; but still she did not follow.

Durak came to a stop beside Tuschka. He rubbed his chin against her to reassure her. Then he backed up a little and gave her a gentle nudge forward in her armpit. Tuschka knew that her companion had no intent to harm her, but she was not ready yet. She ducked down and swam away from the gate. He followed her, but as he tried to come alongside, she sped up. It was obvious he had pushed it a little too much.

Some trainers had been watching the attempts of the male to entice the female through the channel. They were happy with it. Perhaps Durak could accomplish faster what they as yet could not. Being of her kind, he was closer to her than anyone of them could ever hope to be.

In the night, Durak finally managed to persuade Tuschka to pass through the gate. It was in the absence of the trainers that she dared to entrust herself to her guide. Durak would not close the gate behind her as the humans might do. Tuschka inched her way forward, chin to chin with the big male, who made his way backwards as fast as her courage would permit. The short passage gave access to a tank that was smaller and a little less deep than the one she was used to, but still a good size. Durak went to a corner away from the gate and called for her. Tuschka passed him twice. She wanted to be with him, but she still felt a little uneasy in the new tank. She sensed his self control as he remained in his corner away from the gate. He was obviously giving her time to adjust.

Tuschka could no longer resist him and glided at his side. He nudged her warmly and caressed her with his pectoral fin. She nudged him back and answered his gentle call with a squeak of delight.

264

Half-way December, Tuschka had become comfortable moving back and forth between the gates. After her first hesitant pass, it had taken two weeks before she did it at the trainers' request. To Tuschka's regret, she had been given much less time with Durak. Since they had played together, however, the attitude of the dominant female had suddenly changed. Until then, only her offspring had looked at Tuschka with curiosity, but now her dominant mother often joined her at the gate.

Durak and Kiki were Shachi's small pod. After Kavja had died, several months ago, Shachi had become the dominant female. With the adult male, a relatively new arrival, and her own little offspring, it had not been difficult to take that position. The coming of the new adult female had cast a different light on the situation. Shachi was not happy with the prospect of having her new position challenged. As long as Tuschka was kept separate, she posed no threat to the relationships in Shachi's small group and without the need to face another change, Shachi had virtually ignored the newcomer. The young mother had heard how the first tentative vocalizations between Durak and the new female had gained confidence. They had even begun to convey affection, but it was not until they had been together that Shachi felt true concern about the relationships in what had now become a group of four. The smooth skin of the new female had put her on guard too, but soon she had discovered that her behavior did not match her appearance. She was well aware that the male had taken a liking to his new companion and she did not want to lose her control over him. When they had engaged in exuberant play, she had clearly voiced her disapproval.

Now, Shachi was watching her peer in the adjacent tank. She was obviously shy and showed no intent to exert any dominance. Despite her offspring's open interest, the new female did not come over and stop. Gaining confidence in the fact that she would not have a hard time keeping her position in the hierarchy, Shachi began to look at the newcomer as a potential companion. Kavja had been a dominant, but stable and warm personality. She missed her now. Although it would be different, it would be good to have the companionship of another female of her own age again. Durak could not take that place. When they were together for any length of time his interest in her as a mate always ended in advances that Shachi did not always welcome. She could easily put him in his place, but that inevitably caused some tension, preventing her from relaxing fully. It was not the same as another female, who had the same natural inclinations as herself.

Tuschka was very aware of the change in the mother's attitude. It made her curious, but she lacked the confidence to take any initiative. Kiki called from behind the gate. Tuschka looked at her as she swam by, but did not respond. To her surprise, the mother repeated the call. Tuschka looked again and slowed down. Both whales remained at the gate, in contrast to the past when the juvenile was often called away by her mother. The voice of the adult female sounded self-confident, but not aggressive. Tuschka felt the vibrations of the juvenile's echolocations on her body. From a small distance, Tuschka took the mother whale in. There was a slight bulge in her streamlined body. She echolocated in return and detected a second heartbeat, faint and fast. There was new life growing inside her.

The two watched each other in silence for a short while, but as Tuschka made a move to turn away, the mother called to her again. The call was not from a dialect that Tuschka knew, but it had an imperative sound. Instinctively, she turned back to face the two whales again. Shachi voiced her approval. Although the other orcas could not enter her tank, Tuschka felt their presence strongly. She was uncomfortable ignoring the dominant female and found herself responding to her. A strange mixture of stimuli was drawing her closer to the gate. She sensed strongly that the mother orca wanted her to come over, but a different voice inside made her stay away from a presence that wanted to force her will on her and was challenging her independence. Yet, there could also be security and guidance in submission, if... the leadership was good. Tuschka did not know what to think of the female on the other side of the gate. It was unsettling to go close and yield to an unknown personality, but somehow she feared enmity with the dominant female more.

Tuschka stopped just a foot short of the gate. She felt judged as the two looked at her. They made a few calls. Tuschka felt as if they were making up their mind about what to do with her. Whatever the mother decided, the juvenile would follow. After a while, when the two orcas left the gate, Tuschka backed up slowly and swam away. The influence of the dominant female went beyond the physical barrier of the gate. Tuschka knew that she could no longer look at them as just two orcas in another enclosure. It had been Shachi's former indifference that had given Tuschka her relative mental freedom. She wondered why the dominant mother had suddenly taken an interest in her. Tuschka settled in a corner where she could not directly be seen in an attempt to escape the mental grip by escaping from sight.

* * *

It was a quiet morning in January, three months after Gunda had arrived at the park. Janet sat in front of her, keeping her stationed while Brian and Mark tried to make Durak move to another tank. But the male was reluctant to leave, and Gunda was becoming impatient. Janet tapped her rostrum and began to caress her and rub her gums. When she bent over to press her cheek against Gunda's rostrum, Brains' sharp warning startled her. The head trainer had caught her off guard. She immediately stopped her private interaction and assumed the required, more formal attitude. She was supposed to just keep Gunda stationed, but she had taken the liberty of doing more than that.

The rules were very strict, especially since several accidents had happened in other parks. They were translated into measures that even the most inexperienced trainer would know to respect. The regulations did not only serve safety, they also served reliable performance. One aspect of control was that each animal would cooperate with a variety of trainers. If one orca highly favored a particular trainer, performance was at risk by becoming dependent on that trainer's presence. Any private attempts to win more of a whale's sympathy were not allowed. The regulations were based on a carefully thought-out theory, including considerations ranging from psychology to liability. Yet it was theory, and the rules that enforced it left little room for the feelings, interpretations, and judgments of those who interacted with the orcas on a daily basis. Janet and most of her fellow trainers knew that their sensitive and intelligent friends had unique personalities and moods that required a spontaneous and personal response. They were entrusted to their care. To care well for them was the least the orcas were entitled to, and how much were they willing to do just that!

Janet had immediately sensed that Gunda was a little tense and nervous. She knew a little reassurance would boost the orca's confidence and cooperation. She sighed softly as she looked at Gunda, knowing that the whale was unaware of her contemplations. She recalled the night when she had let Sheila play freely with her friend. How beautiful, how touching it had been. That same Gunda was in front of her now, capable of all that warmth and enthusiasm. Janet wondered if she would ever share it. It would require spontaneity on both sides, and although the orca could refuse it, Janet knew that she would be denying Gunda far more than the orca would ever deny her.

Janet realized she had been romanticizing her career as a whale trainer. She had been dreaming of the beautiful intimate relationship that would grow between her and the orcas. In the beginning, it had all been so wonderful. The first recognition and acknowledgements of Kavja had raised her enthusiasm sky high. She had been thrilled with every small step forward, finding it self-evident that her freedom of interaction kept pace with her progress as a trainer. But at that time she had thought that the sky was the limit. She had looked with longing at the seasoned trainers, who did the most fantastic water work with the whales. To swim with an orca had seemed the ultimate closeness to the magnificent creature. There could not be any barrier when trainer and whale acted as one.

Janet remembered her first swim and felt tears sting her eyes when she thought of Kavja, who had carried her so gently on her back. The experienced female orca had no doubt known how inexperienced she was and yet she had not taken advantage of it. On the contrary, she had somehow communicated to her that she need not fear. Now, she had become one of those experienced trainers herself, admired by the younger ones, but the limit had not been the sky. There was indeed a relationship between mental contact and physical interaction: without the first, the latter could hardly be more than a rub. But Janet knew now that there could be a far deeper bond than their controlled physical interaction required. The secret lay in spontaneity, and so Janet was always alert and ready to steal little intimate moments with the orcas. Some of her best friends did the same thing. During such moments, a little nudge or a subtle touch conveyed more than all the big predictable rub-downs of a whole show. It was then that she shared her greatest joy. Those were the moments that proved her dream true. The orca lived up to it. If there was anything unrealistic about the dream, it was because man had made it so...

* * *

Tuschka tensed as the mother and her offspring glided into her tank. She knew the two would not ignore her, but she had no idea what they were up to. They stopped a few yards away from her in front of their trainers, but they were very aware of her presence. Tuschka looked at them and saw the dominant female watching her. Kiki's head was behind her mother's, but the curious juvenile briefly sank down to take a peek from beneath her mother's belly. Tuschka tried to concentrate on her own trainer. As long as the trainers were there, they would be leading the situation.

Tuschka rose up higher and closer to the young woman in front of her. She called imploringly, not wanting her human companion to leave while the other two whales shared her tank. They left as smoothly as they had come and Tuschka relaxed when the gate was shut again. Her trainer was obviously pleased and after a tender rub, she got up and left. Tuschka followed her along for a few steps and then saw the other two orcas being fed in the other tank.

Tuschka had retreated in her own corner, but the imperative voice of the dominant female respected no visual barriers. It pierced Tuschka's ears loud and clear. Her heart beat faster. She did not want to come, and waited. One more time, the call sent a shiver through Tuschka. Then, it fell silent. The subtle sounds of turbulence and the blows of the orcas told Tuschka they had moved away from the gate. She looked towards the gate to the other adjacent pool. The male was in it, but he was not showing himself. Tuschka wished he was with her now. Hesitantly, she glided over to that gate, but refrained from calling him, lest she arouse the attention of the other two females. He slowed down and stopped in front of her. "Aaaieeee..," the dominant female sounded loud. Tuschka stiffened briefly and saw her companion back away. She sensed that it was in response to her call. Despite his size, he was clearly submissive. Tuschka realized they were both in the mental grip of the dominant female.

Several hours later, a shiver went though Tuschka when she heard the gate open. She watched with apprehension as the mother and her calf entered her pool again. They started circling, but they were coming closer to her now. The juvenile was obviously curious, trying to look at Tuschka while her mother kept her on the inside. The young orca was squeaking a lot and poking her mother frequently. With each circle, Tuschka saw the mother orca pass closer to her, and she barely moved in fear of triggering aggression. To yield to a higher-ranked female came naturally to Tuschka, but the presence of this unfamiliar dominant personality drained her confidence. It had been so different with the male.

The mother whale slowed down and turned her head sideways towards her. Her eye was wide open. She called. Tuschka only listened. Then she made a short circle and repeated the sound. When Tuschka did no more than just watch, the female gave a slight jerk with her head. She had not yet shown her teeth, but Tuschka took the hint that the female wanted her to do something other than just sit there. But what did she want? Did she want her to move? Where could she go?

Tuschka moved forward. She felt the orca catch up behind her, but she suppressed a sudden urge to speed away. That would not be submissive behavior and the chase that might follow would not be a game. The mother orca came alongside and slowed down to match her speed. Her voice was calmer now. Sensing a slight lessening of tension, Tuschka kept on swimming. The female was noticeably smaller than the male, but strong and well fed. The top half of her dorsal fin was drooping, although not as much as in the male. Under water it lifted up a little. There were some scars on her skin, but most of those were healed over. She had not been seriously raked recently. The few that were relatively fresh were very shallow with small distances between the lines, revealing that her own offspring had made those in play.

The juvenile orca swam on her mother's other flank. Although she was restless, her mother was very tolerant towards her. Tuschka had not yet seen much of the way they normally interacted, but the mother displayed a very caring and warm attitude towards her offspring. There had to be a very harmonious and strong bond between the two. It was strange to be so close to the tiny family and be an outsider at the same time.

Although there were several familiar intonations in the calls of the two orcas, Tuschka paid very close attention to their movements. Their body language was easier to read than their calls. As Tuschka watched the adult female gently nudge her calf and caress her with her flipper, memories of her own mother surfaced. How she longed to be in the youngster's position: to be loved and wanted at all times. Tuschka felt drawn to them. She felt a strong desire to be part of the little family. Remarkably enough, this mother had taken the initiative and had almost ordered her to swim along, but obviously on her terms. The adult female commanded respect and Tuschka had no wish to challenge it. She swam along in silence, hoping that she would experience not only dominance, but also a little of the sympathy that this mother orca was so generously capable of giving.

It was no surprise for Shachi that the new female did not immediately respond to her commands. Since her arrival it had been apparent that she had come from a different pod. Although there was no opposition in her hesitant behavior, Shachi wanted to leave no doubt about her rank. She was curious about the personality that would unfold, but it was her first concern that the newcomer would become a compliant companion… and for that she had to accept the role of subdominant female. Shachi looked at the young adult orca at her side. She had already assumed a docile attitude. Shachi understood how she felt and noticed how eager she was to avoid conflict. She wanted to confirm her dominance, but not through fear. Calling the new female to swim at her side was her way to accept Tuschka as a new member of her little pod.

In the first two days Shachi and Tuschka had barely touched each other. Tuschka tried hard to understand when her company was wanted and when the mother and her offspring preferred to be by themselves. Despite the relatively distant behavior of the dominant female, Tuschka sensed no hostility in her attitude.

As they swam together, both females felt a desire for more closeness, but they lacked the natural bond from sharing the same pod. In that matriarchal society, the complex relationships between the females were based on age, matriline, and experience. Being Shachi's offspring, Kiki's position was clear. In contrast, Tuschka and Shachi each had a past that was unknown to the other. They were both motivated to establish a good relationship, but there was a large gap to be bridged. Shachi had been in Tuschka's position several years ago when she was introduced to Kavja. She had learned much from Kavja, who had been a good leader to her. Now, drawing from that experience, Shachi had a natural authority. She tried to gain the other's trust by finding the balance between mildness and dominance. Too much emphasis on dominance would foster more fear than trust, and being too mild would jeopardize her position. Tuschka, on her part, tried to win Shachi's sympathy by showing her willingness to comply. While Shachi and Kiki had been resting, Tuschka had quietly been hovering near one of the gates. She had refrained from swimming circles, lest she disturb the two. When they awoke from their slumber and started to swim, Shachi passed close and signaled her to join them. Tuschka gracefully turned and glided by her side. Then the dominant female came a little closer, lifted her flipper and touched her lightly. Tuschka felt a wave of warmth and excitement with the subtle gesture of affection. It meant much more than acceptance. Knowing that her company was appreciated she felt her tension ebb away. Tuschka learned quickly to read her new leader and as Shachi became more convinced about the gentle and submissive personality of her new companion, she began to show more of her warm nature.

25.
Wobke

In the weeks that followed the trainers worked as much as possible with the two adult females together. One aim was to have the two females become attuned to each other. With the impending birth of Shachi's calf it was important that the two orcas would get along well. The trainers wanted Gunda to assist Shachi during her labor and to learn from her maternal behavior at the same time. The second goal was to accelerate Gunda's progress with the examples of the experienced female. She had to learn as many skills as possible to fill in for Shachi in the weeks following the birth.

As the bond between Shachi and Tuschka grew, Shachi allowed her offspring more interaction with Tuschka. The juvenile orca was about three years old and very playful. She often rubbed along Tuschka's flank, cut her path, or bumped her to entice her into a chase. Although Tuschka had a playful nature, Kiki proved insatiable. The young orca demanded much of her attention and often went on when she wanted some quiet time. Shachi was remarkably playful for a mother, but when she had had enough, she simply told her calf to stop. Only rarely did the mother orca need an extra signal to end Kiki's exuberance. There was a perfect balance between love and dominance. But Tuschka did not have that dominance and there was no doubt that Kiki took advantage of this. She often ignored Tuschka's hints to leave her alone. Upon any sign of aggression, mother would protect her. Tuschka envied Shachi for the control she had over the young orca. When she grew tired, Tuschka was grateful when Shachi called her calf to order or when the trainers brought relief by giving her time by herself. Although Tuschka was happy to have companions of her own kind, she savored such quiet moments.

The gate to the performance pool swung open. Only recently had Tuschka become familiar with the deep and large space where her companions performed. Although it was a great place to frolic and play, she was not yet used to the many people watching her through the big transparent semicircular wall. Kiki loved the attention of the visitors. She had discovered that they always came to her, but that they would squeal and jump away when she squirted them. The adults usually stayed away after being splashed, but the younger ones seemed to view it as a game and often came back.

Kiki broke away from her mother and raced away into the big pool. Not finding any playful visitors, she quickly returned and began to bump her mother to come and play with her. Shachi wanted to stay with Tuschka, but Kiki bumped her flank again. She could easily command her calf to be quiet, but Kiki had been so patient during their resting time that she did not want to ignore her request. With a little reluctance, Shachi veered away in the direction of the open gate. Kiki sped away when her mother approached. She raced through the pool, diving deep, turning fast, and dashing towards the surface in half breaches. Shachi was agile and physically superior to her offspring, but she deliberately engaged in the game.

Tuschka was watching it from the channel. It was great to see the two orcas enjoying each other and the larger space. Shachi knew her daughter's style of playing very well. The mother orca seemed to always know what the juvenile would do next and chose strategic moments to chase her calf. Occasionally, Shachi made an unpredictable dash for Kiki and if she paused too long, the young orca ventured near to challenge her mother again. Shachi was fast and a few times her pursuit squeezed Kiki's adrenals and sent waves over the edge. Soon, Kiki was catching up on her breath. It was while the youngster was taking a pause at the surface that Shachi turned belly up and rose to lift her baby up on her chest. Briefly she carried the juvenile orca, who squealed her delight. The warmth between the mother and her calf touched Tuschka and stirred memories of times when she had enjoyed similar play and expressions of love. It was tempting to join them, but she held back. Although she had been accepted by the two orcas, this was an intimate moment between the mother and her calf into which she would not intrude.

On a late afternoon, Tuschka was woken from her slumber by a bump in her flank. It was Kiki. The show was still going and the juvenile had sneaked away to surprise Tuschka. It was not often that the gate was open during a show and, as a result, Kiki's appearance was totally unexpected.

As soon as Tuschka paid attention, Kiki started to rub her lightly, nudging the big orca under her pec. Tuschka was well rested and quickly realized that the young orca's mother was performing. It gave her a feeling of more freedom to interact with Kiki. She anticipated that the juvenile would become more exuberant if she gave in to her, but she also realized that showing her superior strength might cause Kiki to respect her more.

Tuschka waited almost motionless until the youngster began to grow impatient. Then she suddenly turned in her direction. Kiki was clearly taken by surprise, but she reacted quickly. She darted off and looped around, challenging Tuschka to chase her. It was not long before Tuschka kicked her flukes and went after the smaller orca, who had already spent some of her energy. Kiki was agile and turned fast, but Tuschka was faster. Soon, she found herself being chased into every corner of the tank. A few times, Kiki jumped out of the water to escape her pursuer.

Kiki liked to be chased, but her big companion was swifter than she had anticipated. For Kiki, no orca had ever shown more dexterity than her own mother. Although big Durak was stronger, he was less agile, and the gentle but ailing Kavja had never really participated in wild games. She had never known the matriarch in her prime before the lung disease had started to sap her strength. Over the last few months, Kiki's physical skills had been approaching her mother's rapidly and her confidence had grown equally fast. Yet her mother's advancing pregnancy had been responsible for most of her relative progress. Now Kiki realized that their otherwise fairly quiet companion was physically her superior. She began to realize that she was no longer in control of the chase. The muscular streamlined female was undoubtedly swifter than her own heavily pregnant mother.

Tuschka began to sense the change in the juvenile's behavior. Kiki's confidence was being shaken. Adrenaline surged through the young female's veins and made her heart beat even faster. She suppressed her impulse to call for her mother, lest she draw attention to her naughty behavior. Kiki, too, had wanted to take advantage of the absence of her mother's watchful eye. She had been thrilled at the prospect of leading the game, but the chase was getting out of hand. What was her pursuer up to?

Suddenly, Kiki took a sharp turn and dashed forward again. Tuschka followed as if she were tied to the younger whale. She gained rapidly on the youngster and was within inches of her tail flukes when Kiki sped through the gate, into the show pool. Tuschka broke off the chase and veered sharply. She had already pushed it and didn't want to trigger Shachi's disapproval more than she might already have. Yet, Tuschka felt excited at the feeling that she had commanded at least Kiki's physical respect.

* * *

Long before the trainers had sensed it, Tuschka had noticed a strange tension in Shachi. The dominant female was more irritable, but strangely enough she was keen on her company. It was also obvious that Kiki's bumping against her belly caused her discomfort and she often rolled over even before her offspring could touch her there.

This morning just before dawn, the early morning guard had seen the pregnant whale make strange bending and stretching movements. Upon closer inspection, there seemed to be some milky discharge from her swollen mammaries. His notice had brought a large number of people to the whale exhibit. Virtually all the trainers, two veterinarians and assistant staff, cameramen, and park officials surrounded the tank.

Reluctantly, Tuschka acceded when a trainer gave her a cue to enter the main pool. Although the laboring whale wanted her to remain at her side, the tension in the matriarch made Tuschka uncomfortable. To her surprise, Kiki was left in the holding tank behind the gate. The young orca was tense and eager to join her mother. She wished she could trade places with her. Tuschka hovered at the surface near the empty holding tank. She wanted to remain inconspicuous and not to be near Kiki, who was vocalizing a lot to get her mother's attention.

Shachi was well aware of her calf. She voiced her acknowledgement to her almost every round and, occasionally, she would stop briefly near the gate and call softly to her. She was not only aware of her offspring. It annoyed her that the one adult companion in her tank stayed aloof instead of being at her side. Kavja had been very caring when Kiki was born. It was obvious to Shachi that Tuschka was nervous and unfamiliar with the situation, but she needed her now. If she had to learn her task now, it had to be. She wanted her to be right there when her calf would be born.

The tail flukes of the tiny baby orca were already visible. In between two contractions, Shachi came close by and called sharply to the shy adult female in the corner of the tank. Tuschka hesitated, waiting to see how persistent the dominant female would be. Shachi had little time for patience. She gave Tuschka a nudge that left no doubt. Reluctantly, Tuschka joined her. Shachi bent and stretched, discharging milk from her swollen mammaries. Both Tuschka and Kiki tasted it. To Kiki, the rich sweet taste of milk triggered recollections far more recent than those of Tuschka, but both whales had an equally strong association with security, tenderness, and affection.

Shachi pumped her tail and twisted around like a corkscrew. Then, in a cloud of red, it suddenly burst out of her. The tension was gone, the pain faded. As one, Shachi and Tuschka swung around and rose on either side of the miniature newborn orca, helping it on the last few feet of its way to its first breath. All apprehension in Tuschka had vanished. Something had touched the right chord in her. A mixture of memories and motherly instinct was guiding her to assist the exhausted mother and her vulnerable little calf.

The unpleasant distance between the two adults was instantly forgotten. They slowly circled the tank with the baby in between them, each holding a pectoral fin under the calf, lest it grow tired and sink down. That had happened to Kiki, right after birth, and it had been Kavja who had been faster than the exhausted mother to pick her up and bring her to the surface. Kiki's birth had been long and difficult for the first-time mother. Hours of strenuous labor had preceded the unusual head-first delivery and taken its toll on both mother and baby.

Little Wobke was raising her head high while she took her little breaths of air. Her dorsal fin was still soft and folded against her back. She pumped energetically with her equally soft tail flukes to keep up with the two big orcas, who glided effortlessly on either side of her. The baby in between them was already making progress in her breathing skills. Still lifting her head high, she exhaled in little puffs, much more frequent than her companions.

276

Suddenly, Shachi and Tuschka became aware of Kiki's squeals. She too had seen her little sister being born. She wanted to be with them and share their closeness, but the heavy steel gate was unforgiving. Shachi acknowledged her and called to her reassuringly, but she did not stop. She would not do so until her little infant would be ready for it.

It was late March, and for about a week, Shachi and Wobke had been occupying the performance pool, giving the visitors a good look at the antics and nursing of a brand new orca baby. The shows had been replaced by short educational sessions during which the trainers explained the behavior of mother and offspring, supplemented with information on the breeding program and how pregnant females were prepared for motherhood. But no matter how special it was to have a baby orca, the majority of the audience did not appreciate it as such. Many complained and others left half-way through the presentations. They had come to see man interact with the killer whale, the savage predator of the ocean. Fearing a decline in attendance, the management had urged the shows resume as soon as possible.

There was no question that Gunda and Kiki would be capable of doing at least a decent show together. Neither of them did the spectacular jumps with the trainers, but some extra breaches and splashes would certainly satisfy a crowd comprising mostly of first-time visitors. Yet there was some concern about Kiki. The young orca had been whining at the gate for much of the time. She had not shown much interest in the trainers, who had tried to divert her with extra training and play sessions. What could they expect of her in a show? Never having been by herself for such a long time, Kiki was craving for her mother's attention. Reuniting her with her family would certainly lift her spirits. Shachi would surely be able to handle it. Although her presence would be more demanding for the busy mother, there was more concern as to whether Kiki would separate again for the show. The juvenile would be glued to her family for at least some time to come. Putting Kiki with Gunda had been considered an option, but chances were that the youngster would give the subdominant female a hard time. For the next few days, all hopes would be on Gunda, assisted at the end by Durak, whose size and power would be awe inspiring.

It had been a while since Tuschka and Durak had last been together. Durak was eager to join her. As he glided by her side, Tuschka sensed a change in him. He was warm and friendly, but he was more exuberant and self-confident than she had known him to be before. She did not give it much thought. She, too, was happy with his company and returned his affectionate rubs. Soon, the two orcas shared their enthusiasm in fast laps and short chases. They rolled over, glided under each other, dived and turned.

The two orcas were barely aware of Kiki, who was overjoyed to finally be back with her mother and baby sister. Her mother welcomed her warmly.

Kiki rubbed and pressed herself against her, squealing her joy. She wanted to explore her little sister, but her mother gently nudged her away when she tried. Kiki snuggled close to her mother's other side and tucked her head under her pectoral fin. She was aware that she had to share her mother's attention with the little orca baby, but her mother's tender caress and gentle motherly authority reassured and comforted her.

By evening the orcas had all calmed. Tuschka and Durak rested side by side, while Shachi slowly circled around in between her two offspring. The little puffs of the baby orca contrasted heavily with those of her big companions.

* * *

Tuschka was very aware of the importance of her solo performances. She could make or break the show, and she sensed how eager her trainers were that she did well. And she did. The enthusiasm in their rewards stimulated her even more, and she was thrilled with the challenge of learning to work with her trainers in the water.

Recently, Tuschka was learning how to pick up her trainer under water and push her straight up, high above the water. It was a challenging behavior that demanded delicate physical cooperation, but she and Janet were close to perfecting it.

It was early morning in June, still before public hours, when Tuschka arched up from the tank floor towards her friend. As her hands took hold, she kicked her flukes and pushed up. Feeling the pull of the woman's body, she became aware that her hold was at the very tip of her rostrum while her feet searched for a foothold on her pecs. Fearing her friend would slide off, Tuschka broke off her jump and sank back just after breaking the surface. She felt her trainer's gentle taps before she swam to the platform. Tuschka followed and nudged her as she pulled herself onto stage.

Tuschka rose up only to find her friend avert her gaze. It struck her hard, for it was a gesture of disapproval. Why was her trainer not rewarding her? She was aware that she had not completed her cue, but she could not help the fact that her friend had been about to slide off. Tuschka could not suppress her frustration with Janet's response. She opened her mouth and kicked her head towards Janet. Again her trainer turned her face away, but within seconds, their eyes met and held. Somehow, Tuschka sensed a hint of regret in her friend. Her face was slightly tilted and her expression revealed empathy. Happy with the restored contact, Tuschka squealed and rose up towards her. Janet knelt down in front of her and laid her hands on each side of her mouth. She barely moved her fingers, but Tuschka cherished the subtle caress.

Tuschka saw Janet rise and point her finger at her. She had seen the gesture before. It meant that her trainer needed all her attention and cooperation for what was to come. Then, she gave the same cue as the one she had just broken off.

Tuschka was happy. She was determined to do it as best she could to show her friend that she knew it well. She darted off to the corner of the pool, rose in a high bow, and dived down to meet her trainer again. When only a few feet separated them, her friend suddenly raised her hand in front of her. Tuschka abruptly slowed, confused with the unexpected gesture. Then, in an instant, her friend took a hold on her rostrum and placed her feet on her pecs. With all doubt gone, Tuschka gave a thrust and accelerated toward the surface. Attempting not to lose her friend, she concentrated on making her movements as smooth as possible. She broke the surface and rose up high. Momentarily, Tuschka seemed to balance erect on her tail flukes. She felt the weight of the woman, who was standing on her pectoral fins near her chest. She squealed in delight as they went almost straight down again. There was no doubt about her trainer's satisfaction now.

Janet embraced her warmly when she surfaced. Their mutual achievement filled Tuschka with excitement and satisfaction. She pushed her friend to the edge and lifted her up onto the platform. Enthusiastically she swallowed a handful of fish and was eager for another cue. But none came. Tuschka watched impatiently and listened as her friend communicated with two others, who had been watching. She was gesticulating while she made her typically human sounds. Somehow, Tuschka saw that something had upset her. She called to her trainer to get her attention again, but as the woman turned, empathy and sadness were in her eyes. Tuschka followed her a few steps and watched her leave. When the trainers had disappeared, she blew and dived with no option but to wait for her friend to return.

"But this was different!" Janet said, frustrated that the curator of training did not share her view. The conversation was almost taking on the tone of an argument. "There is no excuse for repeating a cue after an open jaw jerk," the curator said sternly, "and you're not going to convince me that this was not a sign of irritation, if not aggression. All your colleagues must know that we take this very seriously. You'll be suspended for the next two days." Janet flushed. The other trainers in the room were silent. Most of them looked down and avoided her eyes. Inside, she boiled with protest, but it was no use fighting the decision. She wondered what the others were thinking. No one had said much, but she hoped that at least some of her colleagues would understand.

The meeting was called off and everyone was leaving except Brian. He looked at her with understanding. "Janet, these animals are so powerful. We can't take any risks when a whale shows aggression. All trainers, including the most inexperienced among us, must recognize the red sign behaviors and know how to act." Janet nodded with a sigh. "But Gunda wasn't annoyed with the cue. I just know that she was being careful with me when she broke off. The behavior is relatively new for her and she doesn't slow down much for us to get our hold. You know how hard it is. I was a bit late with my foothold and all the pull was on my hands. It must have felt unfamiliar for her. Immediately after she stopped, she came over friendly. There was no sign of aversion or annoyance. It was hard enough for me to withhold her reward and look away. I had no option but to give her another chance. To do otherwise and walk away from her would have been unfair... and you saw how well she did the second time. She has never before been so steady." "Janet," Brian said empathically, "Gunda showed aggression. What matters is that such behavior must be discouraged, no matter what reason the whale has to show it." "But... what if we make a mistake? What option do the whales have to tell us, without having us turn our backs on them?"

Janet knew that the head trainer had no option but to heed the rules, but what did he really feel? She looked at him questioningly, craving more than just the management's official line. If he would only speak to her as orca friend to orca friend. "Brian, irrespective of what I should've done, don't you think that my judgment of Gunda was right? Do you never feel such frustrations?" Janet paused and looked at him to emphasize her words. "More and more, the rules frighten me," she continued. "They leave so little room to respond to the whales in a personal way. It's not only frustrating to be unfair towards an orca. I've the feeling that stricter rules won't necessarily make our work safer. Ultimately such rules may achieve the contrary. If I had simply walked away from Gunda, she might not be so considerate with me next time. She might decide to complete her cue, no matter whether I held on or not."

The head trainer paused. Finally, he nodded. "Janet, I do believe that you judged Gunda right. Probably most of us share that belief, but it'll not change the rules." "But, why can a trainer's freedom of interpretation not grow with his or her experience? Why must we all act like we have been just hired?" The question was not easy to answer. Brian was aware that there was much truth in Janet's words, but the rules had been made by others and were largely based on fear of liability and possible discredit of a big company. "I understand what you're saying Janet, but the ideal situation is hard to put to practice. It's not a simple matter of saying who has which permissions in general. As you know, every orca and every trainer is different. You and I may be fairly self-confident, but many of your colleagues don't have that subtle understanding, that rapport that you usually have. They're good trainers, but they need guidelines to deal with unforeseen or difficult circumstances." "But I was so certain about Gunda. I knew it and she showed I was right." Brian looked at her intensely. "You have a bond with Gunda like no one else, but even you experience fluctuations. Sometimes it's easier to read a whale than at other times. "Do you think that, if we feel confident, we're always right? If you were responsible, would you feel comfortable saying: act upon your insight and if it fails you fall back upon the rules?" "No, I wouldn't," she whispered.

Janet was grateful for his listening ear, for his understanding and the effort he took to make it all more understandable for her. Yet she knew deep within that forcing the whales to comply with man-made rules would be an ever-present source of frustration for them. The orcas had not chosen to be there. They were

280

magnificent creatures, pre-eminently adapted to roam the world's vast oceans. Orcas did not need man to survive. Man had made these whales dependent by depriving them of the environment and company that enabled them to use their survival skills. How frustrating it had to be for these intelligent animals when humans try to make them feel bad if they don't jump at their cues. Janet began to see ever more clearly how much her vision had been blurred by what she had been taught over the years. Could one speak of 'bad behavior'? Wasn't that a purely human concept? She had to admit how special and touching it was to befriend an orca. It was a relationship she did not want to think of giving up, unequalled as it was in depth and purity, but it was not balanced: it was not an equal give and take. It moved Janet deeply that the orca, after all it had lost, was still so giving, so patient, so mild.

Brian's voice interrupted her reflections "I'll call a meeting and we'll discuss it with the entire group. I want all trainers to ask their questions and to have no doubts about the policy. It's unfortunate, but this company is too big for fine-tuning. We must use our insight to make the best of it. I view it as my task to help everyone to do that in a way that suits him and the orcas best. And Janet," Brian continued, "you said that walking away from her would have been unfair, but you did not need to walk away from Gunda. You could have given her a different cue. That would probably have satisfied Gunda almost as much." "But it might still have discouraged her caution with the push-up," Janet brought up. "It might, but probably not, even if you had restored the bond differently. Frustrations will be a recurring thing, Janet. We can only try hard to avoid them as much as possible."

Janet left, glancing at Gunda, who was resting near the gate with Durak on the other side. She relived the incident in her mind, recalling how well Gunda had picked up on her hand-signal. Her slowing down had given her just that extra time for a good hold and her subsequent ascent had been so delicate and steady. Janet thought about this and of numerous other occasions when she had not been free to act spontaneously. Training, separating, even playtime was controlled. Indeed, the truly precious moments were rare, but they made it both rewarding and justifiable to continue. The least the orcas deserved was to be taken care of by people who would seek every opportunity to give them joy.

26.
Kiki's Farewell

During the first several months after Wobke's birth, Tuschka continued to do the majority of each show. Although Shachi would interact with the trainers in the water and carry them around, she was not yet asked to do any of the spectacular jumps in order to avoid accidents with the baby orca. Those months were more demanding for Tuschka, but it excited her to be the primary performer and to do it well. Yet Wobke was growing and learning fast. She followed her mother in almost everything. It was amazing how fast the little orca picked up show behaviors as part of a natural inclination to imitate her mother.

Kiki loved her younger sister. Their playtime seemed to be limited only by the trainers or their mother. Although there was more activity overall, Kiki did not demand as much of her mother's attention as she had before. Often, Shachi and Tuschka circled together keeping an eye on the two young orcas. Shachi was remarkably tolerant when they bumped her flanks, rubbed against her belly, and tried to involve her in their games. Only when they became too exuberant would she call them to order. Kiki was considerate of her sister's small size and lesser skills, but since she was much larger than her sibling, the caring mother always kept a watchful eye on her, lest her exuberance make her less careful and cause harm to little Wobke.

Kiki and Wobke loved the attention from the visitors before and after the shows. They were swimming together along the long transparent wall. Every time, they stopped, people gathered to look at them. Wobke saw that there were big and small people, and especially the small ones tried to keep up with her when she swam along. One moment, Kiki squirted a mouth full of water at them. They squealed and yelled and some jumped aside. Wobke waited for her sister to do it again, but Kiki moved over a little away from her and stopped again. Wobke saw some people follow her sister, but many stayed with her. She filled her mouth and also tried to throw some water over the edge. There were some squeals of excitement, but the reaction was not nearly as exciting. Wobke moved over to Kiki again, hoping for another surprise. Her sister swung around in a small circle, and suddenly almost all people screamed and jumped aside as a fair amount of water landed on them.

In the corner of her eye Wobke had seen Kiki roll over on her side and swing her tail towards the edge throwing up quite an amount of water. This was great!

She waited for Kiki to repeat it, then tried to imitate her. There was a lot of giggling, but the people barely stepped aside. Wobke was a little disappointed with the little response, but somehow, most people crowded near her. She began to swim and delighted in the small ones following her. They loved the game. Wobke swam back and forth, watching them follow her. Then, she rolled on her side and tried to splash them with her little tail flukes. To her great surprise, most people screamed and the adults jumped away, but their wet offspring jumped enthusiastically up and down as if to encourage her. Then, Wobke felt Kiki's nudge. She had not noticed her bigger sister close behind while she had been fully engrossed in her spectators. Kiki had been watching and when she saw Wobke set up for the splash, she quickly joined in, timing her own exactly with her younger sister. Kiki took delight in seeing the little whale's excitement. Wobke realized Kiki had helped her and wanted her to do the great trick with her again.

Both big and small loved the antics of the little orca. They found it adorable to see the juvenile roll over and fling her tiny tail flukes at them or squirt them from her mouth. The children loved the splashes. For them it was the wetter the better, but their parents quickly grew wary of the bigger orca. They rather stayed with the baby whale, watching her harmless attempts to learn the tricks. But the fun was not as long as both people and whales had wanted. Kiki paid no heed when she heard a loud tap on the water, but then Shachi called an end to the game. Reluctantly, Kiki and Wobke joined their mother and followed her into the adjacent pool.

In July, as Wobke began to make little bows in unison with her mother, Shachi became more involved in the shows again. The leading female had sensed the change in her companion's attitude. Her boosted confidence and motivation to excel in her performances made Shachi aware that Tuschka was enjoying the increased recognition. Now it was time for the mother orca to re-establish her dominance, lest her companion consider challenging her.

Tuschka was taken by surprise when Shachi suddenly appeared from out of the holding tank and shot by. The mother orca snapped a command at her to join her in the other tank. Tuschka felt an impulse to follow, but stopped. She was in the middle of performing and she had no wish to pass up her reward. She returned to stage, expecting to be given another chance. It was the same cue for a good tail splash at the public. She turned and dived, but as she set up for a powerful thrust with her flukes, Shachi came out of nowhere again to block her way. There was no question that she wanted her to follow.

For some reason, Shachi was not in the mood to perform and had left the performance tank shortly after the beginning of the show. Tuschka immediately felt that the trainers' hope was on her. It was an exciting feeling that she could make the show and she was determined to perform well. But she had not reckoned with the envy of the dominant female.

When Tuschka left the main stage for the third time on her trainer's command, Shachi appeared as a torpedo and bumped her flank hard. She left almost as fast as she had come, leaving Tuschka in confusion. She hesitated. No matter how much she wanted to continue, Shachi was not going to let her finish the show. Pushing the dominant female any further would only make it worse. Reluctantly, Tuschka turned and left the main pool to join the mother orca and her baby. Shachi remained silent as Tuschka took her side. Yet there was no doubt that this was exactly what she had wanted her to do. After a few laps around the holding tank, Shachi turned towards the open gate and entered the main tank, but not to present at stage. Instead, the three of them circled around and passed by the stage as if reminding the trainers who was ultimately in control.

Shachi's recalcitrant behavior did not last long. As soon as Tuschka gave up her resistance, the leading female relaxed and reassured her companion. To Tuschka, a harmonious relationship with the other orcas was more important than anything else, but such harmony with Shachi was not compatible with prime recognition during the show. To her regret, she had to take a step back during the shows. Performing less than she was capable of was demotivating for Tuschka. Physically she was superior to the leading female, but respect for Shachi dictated that she jump lower and swim less fast than she really could. The thrill and satisfaction of pushing herself to the limit to reach perfection became a rare experience.

As Shachi's part in the show increased, Tuschka's shrunk. During her quiet moments, Tuschka began to take more interest in Durak. The male orca had not enjoyed much company since the birth of Wobke. When he was brought out at the end of most shows to impress the audience with his size and spectacular splashes, he was kept carefully separate from the other whales. It was a precaution for Wobke's safety. The trainers feared the baby orca might get wedged in between the two large bodies, not only when the two adults quarreled, but also when they made love. The male had been given Kiki as company a few times, but she was either teasing him or ignoring him and waiting near the gate in hopes of being reunited with her mother.

It was not lost on the trainers that Gunda was taking renewed interest in the adult male. Now that she had integrated well in the group and had observed Shachi giving birth and taking care of her newborn, Gunda had received an important part of her preparation for motherhood. The trainers would welcome the awakening of Gunda's feminine feelings.

Tuschka was aware of Durak's increased attention. Recently, the male orca had spent more and more time watching her from behind the gate. She had come to feel strongly attracted to him, but Shachi obviously did not want her to linger in his vicinity. The leading female would take position on the outside while they circled or call Tuschka to her side to rest in a corner away from the gate.

284

In early August, when Shachi and Kiki were performing in the show, Tuschka came over to her admirer, feeling a growing desire to be with him. When the show came to an end, Tuschka expected Shachi and Kiki to soon join her again and call her away from the gate. To her great joy, it was not the gate towards the performance pool that opened, but the one that had been keeping her separate from her desirable companion.

Tuschka did not hesitate to join Durak when the gate to the back pool opened. She shivered with excitement when his big body touched hers. She was surprised by her own response. He had touched and rubbed her before and warmed her with his gentleness, but what she felt now was a burning desire that intensified with his every touch.

The feeling was mutual. Instinctively, Tuschka swam ahead of him, drawing even more excitement from his effort to come after her. She would speed up and slow down as soon as he made body contact, enjoying the feel of his soft skin against hers as he glided forward. She drifted, savoring the moment, until he rose up for air. He took a deep breath and when he came down again, Tuschka kicked her flukes and took off, challenging him to follow.

The big male's heart pounded. Without hesitation, he was after his treasure. Tuschka was faster and swifter. She raced along the pool, making fast and unexpected turns. Several times the two orcas passed the channel between the two tanks at high speed. Nothing even hinted at the fact that the agile female had ever felt fear for the narrow passage.

Shachi's voice pierced their ears. The matriarch was not happy with their behavior, but they were too caught up in their activities to pay her any heed. Durak turned the water white in hot pursuit and Tuschka squealed her delight as she surfed on the waves that he created with his large body. The energy and power that he put into his effort aroused her even more, but it was not her intention to push him to exhaustion. Tuschka wanted him close as much as he wanted her. Although the chase excited her, she could no longer resist the desire for his touch. She slowed down, instinctively lifting her flukes and inviting him to glide under her.

Durak took a deep breath, rolled over and approached her from behind. He stretched his flippers wide to embrace his treasure as he glided forward. His excitement built fast as his belly touched the receptive female. He nudged her gently as his eyes found hers. Tuschka felt the caresses of his pecs and something tickling her belly. It sparked a new exquisite experience. She pressed herself against him, encouraging him to continue. She wanted the pleasure to last. He filled something inside her like no one had ever done before. It was the fulfillment of a slumbering longing, that only now overwhelmed Tuschka in its full intensity. She had never experienced such a strong desire, welling up from within, and never such a perfectly matching satisfaction. Their joining was brief, but intense. As they parted and rose to the surface, they rested in silence, savoring their closeness side by side, their bodies touching.

Tuschka peacefully glided along with Shachi and Wobke. The little baby had filled herself with her mother's rich milk after they had been playing together. Since early morning, Kiki had been by herself in the adjacent tank. She was not happy with it, but it did not upset her as much as during the period surrounding Wobke's birth. Although Kiki spent the majority of her time with her mother and little sister, it was not uncommon for her to share a tank with Durak or Tuschka for some time. Only during the past few weeks had Kiki more frequently been by herself for the night or part of the day. Shachi and Wobke came to rest close to her on the other side of the gate. Tuschka was hovering several feet behind them. The orcas exchanged a few soft calls. The proximity of her mother, even behind the gate, was soothing for Kiki.

* * *

Darkness had brought quiet to the park. With barely any wind to whisper through the trees, this calm September night had a special serenity. Only the orcas' blows broke the monotony of the faint background noise of the filtering system as they dozed off in peaceful slumber.

A rumbling vibration woke the orcas with a start. Whether it was her mother's upset call or the sound itself that woke her, Kiki could not tell. There was a disturbing familiarity to the sound. It rapidly grew louder. Wobke sensed the sudden tension in her mother and pressed close. Shachi protectively laid her pectoral fin over her precious Wobke's back. Kiki felt confused. On the one hand she was curious, but at the same time the tension in her mother and Tuschka was unsettling.

Bright spotlights suddenly lit the tanks and the surrounding area. When the source of the sound appeared, it sent a chill through the adult orcas. Shachi called Kiki close, but the gate still separated them. Something seemed wrong, but what? Kiki had seen the large moving thing before. Both times it had brought a new companion to them. She faintly remembered that her mother had been tense the previous time, but nothing unpleasant had happened. When she turned to take a closer look, a sharp call from her mother commanded her to stay. Shachi pressed her rostrum between the steel bars of the gate. Kiki managed to make contact with her mother and touched tongues with her. Kiki saw the concern in her mother's eyes and heard it in her stressed high-pitched voice. She wished there was no gate to keep them apart. Whatever it was that her mother feared, it made Kiki want to be at her side.

Kiki heard a tap on the water. A trainer called her over. It was one she knew very well. Yet it was an unusual moment for a session, be it training or play. When Kiki backed up, her mother protested again. Kiki felt torn. She trusted the trainer and did not want to ignore him. Yet, no one was closer to her than her own mother. The situation was strange with all the lights, the people, and the large roaring objects near the tank. Was it the situation that upset mother? It was not

286

uncommon for her to feel protective toward her under unusual circumstances. Things like these had never happened with them being separated. Or was there more to her fear?

Kiki heard other slaps on the water near the platform in the main tank. Tuschka responded immediately, but her mother was hesitant. They both looked up as a trainer came over. He tapped the water gently on her mother's side of the gate. Kiki saw her mother turn towards him and lay her chin in his hands. He tried to ease her away from the gate, but Shachi felt uncomfortable losing sight of Kiki. Tuschka was receiving a rub-down near the platform. She welcomed the attention from her friend. Janet's relaxed and confident mood stood in contrast with the strange situation. Although it took the edge off her apprehension, Tuschka kept a sharp eye on what was happening. For a while not much changed. Shachi remained restless. She wanted Kiki at her side, but the gate was unforgiving.

Several voices and other strange sounds replaced the initial rumble. A large panel came down almost directly above the gate where Shachi and Kiki were facing each other. Shachi cringed at the sight. She knew the purpose. It was no good. The gate rattled against its hinges as she pressed herself against it to be closer to her oldest offspring. She voiced her protest loudly as two trainers fixed the panel and started to lower it on Kiki's side of the gate. Simultaneously Shachi and Kiki went under, continuing to face each other beneath the lower edge of the large panel. Kiki suddenly realized that she was about to lose eye contact with her mother. Something bad was about to happen and her mother had known it all along. She cried frantically as the last inches she could see of her mother disappeared behind the dropping wall. When she surfaced, Kiki was surprised and relieved to see that the panel was only slightly higher than the gate. She pushed herself up against it, pressing her chin against her mother's. As long as they could see and touch each other, they were still together.

All the whales, except Wobke recognized the big white object that had been lowered in the water. In each of them, it roused different memories. Kiki saw no sign of a new companion this time. Tuschka shivered, feeling the foreboding of leaving. She whined at the woman in front of her, inching away from the scene towards the opposite corner of the tank. She did not want to lose her orca companions again. Janet sensed the orca's fear and tried to comfort her.

"Shachi won't leave that gate," one of the trainers said to Brian, who was trying to coax Kiki away from it. The head trainer nodded. He had not expected much else "She senses what we're up to. She knows it too well. There's no point in trying further." While Janet stayed with Gunda, several men gathered near Brian to discuss how to proceed. It was obvious that Kiki would not turn away from her mother. Instead of head-first, as initially planned, they would bring the sling in from behind. On Kiki's side of the gate, the walls formed a short channel, which stretched half-way the 12-foot body of the 4-year-old whale. "It'll make things easier when she has less freedom of movement," Brian said, "but it's a little more dangerous for those of us who have to put her pecs through the holes of the sling. We must try to avoid getting wedged in between her body and the wall. Always stay behind her pecs," he continued. "I don't expect her to snap at any of us, but with a stressed whale we must be prepared for everything."

Kiki suddenly found the channel with the two men, the noise, and the strange object beneath her oppressive and wanted to back out of it. When she moved her tail flukes down, she hit something. It was soft and gave a little, but it was hindering her movement. She rose up, surfacing in all the confusing noise, and cried for her mother. Shachi's answer acknowledged her, but it did not convey the reassurance of a loving mother in control of the situation. Instead, her voice carried a mixture of protest and helplessness. Kiki cried out several more times. She tried to spyhop, but she was unable to upright herself, and when she tried to move away, she found herself severely restrained. Kiki gave a shriek of distress when suddenly white blocked her view. Then, she felt herself being lifted. A familiar trainer appeared in front of her now and she could just get a glimpse of him. He was stroking her melon gently and speaking warmly to her. Two other trainers slid into the water behind her. She did not understand what was happening. Somehow, she sensed that her trainers were trying to comfort her. She clung to the hope that they would not let her come to harm. Kiki felt increasing pressure on her chest from her own weight. She had been on the platform of the performance tank many times, during training, shows, and even spontaneous play, but then she had never been restrained as she was now.

Shachi saw the white U-shaped object rise above the panel that had blocked her view. Her Kiki was in it. The sight sent a chill down her spine. Her fear materialized: Kiki was going away... She voiced long loud wails, full of despair and grief. Her juvenile girl answered, confused, calling for her help and reassurance, which she was unable to give. Shachi knew what it meant to be parted. She had been carried away in that white object several times. Resistance did no good. She had always found water again and companions: sometimes new, sometimes familiar, as if she had traveled back to the past. But this was different. Her motherly instinct and the bond with her precious Kiki were stronger than any bond she had ever felt. She watched her big baby rise higher and away. They called back and forth, trying to maintain contact and to overcome their physical separation with sound.

Kiki felt a swaying movement. Then it became darker and water relieved her weight. It was cool and soothing. She called for her mother and listened. Her answer was farther away and full of anguish. Mother had lost hope.. Kiki's heart sank. There was no resisting. She let out a soft wail, a helpless trembling cry. She felt the hands of her trainer on both sides of her mouth and his soft lips on her rostrum. He was whispering to her and stroking her gently. Mother's voice sounded again. As she was about to answer, the engine throb intensified and a jerk set her small container into motion. High above all other sounds, Kiki's farewell call rode the nocturnal wind.

Not only Kiki's favorite trainer, had swallowed against the heart rending calls of the mother and her calf. Deep inside, they all felt that they had been involved in something wrong. It had not been their decision to move the juvenile orca, but was that an acceptable excuse? They were grateful that the management had at least waited with the transfer until after Wobke's birth. The rationale was that Shachi could lavish her motherly feelings on her baby, while it was natural for 4-year-old Kiki to explore contacts with other orcas. Yet, it did not give them peace at heart. No one spoke the feelings aloud, but when their eyes met they knew they shared them. They had just cooperated in tearing apart what was known to be the strongest bond on earth: one that only death would end.

Shachi sank down, drifting with her head facing towards the panel. It was being lifted now, but as it rose it revealed only an empty tank on the other side. Wobke bumped her belly, reminding her of one who needed her love and care. She could not fill the emptiness that Kiki had left, but the presence of the precious lovable calf was comforting. The baby had sensed the sadness in her mother and rubbed her little face against her mother's. Shachi acknowledged her with a warm nudge. Then, she slowly turned away from the gate. With Wobke tucked under her pectoral fin Shachi began to circle the tank.

Tuschka had seen it happen. It had revived the memory of long ago when she was so painfully taken away from her own mother. Now, she was among those that stayed behind. Kiki's departure did not mean nearly as much to Tuschka as it did to Shachi, but Tuschka did not miss the grief-stricken mood of the leading female. As mother and baby swam by, she wondered whether they wanted her company or preferred to be by themselves. Shachi and Wobke took several rounds. Then, as the matriarch brushed by her flank, Tuschka took the hint and glided at their side. Although there was sadness, there was also warmth in being a companion for the mourning mother.

27.
A Hefty Blow

In the days that followed, Wobke turned out to be a good diversion for Shachi. Although the mother orca was painfully aware of her elder daughter's absence, the juvenile female lifted her spirits and filled her life with purpose. Shachi showed little interest in doing shows, but she gratefully accepted the comforting attention of her most favored trainers. Tuschka soon felt that the trainers primarily relied on her again during the shows. It was tempting to show what she was capable of, but she kept a keen eye and ear in the direction of the holding tank. The gate to the holding tank was open most of the time, except during the moments when a trainer was in the water with her. Tuschka had no wish to elicit the envy of the leading female.

The trainers also knew that Shachi did not like to be shadowed by another performing companion, but when the dominant female chose not to perform they had to rely on the other orcas to do her parts. It was in the trainers' interest too to avoid irritating Shachi. They tried to give the mother orca some diversion during show time and kept the gate open as much as possible to give her the opportunity to join the performance.

Tuschka noticed the different attitude in the trainers when they rewarded her. They were more subtle, rubbing her gently and speaking with a quiet, but warm voice. She was grateful for it. It was not only that she appreciated a more personal and subtle way of rewarding. Somehow, she sensed that they were conspiring with her, hiding from the dominant female how happy they were with her. Tuschka reveled again in giving the best of herself. Yet she did not express her exuberance in sound, but in eager quick responses.

It was a joy for Janet, and some of the others who worked with her, to see again how well Gunda could perform. No wonder Shachi kept her on a tight rein. With her streamlined musculature and erect dorsal fin, she was the most beautiful and swiftest of all.

* * *

It was early November, and over the past months, Tuschka had shared several more special moments with Durak. Recently, however, she had become less appreciative of his advances. Although she loved gentle physical contact with him, Tuschka discovered that Durak's longing for her was almost insatiable. He

290

almost never tired of rubbing, nudging and probing her, while she just preferred to swim or rest quietly in his closeness. Gradually, his presence became more oppressive. In such moments, Tuschka would swim away or start circling the tank. She knew Shachi would have no problem telling him his place, but she was not as assertive as the dominant female. She did not feel confident enough to give him a clear message by showing him openly when he annoyed her. She was uncertain as to how Durak would respond to such a gesture and she had no wish to provoke aggression in the large male. She wondered why he was not reading her feelings as he had in the beginning. What had changed in him that he was no longer as considerate and patient as in those first times?

Tuschka was not eager to enter Durak's tank when the gate opened, but within seconds, the big male glided into hers. His greeting nudge showed his fondness for her, but Tuschka was not in the mood for what he had in mind. She did not return his affection and moved away. Durak followed. The smaller holding tank left her little room, so Tuschka slipped through the channel to the back pool and started to circle at a fast pace. Durak sensed that Tuschka was not in a receptive mood, but he had been by himself for quite some time. The smooth streamlined body of the beautiful female excited him and he felt strongly attracted to her. Why did she act so aloof?

Durak had no trouble matching her pace. He tried to entice her into play by moving away, then suddenly blocking her path, and rubbing her as she veered. Tuschka felt uneasy. The big male was not going to leave her alone. Tuschka opened her mouth towards him and saw him make a small evasive maneuver. It was a clear message to stay away, but Durak was too full of desire to pay heed to the warning. A little more carefully he rolled over and tried to take her between his pecs. Tuschka kicked her flukes and escaped his embrace. Why was he so pushy? Why did he not respect her as he had done before?

For Durak, the answer to that question was clear. From the first day that the new smooth female had been introduced to Shachi, he knew that she would not try to dominate him. Tuschka had showed immediate submission and now, many shallow rakes reflected Kiki's bold play and Shachi's reminders to keep Tuschka in her place. Durak felt that Tuschka would not reject him like Shachi would if she wanted no part of him. If Shachi had given him the same warning, he might have given up, but not so with Tuschka. He saw little harm in trying, hoping for her to yield and give in his desire.

Tuschka warned him again, but he was not impressed. When they approached a corner of the tank, she stopped swimming, trying to ignore his advances. He had not been rough in any way, but something inside told her that it was not the right time for what Durak wanted. The big orca pushed her gently into the corner, but as he rolled over, Tuschka swung underneath him and bumped him firmly. Durak was taken aback a little. He was just up righting himself and turning when Tuschka suddenly opened her mouth towards his flank. It took less than a second for Durak to know that she was about to rake him. He had pushed it too far. Without giving it a conscious thought, Durak lifted his powerful flukes in a big evasive lunge and thrust them down. He hit something hard and heard a muffled scream.

Hot pain flared through Tuschka's head and jaw as a great impact slammed down on her. She lay dizzy for a moment, then awoke to an excruciating pain that froze her on the spot. She dared not move, lest the pain take her life out of her. Something oozed in her windpipe. She felt an urge to exhale, but hesitated. The oozing continued and her need for air intensified. She had to expel whatever dripped in her windpipe and threatened her breathing. Tuschka carefully took the pressure off her blowhole. Then she exhaled slowly. As she closed her blowhole the sharp pain flared up again. She dreaded the pain accompanying every breath, but in breathing there was life, and Tuschka's will to live was strong.

Durak looked back from the middle of the tank. Tuschka was badly hurt. His former intentions had vanished. He saw the thin red droplets in her breath and knew that she was severely if not mortally injured. Something in him wanted to come over and comfort her, as he had done with Kavja, whom he had gently carried when the strength to stay at the surface almost failed her. But should he approach Tuschka and risk that his presence would only stress her more? Durak watched another painful breath before he heard a slap on the water. Uncomfortable with the situation, he swam over to the trainer who had called him. He was grateful for it. Right now, it eased him to let the trainer decide for him what to do. The cue directed him to the holding tank. He followed up on it without hesitation. The hydraulics of the closing gate melted with Tuschka's rasping blow.

None of the trainers had accurately seen what had happened. Steve had seen something only out of the corner of his eye, while the others had been alerted by Gunda's strange and muffled cry. They stood in shocked confusion for several seconds, until one of them went to call Brian. Another realized that Durak had to be moved away from the scene, and he hurried over to direct the big male into the holding tank.

Janet paled as she watched the little droplets of blood in Gunda's breath. She lay so still and every breath seemed an agony. It was clear to all the trainers that Gunda's life was in immediate danger. Although Brian had heard a brief summary of the accident over the phone, he too was shaken at the sight of Gunda. "We have to get her in the med pool," he said. "The vet is on his way. Call operations to get a sling ready in case she needs to be supported at the surface." The head trainer had someone open the gate towards the medical pool and knelt down at one side of the passage way. Gunda was not very far, but he doubted whether the injured female would respond to him. He tapped the water gently. Her hoarse difficult breath troubled him. It was important to get her into the med pool, where they could lower the water and offer help more effectively. Yet he did not want to stress the suffering whale. He motioned towards Janet, who was standing at the pool side. "Could you quietly enter the water and push her a little? It's the best I can think of to move her into the med pool." Janet nodded. Her voice faltered with emotion.

Steve pulled up the zipper of her wetsuit. She glided into the water quietly. Gunda inched away. Janet kept still, afraid to cause the orca extra pain. "Talk to her Janet," Brian encouraged, but she managed little more than a whisper. "Don't be afraid Gunda. No one will harm you. We know you are in pain and need to help you." Janet was only a foot away from Gunda's flank. Although she wanted to comfort Gunda and make eye contact with her, she figured that the orca would not be comfortable with someone coming close to her injury. She touched Gunda gently. The orca stayed. "It's o.k. Gunda. You're such a good girl. You don't need to swim. Just let me help and push you gently." Brian tapped the water lightly, hoping to help Gunda understand Janet's intentions.

Tuschka tensed as Janet approached. Fear that the woman would cause her more pain was stronger than her desire for comfort. She wanted to turn away a little, but even the slightest movement of her neck was painful. The soft whispering voice of her friend was, however, reassuring and Tuschka felt relief when the woman approached her flank, behind her dorsal fin. Her touch was gentle and she drew comfort from the tender strokes. Tuschka had no desire to move and respond to the taps on the water, but she felt the woman push her towards the gate. She did not push hard, but she was unmistakably urging her on to comply. Tuschka knew she was helpless and sensed the sincere concern in her human companions. She moved her flukes a little. It was not as bad as she had feared. It intensified the constant pain, but it was not the sharp shooting pain that she felt when she tried to move her jaw or neck.

Janet swallowed with emotion as she noticed that the poor orca had understood her hint and tried to cooperate. Within less than 10 minutes, Tuschka and Janet had entered the med pool. The gate closed behind them. Janet wondered for how long, fighting the terrible thought that Gunda might never leave alive.

The medical pool could be completely separated from the rest of the pools and fall back on its own circulation system. It was only 12 feet deep and could be drained and filled in a few hours. They could bring in foam pads to support an orca during certain medical procedures, or they could put a sling under the whale for support.

Janet stayed with Gunda as a large crane positioned the panels to block the two gates that gave access to the small pool. She was not happy with all the activity around them. She sensed it was stressful for Gunda, but at the same time, she knew all these preparations were necessary in order to respond quickly to Gunda's potential needs. She kept on stroking her friend, even when the veterinarian approached to check upon her condition.

"Her heartbeat is regular, but relatively fast. The sanguineous vapor in her breath indicates internal damage, but the extent of it is hard to judge. I don't think her lungs are threatened by serious bleeding." He looked at Gunda's eyes. They were almost closed. The veterinarian inspected her head, jaws, and neck, and observed her breathing. "There isn't any visible injury, but for some reason she doesn't completely close her lower jaw. It'll be too stressful for her now to try to X-ray her and the therapeutic consequences are minimal at the moment. I'll give her an injection for pain relief, but I'm reluctant to truly sedate her, because of her breathing." It was unnecessary for the vet to ask for continuous monitoring of the injured orca. Janet volunteered for the first night. "I'll be back every three or four hours," the veterinarian said as he climbed out of the tank, "but call me if you see any change in her condition."

Brian kept Janet and Gunda company until after sunset. The two didn't say much and unknowingly shared many thoughts. Brian felt responsible for the tragic event. He had given the instruction to put Gunda with Durak after the early afternoon show. Could he have foreseen what would happen? Even more nagging was the question whether he could avoid a similar accident in the future. He could not tell if such a thing would ever happen among orcas in the wild, but he strongly felt that the accident was related to human interference. He had seen Durak's interest in Gunda and he had thought it was mutual because Gunda had recently been paying close attention to the big male's training sessions. His training sessions.... why?... Something in that was odd. Why would the female orca show interest when the male's attention was not directed at her? Had she shown similar interest in quiet moments? He felt ashamed not knowing the answer. Although the trainers briefed their observations every shift, Brian realized he rarely took the time to observe the orcas' spontaneous behavior. A few weeks earlier, Gunda had not been pleased with Durak's advances, but such things could change from one day to the next. The head trainer blamed himself for not paying close attention to the whales' moods and signals and for underestimating the potential danger of failing to read the orcas well.

Janet was burdened with similar thoughts. She had seen that Tuschka had not entered Durak's tank after the gate had been opened. She remembered noticing that Gunda was not happy with his intentions, but she had not given it much thought. Brian had told them to put the two orcas together and it had never occurred to her that a little annoyance could lead to such a severe accident. But annoyance.... Why would Gunda have to suffer annoyance in the first place? Why did they not pay more attention? Why had she not heeded Gunda's hints? It was a frightening thought that damaged her self-respect and made her feel unworthy of the orcas' trust.

Janet realized how frustrating, if not humiliating, it was to decide for these highly developed social creatures in what enclosure to stay and with whom, or when to be by themselves. Surely, free-ranging orcas would be more than capable of handling such things. A female would have room to move away from a male or have support from a higher-ranked female. Conversely, a male would have space to evade the response of an irritated female, and might find other, more receptive females. At least, he would never be pinned into a corner, and be forced to make a strange move to evade a female's serious warning. Without exception, all the trainers were convinced that Durak had not hurt Gunda intentionally. That was not in his nature. He had probably inadvertently hurt Gunda in an attempt to evade some kind of warning from her. Poor Gunda. She would not have hurt him very much, if at all.

Brian felt an urge to ask Janet how Gunda had been acting prior to the accident, but he kept quiet. It would be a direct confession that he had failed to consider his decision carefully in advance. It was a bad thing and he was reluctant to speak openly about his failure. Tuschka's grating breath stung the two trainers deeply. She was in agony. Janet swallowed back tears when she realized how close Gunda had come to rest in front of her. Gunda was facing her, entrusting even her most injured part to her closeness. 'I don't deserve your trust', Janet said to Gunda in thought, 'but I love you so much'.

Brian tapped her shoulder as he got up to leave. A moment later, Janet slowly reached out towards Gunda. She did not back away. Feather light, she touched the orca's glossy rostrum. Gunda kept still. Janet was overwhelmed with the orca's trust. "I'll do everything my dear Gunda to help you pull through," she said in a hushed voice. "I need you as much as you need me now. By letting me comfort you, you comfort me by accepting me with all my shortcomings. You're so mild and so forgiving. I can learn so much from you ... How can I ever treat you as you deserve.. ? How can I find a way to make things better and not be sent away at my first attempt?"

Tuschka was grateful for Janet's closeness, but she did not dare to voice her affection. She could only hope her friend would understand. When she had seen Janet reach out for her she had wondered whether her touch would hurt, but this time, trusting her friend for her gentleness, she risked the pain in favor of comfort. Her touch was light, just perceptible, but it was in that subtlety that Tuschka felt her friend's tenderness and compassion. The whispering, slightly quivering voice of the woman added even more to the comforting and meaningful gesture. Tuschka wanted to acknowledge her friend, but she dared not nudge back. She tightened her blowhole to produce a little call, but pain discouraged her. Tuschka could only stay where she was and hope that the caring woman would understand.

Janet did understand. That the orca had sought her closeness and did not back away was more than Janet had dared to hope. Gunda could not have communicated her trust and desire more clearly. Knowing that Gunda drew comfort from her, Janet responded to the orca's silent invitation and extended her touch for a long time. Growing stiff, she finally drew her hand away and shifted position, but she did not leave Gunda's side.

Tuschka concentrated on her breathing, trying not to intensify the pain. She did not move her jaw. The slightest attempt caused such terrible stabs of pain that she did not even know if she could move it at all. The pain made her slightly nauseous and took away her appetite. Although she felt helpless and vulnerable, Tuschka did not feel truly sick. Her body was full of vitality, if only her head did not hurt so much. As darkness fell, the pain seemed to let up slightly. She realized she could not see through either gate. The situation reminded her of the moment when Kiki was lifted up and taken away. But it was different now. The quiet atmosphere and her friend's presence were reassuring.

By morning, Gunda's breathing still reflected her pain. None of her breaths started with the explosive 'poo..'. Somehow, the orca took away the pressure on her blowhole before opening it, to permit a very controlled release of air. Yet there was no longer a sign of blood in her breath. Whatever had been bleeding, was bleeding less, or had ceased to bleed. Although Janet was exhausted from the long night and emotion, she was reluctant to leave, but fellow trainers managed to convince her that she could do more for the orca if she were to rest and then return.

Janet made sure that those attending to Gunda would be extremely careful around her head. She drew their attention to the orca's breathing and asked them to ask the vet's advice about feeding her and keeping her hydrated. Gunda's body was in good enough condition to go without calories for a couple of days, but without the possibility of extracting fluid from food, dehydration would soon threaten. If Gunda would accept fresh water, the danger of dehydration could be averted, but how could they let her drink when the slightest movement of her neck or head caused her so much pain? Gunda's lower jaw was not completely closed. The small opening would be large enough to squirt in some water, but her mouth was submerged, making it almost impossible to do.

The veterinarian was relieved that the orca no longer had a sanguineous breath. Aware of the danger of dehydration, he realized that the only effective way to give the orca fresh water would be to drop the water level enough to expose her mouth. But such an activity would be stressful and he was reluctant to risk the recurrence of bleeds that might just have stopped. He decided to wait another 24 hours in hopes that the risk of bleeding would be less.

Tuschka lay quietly in a corner of her small tank. She had no wish to move unnecessarily. The pain was a constant presence, but as long as she did not move it was bearable. Every breath required careful control to avoid intensifying the pain. Tuschka was aware of the constant presence of people in her vicinity.

She sensed it had to do with her condition. She did not want to be bothered and stayed in the farthest corner, facing away from the activity. Not seeing the people eased her fear of being the center of attention. Yet during the nights, Tuschka sought the closeness of her friend. In her presence she could relax, without the need to worry about being hurt or pushed beyond her limits. Her patience and understanding were a solace to her.

As Tuschka's belly touched ground a surge of panic came over her. It was not the association with restraint and separation that bothered her most. It was the prospect of being manipulated and the ensuing pain that made Tuschka tense. But the manipulation did not come, and as her friend appeared, she relaxed a little, focusing her hopes on her understanding and gentleness. Tuschka saw the woman handle the big hose that she sometimes used in play to spray water over her body and into her mouth. She brought the hose close, but Tuschka trusted her to be careful. As the water began to flow, she soon felt the fresh water run into her mouth. Tuschka was not quite in the mood for play and wondered what her trainer wanted. The water was rising in her mouth and it was already flowing over a little, but it did not occur to Tuschka to swallow. She was used to having water in her mouth and rarely swallowed for reasons other than feeding.

Janet gently laid her hand on Gunda's side, well away from any spot that might hurt. 'How can I make you understand?' Janet thought. Then, she turned and asked for some small fish. All her hope was on getting Gunda to swallow some fish. Then, in the act, she would also swallow the water. As Janet held a fish close to Gunda's mouth, the orca moved neither closer, nor away.

Janet held a fish close to Gunda, but the pain and the stress of being run aground had all but stimulated her appetite. She bent down to see whether the opening between the orca's jaws would permit her to slip in a fish. Near the front, the opening had enough height. Janet touched Gunda's teeth with the fish, but there was still no response from the orca. With her free hand, Janet gave the cue for Gunda to open her mouth. She made a miniature version of the cue to tell Gunda she needed to do it only a little. "Come Gunda, you must try," Janet encouraged. Inadvertently, she pressed slightly against the orca's jaws to push the fish into her mouth. It intensified her pain, but moving her head away more than two inches was not an option for the injured whale. She let out a feeble call.

Janet interrupted her attempts and looked at her beloved orca with empathy. She knew that the light pressure she had exerted by pushing the fish had caused Gunda pain. She had not voluntarily moved her head, nor vocalized since her injury. Janet sensed she had forced Gunda to voice her agony. She was at a loss. The last thing she wanted was to lose Gunda's trust. She wanted to be the haven to where Gunda could turn knowing that she would not be hurt. The paradox was that she, because of her strong rapport with the orca, had been asked to do something that clearly caused her discomfort. Yet that bond had developed because of her understanding, love, and respect for her. Now, Janet brooded to find a way to achieve one thing without losing the other. She did not know how soon Gunda would dehydrate, but it would certainly be before her pain was over. It was tempting to give in to the orca's protest, but that would not be in her best interest.

Tuschka saw her friend lay the fish on her knee. She was relieved that she had taken her hint, and was grateful for Janet's gentle strokes. A moment later, she saw her trainer tear a small piece off the fish. She tensed when Janet delicately slipped it into her mouth, but this time her friend did not hurt her. Soon, more parts followed. With her sensitive tongue, Tuschka felt the few pieces. Although she had no appetite, she sensed instinctively that feeding was important and gave in to her trainer's prodding.

Janet peered into Gunda's mouth as she started to move her tongue. It was her hope that Gunda would be able to collect the pieces and swallow without pain. Some water poured out of her mouth as the orca finally swallowed. Janet was overjoyed and nodded her head at Gunda in approval and encouragement. She poured in a little more water with a piece of fish and expressed her appreciation again as the orca swallowed it down. There were cheers from the onlookers when they saw that their fellow trainer was having success. It was a tedious job, which would have to be done very frequently, but as long as Gunda would take food there was hope for recovery. The next concern would be to get Gunda to swallow fish while floating at the surface, to spare her the stress of draining the pool.

As the weeks passed, Gunda's condition seemed to improve slowly. Although it was still well below her normal ration, she was accepting more fish. Still, she had unexpected relapses that caused worry and puzzlement. During such days, she was very quiet and reluctant to respond to any attention. Fortunately, the relapses were always followed by improvement that brought her a small step closer to recovery. The big panels that had blocked the gates were removed. It was no longer considered necessary to drain the pool and it gave Gunda the option to have contact with the other orcas. Shachi and Wobke often made a stop at the gate, but the injured female showed no interest. As she slowly fought her way towards recovery, a turbulent discussion developed.....

28.
The Debate

Despite the park's efforts to keep Gunda's injury quiet, the word had got out and heated discussions flared up about whether or not keeping orcas captive was justifiable. Although the topic had been receiving attention for several years, attendance had not suffered much from it. With the recent injury, however, the option of release was receiving increasing support from environmentalists and, through them, from the general public. Gunda had become the focus of attention and park officials felt the growing pressure. Releasing a captive orca would be an unprecedented undertaking and opinions about the outcome were divided. Depending on their background and interests, people approached the issue from many different perspectives, ranging from emotional, socio-psychological, and commercial motives, to biological consequences and new opportunities for research. Apart from all the pros and cons, such an endeavor would involve a lot of costs, not to mention the loss of investments already made.

As Janet sat watching Gunda, the thought of her potential release troubled her. The thought of never seeing Gunda again filled her with dread, but she realized that her view on the matter was blurred by her fear of losing her friend. She tried to approach it from the perspective of the orca, but that did not make it much easier to decide what would be good and what not. First of all, Gunda would have to heal properly, otherwise release would not be an option. But even if Gunda did completely recover, the young trainer wondered how much the orca would remember from her short life in the wild. How much was instinct and how much did orcas need to learn? If contact with her pod were possible, would they recognize her as one of them?

Several years of orca research had revealed tight and consistent family ties. Especially in bigger pods that specialized in hunting fish, no orca had ever left its pod other than through death. Gunda had not died, but Janet wondered if that had made a difference in the way her family had perceived it. She was aware that Gunda had been taken as a young orca, probably about five years old. If she were ever returned to her home waters, it would be as a big adult female; not as the juvenile that was taken from their midst. Janet also wondered whether orcas' voices changed with age. Yet for Gunda, the orcas that were already adult at the time of her capture, would still look the same and have the same voices.

If her mother were still alive, would her voice stir memories deep inside Gunda and thus provide an opportunity for recognition? Acceptance into a pod would be crucial if Gunda were ever to survive in the wild. Without them she would not be able to effectively hunt fish or even know where to go to find food.

Although Gunda was now making considerable progress towards recovery, park officials adopted a pessimistic attitude about her convalescence to gain time in the debate regarding her release. No one could really force them to give up the female orca, but in their opinion they could only lose. Even if sufficient money were raised to pay for the orca and all additional costs, the staff did not know what outcome they should hope for. If Gunda's release were successful, it could very well lead to increased pressure to release their remaining orcas. If the whole undertaking failed and ended in the orca's death, they might be blamed for lack of responsibility. In the worst case, anti-captivity people might accuse them of making the public think the release of captive orcas was not feasible. Failure would then be seen as a deliberate attempt to prevent any further pressure.

Brian was exhausted when he returned from a meeting with management officials, veterinarians, biologists, lawyers, and several activists of various backgrounds. The debate had drained him. Yet he was too keyed up to go straight home. Janet sensed his need to talk and sat down with him after the last show was over. "The pressure was so tangible," he said. "I was invited to answer questions on behavioral aspects and to share my thoughts on training or untraining orcas to prepare them for their life in the wild, but it was by no means an open brainstorming session. Every word I spoke, I felt pressure to speak in the management's interest. But apart from that," he continued, "it was so complicated. Most questions were about things I have never been confronted with. I feel bad about it, but I found myself constantly thinking and searching for answers that were both realistic and not too far from what the officials might want to hear. And you know... if you think too long, they immediately doubt your credibility."

Brian sighed as he looked his colleague in the eye. It was not common for him to step out of his role of head trainer and to talk person to person. Now, he felt an urgent need to discuss some issues in an informal atmosphere. "I still have to find my own answers to most of the questions and I fear some of them might not be what the managers like to hear." Janet saw his meaningful glance at her. She remembered too well their discussion about the rules and the orcas' needs. It was hard to find the balance between speaking up for the orcas and being compliant enough to keep working with them. "How was Gunda today?" he asked. "Quite good," Janet answered. "She can open her mouth wide enough for me to give her a handful of fish, and I have the feeling she's still getting more control over her jaws. She still can't completely close them, however, and I wonder if that'll change much. I also saw her with the other orcas at the gate and I think it's a good sign that her social interest is returning."

* * *

In the three months following her injury, Tuschka had recovered so much that she felt no spontaneous pain anymore. She could breathe without difficulty, allowing her good quality rest. Only the opening and closing of her jaws and sideways movements of her head caused her some discomfort.

Tuschka's heartbeat quickened when she heard the sound that preceded the opening of the gate towards the pool where Shachi and Wobke were. The other orcas shared her excitement. As Tuschka finally left her small enclosure, she was greeted warmly by the other two orcas. They nudged, rubbed, and caressed each other. But not for long. As exuberant as Wobke was to have their companion back, she darted over and under Tuschka, bumping against her to entice her into play. Shachi saw that Tuschka was not quite ready for such lively interaction and called Wobke to a halt. The impatient juvenile took position at her mother's flank when the three started to circle the pool. Wobke was nearly a year old now and although she was accepting fish, she was still nursing.

As they swam along, a frayed strand of fish caught Wobke's eye. She dived down and skillfully sucked it in. In a few seconds, she was back to block her mother's way, offering her the little treasure. Shachi took the other end and a little game of spit and suck ensued. The little female had enjoyed the game since the beginning when her mother had used it to teach her the taste of fish and to awaken in her the inclination to pursue prey. But a true opportunity to hunt had never come. Instead, Wobke treasured every opportunity that involved chasing or tugging at something. She also came over to Tuschka with her piece of fish and spit it out in front of the big female. Tuschka sucked it in without effort, but she had to catch it between her tongue and palate to prevent it from slipping out of her mouth again. Wobke was nudging her jaws and eagerly waiting to get it back.

Tuschka engaged in the game briefly. It was not as easy to play as she used to because she was no longer capable of completely closing her jaws. Right now, her physical condition caused her more problems. After spending several hours with the mother and her offspring, Tuschka felt an increasing need to stop and rest, but they would not let her. Every time she turned away or slowed down, Shachi urged her on. Eventually, she ignored the prodding of the adult female and the bumps of the young orca. As much as she had longed for their company, so much she longed for quiet now. Her stomach was growling. In the weeks following her injury, the pain had masked her appetite. Now, able to feed well again, she was craving to recoup her losses.

When Janet saw Gunda facing the gate, breathing more frequently than normal and ignoring the presence of the other orcas, she understood that her favorite whale was not yet physically ready to spend much time with her companions. This time, she did not lead Gunda into the small medical pool, but into the much larger pool in the back. They hoped, that with much more room to swim, Gunda would be able to rebuild her stamina.

Although no one knew what Gunda's future might hold, the staff closely monitored Gunda's progress. It was still not very clear if Gunda lacked the strength to close her jaws, whether it was still painful, or whether it was an anatomical artifact following the injury. Janet wondered if Gunda would be capable of grabbing a fish and holding on to it. Although Gunda's teeth still overlapped, she would need to select a fish that was bigger than the opening between her jaws. Otherwise, it would be hard to test Gunda's ability to hold on to something.

Janet did not need to call the orca over when she appeared near the tank with a bucket. She had noticed Gunda's increased appetite and was happy that she was finally eating excess food to regain her original weight. She fed her several normal-sized herring before she held out a big salmon. Gunda rose up, showing her eagerness to eat the fish. Janet realized the orca would be surprised to find her trainer holding on to it, and in the meantime she was reluctant to cause Gunda unnecessary pain. She regretted now that she had never used some kind of object to play tug with the orca. Gunda's impatient squeal triggered a sudden idea. Janet quickly turned the fish and fed it tail-first instead of head-first. Orcas always swallowed big fish head-first and the way Gunda manipulated the fish would tell her much. How much more elegant than holding on to it!

Gunda closed her jaws on the fish and sank down under water with it. Janet watched Gunda release the fish and, as it drifted in front of her, make another grab closer to the head. Still not satisfied with her grip, the orca released it again. Her final bite was resolute and she swallowed the fish with no visible effort. Janet recalled from previous observations that the whales often positioned a big fish with a few yanks of the head, barely losing contact with the prey. Gunda was clearly avoiding sharp sideways jerks of her head to position the fish. It was an indication that her neck movements were not yet without pain. At least it was encouraging to see Gunda bite into it three times. From now on, Janet would offer big fish more regularly to see if any change would develop.

Although Janet wanted Gunda to recover, thoughts at the back of her mind made her shiver. Was she truly hoping for full recovery... or was she hoping for a partial recovery as long as Gunda suffered no pain? In the latter case, her life in captivity would differ little or not at all from the past and she would not have to part with Gunda. Yet there was no question Gunda was deprived of many aspects of a wild orca's life. If there were a fair chance for Gunda to return to her family in the wild, she should have it. 'It is not important what I hope or think is feasible', Janet thought. 'It is my duty to help Gunda regain as much of her former strength and skills as possible, no matter what the outcome will be.'

The situation troubled Janet. Who would be capable of judging the chances for Gunda to survive in the wild? What if public pressure would lead to decisions and actions that would mean a premature death of her beloved orca? But premature was a relative thing. If Gunda stayed where she was, which was still most likely, she would probably not make it far into her thirties. In the wild, she could have a life expectancy of 50 years or more. Janet could not bear the thought of her Gunda wandering the seas alone, rebuffed by others of her kind, unable to find food, and slowly wasting away to finally wash ashore or vanish in the depths. But the alternative, to share again the fullness of their togetherness, would be an unspeakable fulfillment for Gunda and her family.

While Gunda's condition improved steadily, the debate regarding her release was in full swing. All hope that it would blow over was gone. The issue had been in numerous newspapers, news clips and dedicated broadcasts. Gunda had become famous worldwide. Funds were being raised and several scientists had designed release plans and offered their expertise. Some were even willing to take responsibility for the release project. Despite the negative publicity regarding captivity for orcas, attendance had been noticeably higher because of all the people who wanted to meet the whale. Transfer of the orca to another park was no longer an option. No one wanted to buy a whale that would be accompanied by so much public pressure.

Although Gunda's accident had caused the debate to flare up, the possible future risk of such an accident in captivity played only a minor role in the discussion. No one knew the risk of such injuries in the wild. Although there were equal or even better candidates for release than Gunda, because they had never been injured, the sequence of events had stirred emotions and evoked sympathy for the wounded orca. It had fueled a widespread desire to make up for her suffering by giving back what she had lost.

Emotional motives alone did not justify a release, however, and neither did funds. The most pressing questions involved the orca's chances of survival and the potential risk of transferring disease germs to the wild population. Gunda's caretakers still brooded about the consequences of a good and a bad outcome. If another party were to take the responsibility for her release, a party that would have the public's trust, they were not likely to be blamed for any failure. A successful reintegration in the wild could put extra pressure on their remaining orcas, but some understanding for that fear had been expressed. It had been argued that the goodwill to be gained by offering Gunda for release, would ease their future situation.

The carefully designed plans involved Gunda's thorough medical screening, a search for her native pod, the selection of an area for gradual rehabilitation, long-term monitoring of the orca, and a back-up scenario in case she failed to proceed through all the stages of the rehabilitation plan.

The final word came from Gunda's owners, the park that had sent her on breeding loan 15 months ago. After thorough consideration, they gave their consent for Gunda to take the first step on her way to freedom. They had become more and more convinced that they would never again keep an orca by itself. They would either have to bring back the mother with one of her calves, or none at all. It had been agreed that the whale's second calf would be theirs, but even bringing mother and baby back would still mean separation between Gunda and her first offspring. They had considered selling the second calf to let it stay with its mother, but no one could guarantee that mother and offspring would never be forced to part, as had happened with Shachi and Kiki. They had taken Gunda from the wild and had known her intimately. They had sent her for her own well being then, they would send her for her own well being now and keep their fingers crossed.....

Everyone had been aware that the debate had been developing towards a climax, but the decision had still come as a surprise, especially to those closest to the orca. Janet sat down with Brian as she watched Gunda through the windows of the trainer's lounge. "Can you believe it?" she said to her supervisor. "Can you imagine Gunda swimming gracefully amidst a pod of free-ranging orcas? I'll miss her so much, but I think such a reunion would bring me joy and give me peace with our parting of the ways. It's just my worry about all the risks and potential problems that she may encounter."

Brian nodded with understanding. A frown wrinkled his forehead. Was he more pessimistic than she or did he have reason for extra concern? "Gunda is pregnant," he said with a serious look on his face. Janet's eyes opened wide with surprise. "For how long?," was her immediate question. "Probably over three months," he said. "She must have been sired during her last cycle, which was approximately six weeks before she got injured." "Could the early pregnancy have had anything to do with her accident?" she asked Brian. "Not so much the pregnancy," he said, "but rather the fact that she was not cycling anymore. It's not uncommon for females to reject the advances of males when they are not receptive. However, I expect that injuries rarely.." He stopped mid-sentence, only to read the remainder of his words in his colleague's eyes. Where was his attitude of head trainer?

Brian had caught himself in other slips of the tongue lately. The many weeks of stress and uncertainty surrounding Gunda had confused him. He realized now that his own thoughts were piercing the layer of education he had received at the start of his career. The debate... the many questions never asked before....

it had sparked his own thinking and the results of that had caught him unaware, as had the desire to share those thoughts with others. His new awareness would make it only more difficult to control his tongue.

His silence brought a myriad of thoughts and questions to Janet's mind. What did the pregnancy mean for Gunda's release? Would they transfer a pregnant female or wait and.... separate mother and calf? She did not want to think of the latter, but she had no idea if reintroduction for both of them would be a realistic option. "What will they do?" she asked. Brian looked up with a start, aware of his introspection. "Uhh, if it has been decided, I'm not aware of it yet," he said. It was the typical answer of a head trainer, but now it came unexpectedly. He had been sharing so many of his thoughts with her lately that she had expected a more personal answer. Janet did not press for more. She sensed he had not yet resolved how far he wanted to go.

In the days that followed, tension was tangible. It was obvious that Gunda's transfer had to be either very soon or well after the calf was weaned. No one spoke openly of a separation of mother and calf, but Janet feared the worst in case they chose the latter. Her thoughts jumped to the future. If they waited for the calf to be weaned, Gunda would stay with them for more than two years... and the environmentalists were against separation of mother and calf! They would not press for a release if it meant separation. Janet suddenly blushed with inner shame. Was she wanting the best for Gunda or for herself? It was so complicated. All options had pros and cons and emotions only blurred her view.

Although the trainers had no say in the matter, they eagerly absorbed any information that trickled down, and engaged in a lively discussion among themselves. Everyone agreed that once her pod recognized Gunda, they would accept her calf too, but how would the presence of the calf affect her chances of being recognized in the first place? "I don't think the calf will be the biggest obstacle to recognition," one of the older trainers said. "I think her size is a bigger problem, and perhaps changes in her voice. Does anybody know about age-related changes in the voices of orcas?" Brian shrugged his shoulders and some others shook their heads.

Janet had been thinking about this for quite a while and spoke up. "I hear you all approach the matter from the viewpoint of Gunda's family, but.." "Of course," a younger trainer interjected. "They have to take her in!" Brian silenced him. "Let Janet speak her thoughts," he said, but she suddenly lacked the wish to continue. The matter was so fraught with emotion for her that she did not want to put herself in the vulnerable situation of a heated discussion. With a motion of her hand, she gave the word back to Brian. A sea lion trainer who had been listening to the discussion broke the brief silence. "I know little about orcas, but I do know that it's a very natural thing for young animals to grow up.

Is it truly so uncommon for an orca to leave its group and return to it later?" "I can't say for sure it would never happen, but most studies indicate that orcas maintain life-long bonds. The more unnatural the circumstances are, the more difficult it is to predict how animals will respond to them." The question of when it all would happen hung in the air, but no one mentioned it aloud. Of all the answers they would get it would probably be the very last.

* * *

Tuschka squeaked in greeting as she saw Janet approaching. Every form of attention had become a welcome diversion for the rapidly recovering orca. Tuschka spyhopped impatiently, eager to know what would happen. She watched her friend bend down to pick up a heavy long rope and drag it towards the edge of the tank.

Tuschka had come to know the object only a few days ago. It was a long strand that would float on the surface with one end free. It had a strange taste and a rough surface. It had soon sparked Tuschka's curiosity and sense for play. Loving the element of surprise, Tuschka had held on to the string and had rediscovered the fun of playing tug. After all she had been through, she had been careful and had discovered with relief that biting the big strand caused her no pain. Although her trainer was no match for her, the new game boosted her confidence in the strength of her own jaws. It was fun to push her friend to her limits.

As usual, Tuschka waited for her trainer to take a good hold on the line. She slowly pulled the cord taut. To pull the cord out of her hands with a little yank had proven too easy and no fun. Gradually, Tuschka increased the tension. She watched closely as the woman braced herself behind the railing, straining hard to hold on. When Tuschka felt the slightest hint of the cord slipping through the woman's hands, she gave a little slack and started over again.

Janet was delighted with Gunda's response. Although she knew her physical strength was nothing compared to that of a healthy orca, she hoped it would at least compare to struggling fish. If Gunda could hold on to a fighting salmon, there was hope for her to learn to take live prey again.

Steve had come to watch and smiled at the vigor that Janet had put into the game. "What if I help you," he offered. "Together we may count for a halibut!" he said with a naughty grin. Janet took the hint. "Why not," she replied. "It's Gunda who decides what her limits are." He took position behind her and took a firm hold on the rope.

Tuschka was watching the two trainers. She took the free end in her mouth and started to back up. A little tug told her that the game could begin. Slowly, she backed up further. The cord was taut now. As Tuschka increased her pull, she felt more resistance than before. As she inched backwards, the man and woman started to groan and strained to hold on. Only a moment later, she felt the cord slip a bit. She waited a few seconds and then suddenly released it. Screams startled her as she saw the two falling backwards on the ground.

"Are you hurt Janet?" Steve asked. "I'll have a bruise on my hip, but otherwise I'm okay. How are you? I am sorry, but she's never done that to me." Steve was rubbing a sore elbow. "I'm happy I'm still wearing my wetsuit. How stupid that I hadn't thought of this possibility." Janet nodded. "As I said, she hasn't done this before, but Gunda is always full of surprises. I should've been prepared for it." The two suddenly laughed as they looked at each other. "I wouldn't want to be a halibut swimming before her mouth," Steve said. "That whale is getting stronger every day. I wonder how many of us it will take to match her strength." "I wouldn't want to push her to her limits yet," Janet replied, "but I've little doubt that she can seize something and hold on to it."

Tuschka saw the two humans get up, groaning a little and rubbing themselves. Somehow, she sensed something had hurt them. She had come closer to the edge and was relieved when the two started to speak again. As the man walked away, Janet knelt down in front of her. Her attitude was no longer inviting play, but her voice was soft and gentle. Tuschka nudged her outstretched hand and gave a little squeak. She wanted to reassure herself that nothing had put distance between her and her friend.

Janet read Gunda's intentions unerringly. She could not blame the orca for what had happened. It had not been an act of aggression, just an experiment by a playful whale. "You're a strong lady, my Gunda," Janet said, "and you've taken me by surprise. I'll be more careful next time." She rubbed Gunda gently and felt the whale rise up, to be closer to her. "It's alright Gunda. You're my big strong lady. I'm so proud of you." Janet felt a lump in her throat as she spoke the words. Then, she bent forward to kiss Gunda. It touched her deeply to feel the orca press herself gently against her cheek. "We've gone through so much together and there is so much yet to come..."

Tuschka had sensed the sudden change in her friend's mood. Something had triggered her emotions, and although it had brought a precious moment of closeness, there was also a hint of sadness.

Although Gunda's jaws did not close completely, her recovery had progressed so well that her health no longer formed an obstacle to her release. Her pregnancy, however, added a risk to her transfer that would only increase with time. None of the veterinarians wished to subject an orca to transfer after 10 months of gestation. Hence, the timing of Gunda's transport had become an urgent topic in the discussions regarding her release. Some veterinarians suggested waiting until after the birth, but most of the scientists advocated a scenario in which the whale would have her baby in her home waters. In the latter case, there would be little time to lose, and so all parties involved were discussing how the timing of the release plan would affect the chances for mother and calf.

"If you wait until after the birth, how's the calf going to be prepared for release?" one of the scientists asked the veterinarian, who was in favor of waiting. "It can be trained, just like the mother," he countered. Greg Fern, one of the leading scientists shook his head. "You would have to wait until the calf is beginning to wean. Before then it makes no sense to teach it to go after a fish. But even then, young calves have a very short attention span. It will not only be difficult to teach it something, it will be impossible to teach it all that it needs to know. Neither can we teach the mother all the necessary skills, but her rehabilitation is focused on reviving whatever is left of her memories. If she's accepted, the pod will have to do the rest. Yet that calf will have no background at all. If it is to survive, it'll have to learn in the pod." "So when and where should she have her calf then?" the curator asked. "Preferably after she has been accepted by her family," Fern replied.

A mixture of laughter and muttering filled the room. "You're a true optimist, man. How do you think to time this all?" Fern cleared his throat. "It's the only option if the calf is to stand a chance. While it learns it has to be able to fall back on its mother's milk. When it's already weaned it'll have starved before it knows how to hunt." Just before someone wanted to voice his opinion, Fern continued. "It'll be a tight schedule, but we don't have to start from scratch. A potential site for her rehabilitation has already been found and permits are in the works. We've not been idling while the decision about her transfer was still to be made. Everyone who has read the release plan knows Gunda can retire in a natural sea pen in case her family does not accept her. With her calf would be even better." "But what if the calf is born and her family does accept her and not the calf?" "Or if the calf has little chance because it is weaned by the time of their acceptance?" Fern finished for his opponent. "In that case," he sighed, "the calf has to live its remaining life in human care."

A wave of protest made it impossible for him to continue. He waited patiently until the chair gave him the opportunity to respond…. "Does that differ much from the plans that favor separating mother and calf beforehand?" The ensuing silence was in sharp contrast with the former protest. Fern continued. "All other scenarios provide such poor chances for the calf that separation is likely to happen at some point; either by death, or by separating mother and calf. What will it be? Do we want a chance for mother and calf to survive in the wild together... or do we deny them that chance beforehand because .... well, you may finish that one for me, because I wouldn't know the reason." No one spoke. The chair called the meeting to an end. They had to prepare for a decision soon.

* * *

Tom woke with a start as the phone rang. It was almost midnight and he had just fallen asleep. The unusual hour made him fear some kind of bad message. "Greg Fern speaking, you're one of Gunda's former trainers, right? If he had been only slightly drowsy, the word "Gunda" now had all his senses alert. "Uhh yes," he said. "Is something wrong?" "No, she's fine, but I assume that you know about her potential release," the man continued in a deep voice. Tom did know about it. He had collected every scrap of information about his beloved orca that he had been able to lay his hands on. "I sure know about it," Tom replied, unable yet to bring structure to the many thoughts and questions that flooded his mind. He had no need to. Fern was straightforward and in control of the conversation. "Would you give it a chance…?"

The question was so direct that it startled Tom. He had thought about the feasibility of rehabilitating Gunda many times. Although he found it hard to predict her chances, the idea appealed to him. 'Imagine it would work', he had thought, 'how wonderful would it be for her to return to her family and once again share their rich and challenging life.' But until now, his thoughts had been without any consequences.

"I find it hard to predict her chances, but…" Fern interrupted. "I'm not asking you to take responsibility. I would rather know if you're in favor of seriously trying it." "Yes, sure," Tom replied. "I've been thinking about her release since I first heard it proposed. I do indeed feel incompetent to take responsibility for such an undertaking, but if I can help Gunda to join her family again, I would spare no pains." The voice on the other side changed in tone. "Then I hope you'll join my team in case Gunda is entrusted to me. I want to surround Gunda with the best people possible. Your expertise and deep understanding of this particular whale are essential, but as such that isn't enough. Only if you put your heart into it, will Gunda have a chance." Tom was impressed by the insight and sincerity of the scientist at the other end. Somehow, he felt that if a man could bring her back, it would be Fern. "I'll be your man," Tom said. "Gunda can count on the best I have to give." "That's what I hoped to hear. I appreciate your offer and so would Gunda if she knew of our intentions. I'll send you my detailed plans and will keep in touch."

Tom sat stunned. It was so unreal. He realized Gunda had been in his mind every day since he had first met her. Even after his job at the marine park had ended, she had stayed on his mind. Although he had recovered relatively well from his paralysis, he no longer had the stamina required for a marine mammal trainer. After management had strongly advised him to look for another job, he had been happy to find administrative work at the zoo. In the new job, he was close to animals and people working with them. Soon, the veterinarian and some of the caretakers had noticed his interest and natural understanding of animals. They shared special experiences with him and took him behind the scenes to assist them with small tasks. For Tom, those moments were a welcome diversion from his daily work.

All his colleagues knew about his past as a dolphin and orca trainer. Many of them had been fascinated and had asked him questions, but only with a few had he shared his more intimate moments with Gunda. Lately, he had talked with them about Gunda's chances if she were released. The veterinarian had been a little skeptical, not so much for medical reasons as for social rehabilitation. Suddenly, he thought of Sheila. Would Fern have approached her too? What if he had not..? It would be hard for Sheila not to be involved.

Tom had kept in touch with her ever since. She was his closest friend and still worked at the park. Together they had discussed several times how to untrain a whale and revive its original wild interests. It would not be an easy thing. Although Tom had been the first to make mental contact with the young wild orca, her behavior at the time did not give him much of a clue. Completely deprived of all that was familiar to her, she had been shy and uncertain. It had been an understandable response. Orcas were such social creatures. He wondered if it would be different on her way home. After so many years, life in a tank had become familiar to her. Tom realized that he as a human could play only a minor part in preparing her for life in the pod. He had given himself a part in all release scenarios that he had conjured in his mind, and yet it was unreal for any of them to become reality. He went back to bed, but sleep did not come easily. After many wakeful hours he finally entered a fitful sleep, interspersed with flashes of orcas, tanks, and the high seas.

Although Fern had gained support, the matter remained complicated. Gunda's rehabilitation required the identification of her pod, a spot where she could meet them, and sufficient physical and mental preparation to face a life in the wild. Gunda had about 12 months of pregnancy left, but that didn't mean all that time was available. The wanderings of the pods were seasonal and there were only two periods during which orca pods were known to regularly venture close to shore. From May through early August, some orcas were known to follow salmon runs towards the Laxava and several other smaller rivers on the southern shore of the big island. Then, in fall and early winter, the pods would hunt for herring near the rugged and inhospitable eastern coast.

It was February now. If Gunda were to have her baby in the pod, the latest chance for acceptance lay only nine or 10 months ahead. Yet it could have been worse. Had it been summer, a release plan for mother and calf would not have been feasible at all. But how would they track down Gunda's family? The only certain thing was that Gunda had been taken in November, not close but in sight of the eastern shore. With this tidbit of knowledge, the sensible thing would be to find a place for Gunda's rehabilitation near the spot where she had been taken, though the logistical consequences of that were numerous. The fjords that some orca pods were known to visit, were remote areas, none of them accessible by plane and only a few by road. To bring the orca over would require a lot of organization, and so would providing food for her as well as room and board for the accompanying veterinarians, trainers, and scientists.

Another practical problem would be Gunda's training. Herring was a type of prey that orcas hunted in a cooperative group, unless extremely high concentrations permitted a more individualistic style of feeding. It would be hard, if not impossible, to teach a solitary orca cooperative hunting strategies. Salmon hunts were different. The actual pursuit of the prey was usually done in individual chases, irrespective of whether the hunt had started as a cooperative effort or not. It would be far more feasible to teach Gunda to pursue salmon. Having regained that skill, the steps to regain the others would probably be smaller. But did Gunda's pod feed on salmon on the southern shore in late spring? It was a nagging question. Only the orcas would know the answer.

The discussion went on and was a hot topic in the media. Every day there were bits and pieces in the newspapers. The information changed from one day to the next and from one newspaper to the other. Either the journalists failed to construct a coherent message or the decision makers were still far from reaching consensus on the release plan. Three weeks later, in early March, an agreement was reached between the fund raisers, Gunda's owners, her current caretakers, and the scientists. Although there was still much opposition, Fern had been given the final responsibility for the release procedure. Despite criticisms of the many assumptions and uncertain factors in his plan, he was the only one who had managed to surround himself with a team of people who represented all the expertise required and who backed him fully. Besides that, his was the only plan that held a chance for both mother and calf to return to the wild. And it was for this that he received the public's overwhelming support.

In late April, Gunda would be transferred to Sigmund fjord, a small protected fjord on the eastern shore. She would be stimulated to take live food and be taught to follow a boat for small and, later, longer trips from her home bay. With luck, these short journeys would trigger valuable memories. There would be continuous monitoring of any interaction that might occur between Gunda and the passing pods, especially in fall. It would be in this period that recognition and acceptance by her native pod had to occur. Gunda's ability to stay in contact with an escort boat would also provide for the possibility to recall Gunda in case she could not keep up with the free-ranging orcas. In the meantime, the release team would initiate attempts to identify her pod, hoping to find a lead by collecting details about Gunda's capture, over 7 years ago.

* * *

It was still dark when bright lights woke Tuschka from her slight slumber. Almost simultaneously, Shachi's voice traveled through the tanks and had everyone on guard. There had been concern in the dominant female's call.

Bright lights in the night predicted unusual events and few of them had been good. Although Wobke had no idea what to expect, the sudden apprehension in her otherwise self-confident mother made her feel uneasy. She snuggled under Shachi's belly and nudged and bumped her mother frequently for reassurance. Tuschka was in the medical pool, but since her injury it had not been uncommon for her to spend time in the small tank. It was the rapidly growing rumbling vibration that put Tuschka on edge. The sound had a disturbing familiarity that conveyed a foreboding of loss, of parting with some or all that she had come to know and trust.

As the large solid panels blocked her view and broke off contact with the other whales, Tuschka sensed that her fear of separation was materializing. She spyhopped high and briefly made eye contact with Shachi, who did the same. Tuschka shivered at the sight of the white cloth unfolding at her side, and backed away. She knew it would take her away.., away from Shachi, Wobke, and Durak. An inner resistance made her body tense. The deeply traumatic experience in her early years had scarred her. Although her latest transfer had brought her friends of her own kind, she could not draw courage from it... only dread of another loss. Tuschka felt an urge to turn away, but a net blocked her way. Tuschka's high-pitched voice rent the air. She voiced protest and surrender at the same time, for she knew that there would be no escape, no way to avert another parting of the ways.

But Tuschka was not entirely alone. As she felt her weight press on her lungs, she found hope and consolation in Janet's gentle touch and comforting voice. It did not take away Tuschka's fear of separation, but it kept her from total despair. As Tuschka called out again, the voice of her friend mixed with Shachi's in response. A little later, she felt her weight lift in cool water. As the rumbling intensified, she shook inside the tiny enclosure. Among the many sounds, Tuschka heard Shachi's voice. It was more distant now, but unmistakable. Wobke sounded an instant later in an almost perfect imitation of her mother. Unexpectedly, Durak joined them. It was rare for him to vocalize. Even more than the other females, his call reflected frustration and loneliness. Tuschka answered them. Her voice was despondent, but affectionate, as it carried her farewell.

Part III

The Return

29.
The Past Revisited

Tuschka did not know how long she had been confined in her small dark enclosure when she felt her weight press on her chest again. The friction on her skin irritated her, but attempts to shift her weight were unfruitful and caused her only more discomfort. As the swaying returned, Tuschka's heart beat faster. The young adult female could not see much with the canvas blocking her view, but it was no question for her that she was outside in the light of day. A gust of wind brushed her skin. Besides a mixture of roars and rumbles, she heard the screeches of birds flying overhead, the sound of the wind, and the voices of humans. Tuschka knew those sounds, but somehow the atmosphere was different. As several of the roars died, she became aware of another sound.... She listened to it intently. It was unlike anything she had heard in years and yet there was a strange familiarity to it. It stirred something deep inside her, but too vague to define. The sound was rhythmic and somehow soothing. She was so absorbed in it that the water touching her belly took her by surprise. As the pressure on her chest fell away and breathing became light again, water flowed in her mouth. The taste... , she knew this taste!

The white structure that had carried and enveloped her sank down beneath her. Tuschka felt an urge to move, but a slight dizziness held her back. People were standing on both sides of her. She heard the familiar voice of her friend and felt her gentle strokes. It was reassuring. Only moments passed before she regained control over her balance and moved her flukes to swim and stretch her stiff and aching body. She looked around, automatically expecting to see the familiar walls of her tank, but she saw none. She found herself in a blue-green twilight and in water that was slightly murky. She echolocated and called for Shachi and Wobke, but the scattered echoes revealed a shallow irregular sloping wall and her orca companions did not reply. Tuschka stopped swimming. She echolocated again.. and again... probing her new environment with sound. She did not know where she was, but her senses were registering things that had been part of her life in days long gone. Yet her memories surfaced in fragments without coherence.

Tuschka did not know where to go. There was no retreat to a familiar place. She lifted her head and looked at her surroundings above the surface. Many people were standing and moving back and forth on a long straight structure that protruded from barren rocks that lined the water's edge. There were many sounds: the roars and rumbling that she had heard for so many hours seemed to come from large colorful objects beyond the rocks and mixed with the many human voices. Tuschka slightly turned to see the end of the long narrow strip that looked like land, floating on the surface. Close to the end, she saw Janet. She tapped the water, but Tuschka needed no encouragement to swim over to her. She was all the orca knew in this strange environment that was new and vaguely familiar at the same time. Upon her friend's touch, Tuschka raised her head a little and nudged her hand. Then, she rose up and pressed close for guidance and reassurance. Tuschka felt her trainer's gentle hug with a subtle rocking movement that emanated affection and comfort. As she relaxed in her friend's arms, the voices and rumbles faded while other sounds began to dominate.... the birds, the wind, and .... the gentle, rhythmic splashing of water against the rocks. Below the surface, the water carried the sounds of life, of miniature creatures, crawling and swimming all around. They were the soothing sounds of nature whispering to her in a thousand voices.

Janet felt her beloved Gunda relax in her arms as she caressed her to comfort her. She was deeply touched by the orca's trust in her and laid her cheek against the whale's smooth melon. She did not speak, lest she disturb the peaceful moment. 'My Gunda,' she said in thought, 'now you seek your comfort with me... but for how long..? It's hard to imagine that some day you may no longer have need of me or any human, but now I will not let you down, my dear Gunda. I'll be with you.'

* * *

Torvil was glancing through the morning's paper when a small header suddenly caught his attention: "Who can help orca to return to her home waters?" Only after reading the first few lines, did the fisherman realize this was a serious plan for the release of a whale that had been taken from the local fishing grounds. His thoughts traveled back to his first season at sea, when he had been struck by the loyalty and caring of an orca pod for a member that had been wounded through his ignorance. Several orcas had been taken from the local waters and each report had filled him with sadness. Torvil had no doubt that the death or capture of a pod member would be a great loss. Yet there were few people who shared his thoughts about the species. Although the orcas could offer a useful lead to fish, many newcomers preferred to rely more on modern equipment than natural signs at sea. They tolerated the orcas as competitors as long as the catches remained reasonable and the nets suffered no damage. Some viewed the local population of orcas as a potential resource that could be economically harvested. The idea of returning one that had once been captured would never sprout from the minds of local people. It had originated in a far land where the captive individuals had evoked feelings that were rare among those who knew their relatives in the wild.

The realization struck him that the people in that far country, most of whom had never seen a wild orca, would be more receptive to his thoughts than most of his colleagues. He wondered why... Was observation in the wild not the best way to learn about a species? It had to be, but learning would require an open and receptive mind, a genuine curiosity and desire to understand. That, certainly, was not the attitude of most local people, who adhered to beliefs passed on from generation to generation and who were driven by the practical consequences of survival, not by curiosity. Torvil suddenly saw an analogy to other species in zoos. People were far more excited to see and learn about unfamiliar creatures than the ones common to their home area. Yet most people in his country had seen less of orcas than he, and he had had only a number of brief glimpses, just a peek into their lives. The lack of interest certainly did not stem from overexposure, but rather from preconceptions passed along in youth.

Although Torvil could find a satisfactory explanation for the attitude of the local people, he was still intrigued by what it was about captive orcas that had earned them such a special place in so many hearts. Indeed, it would be awe-inspiring to see the large, powerful creature up close and to be able to observe it for a while. But there had to be more.... Orcas were being trained like dolphins and those were popular because of their intelligence and gentle nature. He recalled again the two adult orcas, supporting the injured juvenile between them. It had been the loyalty and the warmth in that act that had struck him then. The scene had showed him a side of the species that no one had ever spoken of: it had showed him loyalty and tenderness in what was known as the supreme predator of the sea. He no longer doubted that it was this aspect that had touched the hearts of so many.

The fisherman turned his attention to the remainder of the small column. "... On that day, her pod followed her all the way into Stenavik harbor. Shortly after, they joined another pod and left. Please contact us if you have any information that might give us a lead to that pod." 'Stenavik harbor...', Torvil thought, 'that was close to where we saw the orcas follow that strange boat and where I saw my orca with the scar.' His heart started to beat faster. 'Would this be the event they refer to?' He looked again at the capture date. That November was his third season... A wave of goose bumps traveled up his spine as the realization struck him that Scarback, as he had named the orca with the scar, belonged to the pod they might be looking for. He would recognize that whale out of a thousand!

* * *

Tom had been tense with a mixture of excitement and concern when his Gunda was lifted from the transfer tank into the small bay. There she was, but… so silent. Her first movements in her new home had relieved him and filled him with awe. She still had her sturdy erect fin and the beautiful big streamlined body of a mature female. How slender she had been when she left!

Tom swallowed hard to control his emotions as he watched his beloved orca seek comfort and reassurance from the young woman. The scene revived the memories of his precious moments with her, especially their last time together. Would she still know him? He had high hopes, but he had to wait. Tom had arrived two days before, but it had been decided to let the orca acclimatize the first day in the company of her current trainer. He was grateful that the zoo had given him leave of absence for this special task. Although the prospect of contact with his dear orca filled him with excitement, he knew that it was his task to prepare her for a life without him. Success would mean a parting of the ways. It would be hard on him, but the gain for Gunda would be worth the sacrifice.

That night, sleep eluded him. He lay awake, pondering about his own part in the project. Would Fern expect him to strictly follow a strategy that he had devised, or would he leave much to the insight and initiative of his crew of trainers? Tom dreaded the thought of being forced into actions that would conflict with his own beliefs and intuition. But too much freedom and responsibility was also frightening. He had never 'untrained' an orca. No one ever had. For many weeks he had been brooding on how he would go about it given a free hand. It seemed not too hard to stimulate Gunda to pursue live food and he knew ample cues to build up her stamina, but what more could he do to prepare her for a life in the wild? There were so many things that he could never teach her. Yet one thing frightened him more than anything else: ignoring her to enforce detachment from humans. How he hoped she would take a natural interest in the wild orcas and not out of despair. In that respect, it was a good thing Gunda had enjoyed the company of other orcas during the past one and a half years.

His thoughts went to Janet. She would stay for only one or, at most, two more months. She knew Gunda in ways that he never had. She knew how Gunda interacted with her own kind: how she had integrated and found her place in the dominance hierarchy. Tom was determined to learn as much from her about Gunda as he possibly could. Gunda…. He listened intently, trying to hear her through the sounds of the light wind and the waves lapping on the shore. The latter resembled the blows of distant whales, but they were too rhythmic and too frequent. …"Pooooohuup".. Gunda's blow sounded strong, eliminating all doubt. He listened for several more. Other than breathing, the orca was silent. 'How would she feel?' he wondered. He felt an urge to get up and comfort her, just as he had those first nights after she had been brought in from the wild.

Someone was watching Gunda, ready to alert Fern and the veterinarian if something seemed wrong. Unable to resist, Tom got up, wrapped a blanket around his shoulders and slipped outside. The wooden cabin, in which he was staying, was close to the dock. His eyes scanned the water. The two spotlights provided barely enough light to oversee the netted-off area. The sound of a strong blow directed his attention towards the dock. A reflection revealed her dorsal fin. She was drifting at the surface, very close to the end of the wooden float. As he took a few steps forward, the night watch spotted him and nodded a greeting. Tom raised his hand to acknowledge him, but at the same time his hope for contact with the silent orca evaporated. How he longed to be close to her. There was no doubt she was lonely and yearning for companionship. The way she hung there near the wooden structure told him that. Yet he sensed no despair, as had been present in the juvenile so many years ago. Was it mental maturity or did this natural environment have a soothing effect on her?

A chill made him realize he had been standing there for a while. The northern night was crisp and cold. As the orca blew, he returned the sound. A glimpse of her white eye patch betrayed that she had briefly raised her head. 'She's lying there', he thought, 'seemingly oblivious of her surroundings, but how aware she is...so fully awake. She reacted to my sound. She picked it up among so many others! It would be so easy to make contact with her now...' His eyes met those of the night watch. Had he been aware of what had happened? Just as Tom wanted to turn around and go inside, he noticed movement in the dorsal fin. Gunda was coming closer! 'She must know that a person made the blow sound. She must be craving contact....' The orca came to a slow stop half-way down the dock. The orca's mind was drawing him in an irresistible way. He swallowed hard as he looked at Gunda's round melon, directed towards him. "Just a little patience, Gunda," he whispered to himself. "I'll be with you soon." Quietly, he turned away and rubbed himself warm in bed. The orca's eagerness for contact filled him with anticipation. It was not until early morning that he finally fell into a heavy dreamless sleep.

After daylight had faded and human activity diminished, Tuschka had become even more aware of her surroundings. The sounds of wind and water had not changed much, but the birds had fallen silent. Yet different creatures in the water stirred and scurried about in search of food. The water was fairly clear, but darkness under water was nearly total. Although she had no problems moving around by her echolocation, she felt more comfortable staying near the floating structure from where her friend had come and gone. Tuschka longed for her company, although she did not really expect it during the night.

Something of reasonable size slid close by. As Tuschka echolocated on the object, it disappeared quickly, but the returning echoes revealed something she had encountered somewhere before. It did not take long for the information to find its way to the recesses of her memory ... the shape, the size, its sideways movement..., it had been a dog shark! Her environment was unlike her former tank in all aspects. Other than dolphins and other orcas, she was not used to having other living creatures in her enclosure. Yet their presence caused her no fear. Somehow, she knew immediately that they were harmless to her. Tuschka was excited about her recognition of the creature. Alert and motivated she began to echolocate more, eager to find out what else might be around.

At dawn, light began to penetrate the shallow water and revealed much that had escaped Tuschka's attention on the day of her arrival. The unexpected recognition of the dog shark had brought more memories closer to the surface. She recognized the shape of colorful starfish and followed the movements of crabs of many sizes. Many small fish reflected the penetrating light on their glossy scales. Some were solitary, others moved gracefully back and forth in small schools. Although they were unlike what Tuschka had ever taken as food, they reminded her of her empty stomach. She rose up with her head above the surface to take in her surroundings. Several gulls nearby screamed as they took wing. She was impressed by the size of her environment. There was much more than the dock she had been staying near. Instead of straight concrete edges nearby, the water stretched very far. To the north and west, the water was bounded by high sloping walls filled with dark green fir trees. Towards the south, the slope gradually flattened and stretched out into a low rocky point of land. Just to the left of that point, Tuschka looked at an unlimited expanse of water. It was still a little intimidating.

Tuschka was not yet aware that the space actually available to her was much smaller than the natural boundaries made it appear. The morning breeze rippled the surface and the tiny waves hid most of the small floats of the net that marked her enclosure. She did not venture far from the dock while exploring her immediate environment. It was a welcome diversion to discover that she could flush little creatures from their hiding places. She quickly averted her head as a big crab lashed out at her rostrum with one of its claws. The experience brought back memories from days long gone. They were not unpleasant memories, and yet she felt a sudden pang of sadness. She was alone.. She called for Shachi and Wobke, but there was no answer.

Tuschka lifted her head and saw a lot more activity now than there had been at sunrise. The area at the other end of the dock was relatively flat and virtually without trees. Many of the large noisy colorful objects had gone. There were several large brown structures from which people came and went.

A vibration in the dock caught Tuschka's attention. She saw her friend approach and perked up as Janet voiced her greeting. She rose up close to the dock and lay her chin in her friend's hands. Tuschka quickly accepted a handful of fish, but hesitated a moment before swallowing them. The taste was different from what she was used to, but it wasn't bad. As hungry as she was, Tuschka readily accepted more.

"I'm excited that she's eating already," Janet said, looking up at Tom, who was standing a few yards behind her. Upon her invitation, he knelt down beside her. He had hoped Janet would have stepped back for him to have Gunda's undivided attention. With her familiar trainer right here, he wondered how receptive the orca would be to him. He felt uncomfortable asking Janet in a straightforward way to leave them alone for a little while. He watched in silence. Janet was obviously surprised with his lack of initiative. "You want to feed her some?" she encouraged him. He raised his hand subtly to decline the offer. Janet looked at him questioningly. "Aren't you excited to meet your whale again? I'm sure she'll recognize you!" Tom was at a loss. He felt like a tourist, given the opportunity to meet an orca up close for the first time. This was not the way he wanted to meet his Gunda again.

Tom noticed a little impatience in the way Gunda moved her head. She had been alone all night. She obviously wanted Janet's attention for herself. He suddenly got up and took several steps away from Janet. He knelt down and bent over the dock to tap the water. The orca turned her head in confusion and then back to Janet. She lay her hand on Gunda's rostrum and looked with puzzlement at her male colleague, who had got up and was walking away. She sensed something was wrong. After feeding the whale some more, she covered the bucket and followed him.

"What's up Tom?" she asked before he had reached his cabin. "I'd hoped you would understand.... She's so happy to see you that she is not much interested in anything else. You could see that when I tapped the water." Janet nodded her understanding, a little embarrassed. "I left the bucket on the dock," she said, looking back at Gunda who was still watching her. "She's hoping for me to come back. Let's have some coffee. That'll change her focus of attention."

The two trainers were welcomed by several journalists. It was not as bad as the day before, but for the weeks and months to come, there would always be some of them around. The news that the orca had accepted food on her first morning was eagerly noted for the next press release. Greg came in and sat down with them. "How's she doing Janet?," he asked. "I saw you feeding her. That's a good beginning. Do you think she's ready to meet Tom?" "Yes, she probably is. We were just planning to find out. She cast a quick glance at Tom. "I'll stand back while he walks up to her, otherwise she'll probably focus on me."

Almost everyone followed the two trainers out the door. Greg quickly stepped forward to prevent them from going too close. Janet stayed with him at the beginning of the dock, watching Tom as he walked up to the waiting orca. Tom slowed down as he approached the end of the dock. The whale lowered herself a little but still had half her head out of the water. He walked past the bucket and knelt down at the edge. Tom saw Gunda back up slightly, in an expectant manner. He bent over, but did not tap the water. He just touched the water with two fingers. "Gunda," he said softly, "come..." Tuschka tilted her head slightly and looked at the visitor. She was disappointed that it was not her friend, but there had been warmth in his words and she was utterly lonely. Something about his attitude showed genuine interest. As soon as Tom saw her eyes meet his, he cleared his throat and made the best version he could of their former greeting call. The sound startled Tuschka. It was so familiar... She came closer and directed her chin towards the man. As he repeated it, it all suddenly fell into place for her. The special call, the familiar voice, the outline of the man's face, his eyes... he was a friend she had lost long ago.

The orca's response left Tom no doubt. She came over in an instant, sliding up over his outstretched hands to nudge his face. The enthusiastic greeting threw him off balance. He grabbed for a hold around her rostrum to prevent himself from falling backwards. Within seconds he had the orca's head in a wide embrace. She was still pushing up at him and squeaking her delight. Tom was so engulfed in Gunda's exuberant welcome that he was no longer aware of all the people who were watching him. Nor was the orca. She was so happy with their reunion that she did not notice Janet, who was observing them halfway up the dock. Janet was deeply touched by Gunda's instantaneous and warm response, and wiped a tear from her cheek. There was no doubt how strong their bond was and yet he was destined to part with Gunda, like herself....

Tom felt the gentle force with which Gunda was pushing herself up and nudging him. It was the subtlety in her movements, the mastery of her sheer strength, and the soft affectionate calls that radiated the orca's warmth and tenderness for him. A few tears ran down his face and made contact with the whale's smooth melon. He pressed her close and rubbed his cheek against her. It felt as if the years of separation had melted away. It was as spontaneous and intimate as the many precious moments he had cherished in his heart. After having missed her for so long, living their bond in his dreams, the moment was overwhelming. This was no dream... They were together again.

Only after he had released his tight hug did the orca sink down. He caressed her chin and turned to fetch the bucket behind him. A handful of fish quickly disappeared. As he reached in for a next handful, he suddenly changed his mind and selected the biggest herring. Instead of giving it to the orca, he stuck his hand in the water and started to wiggle the fish. "This is what you'll have to learn," he said with a smile. "You like to catch it?" Tuschka watched him in surprise. What was he up to? She saw the hand pull the fish away from her, twisting it sideways by its tail. Looking up at him on the dock, there was no doubt he was inventing a little game. As he started to walk away from her, she followed him while closing in on the fish. Tom lightly bumped into Janet, who was still standing halfway up the dock. As they both watched, Tom let go of the fish and saw how the orca swiftly sucked it in. Tuschka rose and spyhopped in front of them. She was happy and yet surprised to see her two friends. Two worlds seemed to have come together.

That afternoon, Tom and Janet launched a little rowboat, adjacent to Gunda's area and rowed over to the net. The orca had been watching them from her usual spot near the dock. Tom lifted the oars off their pins and placed them inside the boat. "We can pull ourselves along at the net. Those oars are only in the way." He tapped the water and made his greeting call.

Tuschka saw the small vessel come to a stop near some small objects that floated in the water. She had never seen her trainers in such a strange situation. The little boat was about 70 yards away, but that was further than she had yet ventured from the dock. Tuschka drew courage from their presence as she slowly approached. She was echolocating on the small vessel when soft fragmented echoes beneath it gave her a chill and made her stop dead.

Tom tapped again and stretched his hand towards the orca. "Come Gunda, it's us, it's alright." But the orca did not move. She wailed softly and then repeated more loudly. Tom looked at Janet in puzzlement. "Something is bothering her, but what?" "She responded to your call and then stopped," Janet said. "Perhaps she's not sure it's us. She doesn't expect us to do things like this. Can you make that call again?" Tom repeated his call. Gunda's response was instant, but not in greeting. She uttered another wail that conveyed distress. "I have an idea." Tom's eyes sparkled. "You let me get out to meet her at the dock. Then I will encourage her to follow me so she can watch me as I step into the boat."

Janet liked the idea and Tom quickly rowed ashore. Gunda was tense and it took a few minutes for the orca to relax a little. As he got up and motioned her to follow, she swam along, close at his side. When Tom started to walk along the shore, the distance between them was bigger, but the orca was still coming along. When he was about 15 yards from Janet, he noticed Gunda stiffen. She spyhopped high, wailed her discomfort, and swayed her head in agitation. Tom was at a loss. He looked at the small rowboat and although he could see no harm in it, he wondered if it was the little vessel that was bothering her. Reluctantly, he walked away from the distraught whale and pulled the boat up on the pebble beach. It made no difference. Gunda was as disturbed as moments before...

Tuschka watched the boat scraping the bottom as it was beached. At the same time, her eyes registered what her echolocations had been telling her. It was a maze... restraint, separation... Traumatic memories and ominous feelings overcame her. She had just gone through such an ordeal. She wanted no part of another. Yet something about this maze was even more fearsome than the one she had recently been confronted with. Tuschka froze to her spot, not knowing where to find safety. When her Janet appeared at the end of the dock, she hesitated before coming over. Her confidence was shaken. What were they up to? Why had they tried to bring her close to that terrible soft maze that could shrink around you and would leave no escape? The soft voice of the woman finally took the edge off her fear. It carried sympathy, no threat. Not knowing what else to turn to, Tuschka lifted her flukes and glided towards the woman. As her hand touched her rostrum, she sensed no tension, no foreboding of something sad. She lay there for minutes, gradually relaxing under her friend's caressing strokes.

Tom, who had been tying up the rowboat, sat down beside Janet. "I feel bad about it," he said with a frown. "That step was obviously too much for her. I remember she needed some time to feel comfortable in the performance tank. This is much, much bigger." Tom's remark had obviously rung a bell for Janet. "Of course, she said. It took months before she was willing to enter our show pool. She definitely needed time to acquaint herself with each new pool and I felt she was reluctant to pass through a gate in fear of losing the option of a familiar retreat. It must be the size of this enclosure that is intimidating her. Would it help if we made it smaller? Shall we discuss it with Greg?" "I'll give Gunda some food first. Then let's discuss it inside." Tom assured himself that the orca was overcoming her stressful experience. He did not want to leave her without a sign that she was regaining her trust in him.

As soon as they had left the dock, Tom gave a tug on Janet's arm to make her follow him into his cabin. "The size is probably intimidating her," he started, "but I haven't seen a response that came even close to the stress she showed just now. She has been fairly timid and has not ventured far from that dock, but with time she probably will. Unless...," he paused deliberately, "unless there's more to it than size alone. I don't think we should disturb her with changes to the enclosure unless we have a very good reason for it." "It couldn't have been the rowboat, do you think?" Janet was thinking aloud. "It made no difference when we pulled it up on the beach," Tom reminded her.

Janet suddenly sat upright with a new idea. "What if we dived with her? It would give us an opportunity to explore what is down there and it might reassure her!" Tom shook his head. "We'd have to use compressed air and dry suits. She isn't used to that at all. Maybe we are thinking too far... maybe it's simply the different type of wall: a net instead of ..." Tom stopped mid-sentence. "A net! Could that be it? The shore did not frighten her." Their eyes opened wide as the realization struck them both at the same time. "She's never experienced anything good from a net. Think of her transfers. We used one prior to placing her on the stretcher," Tom said. "Actually, the first traumatic experience in her life involved a net."

Silence fell. That was exactly the trauma they hoped to make up for, although no one could ever give her back the years of lost freedom. As Tom thought of the event that had so dramatically changed Gunda's life, he jerked upright. Janet was startled by his sudden reaction. "Janet, this is a seine net! It's probably the same type as the one she had been captured with! The maze is different from the one we had at the park. Perhaps the rowboat in combination with that net has revived her memory of that tragic experience." The explanation made more sense than anything else they had come up with.

Although they shared their thoughts with Greg, there was no practical solution to the problem. All agreed that it was best to let Gunda explore her enclosure at her own pace. Sooner or later, she would find out that this net posed her no threat. Attempts to help her would probably have adverse effects on her trust in humans.

Although both Tom and Janet had a document with a full description of the steps to be taken in the release plan, Greg filled them in with some more detail. Within a few days, another trainer was expected to arrive. The man had no former experience with orcas, but he had worked several years with pilot whales for the Navy. Those whales had been trained to follow a boat at sea, perform certain tasks and come back on recall. The plan was to eventually train Gunda to follow a boat to build her stamina and to reacquaint her with her home waters. It was especially for this aspect that they needed his experience. At some point, Gunda would have to be capable of swimming 70 miles a day. This part of the plan had met with a lot of resistance and it still did. The main concern was that the orca would swim up to all kinds of boats and put herself in potential danger. Yet many observations indicated that orcas had a very keen and subtle sense for discriminating between boats and that it would not be likely for Gunda to spontaneously follow other boats, especially if such behavior were discouraged during her training sessions at sea.

30.
Chasing Fish Again

The phone rang again. Annoyed by the many calls that interrupted his work, Greg was happy to have a secretary to deal with most of the reporters and to help him with answering the phone. Most calls involved frequently asked questions that could easily be answered by non-experts. His secretary's voice had become a nearly constant soft noise in the background. Greg looked up when she knocked on the door. "It's Johann, the captain of the research team. Somebody called him about that newspaper column and he found it really interesting." Greg raised his brow. He was still skeptical after the numerous reactions that had involved non-specific sightings of what appeared to include orcas, pilot whales and sometimes other cetaceans.

"....the pod followed the seiner, which was doing about 12 knots and heading in the direction of Stenavik Harbor. When his captain asked that boat about the orcas following behind, he received evasive answers over the radio. They followed for a while to observe the whales. With binoculars, the crew saw a lot of activity on the deck around a white canvas-like structure. When they came closer, this crew member, who just called me, recognized the pod by a young male with a scar on its back." " recognized the pod?," Greg asked eagerly. "He claims to have seen that same pod several times," Johann continued. "He wants to come and explain in more detail."

Greg shifted his position. This sounded interesting. "How sure is he about the date of that event?" "He remembers that it was the first half of November. It was his third season and that was exactly the year of the capture. He said he could check the log and see if there is any note on it." "What do you think, Johann?" Greg asked. "I think it's worth checking out. He sounds very convinced and is eager to help us. He must take a special interest in orcas to look at them in such detail. He claimed he would recognize that scarred whale out of a thousand." The skepticism on Greg's face had changed into eagerness and anticipation. "Listen Johann, we have to arrange a meeting with him and Bjorn so that he can look at the catalogues. Please join us if you can. We might need your help. I will have Monica, my secretary, arrange a date as soon as possible. Keep in touch." Greg leaned back and looked at Monica with a twinkle in his eyes. "Imagine this were a lead.... It's almost too good to be true."

In the days that followed, Gunda stayed in the vicinity of the dock. If she ventured a little away from it, it was opposite to the place where she had seen the menacing maze. Tom and Janet knew that the net formed the border of most of her area and wondered if the orca was already aware of that. Fortunately, Gunda had become more relaxed and was willing to engage in little games near the floating dock. Janet had been contemplating whether or not she should give Gunda the cue for perimeter bows or a speed swim. Chances were that the circumstances of a training session would divert her attention away from restraint and transfer, but seeing the net unexpectedly might easily give her another fright. "Somehow, she must learn that this net isn't moving, not closing in on her," Janet said to Tom. "I'm afraid that if she doesn't explore it by herself, she'll be equally afraid next time." Tom understood what his buddy meant, but did not have any idea what to do about it. "Janet, I understand your worries. It may take a while, but it won't take forever."

Janet suddenly had an idea. She told Tom about the tugging game that she had invented to test the force with which Gunda would close her jaws. "A bow cue sends her closer to that net on our command. The challenge is to have her move further away from the dock on her own initiative. It's important that the incentive does not come from us." Tom was excited about it. The orca would be in control of her own movements and nothing in their behavior would hint at their hidden intentions.

Although the diameter and texture of the long line were a little different, Tuschka needed little time to understand what game her friends wanted to play with her. She took the knot in her jaws and slowly swam away from the dock. When she began to feel some resistance, she slowed down and turned to face her friends. It was clear from their stance that they already had difficulty holding on. Suddenly, she saw the woman let go, lose her balance and tumble against the man behind her. At the same moment, the tension in the line was gone. The threesome repeated the game a few times and each time, the orca waited patiently for her friends to pick up the other end again.

Tom and Janet quickly discovered that the weight of the line left them little extra strength to offer the orca any resistance. Tom was happy when his eye caught a cleat around which he could wrap the cord. He did not tie up, but swung it around once, which made it possible to offer much more resistance with less effort.

Tuschka pulled, but the cord barely gave. She pulled harder and it gave a little more. Although she had not nearly reached her limits, she noticed that the two people on the dock were standing their ground without too much effort. When the resistance kept increasing, and backing up was no longer effective, she turned to swim forward with the cord running backwards along her flank. Suddenly, as it went slack, Tuschka let go, wheeled and spyhopped to watch the situation on the dock. She noticed the cord move away and she swam after it to grab it again. Tom and Janet had tried to haul the cord in as fast as possible like an escaping fish, but they laughed at the meager results.

That evening, after her last feed, Tuschka discovered the line extending down and away from the dock. As she followed it over the bottom, the memory of her earlier fright returned. She stopped and looked towards the net. It was not visible. Had it disappeared or was it still there, further away? A little hesitant, Tuschka sent a train of clicks.... Apprehension filled her as she recognized the echoes. She backed away and listened intently, but there were only the familiar sounds of wind and birds, and little waves lapping on the beach. Her tension subsided a little and she had the courage to spyhop and look to where her sonar had detected the net. On the calm surface, Tuschka saw the small floats, gently bobbing up and down with the movements of the water. Motionless, she kept watching them. Vague memories began to stir. She had seen these before... there was something important about them. Tuschka could not put her associations into a coherent framework yet but somehow these objects were related to food and caution.

Still before dusk, Tuschka echolocated again. The maze was hanging there, but otherwise everything was quiet. Slowly, curiosity overcame her apprehension. With caution, Tuschka crept closer until her rostrum was almost in contact with what had recently startled her. The webbing moved in slow undulations with the pull of the tide. As she watched it, her tension subsided. She echolocated and focused beyond the mesh. Further away was only water. Tuschka slowly sank down following the net to find that it extended all the way down to the bottom. The water was deeper than near the dock, but she could still see some detail in the blue green light. The sea floor was fairly irregular with rocky elevations, pebbles, and boulders of various sizes. Most of the surface was covered with a variety of algae, anemones, and other small sea life. Where the maze touched bottom, it folded up and formed a soft band, that followed every contour of the sea floor.

Tuschka noticed a medium sized fish struggle to get free. It was entangled with a pectoral fin and some of its gills. She watched it for a little while. When it rested from its efforts, she revived it with a small nudge. The startled fish dashed forward instinctively and jerked itself free. Tuschka saw it brush the net with its flank, veer away and disappear. There were also several starfish, but their colors were dull in the dim light. Slowly, she began to follow the band of folded mesh. As she rose up to take a breath, she looked for the dock to orient herself. Right next to her was the edge of the net with the typical small white floats at regular intervals. She followed them with her eyes, but as low as she was, they quickly disappeared from sight. Keeping visual contact with the dock, Tuschka began to follow the floats. She noticed that she was swimming in a huge circle, her distance from the dock barely changing.

As Tom walked towards the dock, he did not see the orca in her familiar spot close by. Something made him stop short of the dock. Although it was not uncommon for the whale to be down for a few minutes, he sensed something was odd. Tom's intuition told him to wait and see without alerting Gunda with the sounds of his footsteps on the dock. Perhaps there was something more interesting than a dive near the dock. His eyes caught the thick line with which they had been playing. It was still as they had left it. Just as he began to feel a hint of worry, the orca's blow startled him. The sound instantly led his eyes to the southeast further away from the dock. There she was, at the perimeter near the floats! He suppressed an urge to run back and get Janet. He wanted his colleague to see this, but at the same time he did not want to attract Gunda's attention. He watched for a few more seconds and saw how she was slowly following the floats. Quietly, on tiptoes he turned to tell the news.

* * *

Everyone was filled with eager anticipation when Bjorn, Johann, and the unknown fisherman had arrived. Tom and Janet were disappointed when Greg had expressed his desire to have a small meeting in his office. Later on, he would share the results with the others. Other than stating his name, Torvil had not said a word. He followed the other three men quietly into Greg's office. The many news clippings and orca pictures on the wall told him that everything here revolved around orcas. Bjorn was about to show him a particular page in his dorsal fin catalogue, but Greg signaled him to wait. Upon his host's request Torvil began to tell his story.

"Were you certain that the seiner was heading into Stenavik harbor?" "Not certain," Torvil answered. "We didn't follow them all the way, but they'd said over the radio that they had a good catch and were heading in that direction. As I already described, however, their captain seemed to be hiding something and it didn't look like they were handling fish on deck." "Do you happen to remember the name of the vessel?" Greg asked. Torvil smiled as he turned to grab something out of his jacket. "I brought that day's log. There's a brief note of the pod following the vessel and the strange activities on deck. The name isn't easy to read..." The fisherman handed the log to Greg. The first thing he noticed was the date. "It's the exact date we're looking for," he said with a raised voice. Then his eyes went to the name of the vessel. The writing was not very clear, but Greg's face became radiant as if he had found a treasure. "Hy..tor... That can only be 'Hydetor', the name of the capture boat!" All doubt as to whether the fisherman had actually seen the capture boat had vanished.

Greg shared the eagerness of the others to see if the whale that the fisherman claimed to have recognized was in Bjorn's catalogue. Bjorn opened the catalogue again and handed it to Torvil. His eyes opened wide with surprise as he pointed at an adolescent male. "This is exactly what the scar looks like! It's also the same spot, but.." His audience saw him frown. Tension was tangible. Was something wrong? Was he no longer as sure as he had claimed to be?

Torvil felt everyone waiting for him to speak up. "I've no doubts about the scar," he resumed. "Only the fin in this picture looks so much bigger than I remember from the last time I saw it." Bjorn wanted to explain the concept of sprouting male fins, but Greg interrupted him. Even though Torvil's reaction showed no doubt, he did not want everyone to jump to the conclusion that Gunda's family had been found. His scientific training told him to temper his enthusiasm until DNA studies confirmed such a thing. There was still the possibility that sounds of the captured juvenile had attracted a nearby pod, although it was unlikely that any other than Gunda's own pod would have been so persistent in following the vessel. "Wait," Greg said. This match gives us a very strong indication, but no proof. I don't want the media to spread information we aren't certain about yet."

Bjorn opened an envelope and pulled out some more pictures. He flipped through them quickly, picked one of them, and handed it to the fisherman. "What about this one," he asked. The smile returned to the man's face. "That... that's exactly the orca as I remember it." He paused a moment. "Are there two orcas with such a ... no, it can't be.. When was this picture taken?" "Good question!" Bjorn complimented him. "It was taken one year after Gunda's capture. It's a young male." It was obviously a pleasant surprise for Torvil, but he did not interrupt the scientist. "When do you remember seeing him last?" Torvil sighed. "The last time that I really recognized him is about two and a half years ago. I may have seen his pod after that, but it was too distant to be certain." "This is interesting," the researcher said. "In the summer after you last saw him for sure, we first saw that his fin was sprouting. That means the growth spurt of the fin in all males when they enter puberty. Last summer, he left us in no doubt that he was an adolescent male. Eventually his fin may become as tall as...well, as B1, the mature male in his pod."

Torvil looked carefully at the picture in the catalogue. "He'll be even easier to identify now!" His finger pointed at the label. "Is that what you call him? 'B7'?" "Yes, his pod is designated as B pod and we have given each pod member a number." Torvil could barely believe he was in the company of people who were so interested in these whales that they had documented each them individually for, apparently, many years. He was eager to learn more, but felt uncomfortable asking trivial questions.

Bjorn unfolded a piece of paper with a small table on it. "From the description that Johann related to me, the only possible candidate in my catalogues was B7, so I've looked up all we know since we first identified his pod. In our first four seasons in this area, the youngest member of that pod was a juvenile, B9. We have never seen it since the summer prior to Gunda's capture. At the time, we assumed that the juvenile had deceased. Since the capture was in a different area, we never associated her disappearance with the capture. I brought our best two pictures of B9, but her saddle is not very distinctive. Although we can exclude an open saddle or a finger, some glare hides the detail in the leading edge. This other photo is a little off angle and shows poor contrast."

The photo of the juvenile orca was passed around. The silence was remarkable while the other men took a thorough look at it. Although it was not spoken aloud, no one had missed Bjorn's insinuation. Everyone, even Greg, looked at it as if it were Gunda in her early years.

* * *

By the end of May, Gunda had become so comfortable in her new enclosure that she showed no trace of fear when she approached the perimeter of the net. She often followed her trainers along as they went round to check the floats, sometimes sliding over the floats with her chin as if attempting to get closer to the boat. It would take little more for the whale to swim to freedom. It seemed paradoxical to fear that Gunda might escape while her freedom was their goal, but the orca was not ready for it now. In their hearts, both Tom and Janet knew Gunda would not venture far, if anywhere at all.

Curt, the former Navy trainer, attended as many training sessions as possible and had recently started to do some of the feeding. The plan was that Curt would become sufficiently acquainted with the orca before Janet left. Her employer had given her two months with pay and the option of one more month, without pay. Although Janet had left with the thought of returning to her job, she had begun to feel more and more doubts about her future at the park. On the one hand, she could not bear the thought of parting with Durak, Shachi, and Wobke; but on the other hand, she was reluctant to go back to an environment with so little room for spontaneity and where she so often had to act in conflict with her own insights. How different was it to work with Gunda here, to stimulate the orca's creativity and to gradually revive her instinct to hunt. It was a great challenge that led her to discover aspects of the orca that were deliberately suppressed in a performing whale, but Janet realized very well that the ultimate goal was the orca's independence. The fascinating and rewarding interactions would gradually be reduced until Gunda made contact with her wild relatives. To bring this job to a good end would also have its emotional difficulties, but the sacrifices to be made would be in Gunda's best interest.

Janet was struggling with the question of whether she could or should give up Durak, Shachi, and Wobke, for a few more months with Gunda. Although it was not a welcome thought, Janet knew Gunda's future did not depend on her. Someone could take her place, but who would take her place at the park if she stayed here? What personality would that trainer have...? Would he or she respect and love the whales as she did? In an environment with so little freedom, it seemed not so important, but Janet felt strongly that it was, especially because of that lack of freedom. The same precious moments that gave purpose and joy to her, gave purpose and joy to the orcas. Yet... if Gunda did not make it back to freedom she would retire in a natural bay and have her own calf as company. They would need people to care for them, and the only goal of that care would be to make the two orcas as comfortable as possible. How much more rewarding would that be!

Since there were only a few weeks left to decide, Janet went to discuss the matter with Greg. The scientist proved to be much more understanding than she had dared hope. He told her that he had already started negotiations with Gunda's owners to have Sheila come as soon as possible. "I want you to know that I very much appreciate your good work, but I couldn't simply sit back and await your departure. It isn't a problem to find motivated trainers," he continued, "but I want to have at least three experienced ones, so that two of them are available to work with Gunda for most of the time. Sheila has experience with Gunda, similar to yours. I thought she would be the best candidate to take your place, but Sheila's employers are reluctant to give up one of their key trainers during the peak season. It would be mid-September at the earliest before Sheila will be available." Janet nodded. It did all make sense, but it did not make things easier for her. "Now that I know how much you want to stay and how difficult your choice is, I'll see what I can do. Give me a few days to work on something."

Janet was in hog-heaven when Greg came to tell her that her leave of absence could be extended till the end of September and that he would have a small stipend for her to help cover her expenses at home. She would have two weeks with Sheila before she had to leave, but that was not all. Greg had assured her that he would give her the option to care for Gunda in case she remained dependent on humans. It was a comforting offer which made her decision a lot easier.

Janet was excited about the next step in Gunda's rehabilitation plan. Although Gunda would never hunt salmon in her current location, it was the food that her probable family would soon be hunting. The team was motivated to encourage Gunda to catch live salmon, now that it was almost certain that this would be a natural thing for her to do. As a first step, they had been feeding her salmon for the past several days to reacquaint her with the taste, size, and shape of the local species. Being used to mackerel and herring as main food, the orca had been a little surprised at first, but it did not take long for her to appreciate her new food.

The vibrations of familiar steps on the floating dock were enough encouragement for Tuschka to come over. She spyhopped high in front of Tom who had come to feed her. She was hungry and eager to eat, but instead of putting a fish straight into her mouth, her friend held one up high. Strangely enough, the fish twitched a little while hanging from his hand. It was not uncommon for him to play with her during feeding, but Tuschka was not much in the mood for it now. It had seemed much longer than normal since her last meal and she rose up impatiently towards the fish. Tom made an effort to keep the fish out of her reach and she gave an extra thrust with her tail to rise high enough to take it from his hands. Just as she was about to grab it, he threw it over her head.

Tuschka turned sharply towards the spot where it landed, but she held back when it jerked a little and made feeble efforts to swim. For a moment, Tuschka forgot her empty stomach and watched the movements of the fish with curiosity. She was not used to moving food, but apart from that, the salmon was not swimming with the grace and agility of a normal fish. It looked like an injured animal, struggling along. Tuschka came forward and nudged the salmon, which jerked twice in startled response to her touch. The extra activity was short-lived and soon faded into a feeble quivering swim. The fish was disoriented and erratic in its movements. Tuschka revived it a few more times until it was so weak and exhausted that it barely responded to the touch of its predator.

Having lost interest, Tuschka turned around towards her friend on the dock to have her appetite satisfied. She opened her mouth eagerly, but her friend made no move to feed her. She squeaked in protest and leaned over the edge towards him. He touched her rostrum briefly and pointed behind her. She squeaked impatiently, annoyed that her trainer did not understand and just feed her. Her spirits lifted when he grabbed another fish, but instead of feeding it to her, he threw it over her head again. Tuschka hesitated briefly and then slid up against the dock in hopes of persuading Tom to throw food in her mouth. After a few seconds, it became clear that he had no intention of giving her a fish. All he did was point behind her. Tuschka turned and swam towards the spot where the second fish had landed. It was fairly close to the first fish, which was still moving weakly. The second fish hung almost lifeless in the water, but when Tuschka took hold on it, she felt it move feebly between her teeth. She released it and watched it for a few seconds.

Tuschka had the strong impression that the fish had been thrown as food, not as toys. Trainers had tossed her fish before, but there had never been a spark of life in them. Her empty stomach drew her closer to the fish again. It was strange that they were not dead, and yet there was something vaguely familiar about it. The unexpected situation had made her cautious, but at the same time an inner voice told her that there was nothing wrong with eating these fish. With a sudden resolve, she grabbed the barely moving fish in her mouth. She felt a weak response, crushed it briefly while positioning it headfirst, and swallowed it down whole. It tasted good and she needed no encouragement to take the fish that had been thrown first. It offered more resistance than the other one, but it took Tuschka little effort to kill and eat it.

As soon as she surfaced, she saw her friend clap his hands and raise his voice in an attempt to squeak at her. It was obvious that he was excited about her. Although his reaction had come as a surprise for Tuschka, it lifted her spirits immediately and she squeaked in response. Soon, another fish soared through the air. Even before it landed, the agile orca followed the fish with her head, turning sharply towards it. She saw it move against the greenish background. This fish definitely had more energy than the previous two. Tuschka nudged it to test its reaction. The salmon veered away from her and managed to increase its speed a little. Then, as it slowed down, Tuschka grabbed it effortlessly with a quick sideways lunge. A strange feeling of satisfaction came over her. There was more to it than just consuming food. Her friend on the dock squeaked and yelled again. Was he sensing her mood and sharing her excitement?

Tom was elated by the whale's eager reaction when he had thrown his third fish. Her instant and resolute response told him Gunda's hunting instincts were awakening. It was amazing how close these were to the surface after so many years of eating dead fish from the freezer.

In the days that followed, the trainers fed the orca partly dead and partly live meals. The dead fish were especially used in combination with sessions to build on Gunda's stamina. To kindle Gunda's hunting instinct, they had started with freshly caught salmon that had not yet died. They were injured or otherwise weakened fish that would be easy for even the most inexperienced orca to catch; but Gunda was not inexperienced: she had hunted salmon in her early years. The crippled fish only served the purpose of reacquainting her with live food. As the weakened salmon revived her hunting skills, it soon became apparent that Gunda was ready for more challenging prey.

The orca clearly relished the challenge of the chase. Most pursuits were short, because the disoriented fish ran into the net or lost speed in their attempts to evade it. Some fish, however, demanded more of the orca's stamina and agility: they swam in circles or made unexpected turns. Others managed to find shelter in crevices in the rocks near shore. Feeding her one fish at a time made it relatively easy for the human observers to follow the orca's movements in relation to her prey. There was no doubt she was improving her skills. Speed and agility were no longer her only strategy. A better anticipation of the salmon's behavior helped her to improve her timing and use her energy more efficiently.

Greg observed most of Gunda's hunting behavior. He was elated to be able to watch a hunting orca uninterruptedly at such close range. Although the majority of salmon hunts in the wild started with a cooperative effort, the final chase was almost always an individual endeavor. He wondered if Gunda's progress was a fast version of the way she had learned to hunt as a young calf. There was no way to help Gunda regain her cooperative hunting skills, nor could he provide her with enough salmon to create the concentrations that she might encounter in the wild. Catching a single salmon in a large enclosure seemed more difficult, but a shoal of salmon presented the problem of selecting one as target and concentrating on it among the others. Although it would not be anything like reality, Greg wanted to experiment with at least a small number of salmon at the same time. He wondered if the fish would disperse or attempt to stay together.

Tuschka was completely surprised at the sound and sight of so many fish landing in the water near the dock. There were far more salmon than she could eat in one meal. She wondered why they had given her so many at once. A little confused, she looked briefly at the fish. For a moment, the individual salmon swam indecisively in different directions, then quickly joined up to form small groups. Tuschka spotted a solitary salmon nearby and kicked her flukes to go after it. When she lunged for it, it made an unexpected turn and joined a small group of five other fish. Tuschka wheeled in pursuit, but lost track as the salmon suddenly scattered in all directions. She darted after another small bunch with the same result. She was a little annoyed with her failure, as if she had experienced it before and should know how to deal with it.

After a brief pause, Tuschka looked around and spotted a few fish, heading towards the net. Instead of racing after them, she gained on them slowly, brooding on a better strategy. The fish suddenly went deeper and Tuschka echolocated to aid her vision. They were close to the net now. Suddenly, Tuschka dashed forward in an attempt to chase one or more animals into the net, but veered aside to avoid it herself. The maze was too small for the fish to get stuck, but the unexpected barrier had confused them briefly. While she managed to grab one of them, the others scurried away. Tuschka surfaced for a few good breaths and went down again alongside the net in hopes to find more. Using the net as a trap yielded several more fish and, with her appetite almost satisfied, she went back to the dock to rest.

As long as there were live salmon in her enclosure, The team fed the orca half her daily ration in dead fish during high energy training sessions. The idea was that Gunda's hunting efforts would improve not only her skills, but also her stamina. Apart from the fact that human cues were an unnatural stimulus for an orca to expend energy, one could ask only so much for a reward. The advantage of letting Gunda hunt for herself was that she would decide for herself how much energy she wished to invest. She would not associate any frustrations, that she might experience during unsuccessful attempts, with a trainer who failed to reward her properly.

31.
The Puzzle Comes Together

A phone call from Bjorn had brought excitement to the camp. Several pods, including B pod had been sighted near Rockcove Bay. Greg had left to join Bjorn, Johann, and Torvil to try to get biopsies from some reproductive females, especially from B4, the female that had been seen with a juvenile during the first four years of Bjorn's study. DNA analysis would reveal more about Gunda's probable mother.

Torvil seemed glued to his binoculars. He could not yet believe that no one asked him to help lower the nets. It was almost beyond his comprehension that the orcas were their goal for the days to come and that he could just watch as long as he wanted. Even more, with all the people on board vibrating with excitement, he soon relaxed and gave in to his joy.

The fisherman had been able to tell adult males from females and juveniles, and had been thrilled by his former recognition of the young whale he had shot, by the scar on its back. Now, he watched it all in silence and was fascinated by the way the researchers worked. Although he had been wondering if he would ever see his Scarback again, it had not occurred to him until that first meeting with Bjorn that many of the orcas could be distinguished by their natural markings. Inside, he shared the researchers' eager anticipation of finding the adolescent male.

Greg had been studying the individuals of B pod intensively. When he put down the field guide, Torvil bent down to look at it. The males seemed easier to tell apart than the females, but their fins, too, had different shapes. Some fins were more rounded at the top, while others were fairly pointy. Besides that, part of the fins had nicks in the rear edge that differed in shape and position. Greg saw him look and tapped him on the shoulder. Torvil was taken by surprise and blushed as if he had done something he wasn't supposed to. "I'll explain more about it on the way back," he offered. Torvil's shy expression changed to a smile. "I'd be very happy to learn more," he said. It pleased Greg to see a local fisherman show such genuine interest and he did not want to pass up the opportunity to educate him a little more. It could only benefit the orcas if he passed it on to his pals.

Torvil had taken several pictures in the beginning, but had soon stopped taking any more. He had a very simple camera and was more eager to take it all in without having to bother with equipment. He keenly observed how the team took notes and identified some individuals. He was talking to Ingrid when his attention was suddenly caught by a small group of orcas chasing, bumping and rolling over each other. Several spyhopped as they came closer to the boat. Torvil gasped, swallowing a scream of recognition as he saw a whale with a distinctive scar on his back dive under the boat.

Torvil's sudden reaction conveyed total amazement. Everyone turned around facing in the direction where they expected the orcas to surface again. They came up about 30 yards from the other side of the boat. The whales differed slightly in size. The first two, that surfaced, were obviously immature. As the third whale came up in a high arch, Torvil, still speechless, pointed at the orca. The animal was slightly larger than the two females on his right side, but his fin was noticeably taller than theirs.

As the orcas moved away from the boat, all eyes were focused on Torvil. The young fisherman still looked in the direction of the whales and was suddenly brought back to reality when he saw all the questioning eyes waiting for him to explain. His eyes met Greg's and he read from the researcher's face that he was hoping this was the whale they had been looking for. "That's Scarba..uhh, that's the one! That whale with the scar." Bjorn's mouth turned into a smile. "That young male is B7, the one I pointed out to you in the photo catalogue." Torvil nodded, too overwhelmed to speak. It was amazing enough to see his special whale again after such a long time and in such a different season and area, but it was even more so in the presence of people who understood him, whose work was based on the recognition of individual orcas! How exciting to see them at work with the orcas at sea.

Greg's voice interrupted his thoughts. "Bjorn, I missed the nick in his fin. Perhaps the glare..." "I'm pretty sure I saw it," Bjorn commented before Greg had finished his sentence. "It's about one-third down from the top. We must certainly try to get a good shot of him, but let's try to find the female B4. There are at least two pods here and we have to check on those small groups in the distance. We'll probably find B1 also, but he may be farther ahead."

While Johann tried to catch up with a group of four whales ahead of them, Bjorn seated himself next to Torvil and Greg and pointed out the characteristics of the female they were looking for. "See, her fin is fairly tall with a sharp top and here, just behind the saddle patch, are two faint scratches." Torvil bent way over to see the subtle lines. He looked questioningly at Bjorn. There were so many little spots and lines on the female's skin that it did not make sense to him that the researcher singled out these two. "These markings don't help us much to recognize the whale from the boat, because we can only see them on good photos, but they have been there ever since we first saw her." As Bjorn's words sank in, Torvil realized how distinctive his Scarback was for these people. What had caused disbelief and ridicule among most of his colleagues, was well accepted by them.

"There's B8, with that somewhat rounded fin," Bjorn pointed out. "She was a juvenile when we first met her. She has a strange elongated scar behind her left pectoral fin, but that's visible only when she rolls over or breaches. Without making any effort to photograph the four orcas, Bjorn instructed Johann to head for another small group. "That might be her, Johann," the scientist said with excitement.

As they came closer, there was no doubt they had found B4. Bjorn was immediately busy readying the crossbow for a biopsy and made no more attempts to mention the identity of the other two orcas with her. The biologist had instructed Johann how to position the boat once they had found a candidate for a biopsy. The seasoned captain needed little coaching as he lined up with the female and gradually closed in on her. It was fortunate that the youngest of the three orcas, who was closest to the boat, changed position to swim in between the two older whales. B4 was now in a perfect position. The orcas were traveling steadily at a speed of about five knots and Johann had not much difficulty keeping parallel to them. Bjorn stood poised with the crossbow ready. Johann was still closing in on the orcas bit by bit, expecting Bjorn to shoot as soon as he felt the opportunity was right. None of them had experience in taking biopsies from wild orcas, but Bjorn knew this population best of all.

Only 25 yards separated them now. Everyone was tense. Johann sensed his presence was becoming intrusive. He was almost certain the orcas would change direction and surface somewhere away from them after their next long dive. The first surfacing had been necessary for Bjorn to help him anticipate the next. Yet he did not use the second, nor did he shoot on the third. 'Shoot Bjorn, please don't wait too long', Johann thought to himself. "Poohup," B4's blow sounded strong. Her high arch announced the long dive. Just as her fin angled forward, Bjorn released the dart. As it hit true, the orca slightly flinched, but otherwise seemed undisturbed. As the boat came to a stop, all eyes were on the wake of the orca's dive. Torvil was the first to see the red float of the tiny dart.

A few weeks had passed when Greg received word from the laboratory. In total, he had sent samples of three females in B pod. The results from the DNA analysis revealed 90% certainty that B4 was Gunda's mother. Similar DNA resemblance had been found in captive mother and calf pairs. Greg's reserve could not prevent that most newspapers from all over the world were announcing that Gunda's family had been found. It was valuable knowledge, which had excited him as much as everyone else in the release team, but the big question remained whether this pod would recognize and accept their lost member. Although everyone knew Gunda's pod hunted herring in the fall, based on the site and season of her capture, it was a welcome discovery that they also hunted salmon in late spring and early summer near Rockcove Bay. It meant Gunda would have more options than the fall to meet her family again.

* * *

By early summer, Tuschka had become quite skillful in hunting the live fish in her enclosure. She had rediscovered strategies to chase small groups of fish without scattering them immediately. Sound played an important part. When she slapped the water with her flukes or fins, before the fish could see her, they tended to flee from the noise in one direction. During her experiments of the past weeks, Tuschka had discovered several spots that could serve as a natural trap and each time she detected fish, she herded them towards one of these.

Although cooperative hunting required different skills, it was a milestone that the captive orca had become quite adept at hunting live salmon in a relatively short time. It proved what Greg and his team had been thinking all along: that the orca's instinct, creativity, and excellent memory would enable her to overcome the effects of almost 8 years away from the ocean, and bridge the gap to the past. The time had come to build seriously on Gunda's stamina, to prepare her for swims up to 75 miles a day and to acquaint her with her native waters. When her family returned to these waters in pursuit of herring, there should be no physical limitation for Gunda to join their ranks.

Tuschka was intently watching the strange looking trainer on the other side of the net. She had recognized him when he entered the water, but now a strange object covered his eyes, and he had big round cylinders on his back. Strangest of all were the bubbles that he was blowing under water. The orca knew that exhalations made bubbles when submerged, but only rarely had she seen humans like this, staying down for a long time and blowing so many bubbles. The man was tugging at the net, close to the bottom. Then he started to manipulate small strands of wire and pulled the net away from the rocky shore. Tuschka did not move as she watched the maze come loose and move away like a giant curtain. A large opening formed, more than wide enough for her to leave her enclosure. Although caution held her back, Tuschka felt tempted to explore more of the world beyond. Somehow, it was not so threatening. The open maze had allowed her to see some of the area surrounding the net and to scan it with her sonar. It was similar in many aspects, except for the noisy vessels that moved at the surface with rotating fins. She had come to know the one close to the opening in the net: over the past several days, her friends had been tossing her fish from it.

When the man surfaced and uncovered his eyes, Tuschka was happy to recognize her friend and made eye contact with him. He did not come closer, but swam over to the boat nearby. She watched the strange fins that were attached to his feet. The way Tom was swimming was very different from what she was used to, but it seemed just as efficient, if not more.

The sudden sound of the starting engine did not scare Tuschka, but it kept her from following her friend. She curiously watched him take the cylinders off his back and climb over the edge of the vessel. It had an unusual shape and by the echoes of her sonar, she knew it consisted mostly of air. As it slowly came towards her, she moved a little aside to give it free passage. Although the vessel had been around for the past several days, it had never entered her area inside the maze. Tuschka kept looking at Tom, trying to keep eye contact with him. She was tempted to follow, but the unusual situation made her cautious. As the inflated object moved along the perimeter of her enclosure, she paralleled it in a much smaller circle, keeping quite close to the dock.

The small inflatable came to a stop in a corner, opposite to where they had opened the net. Tuschka did not hesitate as the other trainer tapped the water. The rather robust man was relatively new to her. He was self-confident, but obviously relied more on past experience than on his momentary creativity. Tuschka liked the latter more. She loved true mutual interaction. The more spontaneity there was, the more mental contact. Tuschka was, however, not unwilling to work with the newer trainer. It was still a diversion for her and he often confronted her with new objects or activities.

Tuschka saw the man pick up a fish. She spyhopped in anticipation of the fish being thrown somewhere near her. But he did not throw the fish. He tapped the water instead. The cue was simple enough in itself, but when she was less than half a body length away from the boat, it moved away. Tuschka stopped, partly annoyed and partly intrigued by the situation; they asked her to come over and when she did, they moved away! As Tuschka moved closer, the whistle of approval left her no doubt that she had done what they wanted. The fish was well thrown and landed close to her mouth. When they repeated the sequence, it was clear to Tuschka that they wanted her to follow.

Tuschka was not surprised when the boat moved away through the opening in the net, but the least she had expected was another tap on the water. She started to approach, but stopped just short of the opening in the net. This time, Tom leaned over the edge of the boat and called to her "Eeeeuuup..." Slowly, but without hesitation, Tuschka glided closer. About 10 yards beyond the opening, she touched his outstretched hands. She enjoyed his gentle caress and nudged his cheek in return. "Oh my precious friend, that was great! You are such a good brave girl." "Eeeueee," greeted the orca. "Eeeeuup," answered the man in a much lower pitch. "Eeeeeueee," sounded Tuschka and again the man tried to imitate the slightly different call.

Lately, there had not been much physical contact and Tuschka cherished the affectionate attention. Tom was elated to find his beloved whale so relaxed and so playful. He remembered Gunda's hesitance to enter the performance pool so well. Only after some minutes of mutual rubs and nudges, did Tuschka notice her position. She was in a spot where she had not been before, but the way to her familiar domain was open and right behind her. Tuschka looked up at her trainer again and rose up in his outstretched arms. He was warm and relaxed and she was delighted with his attention. Tuschka softly voiced her disappointment when her friend pointed her back to her enclosure. She sensed their interaction was coming to an end and she was reluctant to part, to give up the precious closeness. Yet she did not want to risk the harmony of the moment by failing to cooperate. Slowly, she turned and swam back inside the net.

Tuschka watched the boat approach and felt a spark of joy when her friend plunged into the water near the edge of the opening. She came close and followed him like a shadow, but she did not interfere while he closed the gap in the net. A little later, she savored his tender caress. Then he turned around with his back towards her. She sensed that he wanted to leave, but as soon as she felt his probing foot touch her chin, she understood what he wanted. Effortlessly, Tuschka pressed her rostrum against the sole of his foot and began to push him.

Tom marveled at the graceful power that propelled him through the water. He was aware of the orca's complete mastery over her streamlined muscular body. The strong strokes of her flukes went pulsing through his own body, making him feel one with the magnificent orca. Tom let out whoops of excitement as he steered wide along the perimeter. The strong explosive "pooohoohup" was right behind him. He knew he had gone beyond the line, but the moment was too exhilarating not to give in to it. He felt how subtle she responded to every twist of his body. He almost knew for certain that the whale would lead him safely underwater if he only had the breath to stay down with her. He made a few more wide loops before he steered towards the floating dock.

The orca nudged him as he climbed up on it. They had both loved the unexpected ride. It was the first for Tuschka since she had arrived in this large new home. She too, had felt a sense of unison, her own power making it possible to glide with her friend in her own environment with the speed and grace of her own kind. She rose up, burning with joy and affection, to be welcomed by a strong and long hug. Tom pressed his cheek against his beloved whale. "My precious Gunda, what you just gave me meant so much to me! How did you read me so well.... For you and me, it was beyond what I ever dared to hope." A twinge of regret sent adrenaline through his chest. "Next time," he said with a hushed voice, "you will be gliding with one of your own family and.. never have to part again...."

"You went too far," Curt said, as Tom came off the dock. The young man was still full of his experience and the former Navy trainer decided to put the subject off until later in the day. Curt was happy with his self-control, knowing that he too needed time to think about how to phrase his objections.

Tom knew his conduct had been completely beyond the limits of physical interaction allowed at this stage of Gunda's release plan. Hadn't they all joined forces to make Gunda less dependent on humans? Why had he not simply swum ashore outside the net? That would also have been the shortest distance. Somehow, the orca had drawn him in some irresistible way to extend

342

their togetherness, and swimming towards the dock had seemed a simple and harmless way to do so. But then, with the whale on his heels, his foot had found her rostrum like a magnet. They had been together again, like that special moment when they first met after his long sickness.

Greg's eyes stood firm and Tom felt uneasy. Had the warm and genuine biologist lost trust in him as a trainer? The young man remained silent. He felt more comfortable in speaking his thoughts after having heard what the others had to say. "We all understand such a weakness Tom," Greg said, "but how well can you resist future temptations? I respect you highly for your skill as a trainer and I do realize how much this task differs from what a marine park expects from you. Perhaps it is easier for you if Curt does the diving tasks, at least for the first couple of days." Tom nodded. "That certainly reduces the temptation." Tom hesitated to continue, but noticed that the others had already sensed that he was holding back. "I'll certainly try to act as much according to our program as possible," he said after a short pause, "but I've been wondering if such interactions would affect her learning much."

Curt cast a quick glance at Greg as if asking him permission to speak from his own insight and experience. "Our work differed from that at marine parks mainly in that we were in open water, but it was similar in the sense that success depended on our control over the whale. Here, we have a situation that is new to us all and contradictory in many aspects. We want to return Gunda to her former life in the wild. That life was not ruled by humans, but by her pod. Strictly speaking, returning Gunda to her former life means we would have to undo all that we have changed in her since the day of her capture and.." "And that's impossible," Tom completed, thinking aloud. "It's important to realize that our aim is not to reverse things," Curt continued. "We can only attempt to revive former skills, to bring back to the surface those behaviors that we have buried under years of captive conditioning. Coming back to what happened today, I believe that to swim with Gunda need not necessarily have a negative impact on her learning curve, but it's not part of a wild orca's life style. It's an activity that she shouldn't expect in this environment. We're using some unnatural strategies for lack of better insights, but we must try to keep Gunda's perspective of the open ocean as natural as possible. All we add to that is a potential source of distraction and may distort some of her future decisions or actions."

Janet and Greg nodded with approval. Their eyes revealed surprise about the clarity of Curt's argument. Tom was silent. He was impressed, and grateful at the same time, because the former Navy trainer had been so full of respect and understanding while he revealed the insight that had been blurred by his own emotion. Tom was relieved that he still had the respect of the team and he felt stronger to resist future temptations for Gunda's own good.

The conversation shifted to boat-following. Of all the strategies they used for preparing Gunda for her return to the wild, this was the most controversial: it was an unnatural behavior that would extend from her enclosure to the open sea. There were concerns about the potential effects on the orca's future behavior, but no one had come up with a better idea to build the whale's stamina and to reacquaint her with the routine of swimming large distances in open water. It was not considered realistic to wait for the arrival of Gunda's pod and to expect that mutual recognition would do the rest. The orca's current physical condition would cause her to drop back from exhaustion before the day was over. Another point of concern was the general reluctance of captive cetaceans to leave familiar surroundings. Gunda had given much evidence in the past that this also applied to her: she had always needed time and encouragement to enter a new tank. If Gunda made contact with her pod, there would have to be as few obstacles as possible to join it.

They all believed training at sea would be essential for Gunda's chances to reintegrate. The main question was how to minimize the potential danger of this type of training. Would Gunda approach and follow other boats in hopes of receiving food? If she did so, people might hurt or even kill her, especially fishermen in fear of damage to their gear and loss of fish. "... but orcas don't approach and interact with any person in hopes of a reward," Janet interjected. "They're very selective." "That's certainly true for experienced performers, but I'm not so sure about that when young or newly captured whales are involved," Tom remarked. "I believe most orcas, when they discover positive responses from humans, will initially generalize and attribute those discoveries to the species as a whole. Experience will teach them that not all humans act the same. Some will stand out by behavior and appearance: these are the ones they will soon distinguish from the rest as being most rewarding to interact with. Just as it takes time to distinguish trainers from other people, it will take time to learn differences between boats."

Greg nodded with understanding. It sounded more than plausible. Tom spoke from the experience of training a young orca that had come straight from the wild. "At sea, orcas show a high level of discrimination when it comes to boats" the team leader commented. "Here, they approach seiners to catch fish, but it's also known that pods remember boats that have been involved in their captures. They seem to recognize and be more accepting of vessels that are frequently present, like those of researchers. Yet there is evidence in the wild too that such knowledge needs to be acquired from older pod members and partially by experience. When a curious and exuberant juvenile comes very close, a related adult often leads it to a larger distance. Gunda was fairly young when captured. How much would she have known about boats at that time and how much of her memory will come back after she has been encouraged to follow a boat?"

Curt felt strongly that it was his turn to speak about his experiences. "The animals we worked with had also been captured relatively young. When we started open ocean training relatively soon after their capture, they showed a tendency to explore other boats. Whether they were motivated by genuine curiosity or hope of receiving food was not certain, but we had to give them extra food rewards to discourage the behavior. If we had not attempted to stop their explorations, they probably would have learned at some point to discriminate between us and others." "But Gunda's situation is different," Greg said. "There will be freedom for her only if she's accepted by her own pod. The other pod members will certainly have a corrective influence on her behavior. The question is how far they'll go in disciplining a young adult female. Even if all Gunda's memories come to the surface, she'll behave like a five-year-old in many ways, but in the body of an adult. It isn't known whether a large discrepancy between behavior and age might increase the chance of rejection."

Janet sat up and raised her hand for attention. She mentioned that Gunda's social development had not completely stopped since the day of her capture. Her introduction to Durak, Shachi, Kiki, and Wobke had exposed her to others of her own kind. She had learned how to interact with the dominant female and her offspring, and she had witnessed her companion give birth and nurse her calf. She had also behaved around Durak as a female, not as a five-year-old. "These experiences include many aspects of what each female learns when she grows up," Janet continued. "Gunda will have a gap to bridge, but it's certainly not as big as 8 years!" Everyone agreed.

Greg broke the silence. "What we'll be doing differs from what Curt did with his whales in that we want Gunda to explore her surroundings. It's important to have sufficient control over her to call her back, but we'll certainly not try to control Gunda all the time. By the time we take her out, she'll be very familiar with the boat and the recall sound. I expect it will take a lot of encouragement in the beginning to lead the whale away from her enclosure. Initially, she'll probably cling close to the boat as a familiar retreat. While she becomes more familiar with the area and gains confidence, she may venture away more. We will have to see then how she will respond to other boats. We will certainly inform vessels by radio when we're working with the whale at sea."

32.
Beyond the Fjord

Tuschka was hovering in the large opening in the net. She watched the vessel in front of her. Again she heard the high-pitched tone, the new signal for her to come over. She felt that something unusual was about to happen. Unlike before she had sensed some tension in her friends when they attached the strange sticky object to her dorsal fin. It had recently become a daily routine. At first, she had tried to rub it off, but without success. Then she had refused to cooperate when they tried to put it on her again, but that had obviously displeased her human friends. The enthusiasm and exuberance they showed when she cooperated was so rewarding that she was willing to accept it. When the initial strangeness wore off, it proved not so bad. Only when she swam faster, she felt water whirl around her dorsal fin.

The boat, the sounds, the people, they were not unlike other days, but their position was...To approach the vessel, she would have to venture farther away from her area than she ever had. In front of her was an environment, so big that she could not even oversee it. Yet it was similar to her domain in many aspects: the rocky floor, the algae, and the numerous small sea creatures. Deep inside, memories stirred: before her lay a world she already knew. There was something about it that filled her with a tremendous longing, and yet it made her shiver with a painful awareness of her loneliness. She looked back as if measuring how fast she could return to her familiar retreat.

Tuschka heard the high-pitched cue again. This time, one of her trainers also tapped the water. As she slowly glided closer, she noticed a new person next to one of her familiar male trainers. Tuschka immediately sensed it was a female. As the woman tapped the water, Tuschka spyhopped, looking questioningly at her. She was not in the mood to interact with a newcomer and she felt a twinge of annoyance at the woman's audacity in expecting her to respond. Tom, however, remained close, not making the slightest attempt to interfere. What did he want her to do?

A small peculiar squeak startled Tuschka. It had escaped from the woman's mouth and was much higher pitched than the calls Tom used to make. The sound took Tuschka completely by surprise. The orca felt her heart beat faster although she could not yet make the proper associations. Curiosity drew her closer to the woman until about three yards separated them. All her senses were tense when the female emitted a second call. Tuschka felt drawn to this person and sensed her sincerity. Instead of making more squeaks, the woman began to emit a lower, melodious sound, with rhythmic undulations in tone. Tuschka crept closer, irresistibly attracted to the gentle sound that revived memories of tenderness and affection. She eyed the woman again and saw her outstretched hand. One more squeak brought all the pieces together. This was another dear friend, who had given her comfort in many moments of sadness. This woman had respected, loved, and understood her like few others... like the man beside her. Tuschka suddenly was oblivious of the circumstances. Her friends were so full of warmth and reassurance that she kicked her flukes and slid up against the side of the inflatable into Sheila's warm hug.

Physical contact was to be completely avoided during sessions at sea, but right now, it was a strong reinforcement for the orca to approach the boat beyond the net. As soon as Gunda would had overcome her initial wariness, rubs and hugs were to be reduced and occasionally saved for reinforcement after returning inside the net. Sheila had felt her heart pound in her chest upon the approach of her beloved whale. What a magnificent creature she was! She was overwhelmed with the sudden and unrestrained response of her precious Gunda. The time that had passed since their last unforgettable swim in the big marine park seemed to have shrunk to one day. Sheila was not only intensely happy with the warm reunion. She was also deeply touched that their bond was still strong enough, after two years, to help Gunda cross a new barrier.

Janet had left the day after Sheila had arrived. It had been a quiet, but tender feeding session when Janet parted with her friend. She had wanted minimal disturbance of the program and the orca's mood. It had been hard on her, but she had comforted herself with the thought that Gunda would either be welcomed by her pod or, if not, be in her care. Sheila had been watching it from the beginning of the long dock. The sound of the orca's blows had sent a wave of excitement over her. In the dark, she had seen the outline of Gunda's melon and the reflections of the lights on her smooth skin. From the little she had seen she had the impression that the orca was in good shape. Sheila had decided not to approach Gunda until after Janet had left. It would spare her fellow trainer the sight of a potential exuberant reunion while she had to part with the orca.

* * *

Gulls were screaming overhead as Tuschka effortlessly sucked in a few herring that landed near her. She was following the familiar inflatable vessel at a speed of about five knots in a two-foot chop. Over the past few weeks, Tuschka had come to feel completely at ease inside the fjord. She often ventured a little away when something caught her interest. She had discovered cod in relatively dense concentrations near the bottom, close to the mouth of the fjord. Although they were not as tasty as the big salmon and the small silvery herring, it was fun to chase them, and occasionally she grabbed one.

Tuschka had just flushed one that had been resting behind a rock when she heard the high-pitched recall cue. She felt a little annoyed at the interruption of her game and ignored it. But soon, a second signal sounded. She knew she had already blown part of her reward, but she did not want to lose it completely. As she turned, she felt a little movement in her belly. It was not uncommon for her to feel a little cramp or ripple in her gut, but this was slightly different and it had recently begun to come more frequently. She concentrated on it when it came again. It did not cause her discomfort. She felt strong and healthy and as it passed, she kicked her flukes in the direction of the boat. Her human friends were obviously happy that she had come over, but the reduced amount of fish that landed near her spoke of their disappointment that she had not responded more promptly.

Tuschka still felt some apprehension when she entered new areas, but less than in the beginning. When she had just started to explore the fjord, she had taken refuge inside the net several times when something unfamiliar startled her. Now, she loved to cavort in the much larger space. The daily trips with the vessel had become a welcome diversion for Tuschka and with every area that she came to know, the step to explore a new one became easier.

Tuschka was surprised by the sudden increase in current and a slight change in taste. The faster flowing water also felt a little cooler, but she did not feel cold. She spyhopped and noticed there was only land on one side. The entrance to the small fjord was behind her. She felt a little uneasy. It was more than a quick turnaround to go back to her enclosure. The only familiar presence was the boat with her friends. Tuschka hesitated no longer and continued to follow at close range. The chop was noticeably rougher and she had to lift her head higher to catch a dry breath. It was not difficult, but it required more concentration. Upon every surfacing she kept eye contact with her lead, and below, the engine sound told her exactly its position and speed. As she moved farther away from home, Tuschka stayed even closer to the boat. Returning on her own was no longer an option for her. She relied completely on the guidance of her human friends. With the engine roar so close to her ears and fully concentrated on every change in direction and speed, she was virtually oblivious to her surroundings.

After a while, they slowed down and came to a stop. Tuschka gratefully accepted a generous number of tasty herring. When she slid up on the pontoon in hopes of an affectionate reward, one of her friends looked away. Then she made eye contact with Tom. He did not avert his gaze, but he did not touch her either. Yet he spoke to her gently. Tuschka called softly, pleading for a reassuring caress, but there was only his voice. She sensed warmth in him. There was contact, but he was holding back. With a disappointed moan, she slid back but hovered close. During her trips with the boat they had touched her less and less, and not at all over the past several days. Right now, after having cooperated so well and being so far from home, she had hoped for a more exuberant reward than fish alone. As she floated near, Tuschka began to understand that rubs and hugs were becoming more and more rare, virtually limited to precious moments near the dock.

Some very high-pitched whistles broke the relative silence. Tuschka blew and lowered herself a little. Where had she heard this before? The sounds made her forget her disappointment and lifted her spirits. Her heart beat faster with excitement. She pointed her head towards the source of the sounds. It did not take long for Tuschka to recall the grey sleek creatures that called and whistled with high voices. They were smaller than herself, but could be fun to play with. She did not know if they were willing to play with her, but she no longer doubted what they were. Tuschka felt tempted to go towards them, but she felt uncomfortable venturing more than a quarter mile away from the boat. She listened intently: they were coming closer. Tuschka emitted a friendly greeting, hoping they might come to her. Silence fell. No answers came. Another painful memory surfaced. Unless they knew her, dolphins had fear of her. How could she tell them that she was not to be feared?

Tuschka blew and heard the screeching gulls and the gusts of wind over the small waves. It was just her and her human friends again. In the sea, every creature feared her, or was too small to be interesting. She almost surprised herself when she called for Shachi and Wobke, but it remained silent. If she could only find companions again of her own kind...

On the way home, Tom knew that he had done the right thing, but he did not feel as happy about the day as he should have. Greg and Curt had been elated with the achievement, but Sheila had sensed his subdued mood when he returned. "It was horrible to refuse any physical contact," he said. "You know how she can beg for it and slide up on the side. She had done so well and we were so far away from anything she knew that it really hurt to deny her even the slightest pet." Sheila nodded with understanding, but nevertheless emphasized that he had been correct. "It must've been hard on her for that moment, but at least you talked to her. You did maintain contact. It's in her own interest that she doesn't slide up on small boats. This first trip outside the fjord was a big step for her. That's why she may have hoped for a physical reward. Soon, Tom, she'll no longer expect it when she's out at sea. You've had the hardest moment today." Tom gave her a warm hug. "You really helped me, Sheila, and I'm also happy that Curt was with me today. I might not have been strong enough to resist her otherwise. Do you think it's acceptable when I go to her tonight?" "I think it'll do her good to end this day positively with you. She looked a little depressed when she returned."

350

Gunda was already hovering near the end of the floating dock. Tom saw her lift her head in the lights. As he knelt before her, the orca looked up at him. She did not rise high as if fearing another refusal. Tom swallowed. All his senses told him how his whale felt. He held both his hands out to her. Slowly, but without hesitation, the orca glided closer and gently lay her chin in his hands. Tom emitted a soft squeak. Gunda answered. She slightly opened her mouth as he probed her lips with his thumbs. Gently, he massaged her gums. As he pulled slightly, Gunda rose up towards his face and nudged him subtly.

Tom felt tears sting behind his eyes. He was so grateful that Gunda had at least understood he had not rejected her, even though he had disappointed her. He pressed his face tight to the orca's head and caressed her tenderly. "My Gunda, you're such a brave girl and so forgiving at the same time. We subject you to plans of which you have no knowing. How can we tell you that it's for your own good? You blindly give us all your trust, and then we deny what is more important to you than anything else: affection and comfort. Gunda, we love you dearly." Tom felt the nudges of the orca in response to his tight hug, and lovingly rubbed cheeks with her.. He held her for a while, wanting the precious moment to last. He wondered how few more of these moments they would be sharing together.

Tuschka was grateful for her friend's affection. Especially at the end of this day, she needed the reassurance of a loving companion. As the man released his grip, she gracefully slid back, still looking at him. She called back and forth with him for a moment longer. Then, she watched him walk away on the dock. Whatever had happened, all was good between them.

Curt and Tom were excited about Gunda's progress. The orca seemed to take each step more easily than the previous one, and it was a milestone to have taken her two miles beyond the mouth of the fjord. Time had come to expand the distance rapidly and build on her stamina. It was easy for the trainers to read where and when Gunda felt at ease. The more relaxed she was, the more she ventured away to satisfy her curiosity. In new areas, she tended to follow the inflatable closely.

In the fjord, the transmitter on Gunda's dorsal fin had proved to work well. The device was attached by two suction cups on either side of her dorsal fin. A strap over the front edge of the fin connected them to prevent them from sliding. To prevent loss, they were also connected to a strap around her body, behind her pectoral fins. Every time the orca surfaced, a signal could be picked up. The team was happy with Gunda's explorations, but they had recalled her every once in a while to keep minimal control over her and to be able to bring her back or call her away from potential danger. Gradually, they made the intervals between the recalls longer.

* * *

351

Tuschka took deep breaths during her high arched surfacings. She was porpoising behind the fast moving boat on a clear autumn morning. It felt good to pump her flukes and feel her heart beat faster. Only recently had she experienced the delight of building speed and keeping on going with no other limits than her own physical strength. The outings with the boat had become daily routine and as her confidence grew, so did her curiosity and playfulness. The sea was full of small and larger distractions and Tuschka did not hesitate to explore them as long as she could see or hear her friends' vessel.

As the boat slowed down, Tuschka veered a little sideways to clear the stern and felt herself being pushed up and forward by the stern wake. As the wave went underneath her, she suddenly lost speed and felt her body slide down on the backside of the wave. She waited for another one, but none came. Ahead of her, she saw the big V-shaped wave roll forward. She kicked her flukes, went after it, and pushed herself over the crest. Immediately, she felt herself being lifted from behind and carried forward again. This time, she wanted the moment to last longer and sped up a bit to stay just ahead of the wave. Tuschka felt herself gain speed with the slightest effort, but soon she was too far ahead to feel the push of the wave. When it came up again from behind, she immediately picked up speed to repeat the game. It did not last very long. The wave flattened out and lost its strength rapidly. Tuschka was startled for a moment when she did not see the boat where she had expected it in front of her, but the engine sound told her instantly that it was approaching her from behind.

Sheila and Tom were delighted when they saw their whale play with the stern wake. The orca was so absorbed in her game that she seemed unaware of gaining on the boat while in pursuit of the wave. "She's surfing, look! She discovered how to ride a wave!" Tom exclaimed with excitement. "She's going after the wave again… soon it will lose its strength… we must give her more!" Sheila suggested. After the orca's game was over, Tom waited until he had Gunda's attention again. He approached her, but hesitated to build up speed again. "Sheila, I wonder if it's wise to stimulate this behavior. She may try it with other boats too." The woman shook her head. "It's a possibility, but orcas are known to sometimes ride wakes. I don't think there would be much harm in it, especially if she were in the company of other orcas. However, we should perhaps not stimulate it too much. Let's see what she does when we do another speed exercise on the way back."

Tom stopped close to Gunda and put the engine in idle. They were about 20 miles from home and about to turn around. He tossed the orca some fish and gave her the signal for a break. She moved a few times back and forth beside the boat as if she was not ready to stop, then disappeared on the dive. Sheila dropped the hydrophone to monitor underwater sounds and Gunda's vocalizations in relation to them. This far into October, it was not impossible for orcas to enter the area.

The signal of the tracking device would tell the two trainers in which direction to look for their orca in case she ventured out of sight. Gunda had gained enough confidence to venture more than a mile away, and in a medium chop, the unpredictable wanderings of the young adult female made it hard to keep a constant eye on her.

Tuschka had been exploring a while when a faint splashing sound alerted her. She stopped swimming and listened. It had to be something relatively big. The sound of the idling engine reassured her. Tuschka refrained from vocalizing. Not yet knowing what it was, she did not want to spook it, nor reveal her presence. She slowly moved in the direction of the sound and came upon a small bed of seaweed. While hovering at the surface, she waited. Two gulls landed near her, but she ignored them. A moment later, Tuschka caught a glimpse of a rounded, spotted form. Something about it looked familiar and she slightly changed position in hopes of a better look. There it was again. The fat creature moved gracefully among the strands of weed and she saw it head for the surface with a silvery fish in its mouth. As the animal shook its head to tear a chunk from the fish, Tuschka recognized the splashing sound that had drawn her attention. Something told her she had nothing to fear from the pudgy animal. As it shook its fish, the gulls competed for scraps. Tuschka was tempted to join in.

Suddenly, Tuschka recognized the creature as a harbor seal. Vague images crossed her mind of weed and rocks and orca companions flushing and chasing them. The prospect of a chase excited her. Without a warning, she darted forward. The seal was so startled it barely evaded imminent collision with the charging whale. Tuschka veered sharply in pursuit and briefly touched the seal's rear fins. Seeing that it was about to leave the protection of the weed bed, the seal turned around sharply and dived, seeking refuge in the weed and the dark. Tuschka followed but was slightly hindered by the strands of weed that dragged on her fins. She had lost sight of her target and listened. The seal had to be near. She faced down and echolocated. It was fairly deep and the weed was floating. For a moment, she wondered if the seal was still hiding near or had escaped on its dive. Then, silence struck her. She did not hear the boat...

Tom and Sheila were a little tense. They had seen her moving off, but for nearly 15 minutes, they had had no sign of the orca. They wondered if she could have moved beyond audible range of her blows. Sheila turned on the direction finder, but received no signal. The two scanned for blows, but saw none. Sheila had suggested moving in the direction where they had seen her last, but after a hundred yards, Tom shut down the engine. It would not only help him to hear blows; it was also a strategy to have the whale look for them. Accidentally, they had discovered that Gunda was comfortable as long as she stayed in contact with the boat. Her acoustic range seemed to be the invisible limit for her wanderings.

When the engine was shut down, the orca had obviously felt uneasy and had always retraced her steps and spyhopped to search for the boat by eye. Since it was part of the plan to interfere with the orca's activities as little as possible, Tom was happy to have this silent recall tactic.

Tom and Sheila were expecting to see the orca pop up any time, but instead, they saw some turbulence ahead between themselves and the shore. Tom immediately picked up his binoculars and noticed the drifting weed. He felt a wave of relief when Gunda's head broke the surface in a big spyhop. She was already halfway between the seaweed and the boat. The relief was clearly mutual. Gunda made an energetic dive and headed straight towards them. The two trainers were happy that no harm had come to their whale and also that the direction finder was functioning. Yet they wondered what had kept Gunda so interested.

As Tuschka rose up towards the surface, the sight of the familiar vessel reassured her. It was not very far away. When only two yards separated them, she rose up again and made eye contact with her friends. She no longer expected to be touched, but she was hoping for some other sign of acknowledgement. Both Tom and Sheila made their own versions of her calls and Tuschka immediately started to challenge them by changing her sounds. She was always excited when she was leading a game. She was the master in this one and always included one or more sounds that her friends could not, or only barely, imitate. She loved to watch them make all kinds of sounds and grimaces in their attempts to copy her. As the man's responses came at longer intervals, Tuschka sensed that he was growing tired of the game. She did not want to frustrate him and she quickly made the call that he knew best.

Tom and Sheila had burst into laughter. They looked at each other knowingly. Gunda loved to have the initiative, to have them respond to her "cues". How strikingly similar were their minds. Just like them, Gunda wanted to end her 'sessions' positively. Tom felt very satisfied. Whenever the orca returned on a silent engine, she perceived it as her own initiative. It was a great way to keep Gunda focused on the boat from time to time. Without the orca expecting a reward, there was room for more spontaneous interaction to make the experience enjoyable for her. Yet the trainers carefully avoided too much spontaneous interaction at sea. They did not want the whale to explore other vessels for possible fun, especially those of sports fisherman, who tended to drift in small boats during spring and summer.

Tom put the engine in gear and sped up. He wanted to give the orca a good workout on the way home. As usual, Tuschka started to follow right behind the stern. She had quickly learned that it was much easier to keep up right behind the boat than to stay at its side. But as soon as she saw the two- to three-foot stern wake, she veered aside and porpoised to get ahead of it. She was lifted up from behind and felt the wave's pushing force. With minimal effort she rode it down and gained speed. Tuschka moved her flukes to gain even more speed. It was exhilarating to go so fast with so little effort. She leaped into the air in pure joy, porpoised ahead of the wave and then glided, waiting for it to lift her up again. Tuschka began to time it better and better. She pierced the wave, rode its crest and then gained speed to take full advantage of the surf. It went on and on. She squealed her delight and barely noticed fatigue.

Tom and Sheila were in awe. It was a magnificent sight to see the young mature female break the surface of the wave head on and ride it down, gaining speed with so little effort and so much grace. They had noticed how fast she perfected the skill and were thrilled to see the beautiful mastery of her sleek and strong body. Her smooth glossy skin reflected the soft sunlight. She arched perfectly while porpoising towards the crest of the wave. The two watched the water run up her white chin and part like waves of glass. Beautiful spray came off the trailing edge of her sturdy fin. This was an orca in her element. For a moment, they forgot that this beautiful creature, the top predator of the ocean, was still in their care.

They continued on for several miles. Tom and Sheila slowed down to give Gunda some rest, but close to the entrance of the fjord, they sped up again to share the joy once more. Gunda glided inside the net without resistance and swam up to the end of the dock where Curt waited with fish. Tom and Sheila were struck by what they saw. They could barely believe that the docile orca at the dock was the magnificent whale that had accompanied them home. More than before they realized the discrepancy between the life they had offered her and what it was meant to be. It comforted them to know they were finally working for her good, even though they could never undo the past.

33.
The Reunion

"Ieeeeuu".. Tuschka woke with a start. Just before daybreak she had dozed off near the net, but now all her senses were alert. The sound was distant, but clear. In an instant she had recognized the voice of her own kind. That in itself doubled her heart rate, but there was more ... It was so familiar. It was not Shachi, Wobke, or Durak. Where had she heard it before? "Ieeeeuu .... Ieeeeuu..," a different voice echoed. Tuschka listened intently. "Ieeeuuee.. Ieeeuuee.." This was a slightly different call, immediately followed by the voice of a young calf. Tuschka blew and quickly sank down again. Fragments of memories from days long gone came to the surface, but she could not yet piece them together. Excitement and confusion overwhelmed her. She felt an urge to call out to them, but apprehension held her back. They were unmistakably of her own kind, but that did not necessarily mean they would welcome her. In a flash, Tuschka remembered the initial tension between herself and Shachi. Only gradually had she changed from a barely tolerated presence to a subordinate, but appreciated, companion.

More voices traveled the sea towards Tuschka's ears. There was a whole pod of them. Among a variety of calls, some were repeated many times. Tuschka had a strong sense of recognition and with it the longing to attract their attention, but fear of an adverse response kept her silent. The voices came from beyond the fjord. Tuschka was not even aware that she drew from deeply rooted memories when she interpreted the sounds. The pod was heading north in a loose formation, calling each other to keep in acoustic contact. She knew they were foraging. A soft miniature moan escaped from her blowhole when the calls of the pod grew fainter. Tuschka did not want them to leave. When they finally grew silent, Tuschka felt desolate. How she had wanted to be with them. In a strange way, she felt left behind.

Greg turned over in his bed when a faint squeak woke him. Two hydrophones had been hooked up so the team could listen round the clock for orca vocalizations. Speakers were mounted in the cabins. As soon as any calls would be heard, they would tape the sounds and accurately record Gunda's behavior. Just as the scientist began to wonder whether he had been dreaming, he heard two other weak calls. In a few seconds, the man was out of bed; he switched the tape recorder on and ran outside to wake the others. In less than five minutes,

357

the team had assembled outside. They kept quiet while they watched the orca, so as not to distract her. The whale was not visible and they waited in eager anticipation of her next blow, or perhaps vocalization...

After what seemed a long time, they heard Gunda blow. The miniature droplets in her breath reflected the light. She was hovering close to the 'gate' in the net. Her dives were long. It was obvious that something under water had her undivided attention. After an hour, and chilled to the bone, they went back inside. Bundled up, Tom reappeared to remain on watch for the next couple of hours. From now on, someone would be on guard during the night to listen and watch for anything that might hint at the presence of other orcas.

It was a bleak day for Tuschka. There was no trip with the boat to lift her spirits and she ate barely half her daily ration. She was withdrawn and did not realize how much she was still absorbed by her early morning experience. Somewhere out there were others of her kind....

No one had missed the sudden change in Gunda's behavior. She was not very interested in a training session of any kind. She seemed depressed and slightly agitated at the same time. It was not unusual for the orca to hover near the 'gate' when she wanted to go for a trip outside, but this day she was glued to the spot. The trainers regretted the order to keep Gunda inside. Now that orcas had entered the area, no one wanted to risk an unfriendly encounter with unfamiliar orcas. Ideally, free-ranging whales would enter the fjord and explore it once Gunda would have revealed her presence. Then, when the ensuing interaction seemed friendly, would they open the net. Right now, Gunda would have to wait for her next trip until that friendly meeting or until no orcas were near.

"It has made a deep impression on her," Curt said. "I wonder why she kept silent, except for that very soft moan near the end of the tape." Greg had made a copy of the recording for Bjorn to analyze. Although he had tapes with calls of various pods, including B pod, he had not been able to reliably identify the pod by the scarce faint calls. "We need a better recording than this to determine which pod went by. It doesn't surprise me that it has a big emotional impact on Gunda hearing others of her kind. Why she remained silent, we can only guess. Most likely it wasn't her pod. In fact, I hope it wasn't. If she doesn't even talk to them, what can we do?" We should at least attempt to identify any pod that passes by during the day.

* * *

After several days had passed, faint distant squeaks alerted Tuschka again. She listened intently, but silence followed. "Eeeeuuueee.." The sound sent a shiver through Tuschka's body. This was one of her own calls! Before she realized what that meant, two others followed in response: "Eeeeuuueee.. Eeeeuuueee..." She pressed her rostrum into the net as if it would bring her closer to the sounds. A turmoil of emotions overwhelmed her. There was an indefinable mixture of excitement and apprehension, of recognition and confusion. "Eeeeuuueee.." There it was again... her call, so strikingly familiar. There was no holding back for Tuschka. Unable to resist her urge for contact, she answered: "Eeeeuuueee…." Her voice traveled out of the fjord and beyond..

Only moments passed when another call sent a chill down Tuschka's spine. There was no doubt about its meaning. It was a strong and imperative demand for silence. Tuschka felt her throat constrict in a wave of panic and impotence. These calls.. this voice.. it had spoken to her before... There was something about it that made her feel close and yet, it had told her to keep silent. Now that she felt an urge for contact, stronger than ever before, they did not want her to speak. Tuschka could not bare the silence, but the command had come from a whale that would admit no contradiction, from a female, who would overshadow Shachi. At a loss, Tuschka waited.

Furka called for silence. It was the distant, but clear call of her own pod that had pierced her ears. They were foraging and using the typical signature call of the pod to keep in touch with each other. But this call had come from the direction of the fjord and from a much larger distance than the matriarch expected from any of her pod members. After several seconds of silence, the matriarch voiced her pod's signature call again, clear and loud.

Tuschka froze. The orca had made her call again, but none of the other orcas echoed it. Tuschka sensed that the call was to announce the pod's presence. In some way, it was an invitation to make contact, but with whom? Vague memories took shape of greetings with other pods. Tuschka was still confused by the earlier resolute command that had followed her own call. The ensuing silence hurt more than Tuschka could bear. She felt so drawn to these orcas that she could no longer hold back. With a slight tremble that betrayed apprehension, Tuschka returned the call. Almost without delay, an answer came, but this time, the voice had a different intonation. It was no longer an announcement... there was a questioning ring to it and it was unmistakably directed at her.

Tuschka's heart pounded. She was excited and confused at the same time. This voice was familiar as if she had known this female before, and yet she could put no name to her. A jumble of contradictory emotions and fragmented memories prevented any coherent thoughts. The prospect of unknown orcas approaching her frightened Tuschka, and at the same time she drew a mysterious consolation from her contact with this female authority. Curiosity and longing were stronger than her fear and Tuschka copied the matriarch's probing call. A reply came and Tuschka answered. They continued vocalizing back and forth, and with every call, the matriarch sounded closer than before. Even when less than a mile seemed to separate them, Tuschka did not hear any other voices.

Was the dominant female approaching her by herself or were the others with her? As confused as she was, Tuschka felt tempted to echolocate, but lacked the courage.

When she came to the surface to breathe, a series of blows ahead left no doubt. A whole pod was coming, approaching her abreast. Tuschka suddenly felt vulnerable and insecure. She backed up, seeking protection behind the dock, but she irresistibly kept answering the matriarch, whose voice conveyed no threat and whose every call gave Tuschka a flare of hope...

Furka and all members of her pod heard the answer coming from the direction of the fjord. They all recognized the typical call, but the voice surprised them and so did the direction and distance from which it had come. Without a hint from their leading female, the orcas gathered around her. They were all there, and yet someone was calling as if she was one of them. Not only Furka had picked up the slight tremble and anxiety in the call. Was the distant whale imitating them? The ensuing calls conveyed more confidence, but they could not comprehend what orca would act like this instead of answering with the call of its own pod.

Slowly, Furka began to move towards the entrance of the fjord. The matriarch was not certain whether the mysterious orca was by herself, but the voice had radiated too little confidence for her to expect any problem. The strange orca intrigued her. It obviously wanted contact as it kept answering, but it made no attempt to come closer. As soon as the pod rounded the cliff that marked one side of the entrance to the small fjord, the voice of the unknown orca sounded clearer. By tradition they lined up abreast with their matriarch slightly ahead, just as they would in preparation of meeting a new pod or one they had not met in a long time.

Furka echolocated regularly as they advanced into the small fjord. A fairly steep rise in the sea floor made her slow down and be attentive to the depth and tide. She spyhopped and noticed several vessels, floating close to shore. Furka made another call. The answer was close now and had taken on the sound of a plea. The uncertainty and apprehension of the strange orca were almost tangible. Somehow, her craving for contact was even stronger, as she kept on answering. Furka sensed the orca was in distress, but it confused the matriarch as to why the orca had so specifically sought contact with them instead of calling out to her own pod.

Suddenly, the returning echoes both startled and confused Furka's pod. The silence was broken by several startled squeaks. The fragmented echoes revealed a big net dead ahead of them with several solid vertical bars further behind. The pod had encountered nets to hold fish in fjords before, but this one was far bigger and stretched all the way to the bottom. There were no fish inside, nor any of the sounds that accompanied similar nets when they were set and pursed at sea.

The next call startled them all as it pierced their ears. It was loud and compelling, and more personal than a strange orca could possibly make. Yet it had not come from any of them, but from the other side of the net.

Tuschka heard and felt the sonar pulses from her position behind the dock. The sudden calls of confusion, surprise, and a hint of fright, startled Tuschka too. She had done nothing but answer the dominant female's call and wondered what had caused so much disturbance among the approaching orcas. It unsettled her even more. Among the brief burst of vocalizations, Tuschka recognized the voice of a young juvenile orca, calling for reassurance. The gentle, comforting answer struck Tuschka with a shock... this voice ... Deeply rooted memories bolted to the surface, bridging the past 8 years in a second. Before Tuschka was even fully aware of the situation, she came forward from behind the dock and blurted the call of her childhood, one of the first she had learned, but hadn't used during all her years away from the sea.

An answer came.. soft and questioning, not from the pod's leader, but from the calf's mother. Excitement and hope flared up in Tuschka, but a wave of sadness followed. Although she could not yet fully comprehend the situation, she knew the voice had come from the orca that had been closer to her than any other ever had, the one who had nurtured and loved her.. , but there had been no recognition in her answer. Tuschka called again, urgent, pressing, as if to wring acknowledgement from whom she knew was her own mother. Suddenly, she became aware of the net against her rostrum. It sent a chill down her spine and revived a trauma from the far past. Separation, parting of the ways, helplessness, she was reliving it all. She began to whine and plead and as the fragmented memories began to piece together, dark shadows loomed up in the greenish gloom.

Tarka stiffened when she heard the loud and unexpected call. The unknown orca had specifically called for her.. as if it were her calf! But the strange whale was no calf. Its voice sounded more mature and the echoes of her own sonar revealed the form and size of an adult female. Yet, there was a familiar ring to the call, something that touched her maternal feelings. The situation baffled Tarka, but she could not refrain from answering. She gave a soft probing, questioning squeak and glided closer to the leading female. The mysterious orca addressed her again. There was urgency in her voice, a need for contact.

Before Tarka could even decide how to respond, a train of vocalizations followed. The orca behind the net was pleading and moaning, voicing distress and helplessness at the same time. But these were no calls of an anonymous whale in need of help. The female cried for them, but more than on the pod, she called upon her.., in the role of mother... Her two-year-old calf huddled close as she glided forward. Tarka began to discern the maze of the net and the black shadow behind it began to take shape. The sight of the female's rostrum, pressed against the maze, made Tarka shiver. It stirred memories that she did not want to relive, but they began to tear open an old wound.

It was already afternoon when the first loud call had startled Greg. Realizing it was Gunda's call he relaxed, but kept concentrated on the speaker. Soft and distant, an echo came. Excitement flared and waned as he figured that it was probably reverberation of the sound against the rocky walls of the fjord. The scientist froze as another distant sound followed almost a minute of silence. This could not be an echo. Then Gunda's voice rang in his ears again. He listened intently and felt his heart beat faster as it became clear that the distant calls were no echoes, but exact copies of Gunda's call by a wild whale. He punched the record button and ran outside.

Gunda was near the 'gate' in the net. Tom came running towards him. Greg's look conveyed so much amazement that no explanation was necessary. Curt joined them. "Should we take a boat out and try to identify that pod out there?" Greg raised his hand in denial. "I don't want to interfere now. Gunda has acoustic contact with them. With luck, they'll come closer and enter the fjord. Let's mount the spotting scope on that hill behind my cabin. From there, we can see the mouth of the fjord and observe Gunda as well. Tom, please bring that portable radio, to listen to the vocalizations while we watch up there."

The team sat watching impatiently, bundled up in the cold wind. Shortly after the distant calls suddenly sounded louder, Curt spotted blows in the mouth of the fjord. Excitement shut out the chilly gusts, but dread filled them as they saw Gunda move away and hug the rear side of the dock. All hope was on Gunda's memory and longing for contact. If she were to hide in silence, there would be no hope for contact with the wild pod. But the calls continued... both close and far. If Gunda was hiding, it was not in silence.

The orcas lined up abreast when they were about half a mile away from Gunda's enclosure. Greg and Tom took turns at the scope, straining to count the whales and to find any recognizable features. "There are two males," Tom yelled as the whales surfaced almost in unison. "A big one and a smaller one. Maybe .. perhaps .. they are B1 and B7!" Greg tapped him on the shoulder. "Don't jump too quickly on a few leading edges, Tom. Even at close range, it'll be hard for us to be certain. We must take pictures of them as best we can if ... they come closer and daylight permits." In his heart, Greg shared Tom's thoughts, but as a scientist he was always on guard for wishful thinking.

Tuschka saw the leading orcas glide into view: two big females, one with a calf tucked under her pectoral fin. She looked at the whale with the baby and saw what her ears had already told her: her contours, the familiar shapes of her white parts, the two old scars on her saddle, in every aspect... her mother..! Tuschka pushed forward, straining against the net in an attempt to bridge the few yards that still separated them. But her mother was not looking at her.

Tarka was grateful when Furka called her away. The leading female felt uneasy in the proximity of a net that held a distressed whale. Feeling more responsible for her pod than the fate of the victim inside it, she wanted to turn and leave the

362

small fjord. As Tarka averted her head to veer away from the frightening scene, Tuschka saw her mother's intention and despair washed over her. She called out to Tarka, conveying her urge for contact with such intensity that she could not ignore it. The compelling call of the orca facing her forced the mother orca to look. In Tarka's mind past and present began to meld.

Their eyes met.. Tuschka read confusion in her mother's eyes and called again, softer and pleading for comfort. Tarka saw the other female's eyes, wide with longing and hope. She had looked into these eyes before, heard these calls before, and seen this rostrum behind a net that had so cruelly torn them apart.... Hesitant, trembling, full of puzzlement, Tarka voiced the name of her long-lost calf. She answered, calling her by name again, conveying hope and encouragement. Tarka read the joy of recognition from the orca in front of her. She repeated the name of her first-born with less hesitance, but still questioningly, asking for another confirmation. It came promptly, personal, leaving no room for doubt. Tarka measured the orca facing her. She was almost her own size and she was carrying new life. Yet in all other aspects, she was her baby: her voice even though more mature, her eye patches, and her eyes, but above all the way she had called her mother. Whatever had happened to her precious calf since that tragic moment was a mystery, but she was here.. her Tuschka!

Tuschka heard the change in her mother's voice and saw it in her eyes. Excitement and joy overwhelmed her as the big female glided towards her. Then, their rostrums touched. Tuschka nudged affectionately and felt the warm response. Gently, and tenderly, her mother called her by name. They caressed each other, rubbing and touching chins, ignoring the strands of netting between them. Tuschka opened her mouth a little and probed Tarka's rostrum with her tongue. The mother orca returned the tender gesture. Tuschka took the tip of her mother's tongue in her mouth and explored it, feeling its familiar features and nibbling on it as she had done in days long gone. She grew quiet as her mother comforted her with her gentle, caring voice. Tuschka felt like the juvenile again and relished the protecting and warm presence of her mother. She pressed close, wanting the moment never to pass.

Sheila grabbed Tom's arm as they heard a sudden burst of vocalizations. "What's happening?" she whispered. "Is it a good or bad sign?" Their eyes met briefly, conveying only questions. Several whales surfaced only 50 yards from the net. Two females were in the lead, one of them with a calf. The big male was not far behind. They dived again. The burst of sound was over, but it was not quiet. A few orcas kept on vocalizing, but it was no longer obvious who was talking, as the calls were equally clear.

Sheila held her breath as Gunda surfaced: she was right by the net, but one of the females was turning.... were the others intending to leave?! Loud whining distress calls filled the team with dread, especially the two trainers who had known the orca so intimately. They could almost feel her despair. Tom sat motionless, with clenched fists and Sheila brought her hands to her face and tensed with frustration as they saw Gunda strain and push against the net. Only moments later, the female with the calf came up, facing Gunda.... touching Gunda! "Tom... Tom... look....!" She lacked words to express what she saw. Tears were flowing freely as she saw the tender rubs and nudges of Gunda and the wild female. They were not only touched by what they saw. The soft affectionate calls radiated warmth and made them almost part of the experience. Tom wrapped his arm around Sheila's shoulder and pressed her close. His vision was blurred with brimming tears.

Furka looked back to see if all her pod members were following. Then, seeing Tarka's affectionate interaction with the whale behind the net, she stopped and watched them. Always vigilant, the seasoned female listened for any sounds that might hint at danger. There were none. With a calm voice, she addressed Tarka to come and follow, but the younger female paid her no heed. She was totally engrossed in her intimate activity. Furka did not press any further. The scene intrigued her.

A high-pitched call and the nudges of the little juvenile, asking for attention, made Tuschka aware of her surroundings again. Tarka reassured the little orca, taking it close to her other side. Tuschka understood that this baby was her mother's calf and she nudged her mother again, competing for the love of which she had been deprived for so long. She noticed the baby bob its head under her mother's belly. The scene revived memories of Shachi and Wobke. As Tarka drifted a little away, Tuschka became painfully aware of the net again. She pushed against it and urged Tarka to follow as she moved to the spot where she had passed through on previous trips out to sea.

The pod's typical greeting call sounded close by and took Tuschka by surprise. Another large female was facing her from only a few yards away. Tuschka took in her familiar appearance and recognized her voice as the one that had spoken to her first. This was the matriarch, their leader... This was ... Furka! Tuschka greeted her, but not with the signature call of the pod. With a shyness that showed submission, she called the dominant female by name. Furka remained silent. She was puzzled, but not as much as in the beginning. The sequence of events had not been lost on her. Somehow, this orca knew who they were and shared their calls. She had addressed Tarka as only a calf would and she had called her, Furka, by name and acknowledged her rank in the pod. But even more convincing was the response of Tarka, who had recognized this young adult female as her own calf, the juvenile they had considered lost for ever.

Furka glided a little closer and measured the orca on the other side of the net. There were familiar features in the female's voice and white patterns. Tuschka hovered in silence. The matriarch's appraising look was tangible and

Tuschka understood the importance of her acknowledgement. Fear of rejection made her tense, but she dared not make a sound. Then, calmly, the dominant female addressed her with a questioning intonation. Tuschka responded by showing submission and answered with a personal, but pleading, call that asked for acknowledgement and acceptance. A wave of relief washed over her as the matriarch came over, glided by, and touched her lightly with her pectoral fin. Tuschka was not yet certain if Furka had recognized her, but she had not rejected her.

Curt's voice broke the silence: "It is B4!, She must be... I saw the scars on her saddle and she's known to have a two-year-old calf." Greg took position behind the scope and watched intently, waiting for the mother orca to rise high enough for him to see a glimpse of her saddle. Finally, she rose a little, possibly playfully being pushed up from below by her juvenile offspring. Greg looked up with agreement showing in his eyes. "The vocalizations, the two males, the scars on her saddle, and this behavior..... It's hard to believe she wouldn't be B4." His voice trembled. Even the serious biologist was deeply moved. "It's almost too beautiful to be true, but I believe Gunda has found her family." He handed the video camera to Curt while he picked up his camera to get a couple of stills. "She's moving to the 'gate'!" Curt said. "Look at the other female.. She's facing Gunda now." A moment later, they saw the second female glide by Gunda while the big male came up to join her.

Tom stood up, raising his hands questioningly at the team leader. "She wants to join them. What do we do? We can't wait too long and risk the pod leaving. I couldn't bear to see Gunda experience her trauma again…" Greg nodded. "We will open the net. These whales won't harm her, but I'm curious whether she'll indeed join them and follow. Anyway, we have to attach the transmitter tag first and ready the large boat. We'll follow and record behavior as long as we can. The inflatable must be on board to be launched if she needs us."

Tom and Sheila ran down the hill to get the transmitter. They stopped halfway down the dock. Sheila shook her head. Gunda would not be in the mood to leave her companion and she was reluctant to ask. Tom understood, but time was critical. "I'll tap once or twice. If she doesn't respond, which I expect, we'll have to use the rowboat."

Tom knelt down and tapped the water firmly. He saw a slight turn in Gunda's head, but the orca did not move away from the net. A few seconds later, she spyhopped and made the pitiful call of a whale that is not unwilling to cooperate, but unable because of fear or commitment to something else. Right now, it was undoubtedly the latter. Tom did not push any further. They quickly took the rowboat that was tied just outside the net and managed to drag it over the floats of the net. Tom took the oars and approached Gunda from behind. He stopped when they were only half a body length away from her. Sheila made splashing sounds with her hand in the water to attract Gunda's attention. Even if the orca did not respond, they would not be sneaking up on her.

Gunda surfaced and slightly bent her head sideways. She was obviously aware of their presence. Then, she spyhopped and vocalized. "She wants us to take her out" Sheila said. "That'll make her more receptive to wearing the tag." She signaled Tom with her hand to maneuver the boat alongside the whale.

The female on the other side of the net bobbed her head in annoyance. Sheila shivered as the big male did two big tail lobs. "They aren't very happy with us here," Tom said. "Be quick Sheila and we're out of here." Gunda did not move away, but her frequent blows and vocalizations gave the impression that she was impatient and slightly agitated. Sheila made soft imitations of some of Gunda's calls to reassure her. As the orca calmed somewhat, she fitted the tag. In a couple of weeks, the metal attachments would corrode, causing the straps to become disconnected and fall off.

Both Sheila and Tom realized this might be their last time with Gunda. They laid their hands on her soft, smooth skin, and caressed her tenderly. The two trainers knew they did not have her undivided attention, but there could not be a better reason for the lack of it. They looked at the female with the juvenile, Gunda's mother.... Who would have thought that they would ever see them together and be so close. Tom saw the other members of the pod and was impressed by their number and the sound of their blows. He smiled at the youngsters and realized that not all of them had known Gunda.

The magnificent male orca was approaching slowly as if keeping watch so no harm would come to Gunda. Tom let his hand glide over the smooth front edge of her dorsal fin, held on to the tip for a second and then let go. Sheila lifted her hand and nodded. Visibly moved, Tom took up one of the oars to back up and upon Curt's signal, he moved over to untie the net. "Take good care of her," he whispered, looking at the orca family into which Gunda had been born so long ago and that had existed only in his imagination, until now.

Although her human friends had only part of her attention, Tuschka appreciated their presence and caresses. She had not wanted to ignore the tap on the water, but she did not want to leave her mother's side and had seen no way but to refuse. Now that they had come to her, they had reassured her of their friendship and affection. Tuschka did not have the faintest idea that there might be a parting of the ways. On the contrary, when she saw her trainer working on the net, she was excited about the prospect of entering the fjord and being amidst these precious companions.

A much bigger whale appeared from the dimly lit waters. Tuschka saw his tall erect dorsal fin and huge broad flippers. He was a magnificent male in his prime. As he glided alongside the leading female, gentle and caring, Tuschka knew he was Sigurd. His demeanor was calm and confident and his presence reassuring.

She felt excitement as he gracefully glided forward. Furka did not call him back. He stopped just short of her and made eye contact. They looked at each other in suspense, their rostrums only inches apart. He had seen and heard what most pod members had witnessed. There was something strikingly familiar about this beautiful female. She acted as one of them.. as Tarka's offspring...

Sigurd eyed the net that separated the young adult female. It worried and frustrated him at the same time. He had seen this before and it had ended in a tragedy. As images from the past surfaced, he felt an urge to free the hapless female. He dived down in hopes of finding an opening in the net, but it went down all the way to the sea floor. He followed it to the right, then to the left, but there was no opening. He saw the orca inside follow him with her eyes.

Tugs on the net disturbed Sigurd and focused his attention again on the small vessel above. He felt an urge to charge it, but it was inside the net. Instead, he vented his frustration with two powerful tail lobs. The agitated gesture startled Tuschka, but it was not directed at her. The big male seemed as impatient to get together as she.

Sigurd hovered close. The earlier scene inside the net had confused him. The people in the small vessel had touched Tuschka and put a strange object around her dorsal fin. Yet she had allowed it all without the slightest sign of distress. The tugs on the net had Sigurd on edge again, but he made no move as long as she seemed not to be disturbed by them. Then, totally expected by Tuschka, but a complete surprise for the large bull, part of the net fell down. The opening was large enough to give free passage to a mature male orca, but it was small in Sigurd's perception.

Tuschka saw the impressive figure of Sigurd in front of her. Nothing was in between them now... She hovered motionless. Her heart was pounding in her chest. In one way, she felt strongly drawn to them, but in another way, she felt vulnerable without the protection of the net. She cast a glance towards the boat. It was near, inside the net, but not buzzing ahead as usual. Tuschka addressed the big male facing her. His answer was gentle, but urging. Then she saw her mother just beside the opening, moving forward a little until her head appeared from behind the net. Her whining call conveyed wanting and anxiety at the same time.

Tuschka was overwhelmed by all that was happening, but she needed no further encouragement. She glided forward and delicately touched the side of her mother's head. Tarka's tender nudge released all the pent-up longing of many years. Tuschka was overjoyed. She rubbed and caressed her mother exuberantly and her excited squeals melded with Tarka's reassuring calls.

Soon, the two females glided side by side and as they turned away from the net, Sigurd gracefully joined Tuschka's other flank. The big male was impressive, larger then any she could remember. He radiated confidence and security. In the presence of Sigurd and her mother the dumbfounded orca felt an inexpressible fulfillment, unlike anything her human friends and even Shachi and Durak had been able to give. Guided by the two caring whales, they approached the matriarch and the other curious members of the waiting pod.

In the dim light that penetrated from the low autumn sun, the black shadows of other whales appeared. There were adult females and several juveniles. Almost simultaneously there was an outpouring of vocalizations and Tuschka recognized familiar voices among them. Furka was the first to come near. The matriarch took another good look at her regained pod member. Then, she swerved gracefully aside to join the others. Tuschka closely followed Tarka's lead. She recognized Tamara in the female that came forward to greet her mother. The older whale showed a mixture of surprise and curiosity as did the others that came over to her. With the first pieces of the puzzle in place, other pieces followed quickly: there was Shaka, Annika, and Skaade...., but she could not recall the adolescent female and the youngsters that accompanied them.

It was a grand moment when Gunda glided forward to meet the wild male and female facing her just outside the opening in the net. There were few vocalizations, but the ones they heard spoke of tender affection. All members of the release team were emotionally moved, but none of them as much as Tom and Sheila, when they saw Gunda and the wild female touch rostrums. Their beloved orca was obviously overjoyed as she rubbed and nudged the other whale's head. The two white chins glistened yellowish in the late sun. Gunda rolled and pushed and caressed what had to be her own mother. The reunion left an unforgettable impression. Each team member had learned about orcas through different experiences, but they all knew the species' capacity and need of strong social attachment. In his or her own way, everyone shared in the joy of the two whales.

Tom's memories drifted back to his first night with Gunda. Seeing her now with her mother on one side and the majestic male on her other, he envisioned her early youth. He needed only to look at the healthy playful calf at the wild mother's flank. It made him realize what tragedy had brought Gunda in his path and how the brave juvenile had pulled through her ordeal. How forgiving and gentle had Gunda been all those years.... It was a weird thought that he had been her closest friend for an even longer time than those of her own kind, than this female that had brought her forth and nurtured her. These orcas were the family to which she belonged and with them Gunda would pick up where she left off and lead again the rich, challenging, and purposeful life of a free-ranging orca. As much as he had shared her grief in the past, he shared her joy now.

The other orcas had not missed the familiar calls of the unexpected arrival, nor Tarka's acceptance and intimate response. In many ways she behaved as

368

one of them. She knew them and radiated something unique to the pod. But they did not all share Tarka's unreserved sympathy, especially two of the adult females. They had not been affected as much as the older orcas by the tragedy of the past. Tuschka's voice and pigment patterns stirred faint memories, but these were blurred by their concern about the newcomer's rank. Annika had two offspring and Skaade was in advanced pregnancy. There should be no question about her rank, but the young female looked big and healthy with few fresh scars. They wondered if she would challenge them.

Tuschka sensed tension in Skaade and Annika. She felt uncomfortable coming closer to them. Something in their attitude was reminiscent of her early days with Shachi, who had become more accepting once she had acknowledged her authority. Tuschka hugged Tarka's side, like a juvenile trying to draw protection from her mother. It did not change anything.... Tuschka did not realize that it was her size and age that made her a potential challenge. Whatever it was, the prospect of enmity or rejection was more frightening now than anything else. Without hesitation, Tuschka avoided their gaze and bent her head slightly down to signal her submission. Soft and hesitant, she asked for acknowledgement. The answer was not overly friendly, but it conveyed their acceptance. The tension abated and Tuschka met their eyes briefly. The two females were relieved, although they were not yet fully convinced that their new companion would not change her mind.

Tuschka was happy when her mother veered away from Annika and Skaade. Tamara joined Tarka's other side, but she radiated nothing to fear for. Of the older females, she was by far the most lenient, probably because she was Tarka's mother. The grandmother whale was relaxed and her evident self-confidence left room in her heart for other emotions than the concerns of the younger females in the pod.

The sudden appearance of another male orca startled Tuschka. He was not as big as Sigurd, but obviously maturing. His approach was fast and straightforward with the brazen attitude typical of adolescent males. Tuschka slightly bumped into Tarka, and startled little Rheia as she tried to take refuge on her mother's other side. Tamara understood and let the little spooked female take position in between them. The young male wheeled, turned around underneath them and rose up slowly to take a good look at the attractive female. He eyed her intently as he glided by on his side.

Tarka had noticed her older offspring's apprehension and voiced a warning to him. Tuschka relaxed as she saw that the young bull respected the hint by keeping a slight distance. He surfaced on Tamara's side, dived down, and took position underneath them again. The tips of his flukes had begun to curl and his pectoral fins were noticeably larger than those of an adult female. Tuschka could not recall a male of his size in the pod, but his calls rang familiar and elicited memories of a rambunctious playmate.

The adolescent male rolled upright, his 4,5 foot fin only a yard beneath her belly. In a shaft of light as he swerved aside and upwards for air, her eye fell on a distinct scar in front and to the left of his dorsal fin. A shiver went through her and visions of danger and a bleeding wound. As he called to her again upon his dive, his identity began to dawn on her... This was Igor, only larger and more mature than she remembered him. Tuschka's eyes followed his every move. He was healthy and strong and unafraid. He was on his way to becoming a noteworthy bull, but he would have a long way to go to even approximate Sigurd in experience, refinement, and self-control. Tuschka returned a shy call, but her response obviously excited him. He made several agile turns near her and darted ahead. Tuschka sensed he was enticing her to play and although she felt a hint of temptation, she felt by no means confident enough to let go and move freely among the pod.

Tuschka had paid little attention to where they were and suddenly became aware that Furka had led them to the entrance of the fjord. It was not their position that suddenly made her restless. It was the absence of the familiar buzz of the vessel that used to be near. She spyhopped, but saw nothing. Dusk had fallen, and below the surface Tuschka could no longer see more than faint patches of white moving with her. Darkness in itself did not frighten her. The sounds around her assured her of the presence of her companions, but she had never left her enclosure at this time of day and without her human friends. She felt an urge to look for them back in the fjord, but was reluctant to part with her gentle and comforting escorts. She decelerated and when her mother and grandmother also slowed down, she turned in hopes they would stay with her. She wanted to bring her precious companions to her own safe place, where she would be welcomed and fed, but it was obvious that they had no intention of following. Tuschka heard the two females call after her and hesitated. Tarka nudged her flank and urged her to turn and come, but Tuschka squealed and pleaded with her mother to follow. Yet, she felt that she was trying her patience.

Tamara had turned to face the pod. The sounds grew weaker. They were falling behind. "Eeeuuee.." The sharp call left no doubt. The matriarch had noticed that the three orcas were hanging back and commanded them to join the pod. Tamara had no wish to resist. Nor had Tarka. She knew that Furka would come over if they did not respond quickly, but the leading female would never change her mind to follow the whims of her new pod member. Although the matriarch had accepted Tuschka's presence in the pod, a bond had yet to be reestablished. Tarka feared Furka might leave her behind if she continued to resist. There was no question for the mother orca as to how much Tuschka wanted her presence, but she dreaded a confrontation with the matriarch and the possibility of being forced to make a choice between the pod and her newly found daughter.

The orcas were about to leave the fjord when everyone tensed. "She's falling behind..," Curt said. "Look, it seems like she wants to turn back!" Greg sighed. "The other two females and that calf are still with her. Perhaps they'll try to make her change her mind," Tom said. Greg nodded. "If they care for her that much already, it would be a good sign. Either they want her to stay or Gunda is hesitant to leave." "She's looking back a bit," Sheila remarked with hope in her voice. "They must be communicating. It seems to me that she wants to go back, but not alone." "That's exactly what I'm thinking," the scientist confirmed, "but that pod isn't going to follow. Let's hope she will..."

"Eeuueee..." The call was closer now. Furka was already on her way. There was little time to lose. Tarka bumped Tuschka hard, then darted forward and cut sharply in front of her oldest offspring. The vocal reprimand, combined with the sudden and rough move of her mother, startled Tuschka. She had pushed it too far. Timidly and a little confused, she turned and followed in Tarka's wake. Tamara brought up the rear. There was no way back... Tuschka wondered what lay ahead, but deep inside, she was touched by the caring and concern that motivated her two companions.

34.
Bridging the Gap With the Past

For most of the night, Tuschka had stayed close to Tarka, little Rheia, and Tamara. She felt accepted by them and was most comfortable in their presence. By dawn, they were far north of the fjord in areas that were only vaguely familiar to her. The farther they swam, the less she was tempted to turn around, and not only because there was no one to guide her home. Even if there had been, Tuschka did not want to part with her caring companions. They were more than a comforting presence. The attachment among the members of the pod was tangible. Their trust was in each other and they formed a team that knew how to survive under the guidance of their experienced leader. Tuschka understood that she depended on them. She would be safe as long as they let her be part of their lives. But not every member in the pod welcomed her as much as her mother Tarka, Tamara, and Sigurd. The juveniles still considered her a visitor, while the young adult females saw her as a potential competitor for their rank. But Furka had accepted her and with the three orcas that supported her presence, she was backed by the majority of the pod's core members. It was a hopeful beginning.

As daylight began to penetrate below the surface, the bodies of the other whales gradually showed more detail. Having calmed down somewhat from the first enervating hours, Tuschka began to pay attention to the travel formation of the pod. The positions of the individual orcas told her much about their lineage and rank. Apart from little sister Rheia, it was only now that she began to understand how the other juveniles were related. Shaka traveled with an adolescent female, Kasimi, who was obviously her youngest offspring. At the age of seven and a half, Kasimi was the oldest of the whales that had been born into the pod since Tuschka had been taken. Not far to the left of Kasimi, swam Annika flanked by her two offspring: four-year-old Lukina, and Njord, a playful almost seven-year-old male who was approaching his mother in size. Skaade traveled at Shaka's other side with her younger brother Igor.

Tuschka looked at Furka, who was in the lead with Sigurd. She radiated the natural authority and mildness of an experienced leader, who had the unconditional trust of her pod members. She was in the lead as a true matriarch, with Sigurd by her side. The majestic male struck a special cord in Tuschka. He was magnificent in size and power. She watched his large curled flukes that moved effortlessly up and down. In their guidance no harm would come to her. Tuschka felt drawn toward him, but made no move to leave her position in between Tarka and Tamara. Somehow she felt it would not be appropriate.

As they continued on, Tuschka began to notice her empty stomach. She could not remember having gone without food for such a long time, nor to have made such a long uninterrupted swim. Gradually, she grew weary and it became increasingly difficult to rise and dive in unison with Tarka and Tamara. She envied little Rheia, who was partly dragged along in her mother's slipstream and even received an occasional sip of her mother's milk.

Having difficulty staying down much longer, Tuschka was the first to rise during the pod's long dive. Tarka followed her and soon it was obvious to the entire pod that their newest addition was having trouble keeping up. Furka slowed the pace somewhat, but she was determined to reach her destination soon. Scattered fish told her and her experienced companions that a large school of herring was ahead. The fish were the forerunners of many more that were about to leave a well-known fjord further north. Furka wanted to meet them relatively close to shore before the density of the school decreased. Tuschka wished she could catch the silvery delicacies, but none of the other orcas made an attempt. The pod kept moving on and there was no way she could spare the energy to even try.

Unexpectedly, Sigurd fell behind his mother and glided alongside Tamara. His presence excited Tuschka and boosted her energy. She wished to be closer to the impressive bull and shyly sought eye contact with him. For a little while the five whales rose and dived together. Sigurd noticed the attention of the young adult female and felt his heart quicken. Although she kept up with them, he was aware of her deep strained breath upon every surfacing. He observed her carefully and was surprised by her relative lack of stamina, which seemed in contradiction to her physical appearance. She looked healthy and well fed, even more so than most others in the pod. Even her advanced pregnancy did not clarify her reduced endurance. Another mystery that kindled his curiosity involved her submissive behavior in combination with the smooth beauty of a highly ranked female.

As Tuschka's spark of energy abated and weariness forced her to rise prematurely again, the large male glided underneath Tamara toward her. Tuschka saw him rise up by her side and followed him to the surface. Already on their way up, she found herself swimming more easily in the suction of his massive body. With a gentle voice, he greeted and encouraged her. Tuschka felt invigorated by his reassuring presence. Sigurd glided within touching range and trailed the tip of his pectoral fin along Tuschka's flank. He felt attracted to the fine female, but respected her advanced pregnancy and position in the pod. It was the tenderness and self-control in his subtle touch that filled Tuschka with a special sense of affection and security.

374

Not long after Sigurd had offered Tuschka the support of his wake, the fish came in denser concentrations. She snapped at some that came close, but refrained from charging after them. She had learned with the salmon in her enclosure that it was hard to catch individual fish without a trap to chase them into, and these fish were much smaller. A few disapproving signals in her direction discouraged Tuschka from showing her interest in the fish. Even the youngest whales in the pod were called to order when they engaged in an occasional chase. They were still traveling relatively tight and Furka wanted no unnecessary activities that might cause the fish to panic and disperse.

Upon the matriarch's signal, they began to space further apart. As Sigurd veered off a little, Tuschka followed him, but the big male motioned her to keep a distance. Although she did not fully understand the sudden change in the big male's behavior, she sensed no aggression or other sign of aversion in him. When Tuschka looked into the other direction, she noticed that Tarka had also created a greater distance. Uncomfortable without the immediate closeness of one of her trustworthy companions, she quickly moved over to join her mother and Rheia. When even her own mother acted the same as Sigurd, Tuschka was at a loss and cried for compassion. Tarka was puzzled by the relative ignorance and dependency of her adult offspring, but she sensed her need for guidance and let her maternal instincts prevail. Tuschka felt great relief when her mother acquiesced in her presence and snuggled close to her.

While the 13 orcas continued on, the density of the fish increased noticeably. The continuous vocalizations of the other members of the pod made Tuschka aware of their positions and movements. Gradually, they had formed a circle around the fish and were closing in. The gaps between her fellow pod members became smaller. They began to swim back and forth and flash their white bellies to make the fish turn away from them towards the center of an ever-tightening ball. The discipline among the pod was tangible. No one was feeding yet and the older females squealed commands to control positions and turns to breathe.

Tuschka shyly followed her mother's example. The silvery fish, moving in unison away from their white bellies, began to revive memories of anticipation, excitement, chasing, and feasting together. Together... The past began to meld with the present. They were with her, right here!... her familiar companions of hunts that suddenly seemed in the near past. Tuschka felt her confidence build and as she noticed the effect of her efforts, she began to participate with a vigor, that befitted a female of her size and power. Tarka noticed and watched her oldest offspring with satisfaction.

A sharp crashing sound blasted through the water. Furka had smacked her tail into the dense ball of fish, killing dozens at once, and stunning as many. Tamara quickly followed. The two whales skillfully sucked in the floating fish while the others kept circling. Tuschka could no longer resist the dense concentration of food and dashed straight into the fish with her mouth wide open. She grabbed several at once and gulped them down. Just as she made a sideways lunge for another batch, a sharp rebuke pierced her ears and she quivered at the teeth of another orca raking her. She immediately retreated and found Tamara and Tarka scowling at her.

Tuschka was completely taken aback and bent her head slightly down in submission. Not knowing what to do or to whom to turn, she remained motionless. But there was no time for any of the orcas to hang in the water passively. All effort was needed to keep the herring concentrated. Tarka quickly understood that the maneuver of her older daughter stemmed from ignorance rather than disobedience. She glided towards the startled female and pushed her forward with an encouraging call. Tuschka was grateful for the reassuring gesture and followed her mother in almost every move lest she upset her or any other member of the pod.

When it was Tarka's turn to feed, she slammed her tail into the fish with great force. Tuschka followed her example, but was not as effective. Her stroke had not only been less well timed and aimed as that of her mother, it also lacked the strong impulse at the beginning of the down sweep. As her mother was sucking up the suspended fish, Tuschka was too shy to take any. Rheia playfully snapped at the dead or stunned individuals, charged after floundering ones, and made an occasional dive into the ball of fish. Tuschka's earlier attempt, however, had not been so well received and she was still holding back. Tarka made another encouraging call to her and spit a fish into her direction to spur her on. Hesitantly, Tuschka took the fish, but her mother's prompt squeak of approval sparked new confidence, and she began taking more. Tarka made a circle and slammed into the ball again. Tuschka tried twice. She obviously had to improve on the skill, but there was enough for the two whales to share and they feasted upon their meal together.

As Tarka called her offspring away from their feeding, Sigurd and Igor closed in to take their turn. While the other whales circled and surfaced, the two males began their attack with unforgiving strokes of their massive flukes. Igor's blows had more force than those of any of the adult females, but Sigurd's impressive thrusts overshadowed them all. Tuschka watched them in awe. In one stroke the large bull killed double the amount that any of the females killed, and sucked them up with a graceful ease that showed his mastery of the skill.

When the ball had become smaller and most of them had taken their fill, the iron discipline began to give way to a more relaxed atmosphere. The organized effort began to break up into individual feeding activities, irrespective of rank in the pod. Especially the younger whales darted around the two males to steal some extra bites. The change in atmosphere gave Tuschka courage and she followed the younger orcas, who darted into small patches of concentrated fish.

376

As Tarka watched her oldest offspring, she was suddenly struck by the similarity between her behavior and that of the juvenile orcas in the pod. The discrepancy between Tuschka's age and skill suddenly took on a special meaning for the mother orca. Her calf was physically adult, but acted like a youngster in many aspects. Like Rheia and Lukina, she still had to perfect her hunting skills and learn more about her rank in the pod. Although Tarka did not understand the reason for Tuschka's retarded development, it seemed not to stem from mental disability. Tuschka was quick to pick up on corrective signals and eager to learn. In the short time she had been among them, she had already adapted considerably. But there was more than the ability to learn. Tuschka had all the emotions of a normal orca and from the moment of their reunion Tarka had been warmed by the sensitive and tender nature of her grown-up baby. Their bond was already too strong to even consider any option other than teaching and guiding her Tuschka to find her place and become a valued member of the pod.

When the fish had become thin and scattered, the hunt was over and most of the adults hovered at the surface to rest. Tuschka lay close to Tarka. She was tired, but the hunt had given her great satisfaction and the meal had strengthened her. Little Rheia was in between Tarka and Tamara. The small orca was quickly bored with resting and dived underneath her mother towards Tuschka, who was still picking up some floating fish parts. The strange object on the female's dorsal fin intrigued her. She inspected it at close range, but did not touch it. As Tuschka turned to see what Rheia was doing, the little orca followed her dorsal fin and soon they were turning in circles.

A little later, Lukina joined them. The four-year-old juvenile had seen glimpses of their newcomer's strange dorsal fin, but it was not until the relaxed atmosphere of this moment that she had felt free to take a closer look. Tuschka stopped moving and looked at the youngster. She had seen Lukina, but had not yet interacted with her. The juvenile female was much bigger than Rheia and proportionally bolder, but the little whale showed no sign of fear. Instead, she seemed to enjoy her bigger playmate and drew courage from her presence. Rheia's spontaneity towards the older juvenile made Tuschka feel more relaxed towards Lukina. The two juveniles reminded her of Kiki and Wobke.

Lukina joined Rheia to investigate Tuschka's dorsal fin. When she nudged the strange object, the feel of it surprised her. It was hard and not at all like flesh. She touched it again and noticed that it gave. Rheia followed her friend's example and started to nudge it too. Tuschka felt the tugs at her fin and pulled it free, but the two younger orcas were not yet satisfied and soon Tuschka was turning and rolling to keep them off her fin. When she was tired of it, she vented her annoyance with a tail lob.

The sound of the impact and the startled voices of the juveniles had Annika appearing within seconds. Tuschka stiffened and felt tension as their eyes met.

Something in the attitude of the older female told her that she demanded submission. Tuschka averted her gaze and waited. Annika glided closer and looked at the object that the two young whales had been after. After nudging it, she took a part in her mouth and tugged gently on it. Tuschka did not move and felt it slide. Her curiosity satisfied, Annika let it go and glided alongside. No longer feeling her rank threatened, Annika's sympathy was stirred by the familiar markings and voice of the new female. She gently brushed Tuschka as she veered away with Lukina into the green twilight. The straps of the tag had somewhat slipped and one of the suction cups had come loose. The dragging and dangling tag had become a nuisance.

Tarka had been watching Tuschka and Annika closely, ready to come to her offspring's aid in case the encounter took a wrong turn. Yet Tuschka had done well to accept her lower rank. Tarka glided quietly at her side and caressed her approvingly. Tuschka felt warmed by her mother's closeness. There was something special about the gentle big female, something she had never felt in Shachi's presence. Her former companion had been accepting and often even affectionate, but deep inside, Tuschka had always felt the loneliness of one without family, one for whom company was not a natural thing, and for whom every gesture of friendship was a welcome bonus. How different it was with Tarka... Tuschka relived the hunt. It had not been lost on her how Tarka had guided and encouraged her after the reprimand, and shared her meal with her. She radiated the unconditional acceptance and commitment that only a mother would give. Deep feelings of affection and reassurance washed over Tuschka: she had truly found her mother again. Finally, she could take company for granted.. the company of the caring female at her side. She rubbed up against Tarka, who returned a warm nudge. Tuschka knew that as long as Tarka lived, she would never be alone.

* * *

Tracking Gunda had not proved easy. The signal could be picked up only when the orca was at the surface within a three-mile range. Heavy weather had forced the team to interrupt their efforts and seek refuge in a small fjord. When the wind abated, they took up the search, despite realizing that finding the pod would be like locating a needle in a haystack. Another concern was whether Gunda's tag was still in place. The device had been a trade-off between reliability for the researchers and safety for the orca, and the latter had prevailed. The fitting had been designed to come off when a part of it became snagged. Although the team had considered the other pod members to be the most likely hazard, it was not acceptable to risk any danger or injury to the released whale. Nevertheless, they were eager to locate her. Finding her among her pod would be a great relief, otherwise they would take her back to her enclosure in the

378

small fjord. Yet, chances of finding her alone were slim, and although Greg did not speak of it openly, he hoped they would not find her pod unless she was with it. Finding nothing would at least leave a spark of hope that she was still surviving.

Greg had drawn hope from his observations during the first week after Gunda's release. There had been no visible sign of her attempting to turn back, but most promising of all had been his observation of Gunda participating in a hunt. Although he had no idea how much of a meal she had managed to catch, he had seen her circle and dive and lunge among the others. During long hours of travel Greg had noticed her periods of frequent respirations, indicating fatigue, but the next day Gunda was still with them and seemed to have recuperated from her endeavors. Video footage of the released orca was studied over and over again. Despite the low light, she was easy to recognize because of the transmitter on her fin. Her behavior was scrutinized to find support for her ability to survive. The scientist knew that the first several days would be most crucial. Her stamina and skill would increase with each day and he comforted himself with the thought that she had already passed the most critical part of the test.

* * *

Tuschka was exhausted after her ordeal in the storm. The white-crested waves had forced each one of them to rise high upon every surfacing to catch a dry breath. Furka would have turned to swim with the wind had she not been quite close to a protected fjord. Fighting the waves and the tide head-on was hard work, but especially for Tuschka. Again, Sigurd's guidance and wake had helped her to cover the last couple of miles to the entrance of the fjord. After the pod had rested from their trek, Furka led them further into the inlet in search of food. In the absence of reasonable concentrations of herring, they dived to scan for cod. The reward came soon as they found a dense layer of the big fish.

Tuschka followed Tamara, Tarka, and Rheia down. The rocky sea floor and the big fish were reminiscent of her exercises with the salmon in her enclosure, but now, the number of fish was incomparably larger. Initially, Tuschka had some difficulty aiming at a target, but seeing her mother and grandmother work, she quickly got the hang of it. It proved more effective to keep still and use the element of surprise than to try to trap an individual fish. Tuschka kept on feeding until she was completely satisfied. She was learning that feeding opportunities were much less frequent than she was used to, but if they had a successful hunt she could gorge herself. Instead of swimming around with a constant appetite and regular small meals, she was learning to accept many hours with a growling stomach for the joy of a complete fill.

Almost a month had passed and lack of endurance had become rare for Tuschka. Having gained more understanding of her own place and the ranks of the other orcas in the pod, most of the initial tension with some of them had subsided and given way for a more candid attitude. The change in atmosphere had boosted Tuschka's confidence and made her far more comfortable with her fellow pod members. Their spontaneous behavior revealed more and more about their personalities. Especially her interactions with the older whales sharpened her memories and diminished the gap between the past and the present.

Tuschka did not realize how naturally she had found her place in the pod again.. as if she had never been away. Having been the youngest orca at the time of her capture, she was higher in rank only to those who had been born after her. Only Kasimi, Shaka's adolescent daughter, had briefly challenged her, but Tuschka's pregnancy had quickly secured her place. The temperament and character of the younger orcas began to unfold while she hunted, rested, and played with them.

Being close to Rheia most of the time, a strong bond developed between Tuschka and the little juvenile. The lively, spontaneous young whale was endearing and awakened her maternal feelings. Sometimes, when Tarka was on a long dive searching for food, Rheia playfully bumped the belly of her bigger sister. On such moments, Tuschka often felt life stir inside and a strange tension around her teats that urged her to expose them. Rheia soon discovered that she was dry, but enjoyed the affection of her new big companion.

As winter came to an end, feeding became more scarce, but the dark months had been rich in herring and the pod was still in prime condition. They were on their final trek south to reach the beaches where soon the grey seal pups would take to the sea.

As they approached the entrance of a small fjord, the sudden familiarity of her surroundings made Tuschka's heart beat faster. The contours of the rocky shore and certain landmarks on the bottom elicited a strong feeling of home and an urge to venture deeper into the fjord. As the other whales spread to scan for food, Tuschka went in farther. She was oblivious to the small patches of cod that had caught the attention of the others. The occasional calls of her companions grew slightly weaker, but still assured her they were there.

When the bottom began to rise, Tuschka spyhopped high and saw the familiar shore and the floating dock. She sank down and echolocated... ahead of her was the maze that had marked her domain for quite a while. It gave her no fright. She remembered the frequent feeding sessions and the often warm and challenging interactions with her human friends. The prospect of finding them and being fed was attractive. As the maze came into view, she quickly found the opening and slipped inside towards the dock. She hovered close for a few moments. Everything was very quiet. She spyhopped again and voiced a greeting. Tuschka pumped her flukes to rise high, but no one came. Nothing stirred in the small cabins on shore and there were no familiar sounds of approaching footsteps. Slowly, she sank back. The quiet waters suddenly revived other memories... memories of long lonely hours.

A faint call from the entrance of the fjord brought her thoughts back to the present. The constant companionship of the other members of the pod and, especially, of Tarka and Rheia, was in stark contrast with the many lonely moments inside the enclosure. Their voices sounded from far away, but they were there. Tuschka's heart beat with joy at the prospect of joining them again. As she turned away from the dock, a sudden ominous feeling came over her. Once inside, the maze used to be closed. Tuschka almost screamed a call towards the pod as she sped towards the passage. A wave of relief washed over her as she found her way free into the fjord.

* * *

Torvil woke with a start when the loud call from the speaker pierced his ears. He had dozed off after lunch and had been unaware of the presence of the whales in the fjord entrance. Having finished his herring season he had offered to keep watch over the fjord for the month of February. After that, orcas were unlikely to pass close. He bent close to the speaker. Had he been dreaming or was it real? Another call sounded. The fisherman grabbed his coat and ran outside. There was nothing to see. As he scanned the waters in the fjord, a blow caught his eye. He sped back to the cabin to report the sighting and ran outside again, armed with a portable scope. Was the whale he had seen entering or leaving the fjord?

On a slight hill, he searched the waters through the scope. There it was again. It was a female, a lone female! Could it be Gunda..? To his disappointment, the orca was moving away, but whoever it was, the animal showed no sign of starvation. Wondering whether the orca was truly alone he searched the waters ahead of her. Then, distant blows and an occasional tiny fin tip revealed the presence of more. There was no question that the female and the other whales were aware of each other's presence, but why had this female ventured so much farther into the fjord? How he wished to be within identifiable range of that pod and find that Scarback was among them.... That would make it likely that the female he had seen was Gunda. The thought was thrilling and he waited impatiently for word of the crew as to when the boat would leave in search of them.

Tuschka's loud call carried a hint of distress and alerted the others, who had been busy gathering a modest meal. They had not been aware that one of them had traveled so far from them. Furka called her companions into a tight formation and turned towards the source of the sound, but Tarka was the first to answer and was already on her way. The call had upset the mother orca. She had almost lost her calf during that terrible ordeal with deafening noise, screams and blood. Then she had truly lost her, ensnared and lifted away. Tarka did not want to experience such a trauma again.

Tarka and Tuschka were porpoising towards each other and the rapidly decreasing distance of the calls turned concern into joy. Tuschka quickly veered as her mother came into view, brushed her lightly and made a full turn to come to a stop. They squeaked and nudged and rubbed affectionately to reassure each other that all was well. Rheia did a playful belly flop to vent her joy. Furka glided by and inspected Tuschka closely. Tuschka felt the matriarch's appraising look. Something in her attitude conveyed her disapproval of her impulsive venture away from the pod. Yet, Furka was visibly relieved that her pod was together again. It reassured Tuschka that the matriarch had come to care for her so much more.

Having calmed down from the incident inside the fjord, the pod suddenly became aware of faint, but clear calls from the south. Without hesitation, Furka turned towards the mouth of the fjord and set a brisk pace. Tuschka felt her empty stomach, but there was no way now to fall behind and get her fill on the cod. The distant calls puzzled her. Something in them was unmistakably familiar, but the excitement in the pod struck her. As they rounded the rocky outcrop that marked the southern corner of the fjord's mouth, the calls became noticeably louder. The other pod was not far ahead of them, but moving in the same direction. Furka called her greeting and broke into porpoising. The answer from the other pod revealed it had reversed its direction and was quickly approaching them. Tuschka felt a mixture of apprehension and excitement: apprehension because she did not quite know what to expect from the other orcas, and excitement because of her companions' unreserved enthusiasm.

When only 50 yards separated them, Furka called the pod to a halt. Tuschka saw her companions position themselves side by side. Ahead of them, there was a similar line of whales, all abreast. Their breaths created a line of vertical plumes, both big and small. Tuschka saw their own leader move forward to meet a big female who was approaching her head on. All except Tuschka, recognized Raina, matriarch of a pod of 16 whales. Tuschka remembered only fragments of the ritual, but she sensed immediately that the other female was of high rank. The two leaders nudged each other friendly. Then each matriarch gave a signal to meet and intermix freely. Without hesitation, her companions, including Tarka, moved forward.

Tuschka held back, watching intently as her companions exchanged greetings and affectionate rubs with the other orcas. They seemed to be familiar with each other, but despite the similarity of their calls, few of them triggered her

382

memories. Soon the members of the other pod noticed her. Shyly, Tuschka stayed close behind Tarka. The other orcas were open and unreserved, but she did not feel completely at ease. They immediately noticed her hesitance and circled her with curiosity. They could not remember her presence in Furka's pod, and yet she spoke their dialect and seemed completely accepted by them.

Tuschka was impressed when a big bull came into view. He was in the prime of his life and took an immediate interest in her. He made a close pass, and after their eyes briefly met, he veered off. Tuschka did not realize that her bulging belly discouraged him to make further advances. Two other bulls came near to inspect her. One of them was fully mature, whereas the sleek, slightly falcate dorsal fin of the other one indicated he was not yet full grown. Tuschka felt a little uncomfortable with the orcas parading past her. The situation was reminiscent of the first several hours among Furka's pod, but there was no tension as there had initially been with Annika, Skaade, and Kasimi.

One of the females, with a tiny calf of at most several months old, hovered close. She radiated a mild and gentle curiosity. Tuschka perceived her sonar pulses on her belly and felt life stir inside. The young mother voiced a greeting. There was a hint of familiarity in her voice and markings, but Tuschka could not put the vague memory in place. She felt drawn to the gentle and patient female, who seemed to take a special interest in her without being obtrusive. She slowly glided closer and touched Tuschka's flank with her rostrum. Tuschka looked back and turned to meet her face to face. Then, she inched forward and returned the young mother's gentle touch.

Aleta had noticed the new female's advanced pregnancy, but there was more to her than just that. She too had sensed an intangible familiarity in her. In the corner of her eye, Tuschka saw her mother move away. Although Aleta was friendly company, Tuschka wanted to stay close to Tarka and avoid to find herself surrounded by whales only of Raina's pod. She gave her fresh friend another nudge and turned away after her mother.

Out of the depths an impressive male glided alongside Tarka. It was Korak. The presence of the big male pleased her. Since their first intimate joining, she had felt a special sympathy for the strong and gentle whale. He caressed her tenderly with his large pectoral fin. Tuschka took Rheia with her and kept a small distance. She was surprised by the harmonious closeness of her mother and the unfamiliar bull. She would never know that he had sired her long ago.

Although they had not seen each other for many weeks, the reunion of the two pods did not last long. Raina was the first to call an end to the social gathering. Reluctantly, Korak left Tarka's side. The relative scarcity of food forced the two pods to part and seek different feeding areas.

35.
Tragedy and Joy: The Cycle of Life

Heavy weather and poor feeding had taken their toll on Furka's pod. The atmosphere was subdued. A few weeks had passed since Skaade had prematurely delivered a baby that had died shortly before birth. Now, the plight of Igor weighed them down. Poor feeding had been hard on all of them, but especially on the two bulls who needed almost twice as much food as the females. Nevertheless, Furka had been forced to give feeding priority to those on whom the future of her pod depended most: the lactating and pregnant females. Sadly, all their efforts had not prevented the loss of Skaade's calf.

Sigurd was lean, but not nearly as lean as Igor. The 16-year-old bull was in the growth spurt of puberty when circumstances had taken a turn for the worse. Desperate for a meal, he had lingered near the beaches where the pod had hunted for weaning grey seals. Just as he was about to catch up with the pod again, he had detected a weakened female. The seal had been an easy target and the young bull had drawn new energy from his unexpected meal. But not for long. Igor had suffered from the long periods of fasting and had failed to successfully fight the massive amount of disease germs he had ingested with his prey. He looked wasted and was gravely ill. The area behind his blowhole was sunken and the contours of his shoulder blades were visible. His sturdy fin was slightly leaning to the left, but still bespoke his former strength. Fever had quickly depleted what was left of his reserves.

The orcas were traveling in loose formation as Furka led them to a bank in hopes of finding mackerel. If only there were enough, they could hunt for their ailing member, who was far beyond hunting for himself. But the rich feeding did not come. Despite his progressive sickness, Igor had initially managed to keep the pace, but recently he needed more frequent pauses to rest. These days, her task as leader was hard on Furka. Whenever the weakening bull needed rest, she had to make the trade-off between leaving him to search for food and resting to stay with him.

When they found scattered densities of cod, the matriarch decided to stay and patrol a small area. The amount of food was not enough to sustain them for long, but in combination with saving on travel, it could at least delay the tragic decision of abandoning their suffering companion for a longer period of time. Since Igor had taken ill, Shaka had participated only partly in the search for food and never ventured far from him. Skaade occasionally traded places with her mother, but when Furka needed all, Igor trailed the pod alone. Shaka, who began to show minor signs of undernourishment, had offered him a fish several times. Reluctantly, he had shared one with his mother, but he was beyond hunger. A little later, he had brought it up again.

Several weeks had passed since his first sign of illness. Since morning Shaka had not left his side. Their attachment was strong. He used to be near his immediate family most of the time and had always been right there whenever he sensed their need for his help and protection. The two whales brought up the rear of the pod. Skaade, and Annika with her offspring, were traveling in front of them. Furka had slowed down to match their low pace. Igor swam in his mother's slipstream as he had done so many years ago. Slowly, he moved his wide curled flukes up and down. They felt heavy. He surfaced with his mother, but labored to breathe. Every time he came up, gravity pulled his fin in a slight tilt. Tuschka fell back and joined Sigurd as he briefly came alongside the twosome. It was a tragic sight.

When evening fell, Igor's heartbeat became fast and irregular. He felt drained of energy, but willed his flukes to continue. Despite his waning strength, his movements were still graceful. Shaka slowed down even more, trying to keep physical contact with him. She would feel his chin touch her back or she would brush him lightly on the upstroke of her flukes. Then upon a dive, she did not feel him behind her and came to a stop. She felt his chin glide upon her back. Igor was exhausted and rested. The closeness of his pod and especially his mother had given him the will to live. They were his purpose and his hope. He had fought against the impending danger of falling behind, sensing it would be their final parting of the ways. For days he had pushed on and on. Now he could no more. He felt his mother's strong heartbeat and her soft comforting voice. He closed his eyes and undulated his flukes just enough to stay with her. As he felt how she lifted him for support, he relinquished himself to her care. The fight was fought. Now, there was only their precious, comforting togetherness.

The young male's breaths were quiet and shallow, but not strained. He vocalized. His frail voice conveyed a special tenderness and Shaka felt his feeble nudge against her sensitive skin. Then she felt him slip and maneuvered to support him better, but in the way he slipped again she knew that life had left him. Grief stricken, she voiced her anguish. Igor's body had tilted and was sinking. She glided underneath and lifted him. Feeling the warmth of his fever, it was as if he was still with her. Skaade came alongside and helped carry her younger brother. Quietly, they moved to where the pod had been waiting. All knew they had lost their precious loyal pod member who had hunted and played with them, shared their tribulations and their joy. Shaka cherished the closeness of her beloved offspring, who had been at her side most of his life. Her companions took them in their midst and surrounded them as they slowly continued west.

* * *

Several successful hunts for mackerel had kept the pod from more losses. Time for the first salmon runs was still a while away. Sigurd was still lean with a dip behind his blowhole, but otherwise he was strong. Skaade was almost continuously at her mother's side, but she could not fill the emptiness in Shaka's heart. They had both experienced a loss and although one was far greater than the other, the two tried to seek comfort in each other's closeness. Igor had not only left a void in his immediate family: the whole pod dearly missed the presence of their loyal, lively, and often playful companion.

It was late March when Tuschka felt strange sensations in her belly. It pulled tight for brief moments, followed by increased movements inside. Instinctively, she drew close to Tarka and was relieved when Tamara came alongside and took Rheia away, whose playful bumps were unpleasant to her tender belly.

A strained call pierced the silence of the dejected pod. Furka fell back and echolocated on the young female. Tuschka had come into labor and the first feeble contractions had become stronger and more frequent. The 12 orcas formed a tight formation and moved closer to shore. Sigurd took position next to Tarka to flank them on the outside. The atmosphere in the pod was one of restrained excitement and suspense. Tuschka was about to become a first-time mother and she was still relatively young. At her age, it was not uncommon to have insufficient milk. Two months of poor feeding made the situation even more unfavorable, but Tuschka had started out with good reserves and Tarka had not yet gone completely dry.

They were entering Kivogur inlet on the south shore when Tuschka's contractions became long and painful with little solace in between. Furka and the other experienced females were relieved to have reached a protected place where they could await the birth in calm waters. Now, Tuschka could save all her strength for what seemed to become a long and difficult ordeal. She breathed frequently. Her flanks were aching and she barely dared to move in between her pains, lest they come even sooner. Tamara and Furka keenly observed the laboring female.

More than three hours had passed since Tuschka had begun to push. She was growing tired, but it was not the first ordeal in her life. She was not ready to give up now. Tamara glided underneath Tuschka and pressed her head against her belly to encourage her even more. The belly button of the tiny orca appeared. With bated breath Tuschka pushed with all her strength. Sudden relief came as the calf slipped out of her. In an instant, she looked for her baby. Her vision partly blurred by a cloud of blood, she saw Tarka glide underneath it, but the newborn orca needed no help. The little male headed for the surface with strong strokes of his still flaccid flukes. He broke the surface like a little rocket with half his body in the air for his first breath. He took several in a row before he made a small dive.

In the green twilight of the cold water, Tuschka glided at the little baby orca's side. He drew close to her and bumped her belly lightly. Then, he came up again and lifted his little head high to catch a dry breath. Tuschka was filled with relief as she heard the healthy puffs of her newborn. Caringly, she held her pectoral fin under his belly for support. In a moment, Tarka came up close and did the same on his other side. Frey was a perfect miniature orca and filled Tuschka with an intense feeling of satisfaction and affection. She felt proud of his every movement. Already, in the first moments of the baby's life, Tuschka felt a strong desire to protect him and care for him.

Although there was barely any food, Furka let them stay near the entrance of the small inlet for two days. It was valuable time for Tuschka to rest and to practice nursing and swimming with her little calf. Tuschka's milk supply was scanty the first day, but soon increased.

Need for food forced Furka to lead her pod to new feeding grounds. The birth of Tuschka's healthy calf had lifted their spirits. Little Frey surfaced in high strong arches in his mother's slipstream as the pod moved on in a westerly direction.

It was a crisp moonless April night with the orcas' fins cutting the calm water. Their fluke prints were all that disturbed the smooth surface of the sea. Nothing in the orcas' dark passage revealed the scene below.

As the pod was traveling tight, Frey marveled at the beautiful green light that enveloped each of his companions. The light was also glowing right by his eyes and intensified when he swam faster. The little calf wondered where it came from and his squeals of amazement broke the silence. Tuschka's voice was more than reassuring. It conveyed excitement to the baby orca and sparked his curiosity even more as a stream of green bubbles whirled up from his big mother's blowhole. Frey rose up for a breath and while he came down, he nudged the bright glowing tip of his mother's dorsal fin. Sigurd had come closer upon the baby's baffled squeaks. The body of the majestic male was outlined with lustrous green and graceful swirls of light trailed his flukes and fins. When little Frey squeaked again, Sigurd's answer sent another stream of radiant bubbles to the surface.

Although Furka's pod was familiar with bioluminescence, the experience was almost as much a revelation to Tuschka at it was to her little offspring. The young mother was enthralled at the sight of Tarka and Rheia with the little green form bumping the belly of the large one. Rheia, Lukina, and Tarka picked up on the excited mood of their two newest additions and engaged in a little chasing game. It was a mesmerizing underwater ballet of extraordinary beauty and grace. Swirls of green whirled and mixed in the trail of the green forms that marked the invisible bodies of the frolicking orcas. Tuschka was filled with awe and delight when she saw the majestic shape of Sigurd nudge a miniature version of himself, seemingly helping her baby catch the large bubbles he had made for him. Having shared sympathy for each other from the beginning, she fully trusted the large male with her little one. Feeling charmed, she glided at their side, almost surprised when the forms materialized upon her touch. Even before dawn unveiled the orcas' familiar white markings, the green light faded and silence returned to the pod.

Since Igor's passing Njord had been quiet and much of the time by himself. He missed the challenging chases and games with the maturing bull. Yet Sigurd sensed his need for a male companion and the importance of guiding and training him. The sad juvenile male had been withdrawn and ignoring the gentle hints of the older male. Now, Sigurd surprised him from the dark depths. As he felt the teeth of the large male rake his peduncle, he kicked his flukes to evade him. It was not enough. Sigurd came again and forced him into a full chase. Njord pumped his flukes, made sharp turns, and finally sought his refuge in full porpoising, but he proved no match for the experienced, agile, and clever male. It was then that Njord found his new master. The refinement and supremacy of the majestic bull both impressed and inspired him.

Sigurd was in his prime. He had seen how Igor used to challenge the younger male, just as he had done with Igor. He had seen how much the maturing bull had loved the games with his younger companion. Igor had thrived on being physically superior, while Njord had valuable learning experiences to perfect his skills. Now it was time that Njord learned from him. As Sigurd slowed down, the young male joined him quietly, with a renewed spirit.

* * *

Greg, Tom, and Torvil were tense as they headed towards the area where Johann had reported orcas. It was early in the salmon season and Bjorn and his team had not yet arrived for their annual census. Johann had learned to recognize most pods by the presence of certain distinctive animals, but he was not certain about the identity of the pod that was approaching Rockcove Bay from the east. "The male looks like B1," he told Greg over the radio, "but since B7 is nowhere to be seen, it isn't easy to know if it is B pod." Torvil's heart sank. He wanted to ask Greg about it, but remained silent. Greg and his crew felt their hearts beat faster when distant plumes came into view, but Torvil had mixed feelings. He was happy to see the whales, but if it were indeed B pod, he worried whether he would see his beloved Scarback again. In a strange way, he sensed the worst.

The orcas were scattered in groups of two or three. The scientist slowed down, gave the wheel to Torvil and picked up the identification guide. He left it open on the page with B pod and scanned the water with his binoculars. It was several minutes until he spotted a large bull. "Head for him," he said to Torvil pointing to where he had seen the whale surface. "Perhaps he'll give us a clue."

Tom and Torvil marveled at the sight of the majestic creature. He had a tall fin with a slight bulge in the trailing edge. His blows were explosive and his massive body created suction in the water. "Could very well be B1," Greg said, "but I too would be more confident if B7 were here. We must strongly bear in mind that it might not be B pod at all. Let's try to take a good look at the females. B5 has a little bump at the base of her fin, while B8 has a small nick."

They left the large male and headed for two smaller fins. It was hard for the fisherman and the former trainer to pick up any details upon the short surfacing of the two orcas. Greg was experienced but not familiar with this population. Still indecisive after a few more surfacings, they headed for another small group. "Look," Tom exclaimed pointing ahead. "There are three whales with a tiny calf!" Without hesitation, Greg took the wheel and headed over. They saw Johann coming towards the same group.

The two boats slowed down when about two hundred yards separated them from the small group. Slowly, Greg approached their side. He held his breath as he tried to get a good look through his binoculars. There were two adult females, a juvenile and a small calf. He gave the wheel to Torvil again and asked him to close in on them. The most comfortable way to identify orcas was still at close range without binoculars. "That calf is very young," he said. "Its white patches are still orangey." Tom was endeared to see the miniature orca that surfaced like a dolphin in playful little bows. It was a magnificent sight to see these wild orcas: unrivalled masters of the sea, tied together for life by a tender bond. He was so full of wonder that he forgot to pay attention to the adults' individual markings.

Greg grabbed Torvil's shoulder. "Look at that female on the outside. Her fin is behind the mother of the little calf most of the time, but I believe that she ..." Tom cut him short. "The mother.... look, it is Gunda! His voice broke. The eye patch is hers and the fin and.. " Greg looked at him, then to the whales again. They had just gone on their dive. "Are you certain?" It was too wonderful to be true. "What I had noticed," said Greg, "were the two small scratches on the saddle of the other female, which is typical for B4."

Greg looked at Torvil, who looked downcast, and gave him an understanding tap on the shoulder. "They are fairly spread out, perhaps he has escaped our..." He stopped and changed his voice. "I understand your dread. Even if the worst is true, he will live on in our memories, Torvil.. and in his family, which is here with us." The fisherman nodded in thought. It was almost certain he would never see his Scarback grow to full maturity, to become an invincible master of the sea. Torvil looked in the guide and his eye fell on B11, a seven- or eight-year-old bull who was Igor's causin. Some day, he would mature to become a strong bull. The thought lifted his spirits. Since he had come to know the researchers and their work, he knew he could learn to recognize the orcas. He would continue to see Igor's family and, in them, the memory of his favorite would never die.

When the whales surfaced again, Tom was confirmed in his observation and was beside himself with joy. He jumped up in the small inflatable and let out a whoop of excitement. The mother of the young calf cut off her dive and slowed down. They all noticed it….

The loud voice of the man on board startled Tuschka and drew her attention to the small vessel. In an instant, she recognized the familiar sound of the small blades that propelled it. She slowed down and lifted her head to look at it. It looked exactly like the little boat that had accompanied her in what seemed a long time ago. Tarka and Rheia wondered why their companion showed so much interest in the small boat. Yet they slowed down with her.

Tuschka was confused. She had felt a spark of excitement, but dread at the same time. The thought of her friends warmed her, but she did not want to follow them to her lonely home from the past. She came to a stop and spyhopped. Only 20 yards separated her from the inflatable. Without thinking about it, Tom squeaked his greeting to her. Their eyes met. The young mother prolonged her spyhop and looked at the man in the boat. It was him, her precious human friend. She crept closer and greeted him softly. He stretched his hand towards her. Her little Frey surfaced in small circles near her as if impatient to continue on. Then, Tarka called to her, not comprehending what was going on.

Tuschka felt a pang of sorrow when she looked at her friend. His eyes spoke of his longing to caress and love her. She felt a desire to be near him and play with him, but she did not want to follow and part with her mother, Frey, and the other members of her pod... Her pod... her place was in the pod: their togetherness was her home. There was no way she would ever leave them again.

Tom leaned over the soft rubber edge and stretched out to reach her. Tuschka inched closer. The bond between her and her human friend was undeniable. Yet it was the certainty of knowing where she belonged that made her realize how final this moment was for them. Her friend could not reach farther. It was all up to her. Tuschka lifted her head, as if to hold off the painful moment of their parting. Then, she rose up and touched his hand. Tom felt her sleek soft skin and relived their first contact. He felt how his precious orca lifted his hand in a subtle tender nudge. Her soft affectionate call touched him deeply. Filled with emotion, Tom's voice failed him. Slowly, she sank down again. He reached to follow, but his fingers slipped. He saw her dark precious eyes disappear below the water, followed by the tip of her white chin. He realized this moment had been more meaningful than all others... Gunda was a free orca and she had come to him on her own terms, of her own free will. Then, as he slowly drew his hand back, Gunda blew and brushed her dorsal fin along his hand upon her dive.

The sound of one of them landing on the water startled the orcas. Furka had breached to call the pod's attention. She was about a mile ahead of most others when she had detected their long-awaited food. Excitement spread immediately. Sigurd kicked his flukes and gained speed as he headed towards the surface. He rose fully in the air. He seemed to hang there for a moment before he bent his streamlined muscular body to the side and fell back in a thunderous crash. Njord followed his example, then Tarka, and Tuschka. Little Frey followed his mother as he built up speed and broke the surface in her slipstream. Water sprayed off his small curved fin. The pudgy male completely cleared the water and moved his tiny flukes in flight. He landed near his mother, who picked him up on her rostrum and playfully pushed him on. Frey was strong and full of energy. Tuschka relished the delighted squeaks of her little offspring and nudged him warmly. As she felt the familiar bumps under her belly and satisfied her baby's healthy appetite, an intense feeling of inner fulfillment came over her. The baby orca was not only close.. he was life out of her life and they would never ever part.

Silence returned among the pod as they came together. A promising hunt lay ahead. The 13 orcas lined up abreast and broke the surface in full porpoising. Water parted under their chins and spray ran off their fins. Frey was elated as he rode the slipstream of Sigurd and his mother. The little curved fin of the miniature orca contrasted sharply with the tall dorsal of the majestic male. They dived in unison, leaving a row of plumes against the western horizon to mark their fleeting passage.

Suggestions for Further Reading

[1]   Dr. Ingrid N. Visser. Swimming with Orca. My Life with New Zealand's Killer Whales. Penguin Books. 2005. ISBN 0-14-301983-X.

[2]   John Stenersen, Tiu Similä. Norwegian Killer Whales. Tringa Forlag 2004. ISBN 82-994577-3-4.

[3]   Robin. W. Baird. Killer Whales of the World. Natural History and Conservation. Voyageur Press. 2002. ISBN 0-89658-512-3.

[4]   Alexandra Morton. Listening to Whales. What the Orcas Have Taught Us. Ballantine Books. 2002. ISBN 0-345-43794-2.

[5]   John K.B. Ford, Graeme Ellis, Kenneth C. Balcomb. Killer Whales. Second Edition. UBC Press. 2000. ISBN 0-295-97958-5.

[6]   John K.B. Ford, Graeme Ellis. Transients. Mammal-Hunting Killer Whales. UBC Press. 1999. ISBN 0-7748-0717-2.

[7]   Graig Matkin, Graeme Ellis, Eva Saulitis, Lance Barrett-Lennard, Dena Matkin. Killer Whales of Southern Alaska. North Gulf Oceanic Society. 1999. ISBN 0-9633467-9-2.

[8]   Sara and James Heimlich-Boran. Killer Whales. Voayageur Press. 1994. ISBN 0-89658-237-X.

[9]   Gerard Gormley. Orcas of the Gulf. A Natural History. Sierra Club Books. 1990. ISBN 0-87156-601-X.

[10] Erich Hoyt. Orca The Whale Called Killer. Camden House. 1990. ISBN 0-920656-25-0.

[11] Rex Weyler. Song of the Whale. AnchorPress/Doubleday. 1986. ISBN 0-385-19938-4.

[12] Ted Griffin. Namu. Quest for the Killer Whale. Gryphon West Publishers. 1982. ISBN 0-943482-00-3.

28182822R00218

Made in the USA
Lexington, KY
08 December 2013